Contents

Photo Credits:
©Jeff Greenberg/Alamy — p.66, p.67 (T), p.71 (T), p.74, p.76, p.91 (B), p.94, p.95 (T), p.171 (T), p.175 (T) and (B), p.177, p.191 (B); ©Karim Shamsi-Basha/Alabama Bureau of Tourism & Travel — p.67 (B); ©Colbert County Tourism & Convention Bureau – p.75 (T) and (B); ©Magnolia Springs Bed & Breakfast — p.69; ©The Birmingham Convention and Visitors Bureau — p.71 (B); ©Andre Jenny/Alamy — p.70, p.83 (B), p.102, p.106, p.107 (B), p.111 (B), p.112, p.131 (T), p.131 (B), p.135 (B), p.139 (T), p.155 (T), p.159 (T), p.197 (T), p.200 (T); ©M. Timothy O'Keefe/Alamy — p.95 (B), p.119 (B), p.167 (B), p.183 (T) and (B); ©Stephen Saks Photography/Alamy — p.103 (T), p.159 (B); ©Florida Images/Alamy — p.105; ©Rough Guides/Alamy — p.91 (T), p.92; ©Wesley Hitt/Alamy — p.82, p.107 (T), p.115 (B), p.117; ©Robert W. Ginn/Alamy — p.109; ©David Caton/Alamy — p.168, p.170 (B); ©Rab Harling — p.77; ©George and Monserrate Schwartz — p.151; ©Bob Pardue/Alamy — p.154, p.170; ©Tom Till/Alamy — p.114, p.200 (B); ©Catherine Wood/Alamy — p.198; ©Ron Buskirk/Alamy — p.103 (B); ©PCL/Alamy — p.130; ©Tom Salyer/Alamy — p.90; ©Robert Harding Picture Library Ltd/Alamy — p.98; ©Byron Jorjorian/Alamy — p.190; ©Thinkstock/Alamy — p.201 (T); ©Frank Vetere/Alamy — p.179 (T); ©Chuck Pefley/Alamy — p.196; ©Chuck Pefley — p.115 (T); ©Scott Mills/Alamy — p.122; ©Visions of America, LLC/Alamy — p.174; ©Lee Foster/Alamy — p.83 (T); ©Purcell Team/Alamy — p.123 (T);

©Arcaid/Alamy — p.138; ©Arkansas Department of Parks and Tourism — p.79 (T) and (B), p.84, p.86, p.87 (T) and (B), p.88; ©Apalachicolaonline — p.96; ©The Florida Keys & Key West - Monroe County Tourist Development Council — p.99 (T) and (B), p.101; ©Cary Wolinsky — p.78; ©Shreveport - Bossier Convention and Tourist Bureau — p.123 (B); ©Cameron Davidson IPN — p.184 (T); ©Scott Warren — p.118, P.120; ©Christian Heeb — p.119 (T); ©The Tunica Convention & Visitors Bureau — p.127 (T) and (B); ©Mississippi Development Authority/Division of Tourism — p.126; ©Tupelo Convention & Visitors Bureau — p.134, p.135 (T), p.137; ©Harrison Shull/Outdoor Collection — p.139 (B); ©Cape Fear Coast Convention and Visitors Bureau — p.142, p.143 (T) and (B), p.199; ©Susana Raab — p.146; ©Winston-Salem Convention and Visitors Bureau — p.147 (T) and (B); ©Charleston Area Convention and Visitors Bureau — p.150, p.151 (T); ©Quang-Tuan Luong — p.155 (B), p.166, p.178; ©Museum of Appalachia — p.158, p.159 (B); ©Knoxville Tourism & Sports Corporation — p.163 (T) ©Robert Harding World Imagery /Getty Images — p.167 (T)s; ©D.J. Dammann/Rand McNally — p.110; © Virginia Tourism Corporation — p.179 (B), p.180; © Mary Lu Laffey/Rand McNally — p.193, p.194 (T), p.195 (T) and (B), p.198 (T); © Brett Gover/Rand McNally — p.191, p.192 (B)

For licensing and copyright permissions, contact us at licensing@randmcnally.com
If you have a comment or suggestion, please call (800) 777- MAPS (-6277) or e-mail us at:
consumeraffairs@randmcnally.com
or write to:
Rand McNally Consumer Affairs
P.O. Box 7600
Chicago, Illinois 60680-9915
Published in U.S.A.
Printed in U.S.A.
10 9 8 7 6 5 4 3 2

USING YOUR GETAWAY GUIDE

? ## How do I find a great place to explore that's just a couple of hours away?

1 Turn to the **PageFinder™** map on inside front cover. Find your general location, then see which regional map corresponds to your it.

3 Once you get to the regional map, you'll see yellow boxes with page numbers attached.

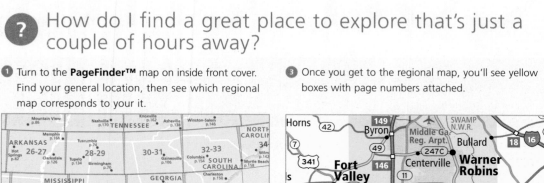

2 See those page numbers? Now you know where to turn for the right regional map.

That's where fun stuff happens, and this book describes that area in detail starting on that page number. There are 30 destinations in the book—one is sure to be close by.

How do I get to that fun place (the one in the yellow box)?

You can use the regional maps (pages 8-59) — a terrific "big picture" — to see what major roads will get you there. You can also go to **randmcnally.com** for directions.

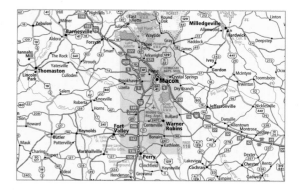

What's happening there?

Read all about what there is to see and do, what the shopping scene's like, where you can stay overnight, the best food to try and where you can find it, and even if there's a festival happening during your visit. These destination sections also offer specially designed maps to help figure out where attractions and restaurants are in relation to each other (and how to drive between them).

Why are some names on the map and in the article purple?

If something's purple, it means it's discussed in the article and also shown on the map.

What are those pictures on the map?

Those pictures (a.k.a. icons) show you at a glance whether something is a place to eat, shopping opportunity, place to stay, or a variety of other specific places to visit.

 Dining   Shopping   Lodging   Casino   Golfing   Museum   Park   Information

How do I find out more about the festivals?

We've included descriptions of the festivals on pages 186-189.

USING YOUR GETAWAY GUIDE

How do I find something that isn't included in one of the destination articles?

The **Point of Interest (POI) Index** lists items that appear on the regional maps. Turn to page 60. Items are listed alphabetically in four categories, with a page and grid reference (map location) to help find them on the map. This list is also great for browsing things to do in the entire southeast region.

How far is it to where I want to go?

This book offers three ways to figure out how far and how long you'll drive. At the back of the book, on pages 220-221, you'll find a **mileage and driving times map**. On the next two pages, there's a **mileage chart** listing distances between 60 cities in the Southeast. And on each regional map, there's a scale bar (for those of you who like to calculate things yourselves).

? What do all those symbols on the maps mean?

Those symbols, such as the rectangles with numbers in them, are explained in the **legend**.

Find the symbol and learn what it means. In the margins of the regional maps, several commonly used symbols are explained in detail.

This book's legend is on the back cover flap.

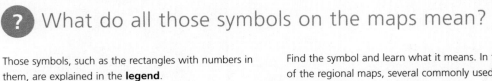

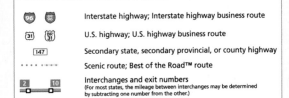

96 85	Interstate highway; Interstate highway business route
31 BR 31	U.S. highway; U.S. highway business route
147	Secondary state, secondary provincial, or county highway
· · · · · · · ·	Scenic route; Best of the Road™ route
2 ☐━━━━☐ 10	Interchanges and exit numbers (For most states, the mileage between interchanges may be determined by subtracting one number from the other.)

How do I find a city or town on the regional maps?

Near the back of the book, starting on page 202, an **index** lists many of the cities and towns located in the southeast region. The index includes page numbers and grid references.

Am I going to run into road construction on my trip?

You can find out using the list of **road construction and conditions hotlines and websites** provided on page 224. You can also get up-to-date construction info at **randmcnally.com**.

Are there any other ways to find great things to see and do?

This book includes four of Rand McNally's **Best of the Road™** drives. They start on page 190. Each drive provides details on the best shopping, attractions, activities, and dining along a route researched in person by Rand McNally editors. (For more Best of the Road™ trips, go to **randmcnally.com/BR**.) You'll find places and faces that make a trip unforgettable.

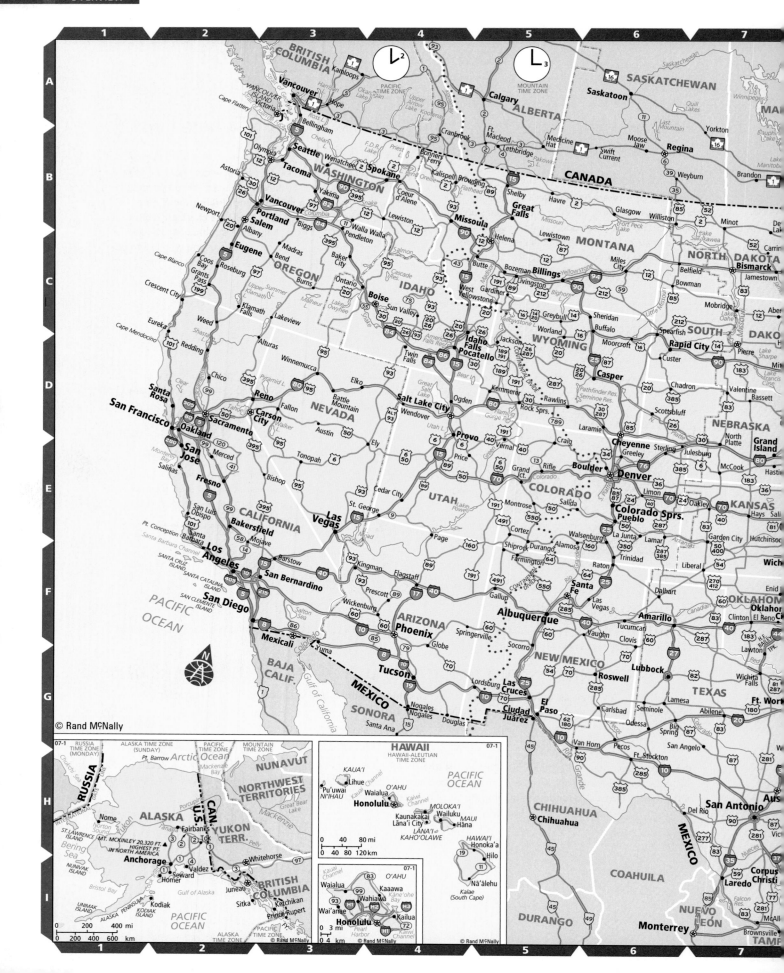

© Rand McNally

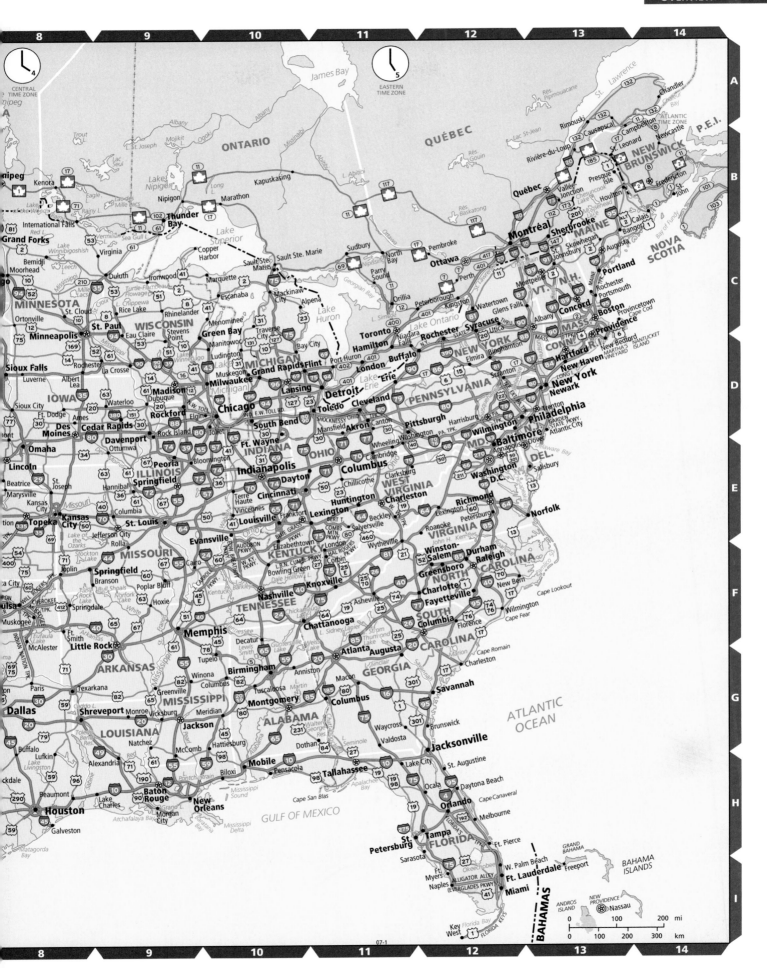

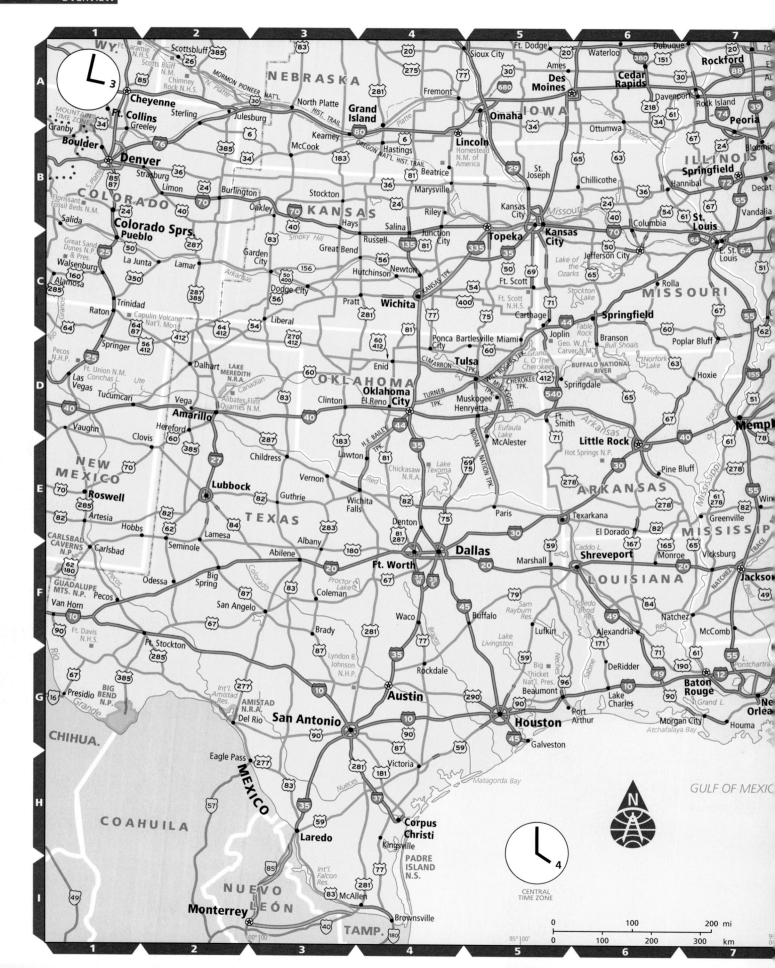

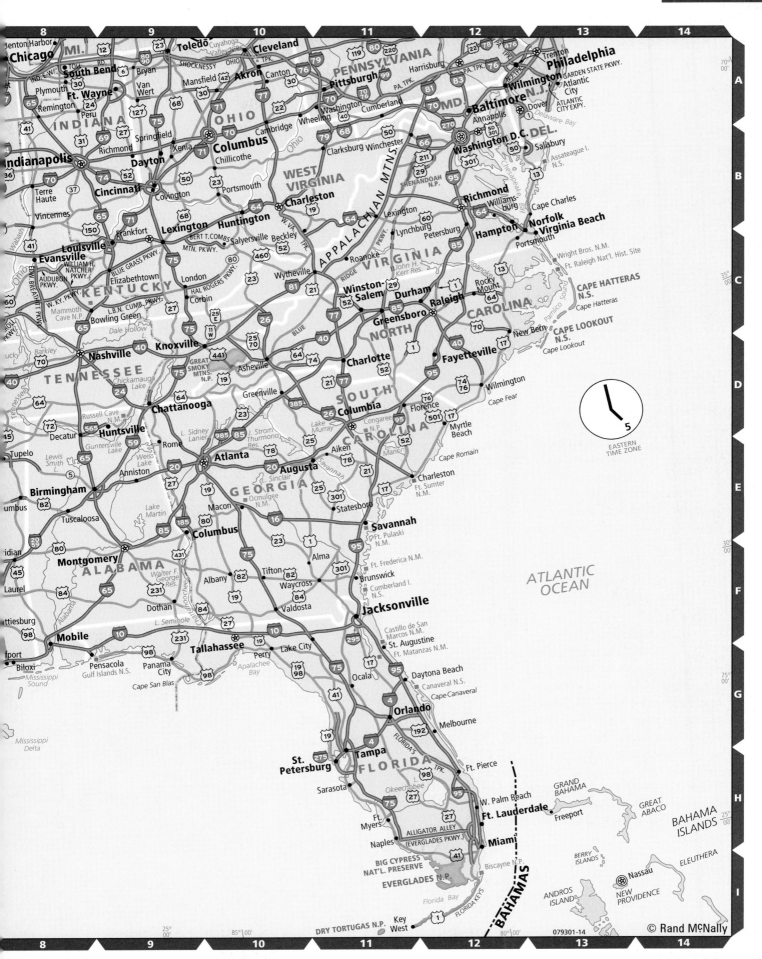

For a complete listing of symbols, see back cover flap.

DISTANCE SCALE

One inch represents 16 miles

0   5   10   15   20 miles

0   5   10   15   20   25   30 kilometers

LOCATOR MAP

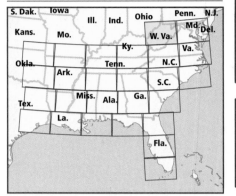

See the Pagefinder™ map on the inside of the front cover for map page numbers.

Why are some city names bigger than others?

The difference in the size of the type helps quickly show which cities are more populous than others. The bigger the type, the more people live in that city. More people means more amenities—food, lodging, gas and shopping.

What are those yellow boxes (with little numbers) on the maps?

That's where fun stuff happens, and this book describes that area in detail starting on the page number you see. Read all about what there is to see and do, what the shopping scene's like, where you can stay overnight, what the best food to try is and where you can find it, and even if there's a festival happening during your visit. These destination sections also offer specially designed maps to help figure out where attractions and restaurants are in relation to each other (and how to drive between them).

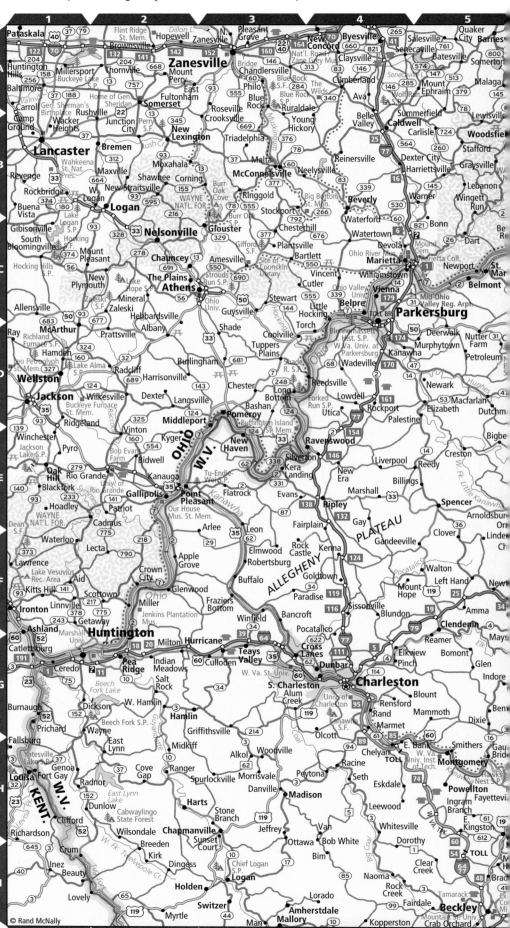

© Rand McNally

When you see this sign ◢04◣, the map continues on the page number indicated.

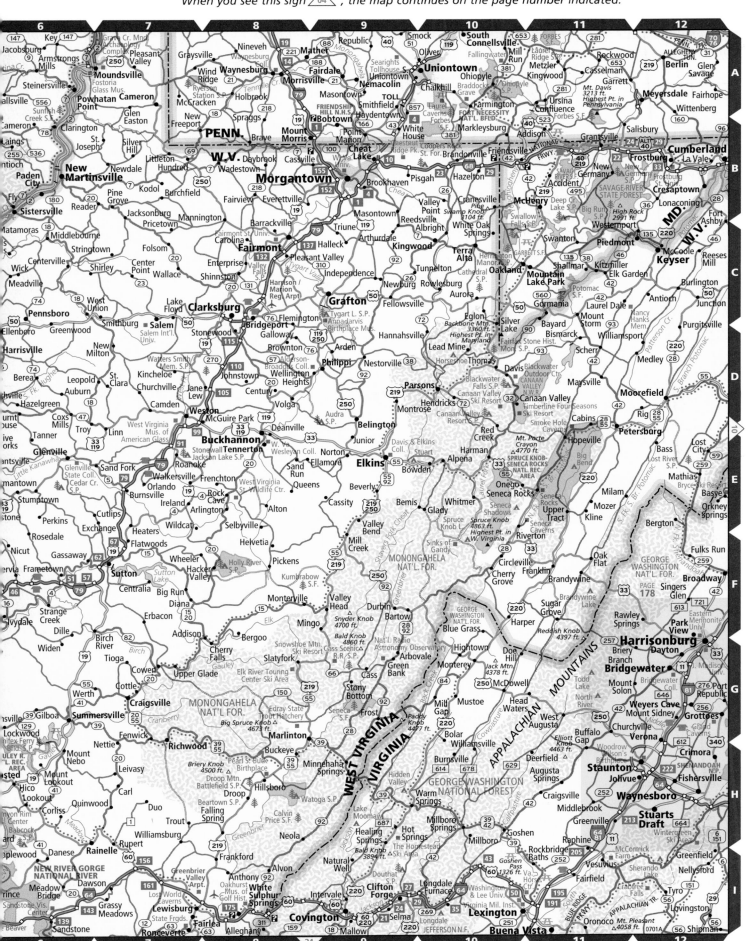

For a complete listing of symbols, see back cover flap.

DISTANCE SCALE

One inch represents 16 miles

0 5 10 15 20 miles

0 5 10 15 20 25 30 kilometers

LOCATOR MAP

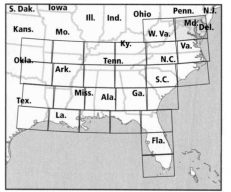

See the Pagefinder™ map on the inside of the front cover for map page numbers.

Why are some of the city dots stars?

Stars indicate the state ✪ or national ✪ capital city. This is where the executive, legislative, and judicial branches of the state or national government work.

What are those yellow boxes (with little numbers) on the maps?

That's where fun stuff happens, and this book describes that area in detail starting on the page number you see. Read all about what there is to see and do, what the shopping scene's like, where you can stay overnight, what the best food to try is and where you can find it, and even if there's a festival happening during your visit. These destination sections also offer specially designed maps to help figure out where attractions and restaurants are in relation to each other (and how to drive between them).

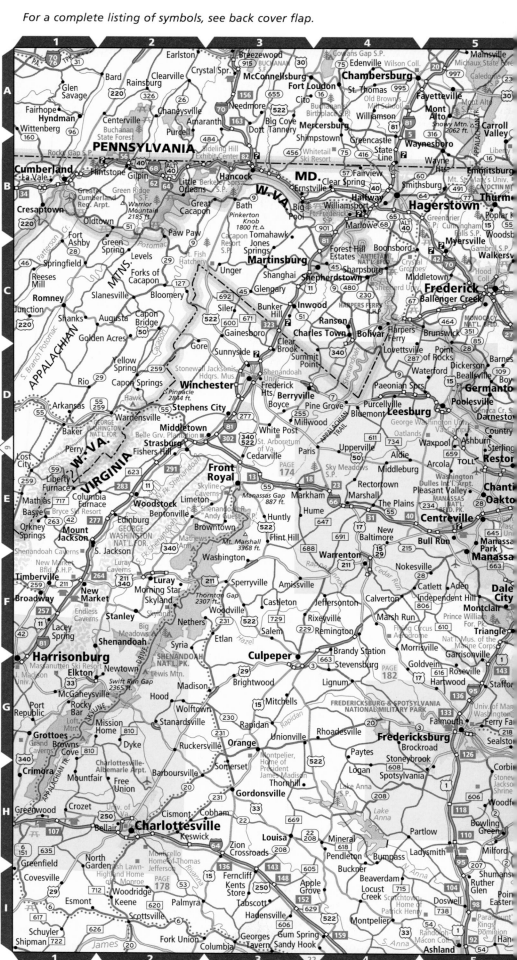

When you see this sign /04\, the map continues on the page number indicated.

© Rand McNally   0702A

For a complete listing of symbols, see back cover flap.

DISTANCE SCALE

One inch represents 16 miles

0   5   10   15   20 miles

0   5   10   15   20   25   30 kilometers

LOCATOR MAP

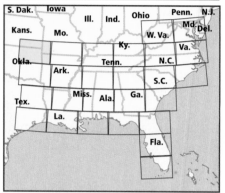

See the Pagefinder™ map on the inside of the front cover for map page numbers.

I wonder why some roads are blue, some green, some red, and some gray.

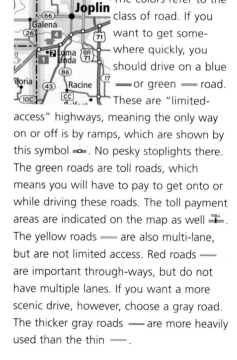

The colors refer to the class of road. If you want to get somewhere quickly, you should drive on a blue ━ or green ━ road. These are "limited-access" highways, meaning the only way on or off is by ramps, which are shown by this symbol ⬦. No pesky stoplights there. The green roads are toll roads, which means you will have to pay to get onto or while driving these roads. The toll payment areas are indicated on the map as well ⬦. The yellow roads ━ are also multi-lane, but are not limited access. Red roads ━ are important through-ways, but do not have multiple lanes. If you want a more scenic drive, however, choose a gray road. The thicker gray roads ━ are more heavily used than the thin ━.

© Rand McNally

When you see this sign ◬ 04, the map continues on the page number indicated.

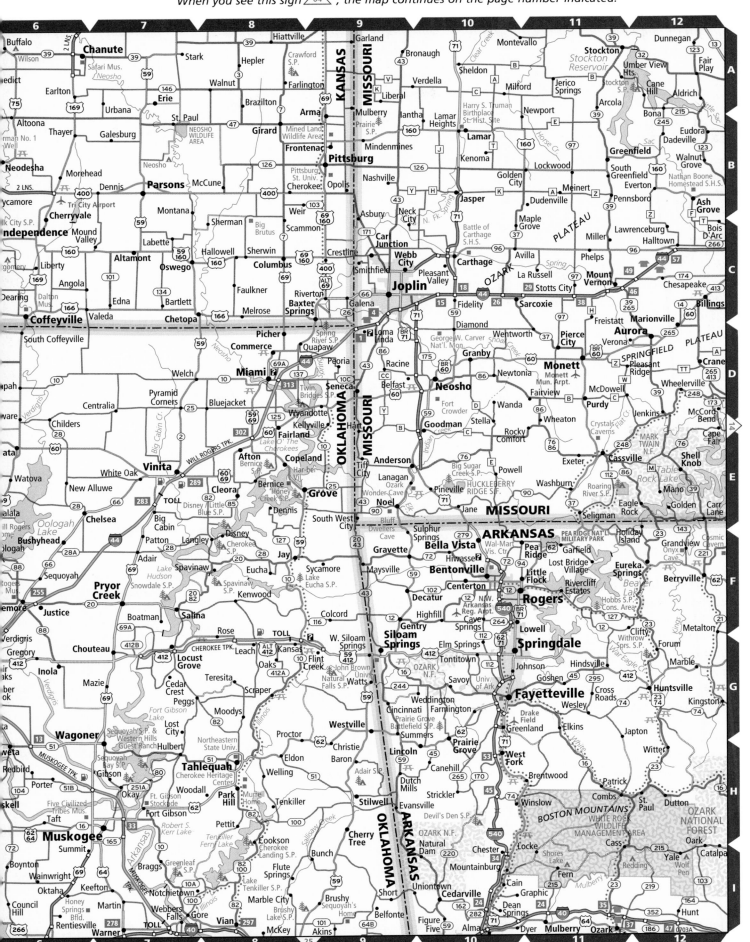

For a complete listing of symbols, see back cover flap.

DISTANCE SCALE

One inch represents 16 miles

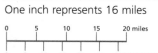

0   5   10   15   20 miles

0   5   10   15   20   25   30 kilometers

N

LOCATOR MAP

See the Pagefinder™ map on the inside of the front cover for map page numbers.

Are there any roads on the map I should watch out for?

This kind of line ═══ indicates an unpaved road. Traveling on these roads may become difficult in poor weather conditions. Take this into consideration when you plan your travel.

What are those yellow boxes (with little numbers) on the maps?

That's where fun stuff happens, and this book describes that area in detail starting on the page number you see. Read all about what there is to see and do, what the shopping scene's like, where you can stay overnight, what the best food to try is and where you can find it, and even if there's a festival happening during your visit. These destination sections also offer specially designed maps to help figure out where attractions and restaurants are in relation to each other (and how to drive between them).

© Rand McNally

When you see this sign ◁04▷ , the map continues on the page number indicated.

REGIONAL MAP 15

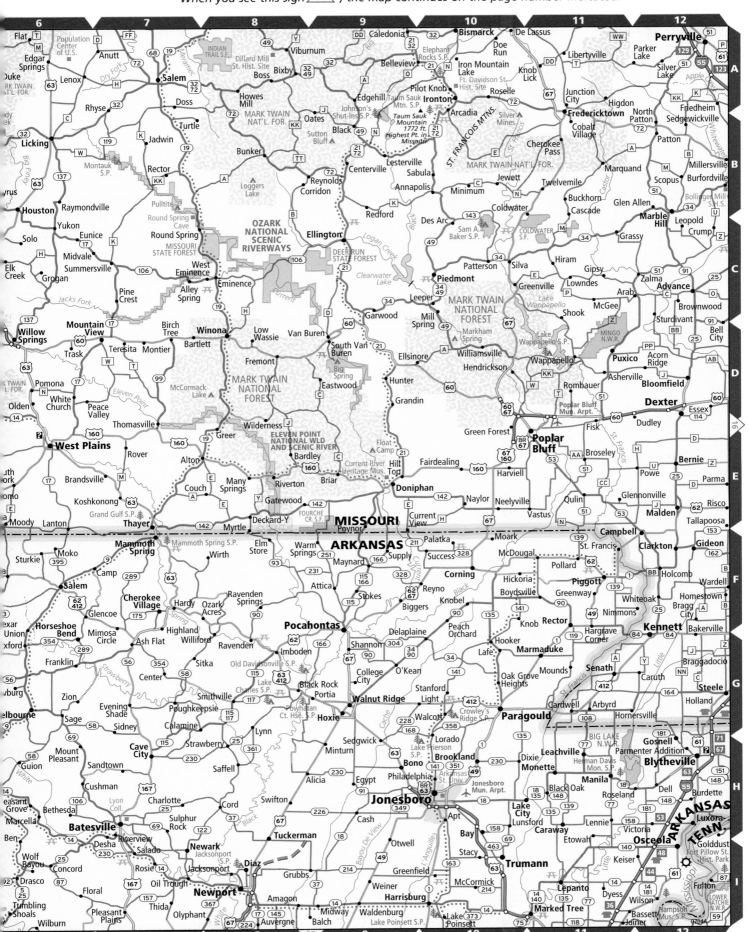

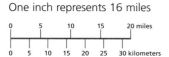

For a complete listing of symbols, see back cover flap.

DISTANCE SCALE

One inch represents 16 miles

0 5 10 15 20 miles

0 5 10 15 20 25 30 kilometers

LOCATOR MAP

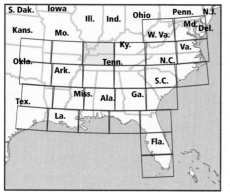

See the Pagefinder™ map on the inside of the front cover for map page numbers.

How do I follow the Great River Road?

Choose roads that have the captain's wheel ☀ alongside them. The Great River Road is one of the oldest and longest scenic byways in the U.S., running through 10 states for 3,000-some miles along both sides of the Mississippi River.

What are those yellow boxes (with little numbers) on the maps?

That's where fun stuff happens, and this book describes that area in detail starting on the page number you see. Read all about what there is to see and do, what the shopping scene's like, where you can stay overnight, what the best food to try is and where you can find it, and even if there's a festival happening during your visit. These destination sections also offer specially designed maps to help figure out where attractions and restaurants are in relation to each other (and how to drive between them).

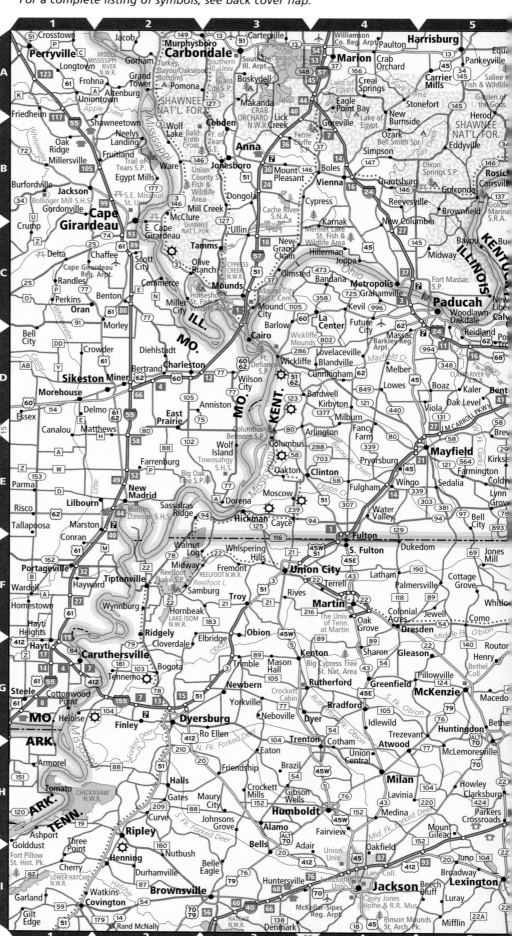

When you see this sign ◁04▷, the map continues on the page number indicated.

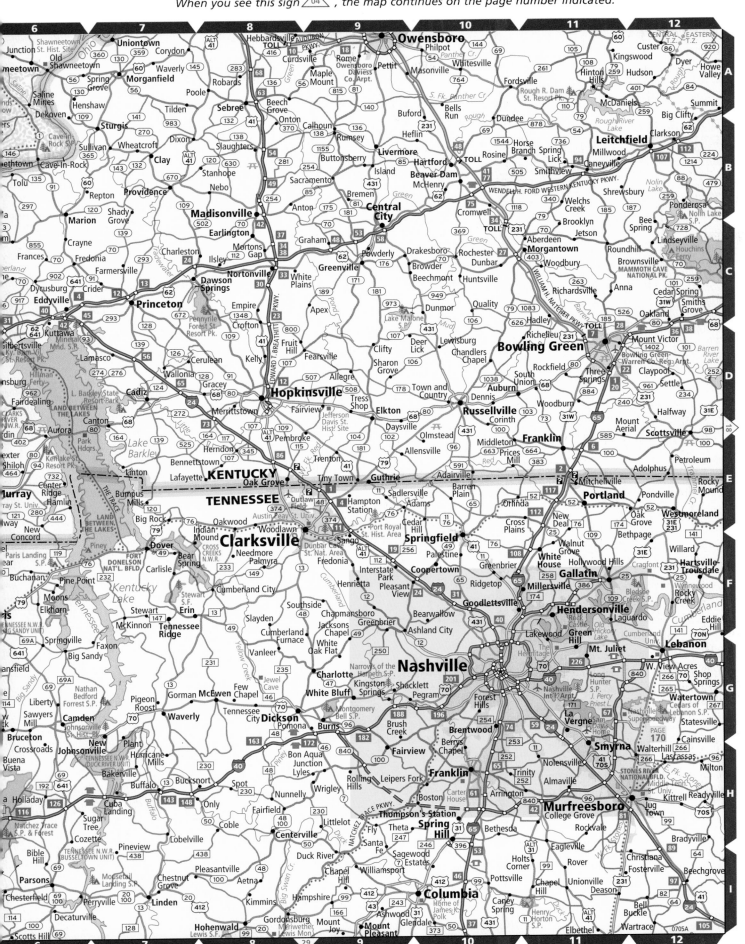

For a complete listing of symbols, see back cover flap.

DISTANCE SCALE

One inch represents 16 miles

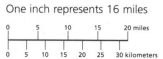

LOCATOR MAP

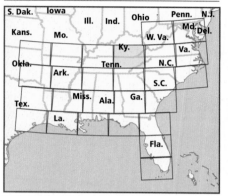

See the Pagefinder™ map on the inside of the front cover for map page numbers.

Does that string of pink dots represent a road?

No—this line ••••• represents the boundary between time zones. Don't forget to adjust your watch when you cross it.

What are those yellow boxes (with little numbers) on the maps?

That's where fun stuff happens, and this book describes that area in detail starting on the page number you see. Read all about what there is to see and do, what the shopping scene's like, where you can stay overnight, what the best food to try is and where you can find it, and even if there's a festival happening during your visit. These destination sections also offer specially designed maps to help figure out where attractions and restaurants are in relation to each other (and how to drive between them).

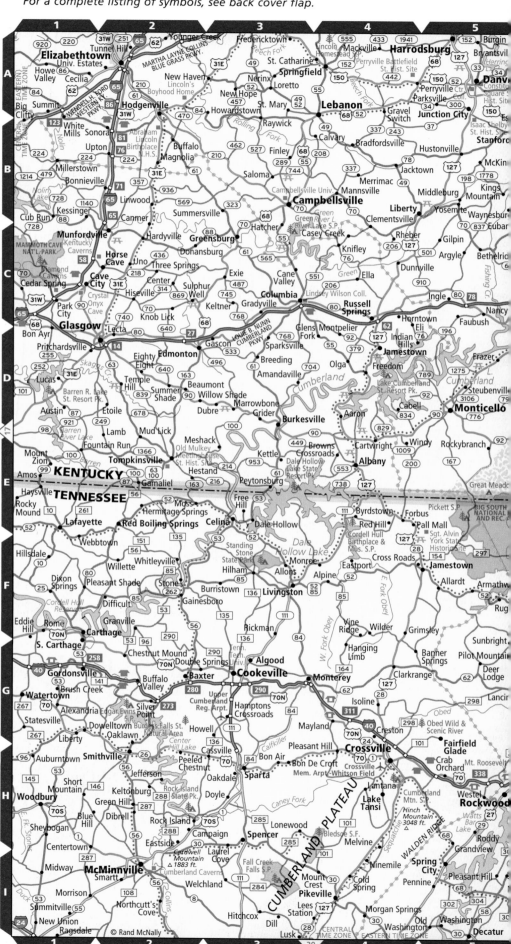

© Rand McNally

When you see this sign 04, the map continues on the page number indicated.

For a complete listing of symbols, see back cover flap.

DISTANCE SCALE

One inch represents 16 miles

0 5 10 15 20 miles

0 5 10 15 20 25 30 kilometers

LOCATOR MAP

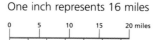

See the Pagefinder™ map on the inside of the front cover for map page numbers.

What are those different shapes on the roads with numbers in them?

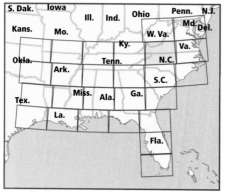

These are called highway shields. The different shapes indicate what type of highway you are driving on. The blue and red shield 96 indicates an Interstate highway; the badge-shaped shield 31 means a U.S. route; a simple circle or oval 18 means a state highway; and a rectangle 147 means a county route. This matters when choosing what kind of drive you'd like: Interstate highways tend to be fast and efficient, while county routes tend to be more leisurely and (possibly) scenic.

What are those yellow boxes (with little numbers) on the maps?

That's where fun stuff happens, and this book describes that area in detail starting on the page number you see. Read all about what there is to see and do, what the shopping scene's like, where you can stay overnight, what the best food to try is and where you can find it, and even if there's a festival happening during your visit. These destination sections also offer specially designed maps to help figure out where attractions and restaurants are in relation to each other (and how to drive between them).

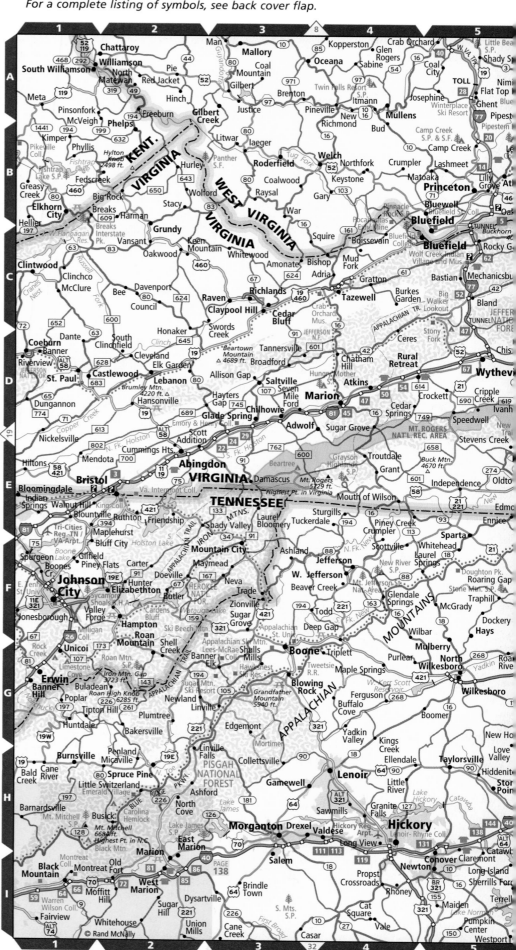

When you see this sign ⌂04⌂, the map continues on the page number indicated.

REGIONAL MAP 21

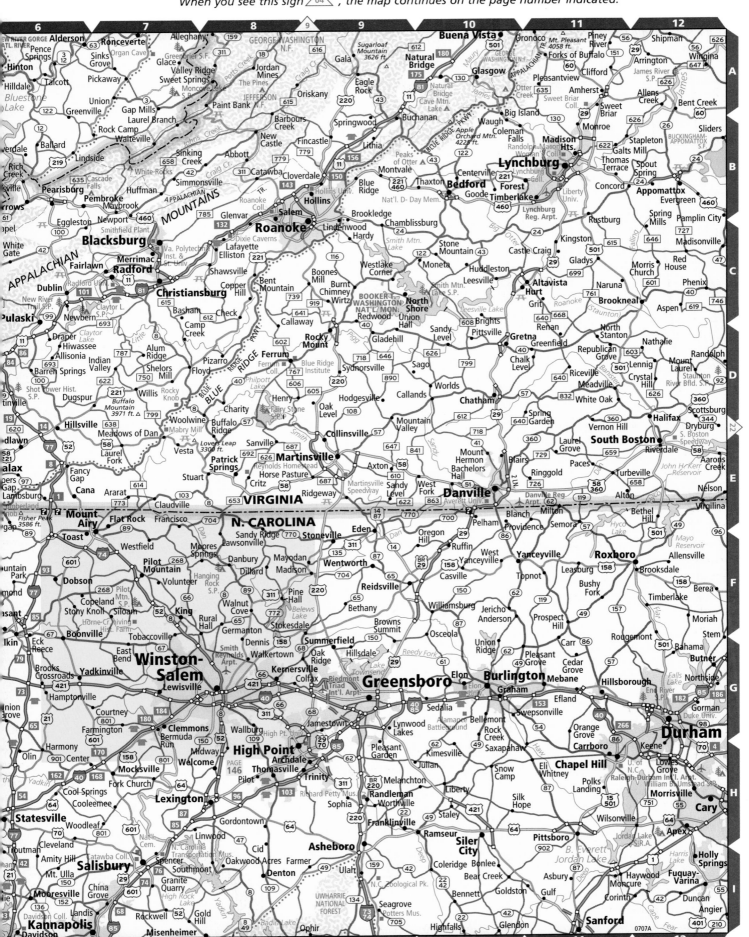

For a complete listing of symbols, see back cover flap.

DISTANCE SCALE

One inch represents 16 miles

0   5   10   15   20 miles

0   5   10   15   20   25   30 kilometers

LOCATOR MAP

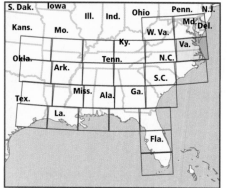

See the Pagefinder™ map on the inside of the front cover for map page numbers.

Why do some highway shields have letters or words inside them?

These letters indicate particular types of highways.

"ALT" stands for alternate route, which provides an optional path to take while going in the same general direction as the original highway.

"BR" stands for business route, which runs through the business district of a city. You will find places to shop, eat and get gas along this route.

"BYP" stands for bypass, which is a route around a major city that avoids traffic snarls.

"SPUR" indicates a way to get directly into the center of a town from a nearby highway fast.

For interstate highways, the shield is also colored green, instead of the normal red, white, and blue.

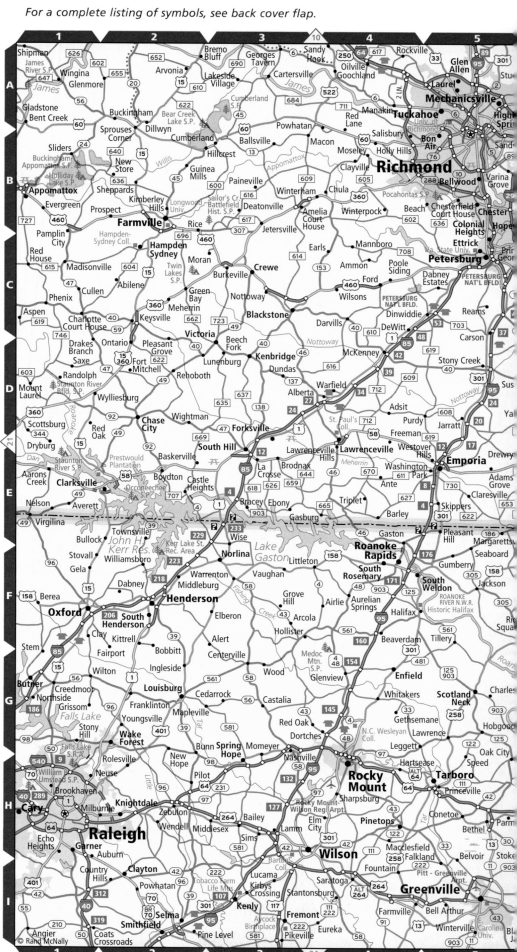

When you see this sign △04△ , the map continues on the page number indicated.

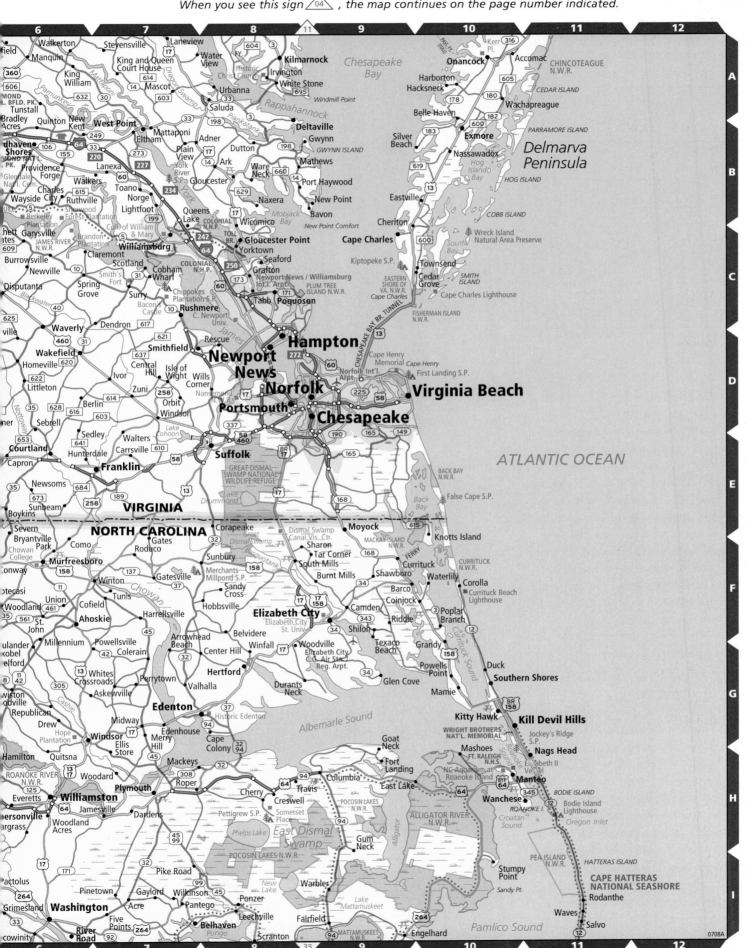

0708A

For a complete listing of symbols, see back cover flap.

DISTANCE SCALE

One inch represents 16 miles

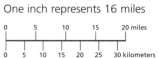

0 5 10 15 20 miles

0 5 10 15 20 25 30 kilometers

LOCATOR MAP

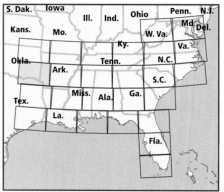

See the Pagefinder™ map on the inside of the front cover for map page numbers.

Why do some routes have more than one highway shield on them?

More than one route follows that roadway. Sometimes when a new route is built, it is easier in some stretches to use the roadway of another, currently existing route, rather than building a new road. Oftentimes, new, federally funded routes will run on older, state funded routes–or vice versa. For a short time, both routes will run along the same road. Eventually though, they will split apart and go their separate ways.

What are those yellow boxes (with little numbers) on the maps?

That's where fun stuff happens, and this book describes that area in detail starting on the page number you see. Read all about what there is to see and do, what the shopping scene's like, where you can stay overnight, what the best food to try is and where you can find it, and even if there's a festival happening during your visit. These destination sections also offer specially designed maps to help figure out where attractions and restaurants are in relation to each other (and how to drive between them).

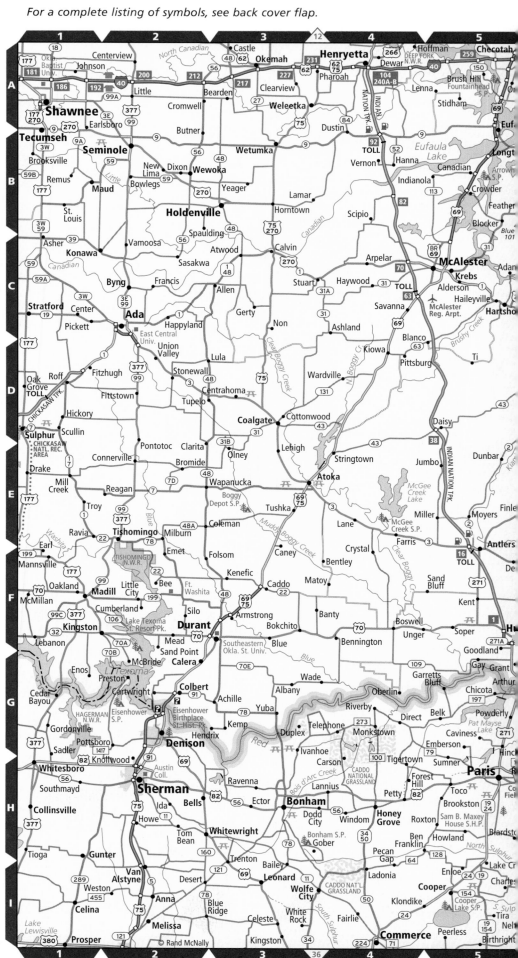

© Rand McNally

When you see this sign △04△ , the map continues on the page number indicated.

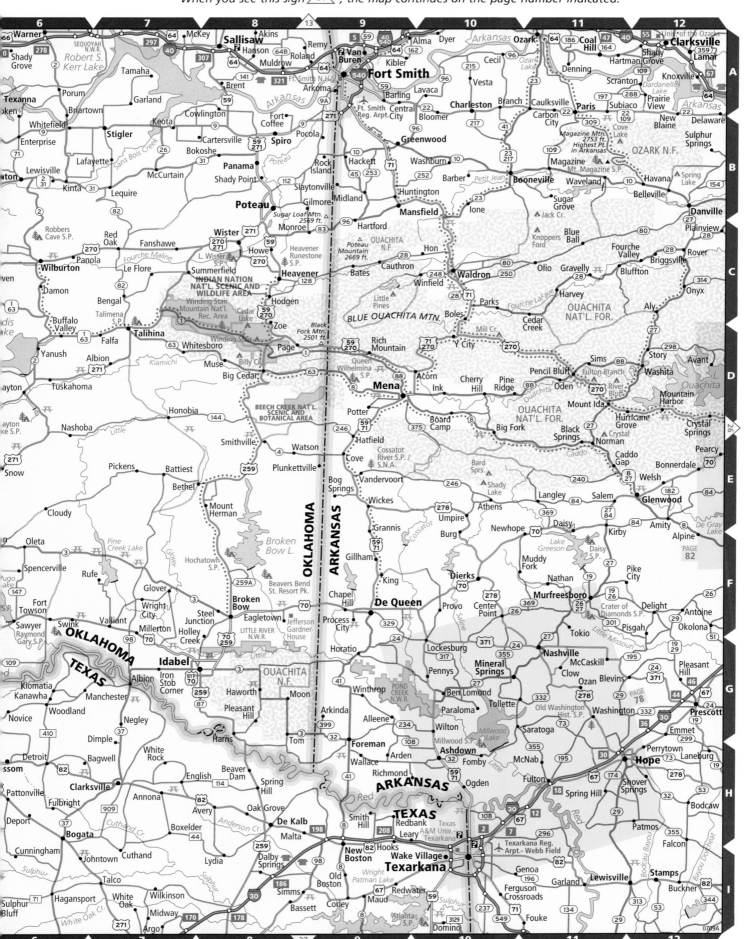

For a complete listing of symbols, see back cover flap.

DISTANCE SCALE

One inch represents 16 miles

0 5 10 15 20 miles

0 5 10 15 20 25 30 kilometers

LOCATOR MAP

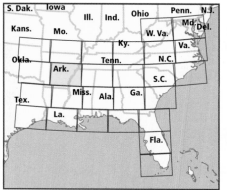

See the Pagefinder™ map on the inside of the front cover for map page numbers.

What are those little green dots alongside the road?

These green dots •••• mean the road is a specially chosen scenic route. You're almost guaranteed great views while driving.

If the dots have a ribbon of color beneath them •••••, the route is one of Rand McNally's Best of the Road™ drives. These drives have plenty to see and do along them. (See pages 190-201 for full descriptions.)

What are those yellow boxes (with little numbers) on the maps?

That's where fun stuff happens, and this book describes that area in detail starting on the page number you see. Read all about what there is to see and do, what the shopping scene's like, where you can stay overnight, what the best food to try is and where you can find it, and even if there's a festival happening during your visit. These destination sections also offer specially designed maps to help figure out where attractions and restaurants are in relation to each other (and how to drive between them).

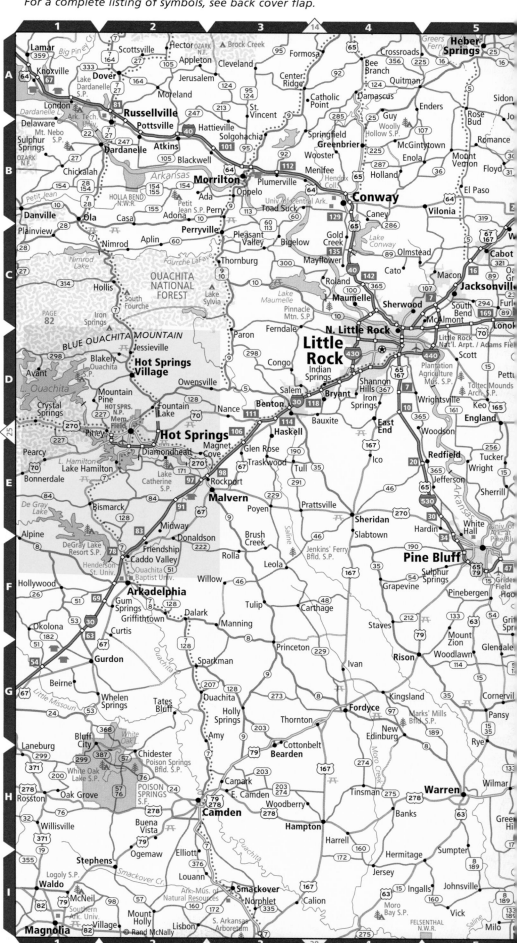

When you see this sign △04△ , the map continues on the page number indicated.

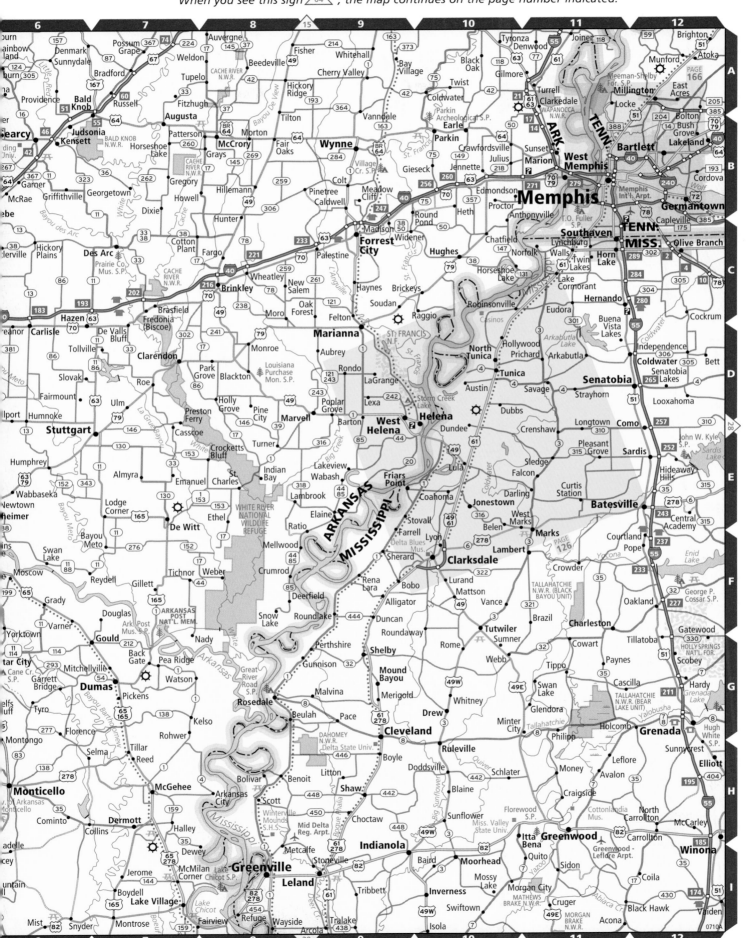

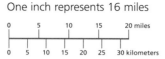

For a complete listing of symbols, see back cover flap.

DISTANCE SCALE

One inch represents 16 miles

0   5   10   15   20 miles

0 5 10 15 20 25 30 kilometers

LOCATOR MAP

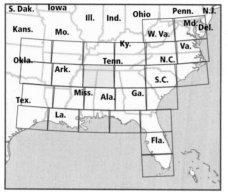

See the Pagefinder™ map on the inside of the front cover for map page numbers.

Why are some roads shown as dotted lines?

Dotted lines, ▬▬▬ or ▬▬▬, indicate a major road that is being built. This route tends to be near completion, but is not yet ready for use when the map is published. Don't confuse these routes with tunnels, which have the entrances marked ▬▬▬.

What are those yellow boxes (with little numbers) on the maps?

That's where fun stuff happens, and this book describes that area in detail starting on the page number you see. Read all about what there is to see and do, what the shopping scene's like, where you can stay overnight, what the best food to try is and where you can find it, and even if there's a festival happening during your visit. These destination sections also offer specially designed maps to help figure out where attractions and restaurants are in relation to each other (and how to drive between them).

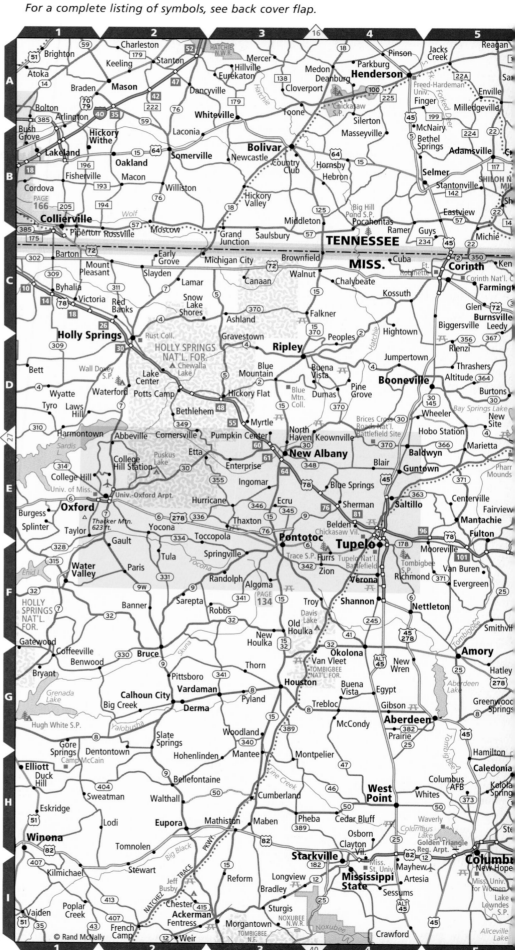

© Rand McNally

When you see this sign △04△ , the map continues on the page number indicated.

REGIONAL MAP 29

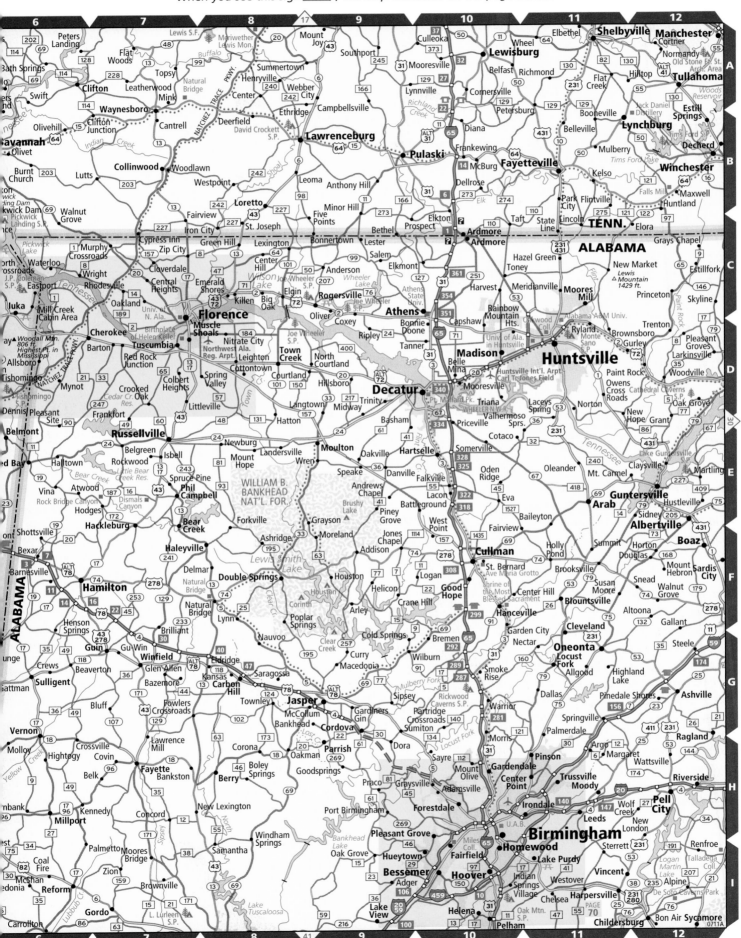

For a complete listing of symbols, see back cover flap.

DISTANCE SCALE

One inch represents 16 miles

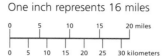

0 5 10 15 20 miles

0 5 10 15 20 25 30 kilometers

LOCATOR MAP

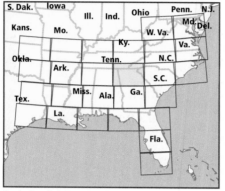

See the Pagefinder™ map on the inside of the front cover for map page numbers.

What are these little triangles on my map?

These indicate the peaks of mountains or hills. A filled-in triangle ▲ indicates the highest point in that state. A clear triangle △ indicates a landmark peak, which can help orientate you on your travels.

What are those yellow boxes (with little numbers) on the maps?

That's where fun stuff happens, and this book describes that area in detail starting on the page number you see. Read all about what there is to see and do, what the shopping scene's like, where you can stay overnight, what the best food to try is and where you can find it, and even if there's a festival happening during your visit. These destination sections also offer specially designed maps to help figure out where attractions and restaurants are in relation to each other (and how to drive between them).

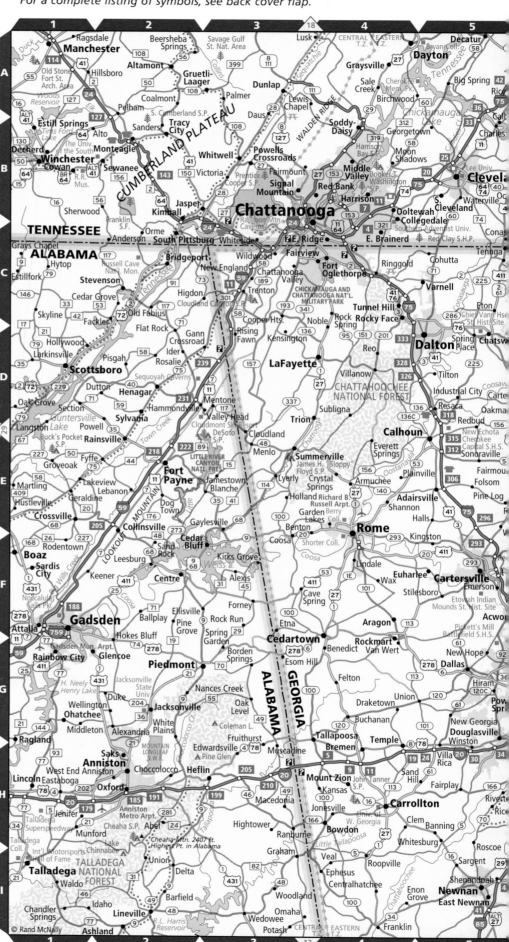

When you see this sign △04, the map continues on the page number indicated.

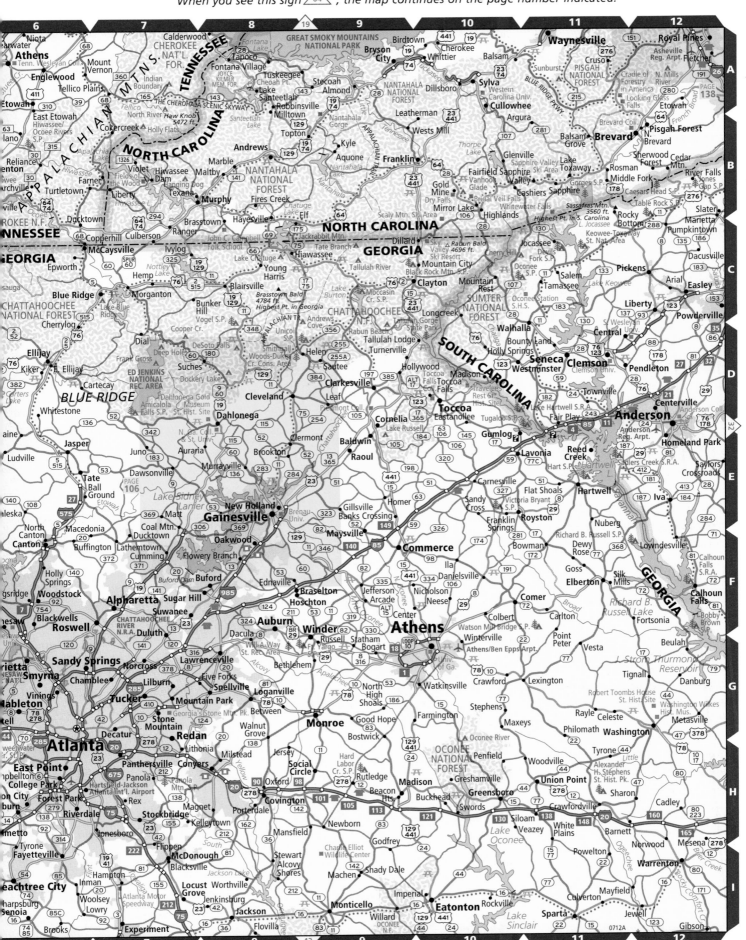

For a complete listing of symbols, see back cover flap.

DISTANCE SCALE

One inch represents 16 miles

0   5   10   15   20 miles

0   5   10   15   20   25   30 kilometers

LOCATOR MAP

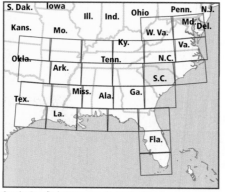

See the Pagefinder™ map on the inside of the front cover for map page numbers.

Why are there question marks on my map?

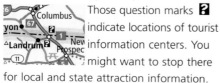

Those question marks **?** indicate locations of tourist information centers. You might want to stop there for local and state attraction information.

What are those yellow boxes (with little numbers) on the maps?

That's where fun stuff happens, and this book describes that area in detail starting on the page number you see. Read all about what there is to see and do, what the shopping scene's like, where you can stay overnight, what the best food to try is and where you can find it, and even if there's a festival happening during your visit. These destination sections also offer specially designed maps to help figure out where attractions and restaurants are in relation to each other (and how to drive between them).

When you see this sign △04, the map continues on the page number indicated.

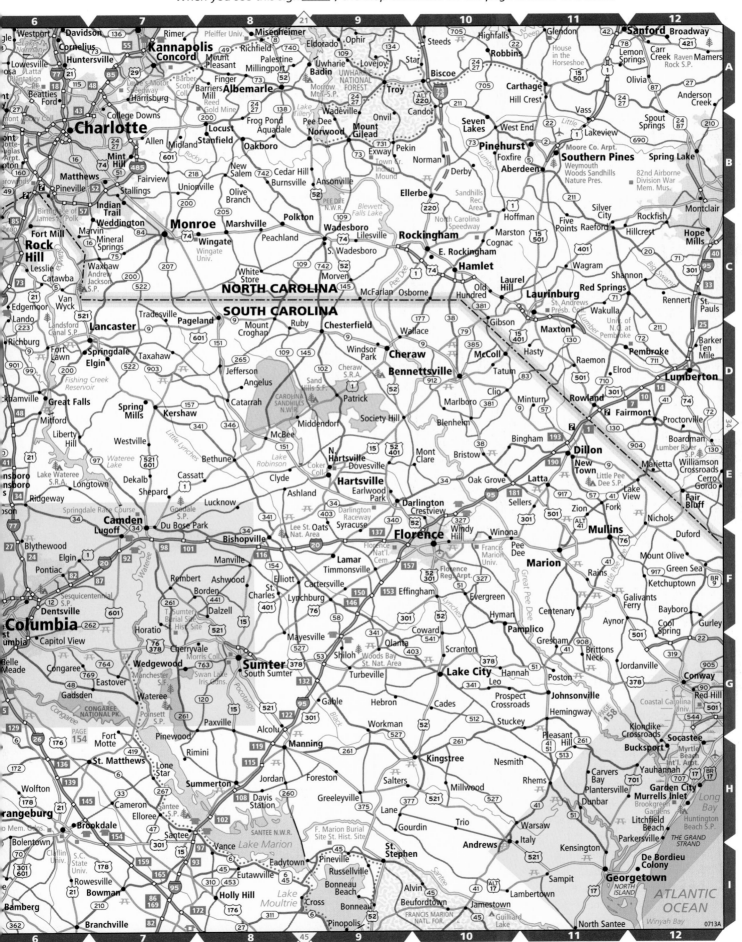

For a complete listing of symbols, see back cover flap.

DISTANCE SCALE

One inch represents 16 miles

0   5   10   15   20 miles

0   5   10   15   20   25   30 kilometers

N

LOCATOR MAP

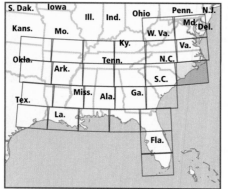

See the Pagefinder™ map on the inside of the front cover for map page numbers.

Making sense of the Interstate highway numbering system (part 1).

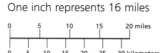

The one- and two-digit signs indicate the main Interstate routes. Even numbers are on routes that run west-east. The lowest even numbers are in the southern part of the U.S; the higher the number, the farther north the route. The major east-west cross-country routes end in a zero. Odd numbers are on north-south routes. The lowest odd-numbered routes are in the western part of the US; the higher the number, the farther east the route. The major north-south cross-country routes end in a five.

What are those yellow boxes (with little numbers) on the maps?

That's where fun stuff happens, and this book describes that area in detail starting on the page number you see. Read all about what there is to see and do, what the shopping scene's like, where you can stay overnight, what the best food to try is and where you can find it, and even if there's a festival happening during your visit. These destination sections also offer specially designed maps to help figure out where attractions and restaurants are in relation to each other (and how to drive between them).

© Rand McNally

REGIONAL MAP **35**

When you see this sign ⟨04⟩, the map continues on the page number indicated.

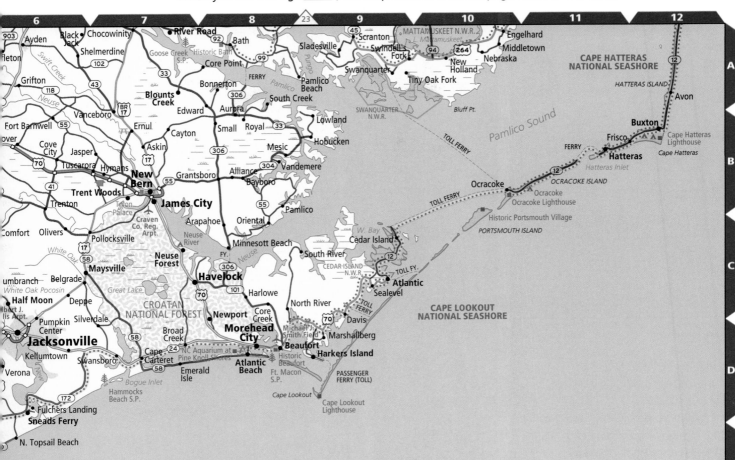

For a complete listing of symbols, see back cover flap.

DISTANCE SCALE

One inch represents 16 miles

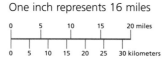

0	5	10	15	20 miles

| 0 | 5 | 10 | 15 | 20 | 25 | 30 kilometers |

LOCATOR MAP

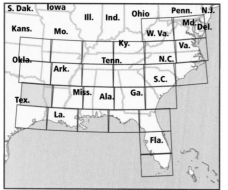

See the Pagefinder™ map on the inside of the front cover for map page numbers.

Making sense of the Interstate numbering system (part 2).

Three-digit signs indicate spur or bypass routes, replacing the abbreviations "SPUR" and "BYP" in the signs. An even first digit indicates a bypass route around a city or its downtown area. These routes eventually reconnect with the main Interstate route to provide a quick way around congested urban areas. An odd first digit indicates a spur into a city that does not reconnect to the main route. Three-digit Interstate routes are always associated with a one- or two-digit Interstate route. For example, I-480 is a bypass around a city that reconnects to I-80.

What are those yellow boxes (with little numbers) on the maps?

That's where fun stuff happens, and this book describes that area in detail starting on the page number you see. Read all about what there is to see and do, what the shopping scene's like, where you can stay overnight, what the best food to try is and where you can find it, and even if there's a festival happening during your visit. These destination sections also offer specially designed maps to help figure out where attractions and restaurants are in relation to each other (and how to drive between them).

© Rand McNally

When you see this sign △04, the map continues on the page number indicated.

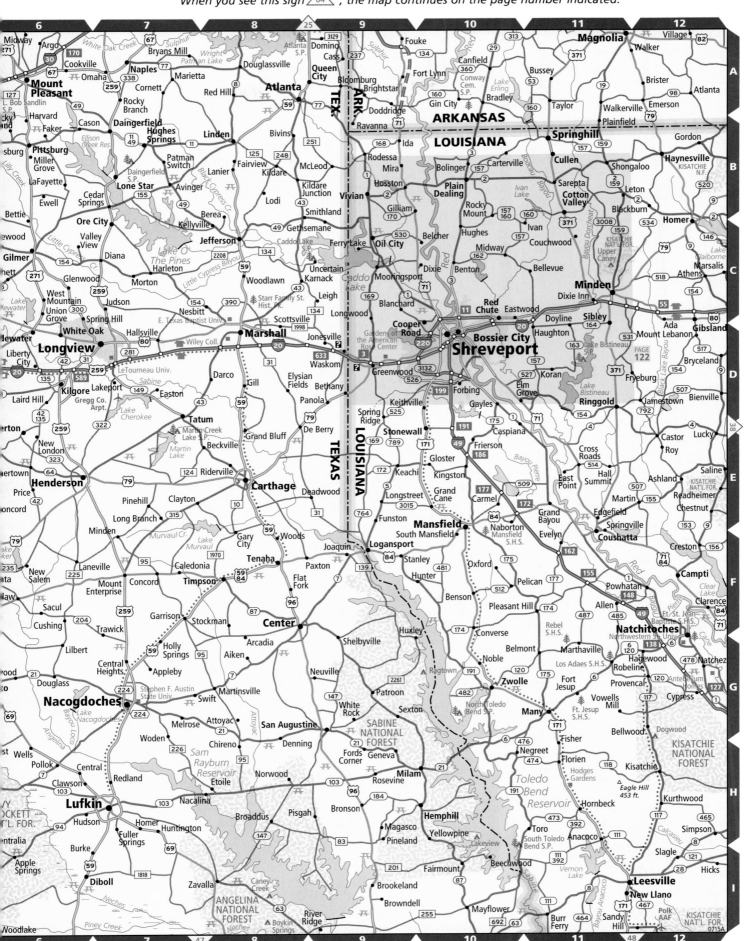

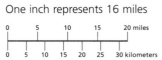

For a complete listing of symbols, see back cover flap.

DISTANCE SCALE

One inch represents 16 miles

| 0 | 5 | 10 | 15 | 20 miles |
| 0 | 5 | 10 | 15 | 20 | 25 | 30 kilometers |

N

LOCATOR MAP

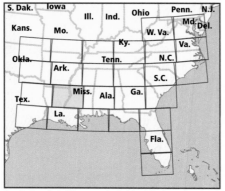

See the Pagefinder™ map on the inside of the front cover for map page numbers.

I need to find a rest stop. Does the map show where one is located?

Look for the picnic tables or little blue huts. Picnic tables indicate waysides. These are pullouts with simple amenities: picnic tables, trash cans, outhouses. Blue huts represent more built-up rest stops, usually with running water, public bathrooms, telephones, and area information. (If the hut has a white spot in it, there are no bathrooms and very few amenities.)

What are those yellow boxes (with little numbers) on the maps?

That's where fun stuff happens, and this book describes that area in detail starting on the page number you see. Read all about what there is to see and do, what the shopping scene's like, where you can stay overnight, what the best food to try is and where you can find it, and even if there's a festival happening during your visit. These destination sections also offer specially designed maps to help figure out where attractions and restaurants are in relation to each other (and how to drive between them).

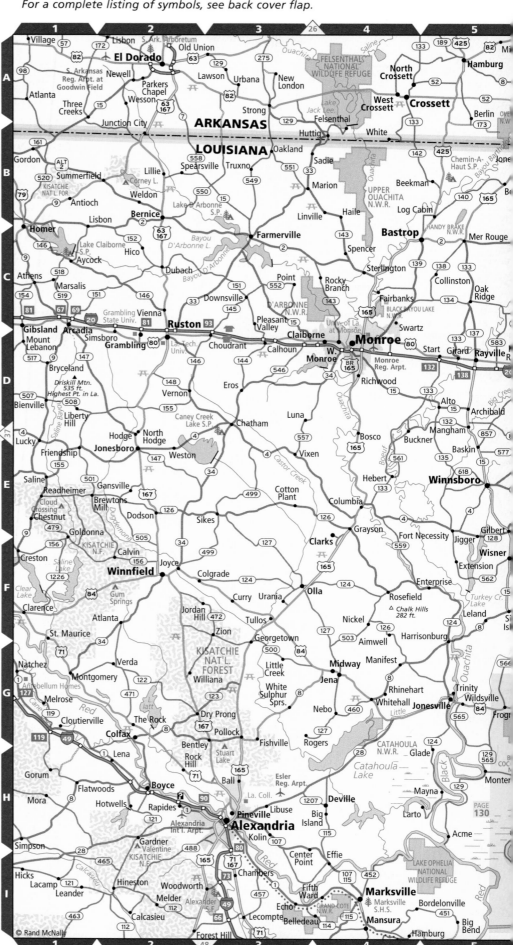

© Rand McNally

When you see this sign ⟨04⟩, the map continues on the page number indicated.

REGIONAL MAP 39

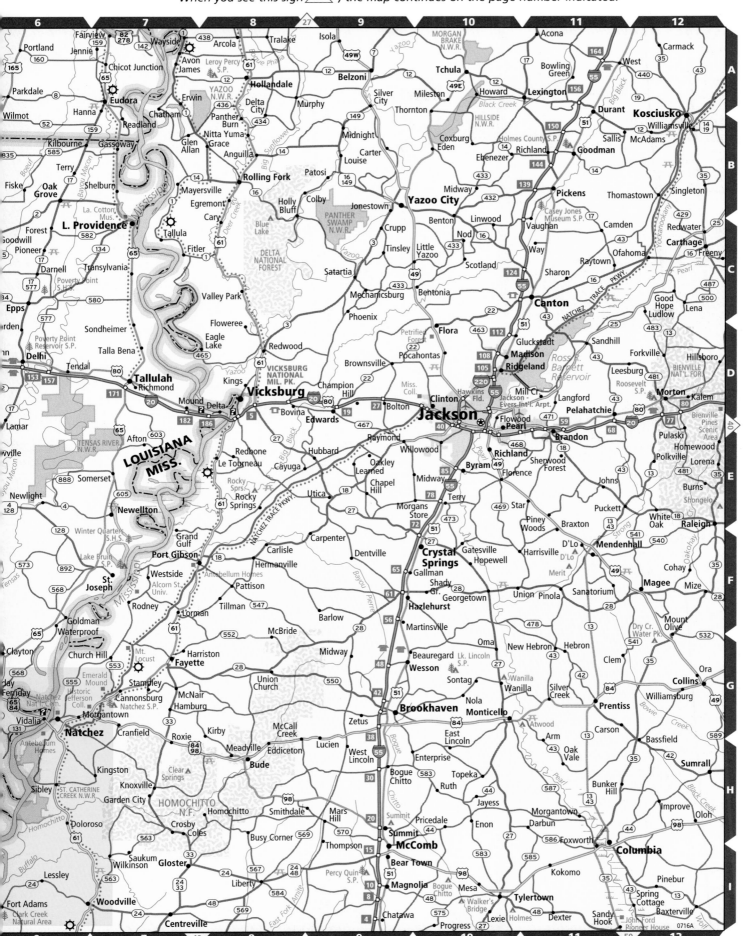

For a complete listing of symbols, see back cover flap.

DISTANCE SCALE

One inch represents 16 miles

0 5 10 15 20 miles

0 5 10 15 20 25 30 kilometers

LOCATOR MAP

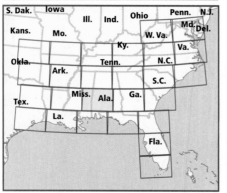

See the Pagefinder™ map on the inside of the front cover for map page numbers.

Looking for something to do along the way?

Keep an eye out for this symbol: ■

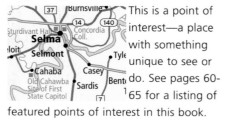

This is a point of interest—a place with something unique to see or do. See pages 60-65 for a listing of featured points of interest in this book.

What are those yellow boxes (with little numbers) on the maps?

That's where fun stuff happens, and this book describes that area in detail starting on the page number you see. Read all about what there is to see and do, what the shopping scene's like, where you can stay overnight, what the best food to try is and where you can find it, and even if there's a festival happening during your visit. These destination sections also offer specially designed maps to help figure out where attractions and restaurants are in relation to each other (and how to drive between them).

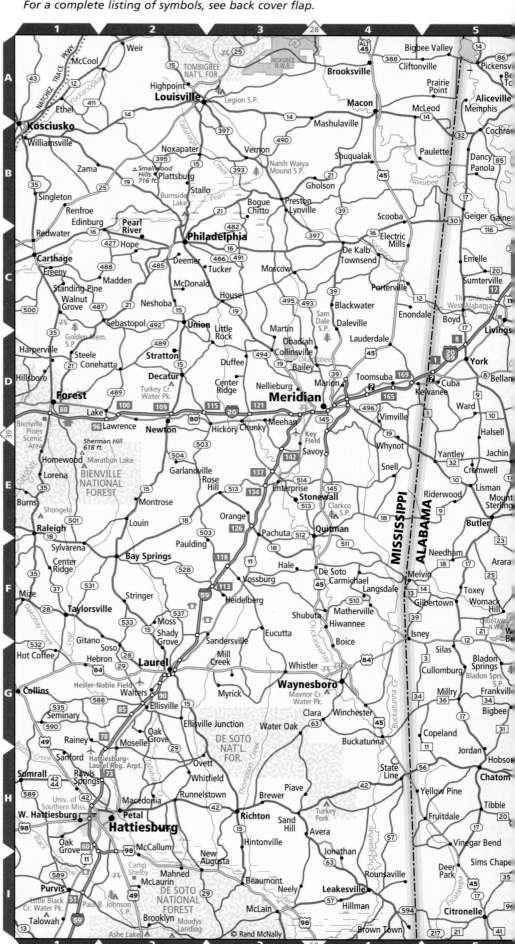

© Rand McNally

When you see this sign ⟨04⟩, the map continues on the page number indicated.

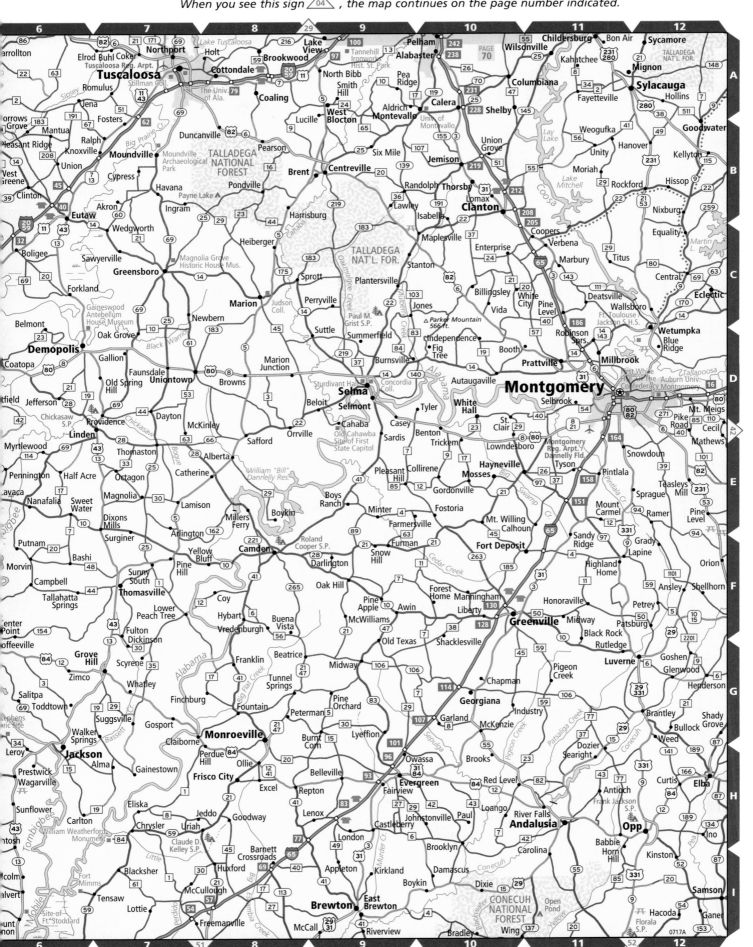

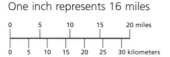

For a complete listing of symbols, see back cover flap.

DISTANCE SCALE

One inch represents 16 miles

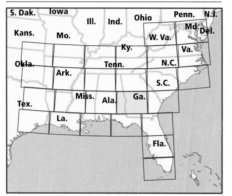

```
0    5    10    15    20 miles
0   5  10  15  20  25  30 kilometers
```

N

LOCATOR MAP

See the Pagefinder™ map on the inside of the front cover for map page numbers.

What are those yellow boxes (with little numbers) on the maps?

PAGE 52 That's where fun stuff happens, and this book describes that area in detail starting on the page number you see. Read all about what there is to see and do, what the shopping scene's like, where you can stay overnight, what the best food to try is and where you can find it, and even if there's a festival happening during your visit. These destination sections also offer specially designed maps to help figure out where attractions and restaurants are in relation to each other (and how to drive between them).

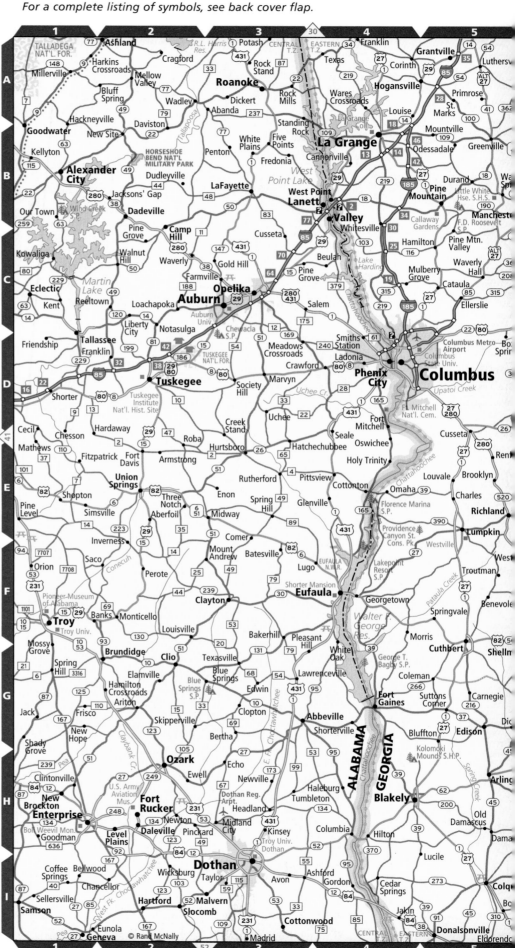

© Rand McNally

When you see this sign △04△ , the map continues on the page number indicated.

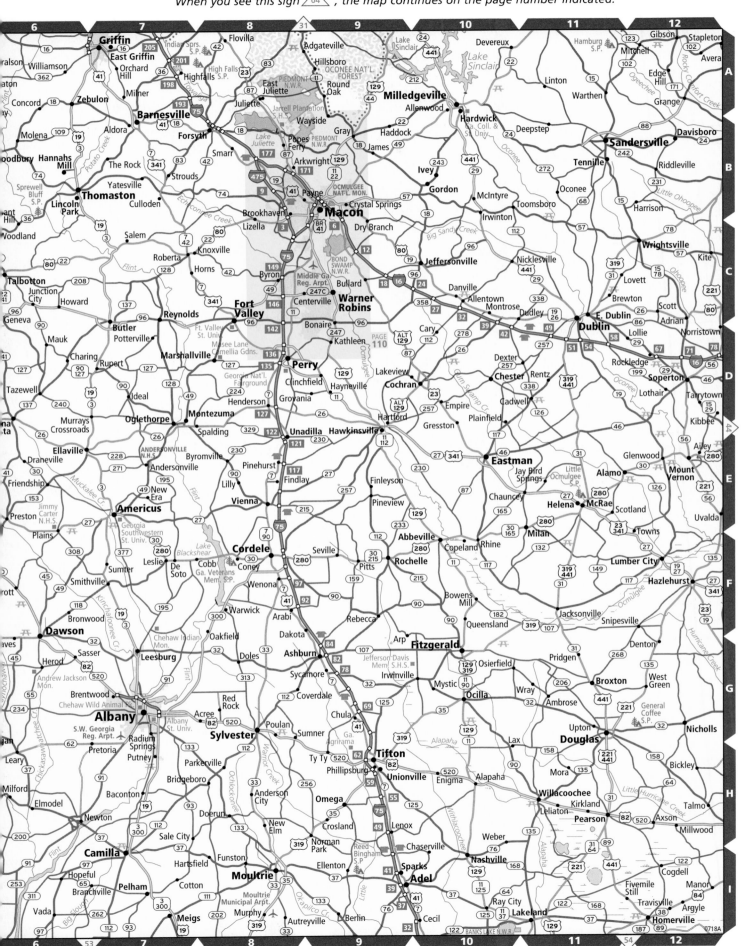

For a complete listing of symbols, see back cover flap.

DISTANCE SCALE

One inch represents 16 miles

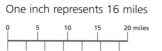

LOCATOR MAP

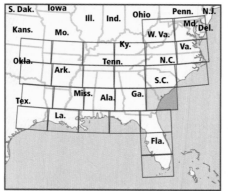

See the Pagefinder™ map on the inside of the front cover for map page numbers.

Why do some cities have orange colored areas around them?

Basically, this color shows where the people are. It does not indicate the city limits. Rather, it shows the extent of built-up urban areas around cities. You'll be certain to find stores, gas stations, hotels, and restaurants in these areas.

What are those yellow boxes (with little numbers) on the maps?

That's where fun stuff happens, and this book describes that area in detail starting on the page number you see. Read all about what there is to see and do, what the shopping scene's like, where you can stay overnight, what the best food to try is and where you can find it, and even if there's a festival happening during your visit. These destination sections also offer specially designed maps to help figure out where attractions and restaurants are in relation to each other (and how to drive between them).

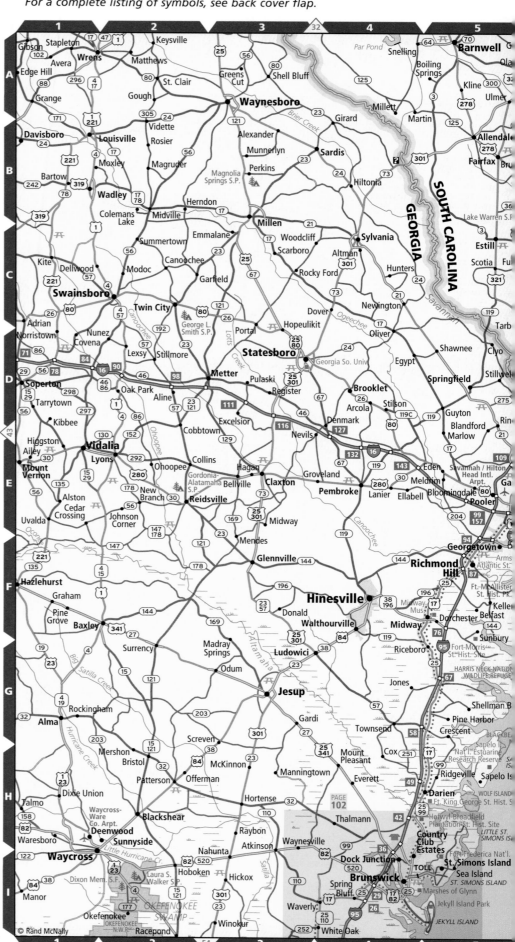

When you see this sign ⟨04⟩, the map continues on the page number indicated.

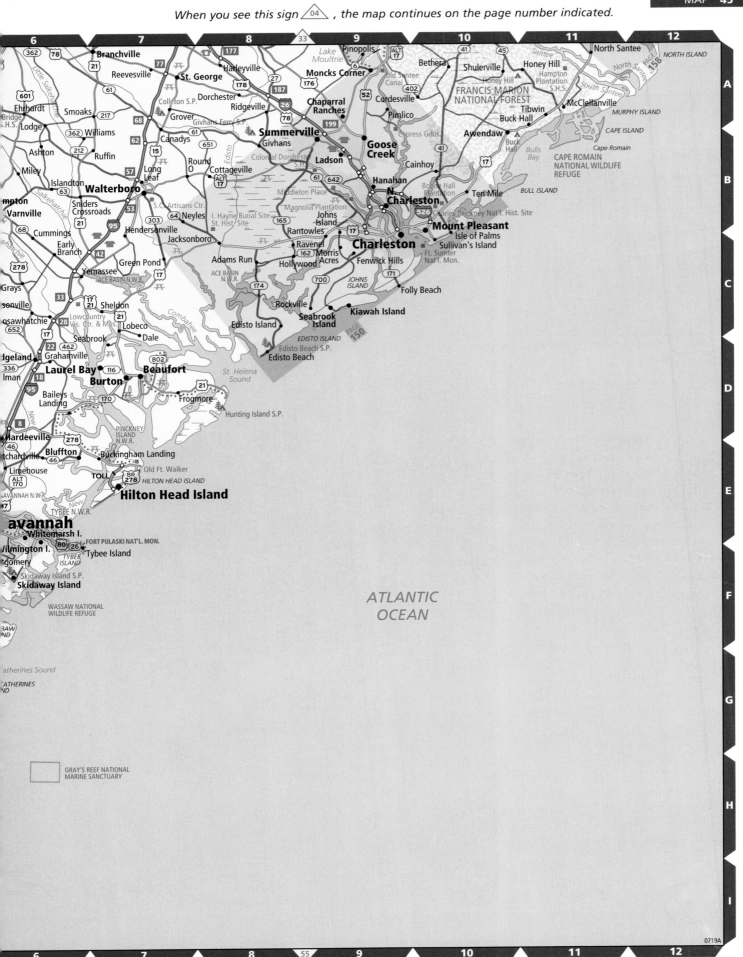

6 7 8 33 9 10 11 12

(362) (78) **Branchville**
(177)
Lake Moultrie
Pinopolis
ALT 17
North Santee
NORTH ISLAND
A

(21)
Reevesville
(77)
Halleyville
Moncks Corner
Bethera
Shulerville
Honey Hill
Santee

St. George
(178)
(27)
(187)
176
Old Santee Canal
Honey Hill
Hampton Plantation S.H.S.
North Santee
PAGE 158

(601)
Ehrhardt
Smoaks
(217)
Grover
Dorchester
Ridgeville
(26)
Chaparral Ranches
(52)
Cordesville
(402)
Pimlico
FRANCIS MARION NATIONAL FOREST
Tibwin
McClellanville
MURPHY ISLAND

.H.S.
Lodge
(68)
Canadys
(78)
Summerville
(199)
Goose Creek
Cypress Gdns.
Awendaw
Buck Hall
CAPE ISLAND

(362)
Williams
(62)
Givhans Ferry S.P.
(651)
Givhans
Cainhoy
(41)
Buck Hall
Bulls Bay
Cape Romain
CAPE ROMAIN NATIONAL WILDLIFE REFUGE
B

Ashton
(212)
Ruffin
(15)
Round O
Colonial Dorchester S.H.S.
Ladson
(61)
(642)
Hanahan
17

Miley
(57)
Long Leaf
ALT 17
Cottageville
Middleton Place
N. Charleston
Boone Hall Plantation
Ten Mile
BULL ISLAND

Islandton
(63)
Walterboro
(53)
S.C. Artisans Ctr.
Magnolia Plantation
526
Charles Pinckney Nat'l. Hist. Site

mpton
Varnville
Sniders Crossroads
(21)
(303)
(64)
Neyles
I. Hayne Burial Site St. Hist. Site
(165)
Johns Island
17
Mount Pleasant
Isle of Palms
Charleston

(68)
Cummings
Hendersonville
Jacksonboro
Rantowles
(162)
Morris Acres
Charleston
Sullivan's Island
C

Grays
Early Branch
(42)
Green Pond
Adams Run
Ravenel
Hollywood
Fenwick Hills
Ft. Sumter Nat'l. Mon.
171

sonville
(33)
(278)
Yemassee
ACE BASIN N.W.R.
17
ACE BASIN N.W.R.
(174)
(700)
JOHNS ISLAND
Folly Beach

osawhatchie
(652)
(28)
Lowcountry Vis. Ctr. & Mus.
(17)
(21)
Sheldon
(21)
Lobeco
Dale
Rockville
Seabrook Island
Kiawah Island
PAGE 150

Igeland
(22)
(462)
Grahamville
(802)
Edisto Island
EDISTO ISLAND
D

(336)
Iman
(18)
Laurel Bay
(116)
Beaufort
Edisto Beach S.P.
Edisto Beach
St. Helena Sound

(95)
Burton
(170)
Baileys Landing
(21)
Frogmore

(8)
Hunting Island S.P.

Hardeeville
(46)
(278)
PINCKNEY ISLAND N.W.R.
Buckingham Landing
E

tchardville
(46)
Bluffton
Old Ft. Walker

Limehouse
ALT 170
TOLL
BR 278
HILTON HEAD ISLAND

AVANNAH N.W.R.
17
TYBEE N.W.R.
Hilton Head Island

avannah
Whitemarsh I.
FORT PULASKI NAT'L. MON.

ilmington I.
(80)
(26)
Tybee Island
TYBEE ISLAND
F

gomery
Skidaway Island S.P.
Skidaway Island

WASSAW NATIONAL WILDLIFE REFUGE

AW ND

atherines Sound

ATHERINES ND

ATLANTIC OCEAN
G

GRAY'S REEF NATIONAL MARINE SANCTUARY
H

I

For a complete listing of symbols, see back cover flap.

DISTANCE SCALE

One inch represents 16 miles

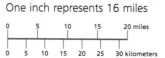

LOCATOR MAP

See the Pagefinder™ map on the inside of the front cover for map page numbers.

Why are some rivers and lakes shown with dotted lines?

These dotted lines indicate a lake or river, such as Sandy Creek in the example to the left, that isn't always wet! Sometimes during the year, the river or lake may dry up. At other times, the river can be a rushing torrent of water, or the lake bed is brimming. If water is present year-round, the river or lake will be shown with solid lines. Many of the year-round lakes are man-made. You can identify these from the presence of a dam symbol, as in the case of the Cedar Creek Reservoir in the example to the left. Major rivers and lakes make useful landmarks as you travel.

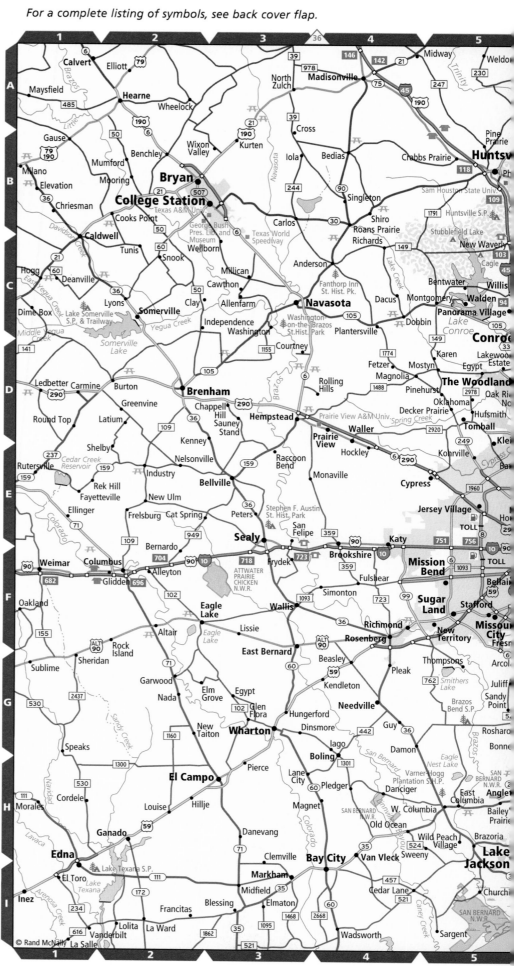

© Rand McNally

When you see this sign △04, the map continues on the page number indicated.

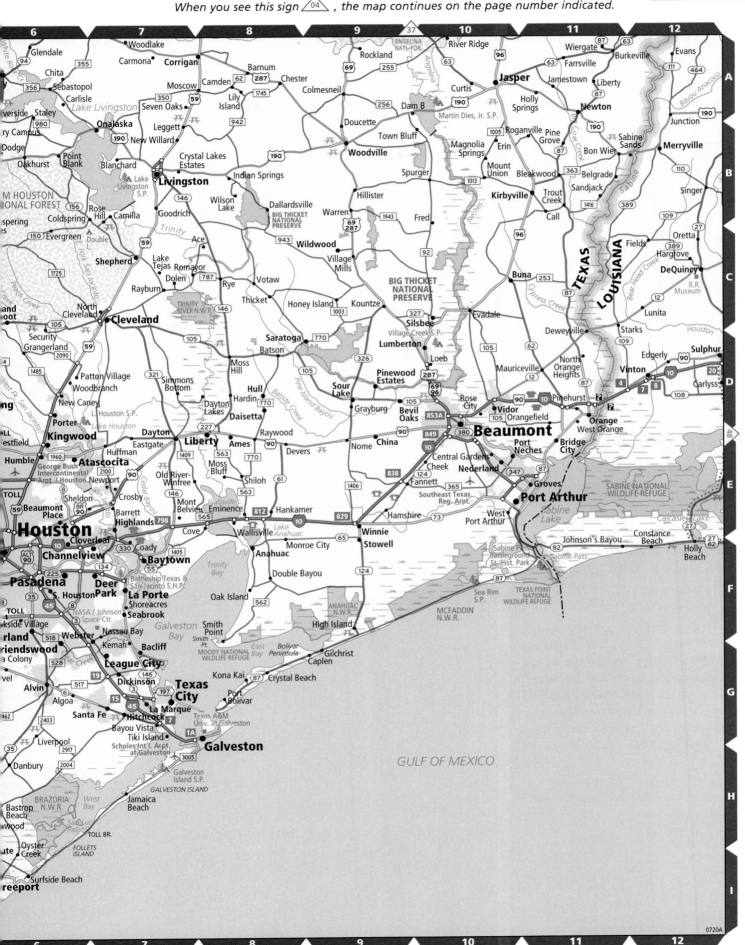

GULF OF MEXICO

For a complete listing of symbols, see back cover flap.

DISTANCE SCALE

One inch represents 16 miles

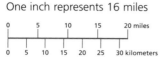

| 0 | 5 | 10 | 15 | 20 miles |

| 0 | 5 | 10 | 15 | 20 | 25 | 30 kilometers |

LOCATOR MAP

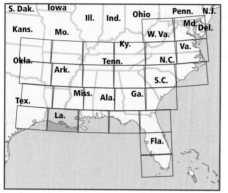

See the Pagefinder™ map on the inside of the front cover for map page numbers.

What are all those short blue lines, some with tufts on them?

When you see this pattern, ≋ you are in an area that has marshes, swamps or mangrove swamps. The terrain is damp, boggy and sometimes even underwater for part of the year. Be sure to stay on the roadways in these areas.

What are those yellow boxes (with little numbers) on the maps?

That's where fun stuff happens, and this book describes that area in detail starting on the page number you see. Read all about what there is to see and do, what the shopping scene's like, where you can stay overnight, what the best food to try is and where you can find it, and even if there's a festival happening during your visit. These destination sections also offer specially designed maps to help figure out where attractions and restaurants are in relation to each other (and how to drive between them).

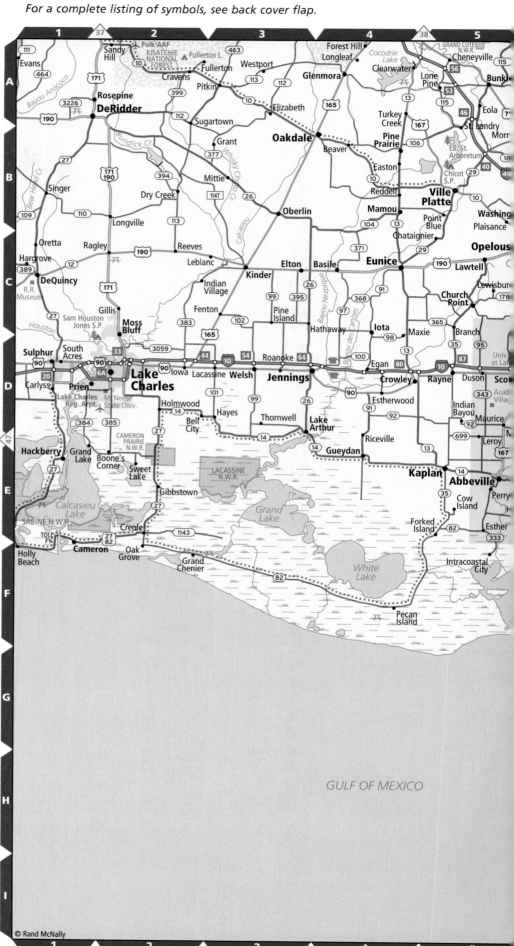

© Rand McNally

When you see this sign △04 , the map continues on the page number indicated.

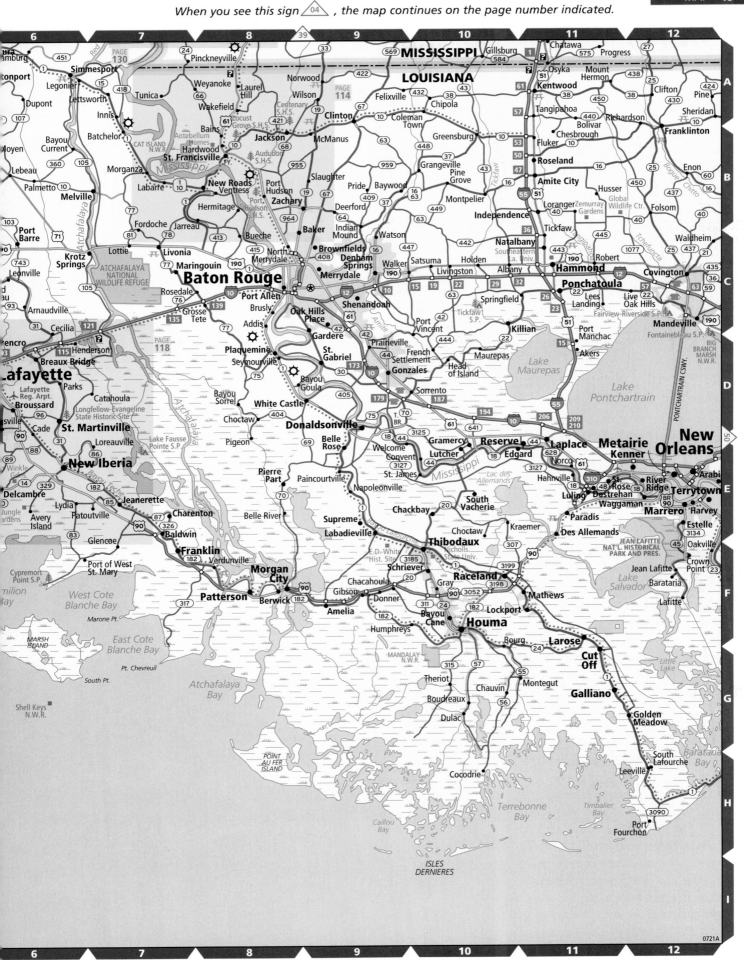

0721A

For a complete listing of symbols, see back cover flap.

DISTANCE SCALE

One inch represents 16 miles

0   5   10   15   20 miles

0   5   10   15   20   25   30 kilometers

N

LOCATOR MAP

See the Pagefinder™ map on the inside of the front cover for map page numbers.

What are those numbers in the green boxes?

Those are exit numbers **10**. You'll see those same numbers in the big green signs over or alongside the highway that say "Exit." In most states, exits are numbered according to how many miles from the southern or western border the exit is located.

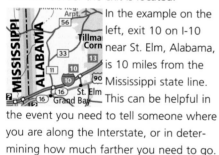

In the example on the left, exit 10 on I-10 near St. Elm, Alabama, is 10 miles from the Mississippi state line. This can be helpful in the event you need to tell someone where you are along the Interstate, or in determining how much farther you need to go.

What are those yellow boxes (with little numbers) on the maps?

That's where fun stuff happens, and this book describes that area in detail starting on the page number you see. Read all about what there is to see and do, what the shopping scene's like, where you can stay overnight, what the best food to try is and where you can find it, and even if there's a festival happening during your visit. These destination sections also offer specially designed maps to help figure out where attractions and restaurants are in relation to each other (and how to drive between them).

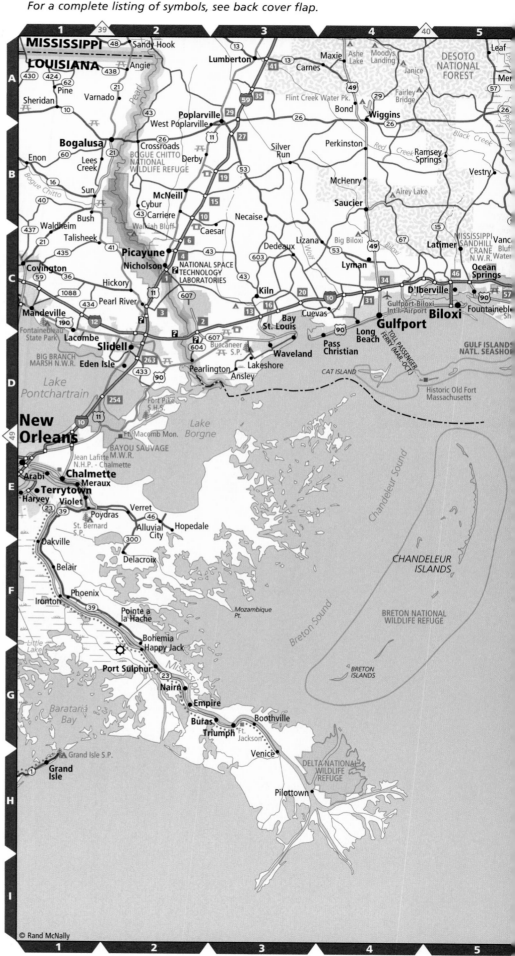

© Rand McNally

When you see this sign ⊿04 , the map continues on the page number indicated.

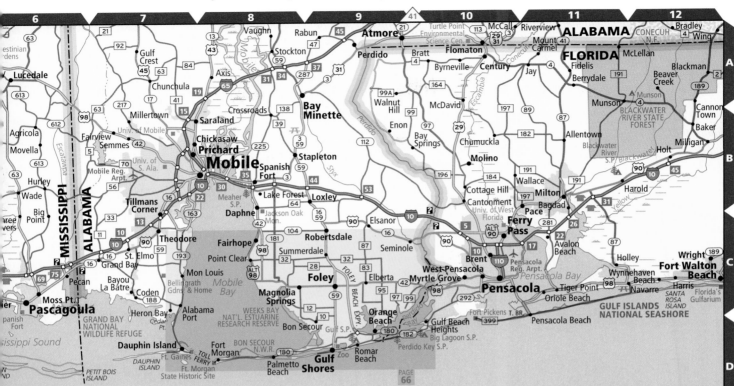

The US 90 bridges across St. Louis Bay and Biloxi Bay were left impassable by Hurricane Katrina and are currently being reconstructed.

GULF OF MEXICO

0722A

For a complete listing of symbols, see back cover flap.

DISTANCE SCALE

One inch represents 16 miles

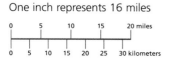

0   5   10   15   20 miles

0 5 10 15 20 25 30 kilometers

N

LOCATOR MAP

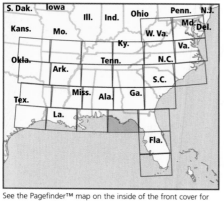

S. Dak.	Iowa		Ohio		Penn.	N.J.
Kans.	Mo.	Ill.	Ind.		Md.	Del.
			Ky.	W. Va.	Va.	
Okla.	Ark.	Tenn.		N.C.		
		Miss.		S.C.		
Tex.	La.	Ala.	Ga.			
				Fla.		

See the Pagefinder™ map on the inside of the front cover for map page numbers.

What can you tell me about the airports shown on the map?

Airports represented by this symbol, ✈, are commercial, have paved runways 5,000 feet or longer, and have regularly scheduled passenger service–though some airports have many more flights than others.

What are those yellow boxes (with little numbers) on the maps?

That's where fun stuff happens, and this book describes that area in detail starting on the page number you see. Read all about what there is to see and do, what the shopping scene's like, where you can stay overnight, what the best food to try is and where you can find it, and even if there's a festival happening during your visit. These destination sections also offer specially designed maps to help figure out where attractions and restaurants are in relation to each other (and how to drive between them).

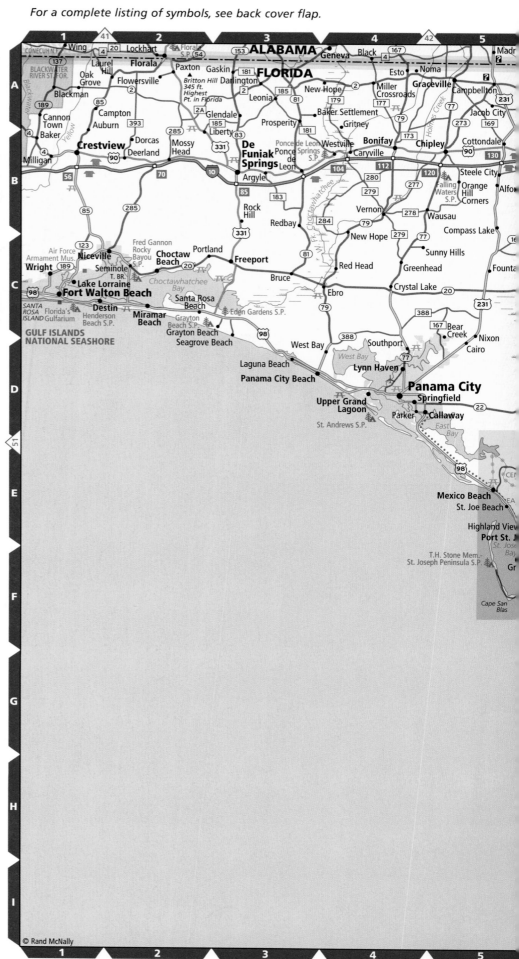

© Rand McNally

When you see this sign ⟨04⟩, the map continues on the page number indicated.

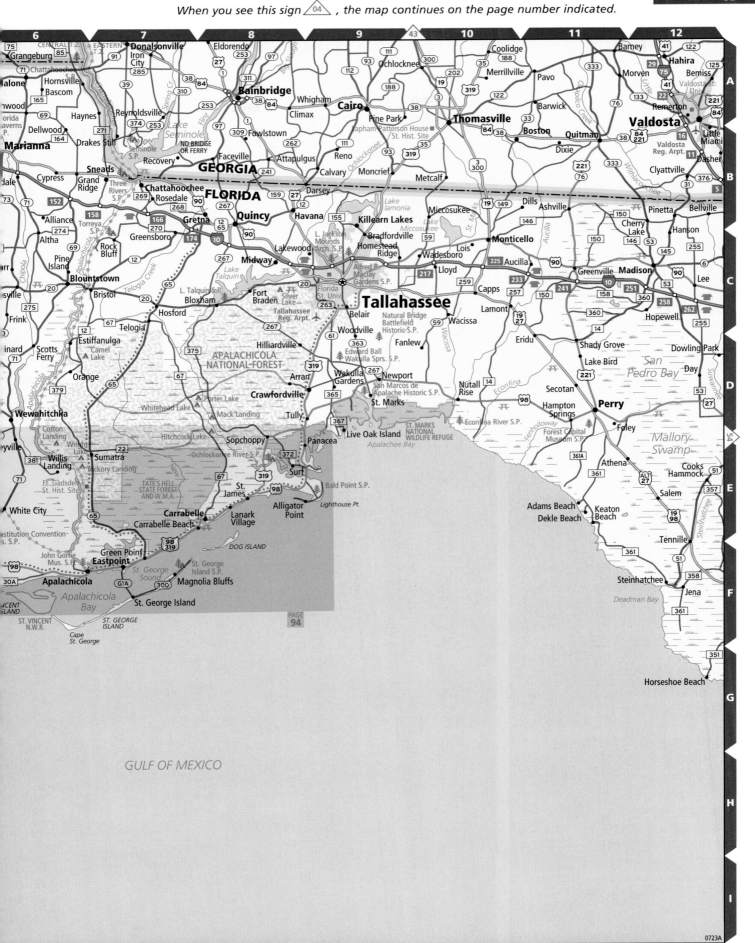

PAGE 94

0723A

For a complete listing of symbols, see back cover flap.

DISTANCE SCALE

One inch represents 16 miles

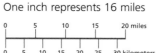

0   5   10   15   20 miles

0   5   10   15   20   25   30 kilometers

LOCATOR MAP

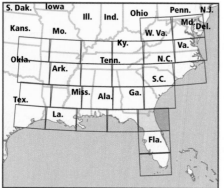

See the Pagefinder™ map on the inside of the front cover for map page numbers.

Where can I find public camping facilities?

Look for the fir tree symbols. These symbols indicate a state-run park, forest, historic site, or recreation area.

A tent next to the fir tree means there are modern public camping facilities (running water, flush toilets and electricity available); no tent means no camping.

A tent all by itself indicates public camping facilities within a federally run park, monument, forest, or recreation area.

What are those yellow boxes (with little numbers) on the maps?

That's where fun stuff happens, and this book describes that area in detail starting on the page number you see. Read all about what there is to see and do, what the shopping scene's like, where you can stay overnight, what the best food to try is and where you can find it, and even if there's a festival happening during your visit. These destination sections also offer specially designed maps to help figure out where attractions and restaurants are in relation to each other (and how to drive between them).

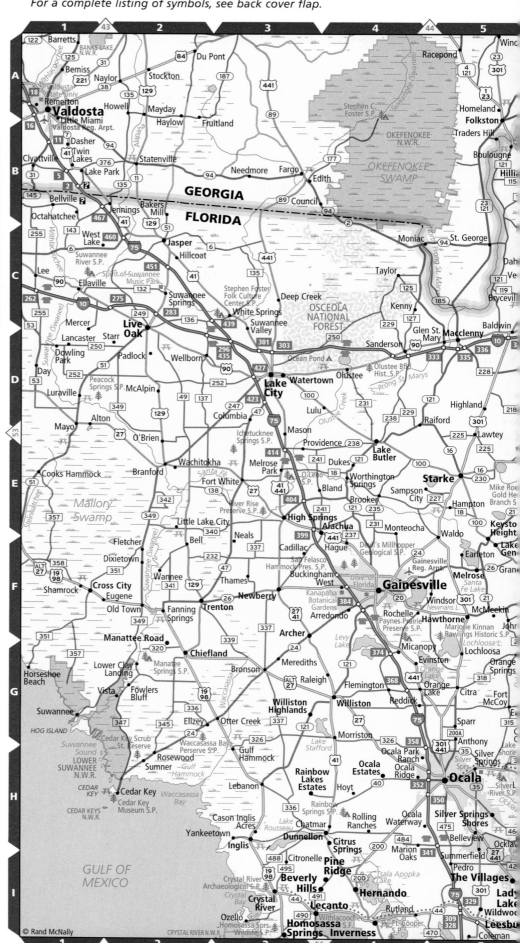

© Rand McNally

When you see this sign ◁04▷ , the map continues on the page number indicated.

**ATLANTIC
OCEAN**

For a complete listing of symbols, see back cover flap.

DISTANCE SCALE

One inch represents 16 miles

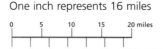

0   5   10   15   20 miles

0   5   10   15   20   25   30 kilometers

LOCATOR MAP

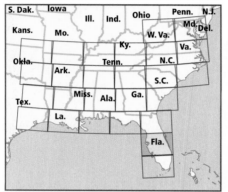

See the Pagefinder™ map on the inside of the front cover for map page numbers.

Why do some shields have more than one number in them?

You won't see these alongside the road, as this is a space-saving trick cartographers use on maps. In this example, this route is both US Highway 17 *and* US Highway 98.

Eventually these two routes will split, but for now they use the same roadway.

What are those yellow boxes (with little numbers) on the maps?

That's where fun stuff happens, and this book describes that area in detail starting on the page number you see. Read all about what there is to see and do, what the shopping scene's like, where you can stay overnight, what the best food to try is and where you can find it, and even if there's a festival happening during your visit. These destination sections also offer specially designed maps to help figure out where attractions and restaurants are in relation to each other (and how to drive between them).

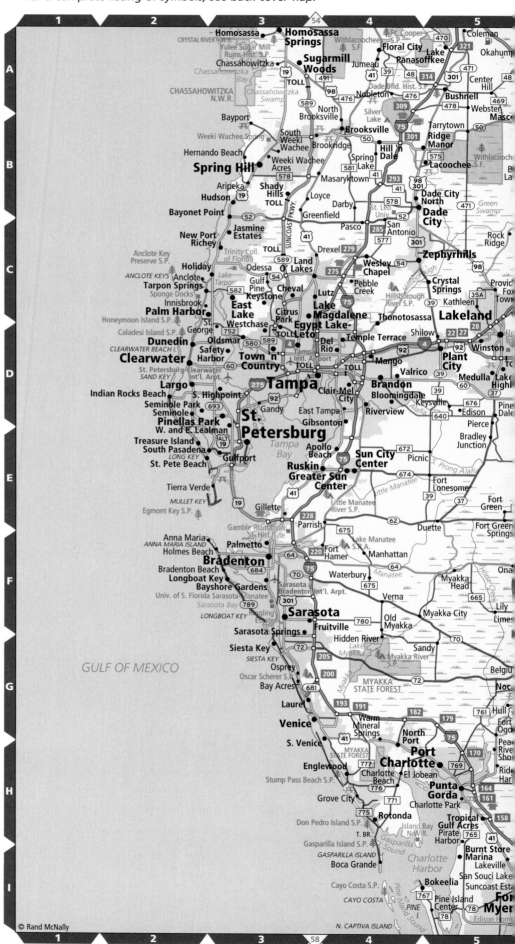

© Rand McNally

When you see this sign △04△, the map continues on the page number indicated.

REGIONAL MAP 57

For a complete listing of symbols, see back cover flap.

DISTANCE SCALE

One inch represents 16 miles

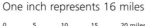

0   5   10   15   20 miles

0   5   10   15   20   25   30 kilometers

LOCATOR MAP

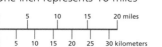

See the Pagefinder™ map on the inside of the front cover for map page numbers.

What do the little blue gas tanks represent?

These symbols will only be seen along toll roads. They represent places where you can stop to fuel up without having to leave the tollway. Here you will find gas for your car as well as food for yourself.

What are those yellow boxes (with little numbers) on the maps?

That's where fun stuff happens, and this book describes that area in detail starting on the page number you see. Read all about what there is to see and do, what the shopping scene's like, where you can stay overnight, what the best food to try is and where you can find it, and even if there's a festival happening during your visit. These destination sections also offer specially designed maps to help figure out where attractions and restaurants are in relation to each other (and how to drive between them).

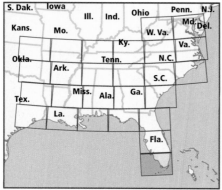

Pine Island Center
NORTH CAPTIVA I.   PINE I.   78   Edison Hor
Flamingo Bay   **Cape Coral**   Vi
CAPTIVA ISLAND   Pine I.   Cypress Lake
Captiva   Sound   Iona
St. James   MATLACHA   Ft. Myers   865
City   N.W.R.   Beach
J.N. "DING"   T. BR.
DARLING N.W.R.   **Sanibel**
The Bailey-   SANIBEL   ESTERO
Matthews   ISLAND   ISLAND
Shell Mus.
Lovers Key S.

GULF OF MEXICO

DRY TORTUGAS
NATIONAL PARK

DRY
TORTUGAS

KEY WEST
NATIONAL
WILDLIFE REFUGE

MARQUESAS KEYS   Boca Grande Channel   BOCA
GRANDE
KEY

© Rand McNally

When you see this sign △04△, the map continues on the page number indicated.

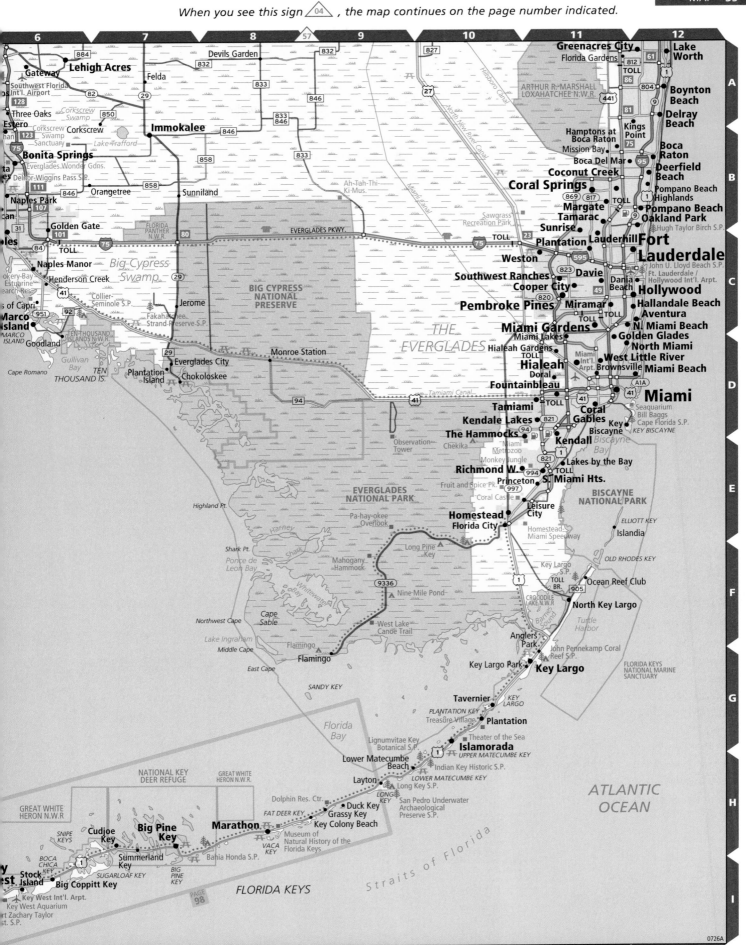

THE EVERGLADES

THE EVERGLADES

Fort Lauderdale

Miami

ATLANTIC OCEAN

FLORIDA KEYS

Straits of Florida

0726A

POINTS OF INTEREST

AIRPORTS

AIRPORT	State	Page	Grid
Albert J. Ellis Airport	NC	35	C6
Alexandria International Airport	LA	38	H2
Anderson Regional Airport	SC	31	E12
Anniston Metro Airport	AL	30	H2
Asheville Regional Airport	NC	31	A12
Athens / Ben Epps Airport	GA	31	G10
Augusta Regional Airport at Bush Field	GA	32	I3
Baltimore-Washington International Airport	MD	11	D7
Barkley Regional Airport	KY	16	C4
Birmingham International Airport	AL	29	H10
Boone County Airport	AR	14	F2
Bowling Green-Warren County Regional Airport	KY	17	D11
Cape Girardeau Regional Airport	MO	16	C2
Charlotte-Douglas International Airport	NC	33	B6
Charlottesville-Albemarle Airport	VA	10	H2
Columbia Metro Airport	SC	32	G5
Columbus Metro Airport	GA	42	D4
Cox Field	TX	24	H5
Craven County Regional Airport	NC	35	B7
Crossville Memorial Airport-Whitson Field	TN	18	H4
Danville Regional Airport	VA	21	E10
Daytona Beach International Airport	FL	55	H8
Dothan Regional Airport	AL	42	H3
Drake Field	AR	13	G10
Elizabeth City Coast Guard Air Station / Regional Airport	NC	23	F9
Esler Regional Airport	LA	38	H3
Fayetteville Regional Airport / Grannis Field	NC	34	C1
Florence Regional Airport	SC	33	F10
Fort Lauderdale / Hollywood International Airport	FL	59	C11
Fort Smith Regional Airport	AR	25	A9
Frederick Municipal Airport	MD	10	C5
Gadsden Municipal Airport	AL	30	G1
Gainesville Regional Airport	FL	54	F4
George Bush Intercontinental Airport / Houston	TX	47	E6
Golden Triangle Regional Airport	MS	28	I5
Grand Strand Airport	SC	34	G2
Greater Cumberland Regional Airport	MD	10	B1
Greenbrier Valley Airport	WV	9	I8
Greenville Downtown Airport	SC	32	C2
Greenville-Spartanburg International Airport	SC	32	C2
Greenwood County Airport	SC	32	E2
Greenwood-Leflore Airport	MS	27	H11
Gregg County Airport	TX	37	D7
Grider Field	AR	26	F5
Gulfport-Biloxi International Airport	MS	50	C4
Hagerstown Regional Airport-Richard A. Henson Field	MD	10	B4
Harrison / Marion Regional Airport	WV	9	C8
Hartsfield-Jackson Atlanta International Airport	GA	31	H6
Hattiesburg-Laurel Regional Airport	MS	40	H1
Hawkins Field	MS	39	D10
Hesler-Noble Field	MS	40	G2
Hickory Regional Airport	NC	20	H4
Huntsville International Airport-Carl T. Jones Field	AL	29	D10
Jackson-Evers International Airport	MS	39	D10
Jacksonville International Airport	FL	55	C6
Jonesboro Municipal Airport	AR	15	H10
Key Field	MS	40	D3
Key West International Airport	FL	59	I6
Kinston Regional Jetport at Stallings Field	NC	34	A5
Lafayette Regional Airport	LA	49	D6
Lake Charles Regional Airport	LA	48	D2
Little Rock National Airport / Adams Field	AR	26	D4
London-Corbin Airport-Magee Field	KY	19	C7
Louie Armstrong New Orleans International Airport	LA	49	E11
Lynchburg Regional Airport	VA	21	B11
Manassas Regional Airport / Harry P. Davis Field	VA	10	F5
McAlester Regional Airport	OK	24	C5
McGhee Tyson Airport	TN	19	H7
McKellar-Sipes Regional Airport	TN	16	I4
Melbourne International Airport	FL	57	C10
Memorial Field	AR	26	E2
Memphis International Airport	TN	27	B11
Miami International Airport	FL	59	D11
Michael J. Smith Field	NC	35	D8
Mid Delta Regional Airport	MS	27	H8
Middle Georgia Regional Airport	GA	43	C9
Mid-Ohio Valley Regional Airport	WV	8	C4
Millville Airport	NJ	11	C12
Mobile Regional Airport	AL	51	B7
Monett Municipal Airport	MO	13	D11
Monroe Regional Airport	LA	38	D4
Montgomery Regional Airport / Dannelly Field	AL	41	D11
Moore County Airport	NC	33	B11
Moultrie Municipal Airport	GA	43	I8
Myrtle Beach International Airport	SC	33	H12
Nashville International Airport	TN	17	G11
New Castle County Airport	DE	11	B10
Newport News / Williamsburg International Airport	VA	23	C8
Norfolk International Airport	VA	23	D9
Northwest Alabama Regional Airport	AL	29	D8
Northwest Arkansas Regional Airport	AR	13	F10
Orlando International Airport	FL	57	B7
Outlaw Field	TN	17	E8
Owensboro Daviess County Airport	KY	17	A9
Panama City-Bay County International Airport	FL	52	D4
Pensacola Regional Airport	FL	51	C10
Philadelphia International Airport	PA	11	A12
Piedmont Triad International Airport	NC	21	G9
Pitt-Greenville Airport	NC	22	I5
Polk Army Airfield	LA	37	I12
Ponca City Regional Airport	OK	12	D1
Poplar Bluff Municipal Airport	MO	15	D11
Raleigh-Durham International Airport	NC	21	H12
Richard B. Russell Airport	GA	30	E4
Rocky Mount-Wilson Regional Airport	NC	22	H4
Ronald Reagan Washington National Airport	MD	11	E
Saint Lucie County International Airport	FL	57	F1
Saint Petersburg-Clearwater International Airport	FL	56	D
Salisbury-Ocean City Wicomico Regional Airport	MD	11	G1
Sarasota / Bradenton International Airport	FL	56	F
Savannah / Hilton Head International Airport	GA	44	E
Scholes International Airport at Galveston	TX	47	H
Smith Reynolds Airport	NC	21	G
Smyrna Airport	TN	17	G1
South Arkansas Regional Airport at Goodwin Field	AR	38	A
Southeast Texas Regional Airport	TX	47	E1
Southern Illinois Airport	IL	16	A
Southwest Florida International Airport	FL	59	A
Southwest Georgia Regional Airport	GA	43	G
Spartanburg Downtown Memorial Airport	SC	32	C
Sussex County Airport	DE	11	F1
Tallahassee Regional Airport	FL	53	C
Tampa International Airport	FL	56	D
Texarkana Regional Airport-Webb Field	AR	25	H1
Tri-Cities Regional Airport TN/VA	TN	20	E
Tri City Airport	KS	13	E
Tulsa International Airport	OK	12	F
Tuscaloosa Regional Airport	AL	41	A
Tyler Pounds Regional Airport	TX	36	D
University-Oxford Airport	MS	28	E
Upper Cumberland Regional Airport	TN	18	G
Valdosta Regional Airport	GA	53	B1
Vero Beach Municipal Airport	FL	57	E1
Washington Dulles International Airport	VA	10	E
Waycross-Ware County Airport	GA	44	H
Williamson County Regional Airport	IL	16	A
Wilmington International Airport	NC	34	E

COLLEGES & UNIVERSITIES

COLLEGE / UNIVERSITY	State	Page	Grid
Alabama A&M University	AL	29	D11
Albany State University	GA	43	G7
Alcorn State University	MS	39	F7
Alderson-Broaddus College	WV	9	D9
Alice Lloyd College	KY	19	B11
Anderson College	SC	31	D12
Appalachian State University	NC	20	F3
Arkansas State University	AR	15	H10
Arkansas Tech University	AR	26	A2
Armstrong Atlantic State University	GA	44	F5
Athens State University	AL	29	C10
Auburn University	AL	42	C3
Auburn University at Montgomery	AL	41	D12
Austin College	TX	24	H2
Austin Peay State University	TN	17	E9
Averett University	VA	21	E10
Barber-Scotia College	NC	33	A7
Barton College	NC	22	H3
Belmont Abbey College	NC	33	B6
Berea College	KY	19	A7
Berry College	GA	30	E4
Bethel College	TN	16	G5
Bethune-Cookman College	FL	55	H8
Bluefield College	VA	20	C4
Bluefield State College	WV	20	B5
Blue Mountain College	MS	28	D3
Brenau University	GA	31	E8
Brevard College	NC	31	B12
Bridgewater College	VA	9	G12
Bryan College	TN	30	A5
Campbellsville University	KY	18	B3
Campbell University	NC	34	A2
Carson-Newman College	TN	19	G9
Catawba College	NC	21	I7
Centre College	KY	18	A5
Chowan College	NC	23	F6
Christopher Newport University	VA	23	C8
Claflin University	SC	33	H6
Clemson University	SC	31	D11
Coastal Carolina University	SC	33	G12
Coker College	SC	33	E9
College of William & Mary	VA	23	C7
Columbus State University	GA	42	D4
Concordia College	AL	41	D9
Concord University	WV	20	B5
Cumberland University	TN	17	G12
Davidson College	NC	21	I6
Davis & Elkins College	WV	9	E9
Delaware State University	DE	11	D11
Delta State University	MS	27	H9
Duke University	NC	21	G12
East Carolina University	NC	22	I5
East Central University	OK	24	C2
Eastern Kentucky University	KY	19	A6
Eastern Mennonite University	VA	9	F12
East Tennessee State University	TN	20	F1
East Texas Baptist University	TX	37	C8
Elizabeth City State University	NC	23	F9
Elon University	NC	21	G10
Emory & Henry College	VA	20	D3
Erskine College	SC	32	E1
Fairmont State University	WV	9	C8
Fayetteville State University	NC	34	B1
Ferrum College	VA	21	D8
Florida Southern College	FL	56	D5
Florida State University	FL	53	C9
Fort Valley State University	GA	43	C8
Francis Marion University	SC	33	F10
Freed-Hardeman University	TN	28	A4
Frostburg State University	MD	9	B12
Furman University	SC	32	C1
Gardner-Webb University	NC	32	B4
George Mason University	VA	10	E5
George Washington University Virginia Campus	VA	10	D5
Georgia College & State University	GA	43	A10
Georgia Southern University	GA	44	D3
Georgia Southwestern State University	GA	43	E7
Glenville State College	WV	9	E6
Grambling State University	LA	38	D2
Hampden-Sydney College	VA	22	C2
Harding University	AR	27	B6
Henderson State University	AR	26	F2
Hendrix College	AR	26	B4
High Point University	NC	21	G8
Historic Jefferson College	MS	39	G6
Hollins University	VA	21	B9
Hood College	MD	10	C5
Jacksonville State University	AL	30	G2
James Madison University	VA	9	G12
Jarvis Christian College	TX	36	C5
John Brown University	AR	13	G9
Judson College	AL	41	C8
Kennesaw State University	GA	31	F6
King College	TN	20	E2
La Grange College	GA	42	B4
Lambuth University	TN	16	I4
Lander University	SC	32	F2
Lane College	TN	16	I4
Lees-McRae College	NC	20	G3
Lee University	TN	30	B5
Lenoir-Rhyne College	NC	20	H4
LeTourneau University	TX	37	D7
Liberty University	VA	21	B11
Limestone College	SC	32	B4
Lincoln Memorial University	TN	19	E8
Lincoln University	PA	11	B10
Lindsey Wilson College	KY	18	C3
Longwood University	VA	22	B2
Louisiana College	LA	38	H3
Louisiana Technical University	LA	38	D
Lynchburg College	VA	21	B1
Lyon College	AR	15	H
Marietta College	OH	8	C
Marshall University	WV	8	G
Mars Hill College	NC	19	H1
Maryville College	TN	19	H
McDaniel College	MD	11	E
McNeese State University	LA	48	D
Middle Tennessee State University	TN	17	H1
Miles College	AL	29	H1
Millersville University of Pennsylvania	PA	11	A
Milligan College	TN	20	F
Mississippi College	MS	39	D1
Mississippi State University	MS	28	
Mississippi University for Women	MS	28	
Mississippi Valley State University	MS	27	H1
Montreat College	NC	20	
Morris College	SC	33	G
Mountain State University	WV	8	
Mount Olive College	NC	34	B
Mount Saint Mary's University	MD	10	B
Murray State University	KY	17	E
Newberry College	SC	32	E
Nicholls State University	LA	49	F1
North Carolina Wesleyan College	NC	22	G
Northeastern State University	OK	13	H
North Georgia College & State University	GA	31	D
North Greenville College	SC	32	B
Northwestern State University	LA	37	G1
Oakwood College	AL	29	D1
Ohio University	OH	8	C
Ohio Valley University	WV	8	C
Oklahoma Baptist University	OK	24	A
Oklahoma State University	OK	12	G
Oklahoma Wesleyan University	OK	12	E
Ouachita Baptist University	AR	26	F

Colleges & Universities - Parks, Forests & Wildlife Spaces

PARKS, FORESTS & WILDLIFE SPACES

Parks, Forests & Wildlife Spaces

Chattahoochee State Park	AL	53	A6
Cheaha State Park	AL	30	H2
Chemin-A-Haut State Park	LA	38	B5
Cheraw State Recreation Area	SC	33	D9
Cherokee Landing State Park	OK	13	H8
Cherokee National Forest	NC-TN	19	H10
Cherokee State Park	OK	13	F8
Chester State Park	SC	32	D5
Chewacla State Park	AL	42	D3
Chickamauga and Chattanooga National Military Park	GA	30	C4
Chickasaw National Recreation Area	OK	24	E1
Chickasaw National Wildlife Refuge	TN	16	H1
Chickasaw State Park	TN	28	A4
Chickasaw State Park	AL	41	D6
Chicot State Park	LA	48	B5
Chief Logan State Park	WV	8	I3
Chincoteague National Wildlife Refuge	VA	11	I12
Chippokes Plantation State Park	VA	23	C7
Choctaw National Wildlife Refuge	AL	40	F5
Clarkco State Park	MS	40	E4
Clark Creek Natural Area	MS	39	I6
Clarks River National Wildlife Refuge	KY	16	D5
Claude D. Kelley State Park	AL	41	H8
Clayton Lake State Park	OK	25	D6
Claytor Lake State Park	VA	21	C6
Cliffs of the Neuse State Park	NC	34	B4
Cloudland Canyon State Park	GA	30	C3
Codorus State Park	PA	11	A7
Colleton State Park	SC	45	A7
Collier-Seminole State Park	FL	59	C6
Colonial National Historical Park	VA	23	C7
Columbus-Belmont State Park	KY	16	D3
Conecuh National Forest	AL	41	I10
Congaree National Park	SC	33	G7
Constitution Convention Museum State Park	FL	53	E6
Conway Cemetery State Park	AR	37	A10
Cooper Lake State Park	TX	24	I5
Coopers Rock State Forest	WV	9	B10
Cordell Hull Birthplace & Museum State Park	TN	18	E4
Corinth National Cemetery	MS	28	C5
Cossatot River State Park / State Natural Area	AR	25	E9
Cove Lake State Park	TN	19	F7
Cowans Gap State Park	PA	10	A4
Cowpens National Battlefield	SC	32	B3
Crab Orchard National Wildlife Refuge	IL	16	B3
Crater of Diamonds State Park	AR	25	F11
Crawford State Park	KS	13	A8
Croatan National Forest	NC	35	C7
Crocodile Lake National Wildlife Refuge	FL	59	F11
Croft State Natural Area	SC	32	C3
Crooked River State Park	GA	55	A7
Cross Creeks National Wildlife Refuge	TN	17	F8
Crowders Mountain State Park	NC	32	B5
Crowley's Ridge State Park	AR	15	G10
Crystal River Archaeological State Park	FL	54	I3
Crystal River National Wildlife Refuge	FL	54	I2
Cumberland Falls State Resort Park	KY	19	D6
Cumberland Gap National Historical Park	KY-TN-VA	19	E9
Cumberland Island National Seashore	GA	55	B7
Cumberland Mountain State Park	TN	18	H4
Cumberland State Forest	VA	22	A3
Cunningham Falls State Park	MD	10	B5
Currituck National Wildlife Refuge	NC	23	F10
Cypremort Point State Park	LA	49	F6
Cypress Creek National Wildlife Refuge	IL	16	C3
Dade Battlefield Historic State Park	FL	56	A5
Dahomey National Wildlife Refuge	MS	27	G9
Daingerfield State Park	TX	37	B7
Daisy State Park	AR	25	F11
Dale Hollow Lake State Resort Park	KY	18	E3
Daniel Boone National Forest	KY	19	C7
D'Arbonne National Wildlife Refuge	LA	38	C3
David Crockett State Park	TN	29	B8
Davy Crockett Birthplace State Park	TN	19	F12
Davy Crockett National Forest	TX	37	H6
Dean State Forest	OH	8	F1
Deep Creek Lake State Park	MD	9	B11
Deep Fork National Wildlife Refuge	OK	12	I4
Deer Run State Forest	MO	15	C9
DeGray Lake Resort State Park	AR	26	E1
Delaware Seashore State Park	DE	11	F12
De Leon Springs State Park	FL	55	H7
Delnor-Wiggins Pass State Park	FL	59	B6
Delta National Forest	MS	39	C8
Delta National Wildlife Refuge	LA	50	H4
DeSoto National Forest	MS	50	A5
DeSoto State Park	AL	30	E3
Devil's Den State Park	AR	13	H10
Devils Fork State Park	SC	31	C11
Devil's Millhopper Geological State Park	FL	54	F4
Disney/Little Blue State Park	OK	13	E8
Dixon Memorial State Forest	GA	44	I2
Dixon Springs State Park	IL	16	B5
Doncaster Demonstration Forest	MD	11	G6
Don Pedro Island State Park	FL	56	H4
Douthat State Park	VA	9	I9
Dreher Island State Recreation Area	SC	32	F5
Dripping Springs State Park	OK	12	I4
Droop Mountain Battlefield State Park	WV	9	H8
Dry Tortugas National Park	FL	58	H2
Dunbar Cave State Natural Area	TN	17	E9
Eastern Neck National Wildlife Refuge	MD	11	D9
Eastern Shore of Virginia National Wildlife Refuge	VA	23	C9
Econfina River State Park	FL	53	D10
Eden Gardens State Park	FL	52	C3
Edgar Evins State Park	TN	18	G2
Edisto Beach State Park	SC	45	D8
Ed Jenkins National Recreation Area	GA	31	D7
Edward Ball Wakulla Springs State Park	FL	53	D9
Egmont Key State Park	FL	56	E2
Eisenhower Birthplace State Historic Park	TX	24	G2
Eisenhower National Historic Site	PA	11	A6
Eisenhower State Park	TX	24	G2
Elephant Rocks State Park	MO	15	A10
Eleven Point National Wild and Scenic River	MO	15	E8
Elijah Clark State Park	GA	32	G1
Elk City State Park	KS	13	B6
Elk Neck State Park	MD	11	C9
Ellendale State Forest	DE	11	E11
Eno River State Park	NC	21	G12
Eufaula National Wildlife Refuge	AL	42	F4
Everglades National Park	FL	59	E9
Fairfax Stone Historic Memorial State Park	WV	9	D10
Fairfield Lake State Park	TX	36	F3
Fairview-Riverside State Park	LA	49	C12
Fairy Stone State Park	VA	21	D8
Fakahatchee Strand Preserve State Park	FL	59	C7
Fall Creek Falls State Park	TN	18	I3
Falling Waters State Park	FL	52	B5
Fall River State Park	KS	12	A5
Falls Lake State Recreation Area	NC	22	H1
False Cape State Park	VA	23	E10
Fanthorp Inn State Historic Park	TX	46	C4
Faver-Dykes State Park	FL	55	F8
F.D. Roosevelt State Park	GA	42	B5
Felsenthal National Wildlife Refuge	AR	26	I5
Fenwick Island State Park	DE	11	G12
Ferne Clyffe State Park	IL	16	B4
First Landing State Park	VA	23	D9
Fisherman Island National Wildlife Refuge	VA	23	C10
Fishtrap Lake State Park	KY	19	B12
Florala State Park	AL	52	A2
Florence Marina State Park	GA	42	E4
Florence National Cemetery	SC	33	F9
Florewood State Park	MS	27	H11
Florida Caverns State Park	FL	53	B6
Florida Keys National Marine Sanctuary	FL	59	G12
Florida Panther National Wildlife Refuge	FL	59	B7
Fontainebleau State Park	LA	49	C12
Forbes State Forest	PA	9	A11
Forest Capital Museum State Park	FL	53	D11
Forked Run State Park	OH	8	D3
Fort Boggy State Park	TX	36	I3
Fort Caroline National Memorial	FL	55	C7
Fort Clinch State Park	FL	55	B7
Fort Cooper State Park	FL	54	I4
Fort Defiance State Park	IL	16	D3
Fort Delaware State Park	DE	11	B11
Fort Donelson National Battlefield	TN	17	F7
Fort DuPont State Park	DE	11	B11
Fort Fisher State Recreation Area	NC	34	G4
Fort Frederica National Monument	GA	44	I5
Fort Frederick State Park	MD	10	B3
Fort Jesup State Historic Site	LA	37	G11
Fort Loudoun State Historic Area	TN	19	I7
Fort Macon State Park	NC	35	D8
Fort Massac State Park	IL	16	C5
Fort Matanzas National Monument	FL	55	F8
Fort McAllister State Historic Park	GA	44	F5
Fort Mitchell National Cemetery	AL	42	D4
Fort Mott State Park	NJ	11	B11
Fort Mountain State Park	GA	30	D5
Fort Necessity National Battlefield	PA	9	A10
Fort Pierce Inlet State Recreation Area	FL	57	F11
Fort Pike State Historic Site	LA	50	D2
Fort Pillow State Historic Park	TN	15	I12
Fort Pulaski National Monument	GA	45	E7
Fort Raleigh National Historic Site	NC	23	H10
Fort Saint Jean Baptiste State Historic Site	LA	37	F12
Fort Sumter National Monument	SC	45	C10
Fort Yargo State Park	GA	31	G8
Fort Zachary Taylor Historic State Park	FL	59	I6
Fountainhead State Park	OK	24	A5
Fourche Creek State Forest	MO	15	E9
Francis Marion National Forest	SC	45	A10
Frank Jackson State Park	AL	41	H11
Franklin State Forest	TN	30	B2
Fredericksburg and Spotsylvania National Military Park	VA	10	G4
Fred Gannon Rocky Bayou State Park	FL	52	C2
Friendship Hill National Historic Site	PA	9	A9
Frozen Head State Natural Area	TN	19	G6
Galveston Island State Park	TX	47	H7
Gamble Rogers Memorial State Recreation Area at Flagler Beach	FL	55	G8
Gambrill State Park	MD	10	C5
Garrett State Forest	MD	9	C11
Gasparilla Island State Park	FL	56	H4
Gauley River National Recreation Area	WV	9	H6
General Burnside Island State Park	KY	19	D6
General Coffee State Park	GA	43	G12
George L. Smith State Park	GA	44	C2
George P. Cossar State Park	MS	27	F12
George T. Bagby State Park	GA	42	G4
George Washington Birthplace National Monument	VA	11	H6
George Washington National Forest	VA-WV	9	H10
George W. Carver National Monument	MO	13	D10
Georgia Veterans Memorial State Park	GA	43	F8
Gettysburg National Military Park	PA	11	B6
Giant City State Park	IL	16	A3
Gifford State Forest	OH	8	C3
Givhans Ferry State Park	SC	45	A8
Glendale National Cemetery	VA	23	B6
Golconda Marina State Recreation Area	IL	16	B5
Golden Memorial State Park	MS	40	C1
Goodale State Park	SC	33	E7
Goose Creek State Park	NC	35	A7
Gordonia-Alatamaha State Park	GA	44	E2
Gorges State Park	NC	31	B11
Governor Hogg Shrine Historic Park	TX	36	C4
Grand Bay National Wildlife Refuge	AL-MS	51	D7
Grand Cote National Wildlife Refuge	LA	38	I3
Grand Gulf State Park	MO	15	E7
Grand Isle State Park	LA	50	H1
Grayson Highlands State Park	VA	20	E4
Gray's Reef National Marine Sanctuary	GA	45	H7
Grayton Beach State Park	FL	52	C2
Great Dismal Swamp National Wildlife Refuge	NC-VA	23	E8
Great River Road State Park	MS	27	G8
Great Smoky Mountains National Park	NC-TN	19	I10
Great White Heron National Wildlife Refuge	FL	59	H6
Greenbrier State Forest	WV	21	A7
Greenbrier State Park	MD	10	B5
Greenleaf State Park	OK	13	I7
Green Mound Archaeological State Park	FL	55	H9
Green Ridge State Forest	MD	10	B2
Green River Lake State Park	KY	18	C3
Greenwell State Park	MD	11	G8
Guana River State Park	FL	55	D7
Gulf Islands National Seashore	MS	50	D5
Gulf State Park	AL	51	
Gunpowder Falls State Park	MD	11	
Hagerman National Wildlife Refuge	TX	24	
Hamburg State Park	GA	43	A
Hamilton Branch State Recreation Area	SC	32	
Hammocks Beach State Park	NC	35	
Hampson Museum State Park	AR	15	
Handy Brake National Wildlife Refuge	LA	38	
Hanging Rock State Park	NC	21	
Harbison State Forest	SC	32	
Hard Labor Creek State Park	GA	31	
Harpers Ferry National Historical Park	MD	10	
Harris Neck National Wildlife Refuge	GA	44	
Harrison Bay State Park	TN	30	
Hart-Miller Island State Park	MD	11	
Hart State Park	GA	31	E
Hatchie National Wildlife Refuge	TN	16	
Hawks Nest State Park	WV	8	
Heavener Runestone State Park	OK	25	
Henderson Beach State Park	FL	52	
Henry Horton State Park	TN	17	
Herman Davis Monument State Park	AR	15	H
Herrington Manor State Park	MD	9	C
Hickory Knob State Resort Park	SC	32	
High Falls State Park	GA	43	
Highlands Hammock State Park	FL	57	
Hillsborough River State Park	FL	56	
Hillside National Wildlife Refuge	MS	39	B
Hiwassee/Ocoee Rivers State Park	TN	31	
Hobbs State Park-Conservation Area	AR	13	F
Hobe Sound National Wildlife Refuge	FL	57	G
Hochatown State Park	OK	25	
Hocking Hills State Park	OH	8	
Hocking State Forest	OH	8	
Holla Bend National Wildlife Refuge	AR	26	
Holliday Lake State Park	VA	22	
Holly River State Park	WV	9	
Holly Springs National Forest	MS	28	
Holmes County State Park	MS	39	B
Holts Landing State Park	DE	11	F
Homochitto National Forest	MS	39	
Homosassa Springs Wildlife State Park	FL	54	
Honey Creek State Park	OK	13	
Honeymoon Island State Park	FL	56	
Hontoon Island State Park	FL	55	
Horseshoe Bend National Military Park	AL	42	
Horseshoe Lake State Fish & Wildlife Area	IL	16	
Hot Springs National Park	AR	26	
House Mountain State Park	TN	19	
Huckleberry Ridge State Forest	MO	13	E
Hugh Taylor Birch State Park	FL	59	B
Hugh White State Park	MS	27	G
Hugo Lake State Park	OK	25	
Hungry Mother State Park	VA	20	
Hunting Island State Park	SC	45	
Huntington Beach State Park	SC	33	H
Huntsville State Park	TX	46	
Ichetucknee Springs State Park	FL	54	
Indian Key Historic State Park	FL	59	H
Indian Mountain State Park	TN	19	
Indian Nations National Scenic and Wildlife Area	OK	25	
Indian Springs State Park	GA	43	
Indian Trail State Forest	MO	15	
Island Bay National Wildlife Refuge	FL	56	
Jackson Lake State Park	OH	8	
Jacksonport State Park	AR	15	
James H. "Sloppy" Floyd State Park	GA	30	
James River National Wildlife Refuge	VA	23	
James River State Park	VA	21	A1
Janes Island State Park	MD	11	H1
J.D. MacArthur Beach State Park	FL	57	H1
Jean Lafitte National Historical Park and Preserve	LA	49	F1
Jean Lafitte National Historic Park-Chalmette	LA	50	
Jefferson National Forest	VA	20	
Jenkins' Ferry Battlefield State Park	AR	26	
Jenny Wiley State Resort Park	KY	19	A1
Jimmy Carter National Historic Site	GA	43	
J.N. "Ding" Darling National Wildlife Refuge	FL	58	
Jockey's Ridge State Park	NC	23	G1
Joe Wheeler State Park	AL	29	

POINTS OF INTEREST 63

Parks, Forests & Wildlife Spaces

n Gorrie Museum State Park	FL	53	F6
n Pennekamp Coral Reef tate Park	FL	59	G11
nson's Shut-Ins State Park	MO	15	A9
nsonville State Historic Park	TN	17	G7
n Tanner State Park	GA	30	H4
n U. Lloyd Beach State Park	FL	59	C12
n W. Kyle State Park	MS	27	E12
athan Dickinson State Park	FL	57	H12
es Gap State Park	SC	31	B12
es Lake State Park	NC	34	D2
dan Lake State Recreation rea	NC	21	H12
ce Kilmer Memorial Forest	NC	31	A8
Coleman State Park	MS	29	C6
nawha State Forest	WV	8	G4
nlake State Resort Park	KY	17	E6
nnesaw Mountain National attlefield Park	GA	31	G6
ntenia State Forest	KY	19	D10
ntucky Dam Village State Resort ark	KY	17	D6
ntucky Ridge State Forest	KY	19	E8
owee-Toxaway State Natural rea	SC	31	C11
r Lake State Recreation Area	NC	22	F2
y Largo State Park	FL	59	F11
ystone State Park	OK	12	G4
y West National Wildlife Refuge	FL	58	H5
ens Pond State Park	DE	11	E11
gdom Come State Park	KY	19	D10
gs Mountain National Military ark	SC	32	B5
gs Mountain State Park	SC	32	B5
topeke State Park	VA	23	C9
atchie National Forest	LA	38	F2
simmee Prairie Preserve State ark	FL	57	F8
lomoki Mounds State Historic ark	GA	42	H4
reshan State Historic Site	FL	59	A6
mbrabow State Forest	WV	9	F8
cassine National Wildlife efuge	LA	48	E3
ke Alma State Park	OH	8	D1
ke Anna State Park	VA	10	H4
ke Barkley State Resort Park	KY	17	D7
ke Bistineau State Park	LA	37	D11
ke Bob Sandlin State Park	TX	37	A6
ke Bruin State Park	LA	39	F7
ke Catherine State Park	AR	26	E2
ke Charles State Park	AR	15	G8
ke Chicot State Park	AR	27	I8
ke Claiborne State Park	LA	38	C1
ke Cumberland State Resort ark	KY	18	D4
ke D'Arbonne State Park	LA	38	B3
ke Dardanelle State Park	AR	26	A1
ke Eucha State Park	OK	13	F8
ke Fausse Pointe State Park	LA	49	E7
ke Frierson State Park	AR	15	G9
ke Greenwood State Recreation Area	SC	32	F3
ke Griffin State Park	FL	55	I6
ke Guntersville State Park	AL	29	E12
ke Hartwell State Recreation Area	SC	31	D10
ke Hope State Park	OH	8	C2
ke Houston State Park	TX	47	D6
ke Isom National Wildlife Refuge	TN	16	F2
ke Jackson Mounds Archaeological State Park	FL	53	C9
ke James State Park	NC	20	H2
ke Kissimmee State Park	FL	57	D7
ke Lincoln State Park	MS	39	G10
ke Livingston State Park	TX	47	B7
ke Logan State Park	OH	8	B1
ke Louisa State Park	FL	57	B6
ke Lowndes State Park	MS	28	I5
ke Lurleen State Park	AL	29	I7
ke Malone State Park	KY	17	C9
ke Manatee State Recreation Area	FL	56	F4
ke Norman State Park	NC	21	H6
ke Ophelia National Wildlife Refuge	LA	38	I5
ke Ouachita State Park	AR	26	D1
ke Poinsett State Park	AR	15	I10
kepoint Resort State Park	AL	42	F4
ke Somerville State Park & Trailway	TX	46	C1
ke Talquin State Park	FL	53	C8
ke Tawakoni State Park	TX	36	B3
ke Tenkiller State Park	OK	13	I8
ke Texana State Park	TX	46	I1
ke Texoma State Resort Park	OK	24	F2
ke Waccamaw State Park	NC	34	E2
ke Wales Ridge National Wildlife Refuge	FL	57	E7
ke Wales Ridge State Forest	FL	57	E7
ke Wappapello State Park	MO	15	D11

Lake Warren State Park	SC	44	B5
Lake Wateree State Recreation Area	SC	33	E6
Lake Wister State Park	OK	25	C8
Lake Woodruff National Wildlife Refuge	FL	55	H7
Land Between the Lakes	KY	17	D6
Landsford Canal State Park	SC	33	C6
Laura S. Walker State Park	GA	44	I2
Laurel Ridge State Park	PA	9	A11
Lee State Natural Area	SC	33	F8
Leesylvania State Park	VA	11	F6
Legion State Park	MS	40	A3
Leroy Percy State Park	MS	39	A8
Levi Jackson Wilderness Road State Park	KY	19	C7
Lewis State Forest	TN	29	A8
Lignumvitae Key Botanical State Park	FL	59	H10
Lincoln Homestead State Park	KY	18	A4
Little Beaver State Park	WV	8	I5
Little Manatee River State Park	FL	56	E4
Little Ocmulgee State Park	GA	43	E11
Little Pee Dee State Park	SC	33	E11
Little River Canyon National Preserve	AL	30	E3
Little River National Wildlife Refuge	OK	25	F8
Little Sandy National Wildlife Refuge	TX	36	C5
Little Talbot Island State Park	FL	55	C7
Locust Grove State Historic Site	LA	49	B8
Logoly State Park	AR	26	I1
Lone Mountain State Forest	TN	19	G6
Longfellow-Evangeline State Historic Site	LA	49	D6
Long Hunter State Park	TN	17	G11
Long Key State Park	FL	59	H9
Los Adaes State Historic Site	LA	37	G11
Lost River State Park	WV	9	E12
Louisiana Purchase Monument State Park	AR	27	D8
Louisiana State Arboretum	LA	48	B5
Lovers Key State Park	FL	58	B5
Lower Hatchie National Wildlife Refuge	TN	15	I12
Lower Suwannee National Wildlife Refuge	FL	54	H1
Lumber River State Park	NC	33	E12
Lums Pond State Park	DE	11	B10
Mackay Island National Wildlife Refuge	NC-VA	23	F9
Magnolia Springs State Park	GA	44	B3
Mammoth Cave National Park	KY	17	C12
Mammoth Spring State Park	AR	15	F7
Manassas National Battlefield Park	VA	10	E5
Manatee Springs State Park	FL	54	G2
Manchester State Forest	SC	33	G7
Mandalay National Wildlife Refuge	LA	49	G9
Mansfield State Historic Site	LA	37	E10
Marjorie Kinnan Rawlings Historic State Park	FL	54	F5
Marks' Mills Battlefield State Park	AR	26	G4
Marksville State Historic Site	LA	38	I4
Mark Twain National Forest	MO	15	D8
Martinak State Park	MD	11	E10
Martin Creek Lake State Park	TX	37	D7
Martin Dies, Jr. State Park	TX	47	A10
Martin National Wildlife Refuge	MD	11	H9
Mason Neck State Park	VA	11	F6
Mathews Brake National Wildlife Refuge	MS	27	I11
Matlacha Pass National Wildlife Refuge	FL	58	A5
Mattamuskeet National Wildlife Refuge	NC	35	A10
McFaddin National Wildlife Refuge	TX	47	F10
McGee Creek State Park	OK	24	E4
Meaher State Park	AL	51	B8
Medoc Mountain State Park	NC	22	F4
Meeman-Shelby Forest State Park	TN	27	A11
Merchants Millpond State Park	NC	23	F7
Merkle Wildlife Sanctuary	MD	11	F7
Mermet Lake State Fish & Wildlife Area	IL	16	C4
Merritt Island National Wildlife Refuge	FL	57	A9
Michaux State Forest	PA	10	A5
Middle Mississippi River National Wildlife Refuge	IL	16	A2
Mike Roess Gold Head Branch State Park	FL	54	E5
Millwood State Park	AR	25	G10
Mined Land Wildlife Area	KS	13	B9
Mineral Mound State Park	KY	17	C6
Mingo National Wildlife Refuge	MO	15	D11
Mission Tejas State Historic Park	TX	36	G5
Mississippi Sandhill Crane National Wildlife Refuge	MS	50	C5

Missouri State Forest	MO	15	C7
Mistletoe State Park	GA	32	H1
Moccasin Creek State Park	GA	31	C9
Moncove Lake State Park	WV	21	A7
Monocacy National Battlefield	MD	10	C5
Monongahela National Forest	WV	9	F9
Mont Alto State Park	PA	10	A5
Montauk State Park	MO	15	B7
Monte Sano State Park	AL	29	D11
Montgomery Bell State Park	TN	17	G9
Moody National Wildlife Refuge	TX	47	G8
Moores Creek National Battlefield	NC	34	E4
Morgan Brake National Wildlife Refuge	MS	27	I11
Moro Bay State Park	AR	26	I4
Morrow Mountain State Park	NC	33	A9
Mound City National Cemetery	IL	16	C3
Mountain Longleaf National Wildlife Refuge	AL	30	H2
Mount Jefferson State Natural Area	NC	20	F4
Mount Magazine State Park	AR	25	B11
Mount Mitchell State Park	NC	20	H1
Mount Nebo State Park	AR	26	B1
Mount Rogers National Recreation Area	VA	20	D5
Mount Roosevelt State Forest	TN	18	H5
Mousetail Landing State Park	TN	17	I7
Myakka River State Park	FL	56	G4
Myakka State Forest	FL	56	H4
Myrtle Beach State Park	SC	34	H1
Nanih Waiya Mound State Park	MS	40	B3
Nansemond National Wildlife Refuge	VA	23	D8
Nantahala National Forest	NC	31	B8
Narrows of the Harpeth State Park	TN	17	G9
Natchez National Cemetery	MS	39	G6
Natchez State Park	MS	39	G7
Natchez Trace State Park & Forest	TN	17	H6
Nathan Bedford Forrest State Park	TN	17	G7
National Key Deer Refuge	FL	59	H7
Natural Bridge Battlefield Historic State Park	FL	53	D9
Natural Bridge State Resort Park	KY	19	A8
Natural Falls State Park	OK	13	G9
Natural Tunnel State Park	VA	19	E11
Neosho Wildlife Area	KS	13	B8
New Germany State Park	MD	9	B11
New River Gorge National River	WV	9	I6
New River State Park	NC	20	F4
New River Trail State Park	VA	20	E5
New River Trail State Park	VA	21	C6
Ninety Six National Historic Site	SC	32	F3
Nolin Lake State Park	KY	17	B12
Norris Dam State Park	TN	19	G7
North Bend State Park	WV	8	D5
North Point State Park	MD	11	D8
North Toledo Bend State Park	LA	37	G10
Noxubee National Wildlife Refuge	MS	40	A3
Oak Mountain State Park	AL	29	I10
Obed Wild & Scenic River	TN	18	G5
Ocala National Forest	FL	55	H6
Occoneechee State Park	VA	22	E2
Ochlockonee River State Park	FL	53	E8
Ocmulgee National Monument	GA	43	B9
Oconee National Forest	GA	43	A9
Oconee State Park	SC	31	C10
Ohiopyle State Park	PA	9	A10
Okefenokee National Wildlife Refuge	GA	54	B4
Okmulgee State Park	OK	12	I4
Old Davidsonville State Park	AR	15	G8
Old Stone Fort State Archaeological Area	TN	29	A12
Old Washington Historic State Park	AR	25	G11
O'Leno State Park	FL	54	E3
Olustee Battlefield Historic State Park	FL	54	D4
Osage Hills State Park	OK	12	D4
Oscar Scherer State Park	FL	56	G3
Osceola National Forest	FL	54	C4
Ouachita National Forest	AR-OK	25	D11
Overflow National Wildlife Refuge	AR	38	A5
Ozark Folk Center State Park	AR	14	H5
Ozark National Forest	AR	13	H12
Ozark National Scenic Riverways	MO	15	C8
Panola Mountain State Park	GA	31	H7
Panther Creek State Park	TN	19	G9
Panther State Forest	WV	20	B2
Panther Swamp National Wildlife Refuge	MS	39	C9
Paris Landing State Park	TN	17	F6
Paris Mountain State Park	SC	32	C1
Parkin Archeological State Park	AR	27	A10
Parvin State Park	NJ	11	C12
Patapsco Valley State Park	MD	11	C7
Patuxent Research Refuge	MD	11	D7

Patuxent River State Park	MD	11	C6
Paul B. Johnson State Park	MS	40	I2
Paul M. Grist State Park	AL	41	C9
Paynes Creek Historic State Park	FL	57	E6
Paynes Prairie Preserve State Park	FL	54	F4
Peacock Springs State Park	FL	54	D1
Pea Island National Wildlife Refuge	NC	23	I11
Pea Ridge National Military Park	AR	13	F11
Pee Dee National Wildlife Refuge	NC	33	B9
Pelican Island National Wildlife Refuge	FL	57	E11
Pennyrile Forest State Resort Park	KY	17	C8
Percy Quin State Park	MS	39	I9
Perdido Key State Park	FL	51	D9
Perry State Forest	OH	8	B2
Petersburg National Battlefield	VA	22	C5
Petit Jean State Park	AR	26	B2
Pettigrew State Park	NC	23	H8
Pickett State Park	TN	18	E5
Pickwick Landing State Park	TN	29	B6
Piedmont National Wildlife Refuge	GA	43	A8
Pilot Mountain State Park	NC	21	F7
Pinckney Island National Wildlife Refuge	SC	45	D7
Pinelands National Reserve	NJ	11	D12
Pine Mountain State Resort Park	KY	19	E8
Pinnacle Mountain State Park	AR	26	C4
Pinnacle Rock State Park	WV	20	B4
Pinson Mounds State Archaeological Park	TN	16	I4
Pipestem Resort State Park	WV	20	B5
Pisgah National Forest	NC-TN	20	H3
Plantation Agriculture Museum State Park	AR	26	D5
Plum Tree Island National Wildlife Refuge	VA	23	C9
Pocahontas State Park	VA	22	B5
Pocomoke River State Forest	MD	11	G11
Pocomoke River State Park	MD	11	H11
Pocomoke State Forest	MD	11	H11
Pocosin Lakes National Wildlife Refuge	NC	23	I8
Poinsett State Park	SC	33	G7
Point Lookout State Park	MD	11	H8
Poison Springs Battlefield State Park	AR	26	H2
Poison Springs State Forest	AR	26	H2
Ponce de Leon Springs State Park	FL	52	B4
Pond Creek National Wildlife Refuge	AR	25	G9
Port Hudson State Historic Site	LA	49	B8
Port Royal State Historic Area	TN	17	E9
Potomac State Forest	MD	9	C11
Poverty Point Reservoir State Park	LA	39	D6
Poverty Point State Historic Site	LA	39	C6
Powhatan Court House State Park	AR	15	G8
Prairie County Museum State Park	AR	27	C7
Prairie Grove Battlefield State Park	AR	13	G10
Prairie State Park	MO	13	B9
Prentice Cooper State Park	TN	30	B3
Presquile National Wildlife Refuge	VA	23	B6
Prime Hook National Wildlife Refuge	DE	11	E12
Prince William Forest Park	VA	10	F5
Providence Canyon State Conservation Park	GA	42	E4
Purtis Creek State Park	TX	36	D2
Queen Wilhelmina State Park	AR	25	D9
Rainbow Springs State Park	FL	54	H4
Raven Rock State Park	NC	33	A12
Ravine Gardens State Park	FL	55	F6
Raymond Gary State Park	OK	25	F6
Rebel State Historic Site	LA	37	G11
Red Clay State Historic Park	TN	30	C5
Red Top Mountain State Park	GA	30	F5
Reed Bingham State Park	GA	43	I9
Reelfoot Lake State Park	TN	16	F2
Reelfoot National Wildlife Refuge	TN	16	F3
Richard B. Russell State Park	GA	31	F12
Richland Furnace State Forest	OH	8	D1
Richmond National Battlefield Park	VA	23	B6
Rickwood Caverns State Park	AL	29	G10
River Rise Preserve State Park	FL	54	E3
Rivers Bridge State Historic Park	SC	45	A6
Roan Mountain State Park	TN	20	G2
Roanoke River National Wildlife Refuge	NC	23	H6
Roaring River State Park	MO	13	E11
Robbers Cave State Park	OK	25	C6
Rock Island State Park	TN	18	H2
Rocky Gap State Park	MD	10	B1
Roland Cooper State Park	AL	41	F8
Rookery Bay National Estuarine Research Reserve	FL	59	C6
Roosevelt State Park	MS	39	D12

Parks, Forests & Wildlife Spaces - Other Points of Interest

OTHER POINTS OF INTEREST

Other Points of Interest

Alabama
Coasting

White sand and clear waters outline Alabama's coastline, where sun, surf, a slow pace, and Southern charm
define the 32 miles of beaches that even back-to-back
hurricanes in 2004 and 2005 could not blow away.
Once battered but now rebuilt, the coastal towns of
Gulf Shores and **Orange Beach** still have sand so
soft (they're 95 percent quartz) that it squeaks beneath
bare feet.

Places for fishing, sailing, sunbathing, parasailing,
canoeing, and kayaking are as plentiful as the stretches
of beach suited to planting umbrellas and spreading
beach towels. (Don't forget your sunscreen.) Additional
delights: lightning-fast rides down a giant waterslide
at Waterville USA (906 Gulf Shores Pkwy., Gulf Shores)
and zoo adventures at Alabama Gulf Coast Zoo (1204
Gulf Shores Pkwy., Gulf Shores), where some 300 animals—big cats, monkeys, alligators, reptiles, and birds
among them—roam in natural habitats. Young visitors
enjoy the petting zoo.

Orange Beach

Fort Morgan State Historic Site

From Scottish-style links to beachside greens, golfers tee off at courses designed by golf legends including Arnold Palmer, Jerry Pate, and Larry Nelson. Some visitors choose to wet a line during a deep-sea adventure with captains who guide them to great fishing.

Time slips backward at Fort Morgan State Historic Site (AL 180 West, Gulf Shores), with its arches of tapering bricks. (Even those who are not history buffs keep their cameras busy capturing the fort's crevices.) The fort's strategic location made it important during the Civil War, the Spanish-American War, and World War II. In the 1864 Battle of Mobile Bay, Confederate and Union naval forces fought for control of the harbor entrance. The fort's adjacent museum offers relics from the past and soldiers' accounts of the harsh life they endured while garrisoned there during the Civil War.

A change of pace awaits at outlet stores, antique malls, and quaint beachside boutiques. Shoppers browse for deals at Tanger Factory Outlet (2601 S. McKenzie, Foley) with more than 120 stores including Polo, Banana Republic, and Tommy Hilfiger. Others scout out what's old and worth taking home at Currier Antiques & Fine Art (25470 Canal Rd., Orange Beach), which specializes in 18th- and 19th-century furniture and accessories.

Seeking a brush with nature? Traipse through Bon Secour National Wildlife Refuge (12295 AL 180, Gulf Shores). The refuge features hiking trails, beach access, and thousands of acres home to migratory birds, nesting sea turtles, and the endangered Alabama beach mouse (cute enough there, but not to be taken home). Off County Road 10, the quaint fishing village of **Bon Secour** is the place to buy fresh seafood from the local market. Sprawling over some 6,000 acres, Gulf State Park (20115 AL 135, Gulf Shores) boasts two miles of beach and nature trails. Grab your binoculars—and pack your patience—before setting out for the six birding loops of the Alabama Coastal Birding Trail. With any luck, bird watchers may spot roosting herons, egrets, sandhill cranes, brown pelicans, sparrows, warblers—or loons that return each winter. Trails and paved paths suited to hikers, bikers, runners, and naturalists lace the area. Observation decks and boardwalks provide additional ways to come close to Mother Nature.

Via mailboxes attached to their piers, residents of historic **Magnolia Springs** (off US 98, about 20 miles northwest of the coast) still have their mail delivered

Cranes on the Alabama Coastal Birding Trail

by boat. A local landmark: Magnolia Springs Bed and Breakfast (14469 Oak St.), operated as an inn in the 1920s and '30s. A street canopied with oak trees and framed by magnolias leads to the home. With a wrap-around front porch, the century-old home provides guests with a wealth of amenities including a stocked guest refrigerator, afternoon tea, and turn-down service. Within walking distance, Jesse's Restaurant (14770 Oak St.) serves fresh seafood, Black Angus beef, and New Orleans-inspired dishes.

Appetites find satisfaction along Alabama's coastline, where fresh-off-the-boat seafood is readily available, whether at seaside family hangouts (where sandy feet are welcome) or at upscale eateries with tables covered with white linen cloths. Nightlife abounds, and music—whether delta blues, country, or calypso—routinely fills the air. Plays, free concerts, dancing, beach bars, and open-air decks add to the possibilities, as do dinner and dolphin cruises.

Lodging Tips

Abundant accommodations include condos, hotels, beach houses, and bed-and-breakfast inns. For details: Alabama Gulf Coast Convention & Visitors Bureau, (800) 745-SAND (7263), www.gulfshores.com.

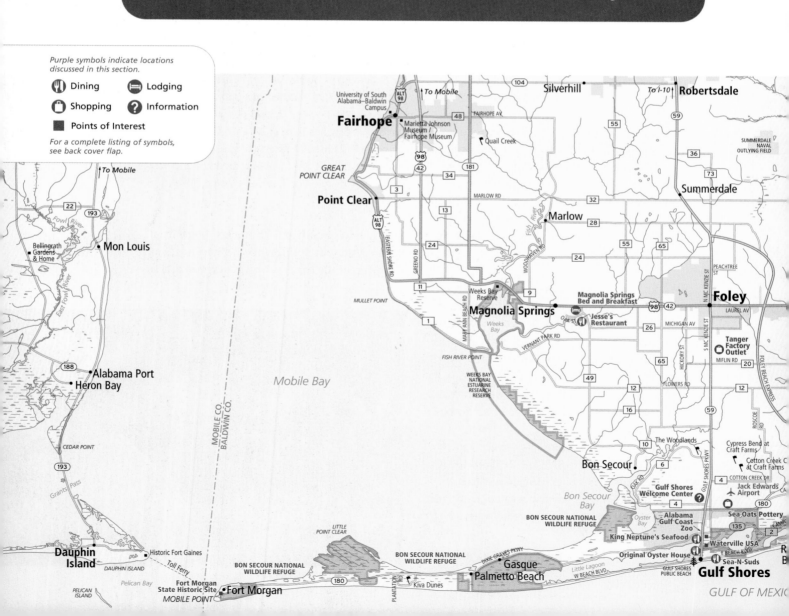

Purple symbols indicate locations discussed in this section.

🍴 Dining　　🛏 Lodging

🛍 Shopping　　❓ Information

■ Points of Interest

For a complete listing of symbols, see back cover flap.

Magnolia Springs Bed and Breakfast

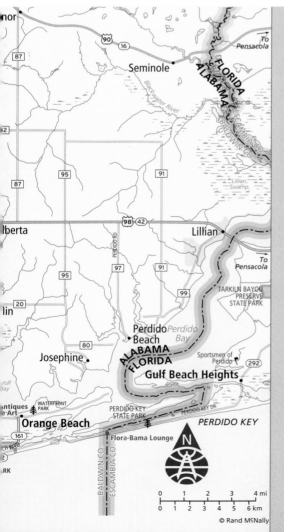

© Rand McNally

🍴 What to eat

Eat Royal Red shrimp, crustacean denizens of the deep water, steamed and with drawn butter and lemon. One of the best places for the "reds": **King Neptune's Seafood** restaurant (1137 Gulf Shores Pkwy., Gulf Shores), where oysters also are outstanding. Gumbo recipes vary but most are based in a thick roux with combinations of okra, tomatoes, onions, shellfish, crab, shrimp, or oysters. King Neptune's serves it, as does **Sea-N-Suds** (405 East Beach Blvd., Gulf Shores) and **Original Oyster House** (701 Gulf Shores Pkwy., Gulf Shores).

📋 What to buy

Seafood houses know how to pack Royal Reds, crab meat, and fish (especially tasty if you caught it) so they will make the trip home in good shape. Steve and Dee Burrow of **Sea Oats Pottery** (1009 E. Canal Dr., Gulf Shores) capture the sea with creations such as tiny sea turtles, shells, shrimp, and other sea life in clay.

❗ What to do

Mullet Toss at the Flora-Bama Lounge, Pensacola, Fla., last full weekend in April.

Annual National Shrimp Festival, Gulf Shores, second full weekend in October.

For more details about these festivals, please see page 186.

❓ *Alabama Bureau of Tourism and Travel*
(800) 252-2262, www.800alabama.com

Birmingham–
Bound

In the foothills of the Appalachian Mountains, **Birmingham** holds museums, parks, moderate year-round temperatures, and places to golf and to dine, whether on hickory-smoked barbecue, fried green tomatoes, or gourmet meals served atop cloth-covered tables.

Much of the after-hours excitement surges a few miles south of downtown in **Lakeview** and **Five Points South**, entertainment districts known for their nightlife, live music, and wide selection of dining and imbibing spots. Pedestrians stroll tree-lined streets or stop at the fountain in Five Points South to consider the whimsical artistry of Frank Fleming's sculpture *The Storyteller*. These places to see-and-be-seen are close to columned homes (many now housing businesses) that intrigue those tantalized by stately mansions. Not founded until after the Civil War, Birmingham has a single pre-Civil War mansion, Arlington Antebellum Home & Gardens (331 Cotton Ave. SW). Built between 1845 and 1850, the restored two-story Greek Revival mansion served as headquarters for Union troops who later burned the University of Alabama, some 50 miles southwest in Tuscaloosa.

For young visitors, attractions abound, including the McWane Science Center (200 19th St. North, downtown) in a renovated department store. The Birmingham Zoo (2630 Cahaba Rd.) houses hundreds of rare and exotic animals. Also at the zoo are a mini-train, children's zoo, picnic tables, and snack bar. During December, the zoo transforms into a winter wonderland awash in more than a half-million twinkling lights.

Frank Fleming's *The Storyteller*

Outdoor explorations await at the urban nature pre-serve Ruffner Mountain Nature Center (1214 81st St. South) and at Oak Mountain State Park (200 Terrace Dr., Pelham), Alabama's largest state park. Oak Mountain features golf, mountain-biking trails, fishing, boating, horseback riding, a petting zoo, a lakeside beach, and a wildlife rehabilitation center where visitors can take self-guided tours.

A starkly realistic lesson in history weaves throughout the city's Civil Rights District, which includes the Birmingham Civil Rights Institute (520 16th St. North) and adjacent Kelly Ingram Park. Once a gathering place for civil rights demonstrations, the park today is dotted with poignant sculptures recalling key events, including the May 1963 incident when police dogs and fire hoses were turned on marchers. (Self-guided audio-tour

Video exhibit at the Birmingham Civil Rights Institute

Birmingham's most visible landmark is the towering statue of Vulcan (1701 Valley View Dr.), the mythical god of metalworking, which stands atop Red Mountain. Second in size only to the Statue of Liberty, the statue —centerpiece of a 10-acre urban green space—was Birmingham's entry in the 1904 World's Fair, where it took top honors. It is a romantic place to share a picnic and to watch downtown lights twinkle.

devices are available at the Institute). Also in the dis-trict sits the Sixteenth Street Baptist Church (1530 Sixth Ave. North), site of the 1963 bombing in which four young black girls died. A few blocks south, the Alabama Jazz Hall of Fame (1631 Fourth Ave. North) honors jazz greats—including Nat King Cole and Duke Ellington—who have ties to Alabama.

The Southern Museum of Flight (4343 73rd St. North) preserves equipment and information from the Southeast's aviation history, while the Alabama Sports Hall of Fame Museum (2150 Richard Arrington Jr., Blvd. North) pays homage to the state's great sports heroes. The Birmingham Museum of Art (2000 Eighth Ave. North) showcases works from ancient to modern times and has the largest museum collection of Wedgwood ceramic outside England. With flora and fauna from around the world, the Birmingham Botanical Gardens (2612 Lane Park Rd.) include a Japanese garden with a teahouse.

Shoppers find plenty of places to exercise their talents. With scores of stores, The Summit (I-459 at US 280) includes Saks Fifth Avenue, Pottery Barn, Restoration Hardware, and Williams-Sonoma. With 200 stores and 11 restaurants, the Riverchase Galleria (I-459 at US 31) is anchored by the Wynfrey Hotel, which offers over-night packages for shoppers.

Birmingham Museum of Art

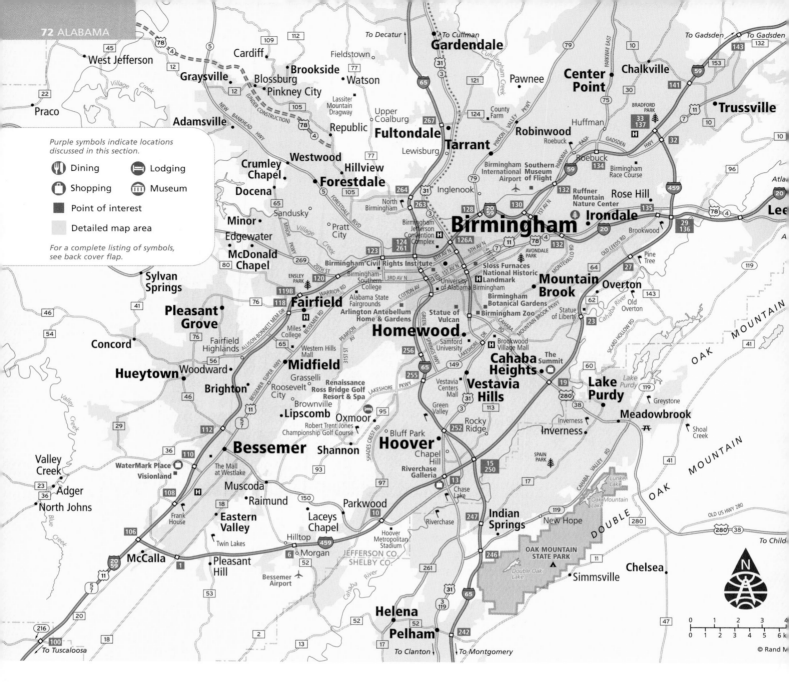

Renaissance Ross Bridge Golf Resort and Spa (4000 Grand Ave., Hoover), open since August 2005, boasts an 18-hole Robert Trent Jones championship golf course, part of the statewide trail of public courses known as the Robert Trent Jones Golf Trail. Overnight visitors enjoy 259 guest rooms (including 11 suites), a European spa, indoor pool, fitness center, and restaurants.

Open seasonally, Visionland (one mile north of I-459 on I-20/59 at exit 110, Bessemer) includes a children's area, a water park, and three roller coasters. Nearby is outlet shopping at WaterMark Place (4500 Katie's Way, Bessemer) with some 30 stores.

Lodging Tips

Birmingham offers most major chain hotels and two historic downtown hotels. Built in the 1920s and restored in 2000, the **Tutwiler Hotel** (2021 Park Place North) holds both Mobil Four Star and AAA Four Diamond awards. Restored in 2000, **Crowne Plaza—The Redmont** (2101 Fifth Ave. North) is the city's oldest operating hotel. With eight guest rooms and within walking distance of Five Points South's restaurants and entertainment venues, **Cobb Lane Bed and Breakfast** (1309 19th St. South) is the city's lone bed-and-breakfast. For details: Greater Birmingham Convention & Visitors Bureau, (205) 458-8000, (800) 458-8085, www.birminghamal.org.

🍴 What to eat

Fried green tomatoes are served at the Irondale Cafe (1906 First Ave. North, Irondale), which inspired writer/actress Fannie Flagg's book-cum-movie *Fried Green Tomatoes at the Whistle Stop Cafe*. **Highlands Bar and Grill** (2011 11th Ave. South) serves stone-ground baked grits.

🛍 What to buy

Vulcan statuettes, letter openers, and wine corks are reminders of the city's most noted landmark, the god of the forge. You'll find these and other Birmingham-related items (including watches and t-shirts) in **The Birmingham Shop** (2200 Ninth Ave. North). Hand-wrought works of metal art by local blacksmiths are available in the gift shop at **Sloss Furnaces National Historic Landmark** (20 32nd Street North).

❗ What to do

Vines & Waldrep City Stages,
Father's Day weekend, June.

Sidewalk Moving Picture Festival,
September.

For more details about these festivals, please see page 186.

❓ *Alabama Bureau of Tourism and Travel*
(800) 252-2262, www.800alabama.com

History and
Music
in Northwest Alabama

Famous faces and historic places await in Alabama's northwest corner. Even though no major battles were fought here, the area brims with Civil War history. Confederate soldiers trained at LaGrange College (eight miles south of Muscle Shoals off AL 157), once known as the "West Point of the South." A pioneer park and antebellum cemetery remain at the site of the state's first chartered college, which was burned by Union troops. The Edith Newman Memorial Museum (Main Street, Waterloo) holds Civil War relics, Native American artifacts, and items unique to **Waterloo**, which was visited by U.S. General William Sherman and burned during the war. Once a stagecoach stop and inn, Pope's Tavern Museum (203 Hermitage Dr., Florence) served as a military hospital during the war. Today it houses antiques and historical items.

Earlier residents are remembered at the Indian Mound & Museum (1028 S Court St., Florence), the Tennessee Valley's largest domiciliary mound—and one that visitors can climb. An adjacent museum holds artifacts that detail the history of the Native Americans who once lived in the area. Downtown **Florence** is suited to self-guided walking tours. The North Court and College Tour runs from the main business area through the campus of the University of North Alabama; the Historic Downtown Tour showcases the National Register Historic District.

Across the Tennessee River in **Tuscumbia**, an important chapter in history was written at Ivy Green (300 West North Commons St.), birthplace of Helen Keller. Built in 1820, the white clapboard house contains many original furnishings and items pertaining to America's "First Lady of Courage." Adjacent to the house sits the well-pump where learning began for a young Helen. Ivy Green each summer offers an outdoor drama remembering

Alabama Music Hall of Fame

Anne Sullivan, the teacher who broke into Helen's dark and silent world. Helen and Anne often traveled through Tuscumbia's downtown depot, an 1880s building that was the town's first to have running water. With interactive exhibits and a buggy once belonging to the Kellers, the red-brick depot opened to the public in 2005.

Like a phoenix rising from the ashes, streets of a revitalized downtown Tuscumbia are lined with thriving restaurants and businesses. On Tuesday evenings from late May through late July, guided trolley tours depart from downtown, wind through the historic district, and include admission into an antebellum home. A trolley routinely shuttles between downtown and nearby Spring Park, where a 51-jet fountain shoots water high into the air during free choreographed light-and-music shows performed on Friday, Saturday, and Sunday evenings. In addition to grassy open spaces, playground equipment, picnic tables, and a mini-train, the park features a man-made waterfall. At its base stands a statue of a Native American, a tribute to the area's early residents.

Civil War re-enactment at LaGrange College

Idol star Bo Bice. Recording here before him: artists such as Wilson Pickett, Otis Redding, Aretha Franklin, and the Rolling Stones. Although no studios offer tours in what is still called the "Hit Recording Capital of the World," music legends receive tribute at the Alabama Music Hall of Fame (US 72, Tuscumbia), which is filled with personal items, wax figures, the tour bus once used by the country music group

Coon Dog Cemetery

No trip through northwest Alabama history is complete without a stop at Coon Dog Cemetery (off AL 247 near the Natchez Trace), which holds more than 185 coon dogs interred among unique headstones and epitaphs. Annually on Labor Day, the cemetery hosts a celebration that includes buck dancing, singing, liars' contest, and barbecue.

Although **Muscle Shoals** no longer boasts a major music recording industry, a few studios prevail and in recent years have witnessed recordings by *American*

Alabama, and a live recording studio. (Even if you can't carry a tune in a bucket, go ahead and record yourself singing; you'll have the tape to take home as a reminder of your visit.)

Among the state's music standouts: W.C. Handy. The W.C. Handy Birthplace, Museum & Library (620 West College St., Florence) contains personal papers and artifacts linked to the "Father of the Blues." Handy is remembered the first full week in August during the W.C. Handy Music Festival.

Lodging Tips

The area offers several chain hotels and bed-and-breakfast inns, all moderately priced. For details: Colbert County Tourism & Convention Bureau, (256) 383-0783, (800) 344-0783, www.colbertcountytourism.org; Florence/Lauderdale Tourism: (256) 740-4141, (888) FLO-TOUR (356-8687), www.flo-tour.org.

Ivy Green, Helen Keller's birthplace

What to eat

Diners find down-home Southern cooking at **Claunch Café** (400 South Main St., Tuscumbia). **The Rocking Chair** restaurant (800 US 72 West, Tuscumbia) whips up a country breakfast complete with grits. **The Palace Ice Cream & Sandwich Shop** (100-B South Main St., Tuscumbia) offers old-fashioned milkshakes, chocolate malts, sundaes, and banana splits.

What to buy

Find down pillows, comforters, and featherbeds (filled half with down and half with feathers) at the **Pillow Factory** (298 River Rd., Muscle Shoals), which produces "Heavenly Bed" products for a major hotel chain and sells them at deep discounts in its outlet store. It also custom-makes products while you wait. The local owners of **Scent-Sations Candle Shoppe** (1123 North Wood Ave., Florence) make their own candles—and the aromas are heavenly.

What to do

Helen Keller Festival, Tuscumbia, third weekend in June.
W.C. Handy Music Festival, Florence, early August.

For more details about these festivals, please see page 186.

*Alabama Bureau of Tourism and Travel
(800) 252-2262, www.800alabama.com*

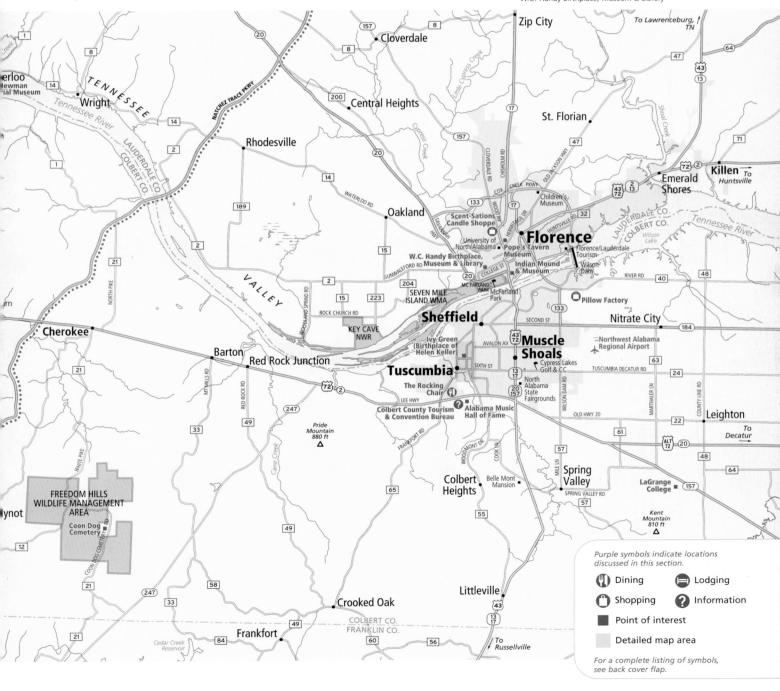

W.C. Handy Birthplace, Museum & Library

Zip City

157   8

Cloverdale

20   8   To Lawrenceburg, TN

64

TENNESSEE   47   43   13

Waterloo
Newman Memorial Museum   14   200   St. Florian   71

Wright   Central Heights   157   47

Rhodesville   14   157   17   Killen   To Huntsville

14   Emerald Shores   43   72   2   13

LAUDERDALE CO.
COLBERT CO.   189   133   Children's Museum   32   72

Tennessee River

Oakland   15   Scent-Sations Candle Shoppe   **Florence**   LAUDERDALE CO.   Tennessee River
COLBERT CO.   Wilson Lake

University of North Alabama   Pope's Tavern Museum   Florence/Lauderdale Tourism

W.C. Handy Birthplace, Museum & Library   Indian Mound & Museum   Wilson Dam   48

204   20   RIVER RD   40

SEVEN MILE ISLAND WMA   McFarland Park   133   Pillow Factory

VALLEY   2   15   223   ROCK CHURCH RD   SECOND ST   **Sheffield**   Nitrate City   184

KEY CAVE NWR   Ivy Green (Birthplace of Helen Keller)   Northwest Alabama Regional Airport   63

Cherokee   AVALON AV   **Muscle Shoals**   TUSCUMBIA DECATUR RD   24

Barton   Red Rock Junction   SIXTH ST   13   17   Cypress Lakes Golf & CC   Leighton

72   2   **Tuscumbia**   13   17   North Alabama State Fairgrounds   22   To Decatur

The Rocking Chair   20   157   ALT 72   20

247   LEE HWY   Alabama Music Hall of Fame   61   48

Colbert County Tourism & Convention Bureau   57   64

33   49   Pride Mountain 880 ft   Belle Mont Mansion   Spring Valley

FREEDOM HILLS WILDLIFE MANAGEMENT AREA   65   Colbert Heights   57   LaGrange College   157

Coon Dog Cemetery   49   55   Kent Mountain 810 ft

21

12   58   Littleville

247   33   Crooked Oak   43

21   49   COLBERT CO.   13   17
FRANKLIN CO.

84   Frankfort   60   56   To Russellville

Cedar Creek Reservoir

Purple symbols indicate locations discussed in this section.

🍴 Dining   🛏 Lodging

🛍 Shopping   ❓ Information

⬛ Point of interest

▢ Detailed map area

For a complete listing of symbols, see back cover flap.

Finders
Keepers
In Southwest Arkansas

Diamonds may be the lure to this corner of Arkansas, but visitors also find an easy blend of southern culture, distant and recent history, and outdoor recreation. It's yours for the taking.

If diamonds are a girl's best friend, there's a great deal of camaraderie among the tall pines of southwest Arkansas. Crater of Diamonds State Park (209 State Park Rd.) is the only place in the world where visitors may keep diamonds they find. Pickings are not exactly slim. More than 75,000 sparklers (an average of 600 a year) have been found in this 37-acre diamond field. These include the "Uncle Sam"—at 40.23 carats, the largest diamond found in North America. It was unearthed in 1924. More recent finds include the "Okie Dokie Diamond," a 4.21-carat canary yellow diamond unearthed by Oklahoma state trooper Marvin Culver in March, 2006, and the "Strawn-Wagner Diamond," found in 1998 and admired for its flawless perfection. The 4.25-carat "Kahn Canary," found in 1997, was worn by First Lady Hillary Clinton at presidential inaugural galas in 1993 and 1997. You can rent or buy simple diamond-hunting equipment or bring your own. Visitors show up with everything from flowerbed trowels to full-scale shovels. Searches can be as simple as walking up and down rows of dirt looking for diamonds lying on top of the ground (most effective after a hard rain) or as laborious as washing soil in a series of screens and patiently sorting concentrated gravel (how Culver found his gem). Don't fret about this volcanic crater being picked over. Geologic action slowly forces diamonds toward the surface, with an assist from park workers who plow the field periodically. If you don't happen upon a diamond, you may find a semi-precious stone to your liking. Amethyst, agate, jasper, quartz, calcite, and barite delight rockhounds too.

Murfreesboro's quaint town square offers down-home eateries and free entertainment on summer evenings. Attractions include the Ka-do-Ha Indian Village (1010 Caddo Dr.), the excavated site of a pre-historic mound-builder village. "Finders keepers" also

Crater of Diamonds State Park

applies to arrowhead hunting on a field set aside for this activity. Neighboring Arkansas Horse Park breeds the Peruvian Paso, introduced to Peru by Spaniards and prized for an even gait that delivers a smooth ride.

Hope is the birthplace of William Jefferson Blythe III, later to become the 42nd president of the United States. Today it draws those embarked on a "Billgrimage" to

—as did an earlier smithy on this site, said to have fashioned Jim Bowie's famous blade.

Within Millwood State Park (1564 AR 32 East, Ashdown), 29,500-acre Millwood Lake is famous for bass tournaments. A fishing hot spot, it attracts leisure anglers as well as tournament pros. The lake produces plenty of panfish: crappie, catfish, and bream. A bass

Kitchen at birthplace of President Bill Clinton

Clinton country. You can tour the Clinton birthplace and view the childhood homes and first schools that Bill Clinton attended in the town where he lived until age eight. During his 1992 presidential campaign, Clinton declared with customary eloquence and emotion, "I still believe in a place called Hope." The Clinton Birthplace Home (117 S. Hervey) offers tours that include the white foursquare house with décor circa 1946 and grounds containing a replica of the White House Oval Office rug and a memorial garden to Clinton's mother. Find Clinton memorabilia aplenty at the Hope Visitor Center & Museum (100 East Division St.), which occupies a former 1912 railroad depot.

Washington is both a town and state park. Established in 1824, it once welcomed travelers on the rugged Southwest Trail to Texas. Sam Houston and Davy Crockett are said to have passed through this frontier boomtown. For a while, it served as the capital of the Confederacy. Old Washington Historic State Park (US 278 NW of Hope) has been restored and recreated to offer insights into a 19th-century community and a glimpse into the territorial, antebellum, Civil War, and Reconstruction eras. Wander never-paved streets shaded by 150-year-old catalpa and magnolia trees. Stop for tour information at the Visitor Center in the 1874 Hempstead County Courthouse (101 Franklin St., Washington) and for chicken and dumplings at historic Williams' Tavern Restaurant, dating from 1832. Visit the blacksmith shop that specializes in making knives

management program has built the population to the point where even a novice angler can enjoy success. The park attracts bird-watchers drawn by the many species seen there, including bald eagles, great blue herons, and mallard and canvasback ducks. Blinds along "Waterfowl Way," a 1.5-mile self-guided hiking trail, provide opportunities to view and photograph birds and animals.

A curiosity in **Texarkana**—which borrows for its name syllables from three adjoining states—is a spot where you can stand with one foot in Arkansas, the other in Texas. It lies in front of the post office, which also straddles both states.

Old Washington Historic State Park

Lodging Tips

Lodging options are limited, unless you travel to Hot Springs or even Little Rock. Hope has several mid-scale chain hotels, while Murfreesboro offers the **Queen of Diamonds Inn** just a block from Courthouse Square (318 N. Washington), combining a Victorian dwelling with add-on motel units.

Williams' Tavern Restaurant

What to eat

"Southern cuisine" includes catfish, fried green tomatoes, and chicken in many forms, including fried and as a partner to dumplings in the ultimate comfort food. Barbecue joints are legion, with preferences ranging from mild to hot, sweet to spicy, tomato- to mustard-based. Hope boasts several barbecue joints, the **Melon Patch** (104 S. Elm St.), and **Cherry's Olde-Tyme Soda Fountain** (225 S. Main St.), which also serves—dare we say it—quiche, as well as fountain creations incorporating the ubiquitous watermelon. Also sample Southern cuisine in Murfreesboro at **On the Square Grill & Deli** (101 W. Main St.) and at Old Washington Historic State Park's **Williams' Tavern Restaurant**.

What to buy

Not lucky enough to find a diamond? You may wish to purchase one (or perhaps a semi-precious gemstone) as a reminder of your trip to this mineral-rich region. Shop for Clinton memorabilia at museum shops in Hope, his birthplace. Goods include cookbooks such as *Downhome Food Fit for a President*.

What to do

Jonquil Festival, Old Washington Historic State Park, mid-March.
Hope Watermelon Festival, Hope, second weekend in August.

For more details about these festivals, please see page 186.

Arkansas Department of Parks & Tourism
(800) 628-8725, www.arkansas.com

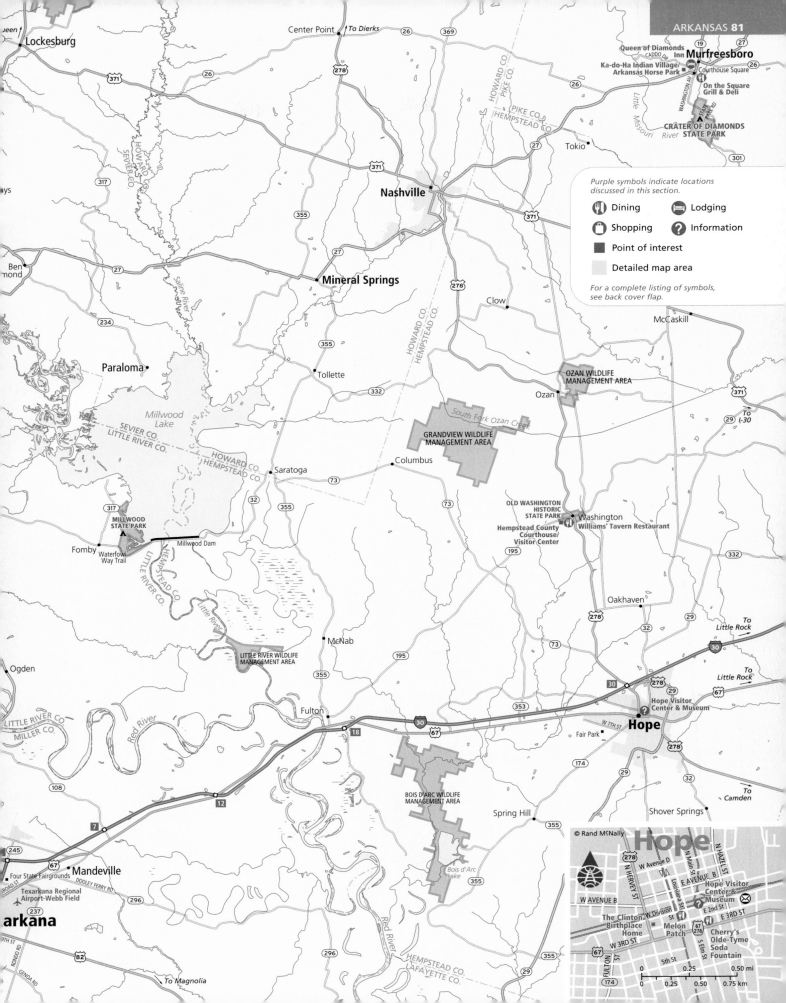

Locksburg

Center Point To Dierks

To Dierks

Queen of Diamonds
Inn **Murfreesboro**
Ka-do-Ha Indian Village/
Arkansas Horse Park
Courthouse Square
On the Square
Grill & Deli
CRATER OF DIAMONDS
STATE PARK

Little Missouri River

Tokio

Ben
mond

Nashville

Clow

McCaskill

Mineral Springs

Paraloma

Millwood
Lake

Tollette

OZAN WILDLIFE
MANAGEMENT AREA

Ozan

To
I-30

SEVIER CO.
LITTLE RIVER CO.

Saline River

South Fork Ozan Creek

GRANDVIEW WILDLIFE
MANAGEMENT AREA

Columbus

HOWARD CO.
HEMPSTEAD CO.

Saratoga

OLD WASHINGTON
HISTORIC
STATE PARK

Washington
Williams' Tavern Restaurant

Hempstead County
Courthouse/
Visitor Center

MILLWOOD
STATE PARK

Fomby Waterfowl
Way Trail Millwood Dam

HEMPSTEAD CO.
LITTLE RIVER CO.

Little River

Oakhaven

To
Little Rock

McNab

LITTLE RIVER WILDLIFE
MANAGEMENT AREA

Ogden

To
Little Rock

Hope Visitor
Center & Museum

Fulton

W 7TH ST

Hope

LITTLE RIVER CO.
MILLER CO.

Red River

Fair Park

To
Camden

BOIS D'ARC WILDLIFE
MANAGEMENT AREA

Four State Fairgrounds

Mandeville

Spring Hill

Shover Springs

Texarkana Regional
Airport-Webb Field

Bois d'Arc
Lake

arkana

DOOLEY FERRY RD

To Magnolia

HEMPSTEAD CO.
LAFAYETTE CO.

To

Legend

*Purple symbols indicate locations
discussed in this section.*

🍴 Dining   🛏 Lodging

💿 Shopping   ❓ Information

■ Point of interest

☐ Detailed map area

*For a complete listing of symbols,
see back cover flap.*

Hope (inset)

© Rand McNally

Hope

N HAZEL ST
N MAIN ST
N HERVEY ST
N ELM ST
W AVENUE D
E AVENUE B
W AVENUE B
Hope Visitor
Center &
Museum
W Division St
Louisiana St
E 2ND ST
E 3RD ST
The Clinton
Birthplace
Home
Melon
Patch
Cherry's
Olde-Tyme
Soda
Fountain
W 3RD ST
FULTON
5th St
0 0.25 0.50 0.75 km
0 0.25 0.50 mi

Hot Springs
Eternal

Whether you long to paddle a kayak into a quiet cove, fish for trophy bass, or simply tour country backroads by car or bicycle, central Arkansas's vast pine forests and sparkling lakes beckon with rejuvenating scenic beauty and idyllic quiet. **Hot Springs** leavens the area with just enough city flair.

Arkansas offers plenty of Bill Clinton sites to go around, from his birthplace in Hope to the soaring glass of the Clinton Presidential Center in Little Rock. But the 42nd president grew up in Hot Springs, and city fathers make the most of it, with banners proclaiming his boyhood home. Local sites range from the high school he attended (destined to become a "cultural campus") to his favorite barbecue joint—the estimable McClard's Bar-B-Q (505 Albert Pike Rd.), founded in 1928.

Hot Springs is comfortable with celebrity—and notoriety. Over the years, a parade of movie stars and politicians have "taken the waters" here, as well as mobsters such as Al Capone. Every year, thousands of tourists from around the world are drawn to Hot Springs and the restorative powers of its thermal waters. The international crowd contributes to the city's cosmopolitan aura. Hot Springs boasts grand dame hotels, stylish inns, classic Victorian architecture, and eateries that go well beyond biscuits and gravy. Choices range from sturdy German and Czech fare to spicy Cajun cuisine to house-made pasta served in an elegant Italian trattoria.

The main attraction, of course: the 800,000 gallons of hot water (143°F) that gush uninterrupted from the earth every day. Hot Springs National Park, incorporating historic sections of the city, is the smallest park in the system; though declared a national park in 1921, it was first set aside as a reservation by Congress in 1832. Visitors head for famed Bathhouse Row, where the restored opulent Fordyce Bathhouse is now a visitor center offering guided and self-guided tours. If you

Quapaw Bathhouse

Fordyce Bathhouse

want to take the waters yourself, Buckstaff Bathhouse (509 Central Ave.) on Bathhouse Row is an option (as are baths for guests at hotels such as the Arlington).

A twisting, scenic drive up Hot Springs Mountain behind the bathhouses takes you to 216-foot-high Hot Springs Mountain Tower. Elevators whisk visitors to observation decks providing 40-mile views of city, mountains, forest, and lakes. Other local diversions include Thoroughbred horse racing at Oaklawn and digging for quartz crystals at Coleman's Crystal Mines (5386 AR 7 N, Hot Springs, equipment supplied).

Slip away from the mainstream with a stay at **Jessieville**, in the foothills of the Ouachita Mountains. The absolute quiet may give pause to city dwellers. Mountain Thyme Bed & Breakfast (10860 AR 7 N) is an eight-room inn designed, built, and furnished by experienced bed-and-breakfast travelers. Enjoy breakfast in the dining room or on the porch. Then stroll around the grounds and visit adjoining Herbs Plus Herb Farm, which sells culinary herbs.

DeGray Lake Resort State Park (2027 State Park Entrance Rd., Bismark) nestles among the tall pines of the Ouachita Mountains on the shores of 13,800-acre DeGray Lake, one of Arkansas's finest water-sports venues. The park offers seasonal guided horseback riding, an 18-hole golf course with driving range, and several hiking trails, including the 3/4-mile Green Heron Trail favored by bird-watchers. Interpretive programs include nature hikes, kayak tours, and snorkeling. Popular special events include spring wildflower walks, nighttime "Owl Prowls," and "Eagles Et Cetera" in January, when chances of spotting a bald eagle are extremely high. Travel a causeway onto an island to the park's 96-room lodge. Relax in front of the lobby fireplace or hike the one-mile island trail, followed by a dip in a lakeside heated pool or hot tub.

"Wildflower Walks," "Eagle Awareness Activities," and barge tours are among the interpretive programs at Lake Catherine State Park (1200 Catherine Park Rd., Hot Springs). Set beside a lake in the forest-clad Ouachita Mountains, it lies just 15 miles from Hot Springs. Rent one of 18 equipped housekeeping cabins, with heating and air conditioning for year-round comfort and a cheerful fireplace for chilly evenings. For those who'd like to try camping but don't own the gear, the Rent-A-Camp includes tent with wood floor, two-burner stove, lantern, and other equipment.

Lake Ouachita State Park (5451 Mountain Pine Rd.) also rents cabins with fireplaces. Lake Ouachita is one of the state's superior fishing lakes, where bass, crappie, bream, and catfish abound and stocked rainbow trout, northern pike, and stripers provide tackle-testing action. With 975 miles of rugged shoreline, the 40,000-acre lake conceals quiet coves ideal for water-skiing, sailing, kayaking, and scuba diving. Interpreter-led kayak exploration tours and overnight kayak expeditions with island camping take place several times a year.

Ozark Bathhouse, Hot Springs National Park

Lodging Tips

In Hot Springs, the **Arlington Resort Hotel and Spa** (239 Central Ave.) is a grand old hotel (circa 1925) with an outdoor mountainside hot tub. **The Austin Hotel** (305 Malvern) is a 200-room, 14-story convention hotel, with live entertainment in its lounge. Lakeside cottages and condos are also popular. For details: Hot Springs Convention & Visitor's Bureau, (501) 321-2835, (800) SPA-CITY (772-2489), www.hotsprings.org.

Arlington Resort Hotel and Spa

What to eat

If you enjoy salads and adore barbecue, try them in combo. Barbecue salad is a version of chef's salad, featuring chilled iceberg lettuce with tomato, onion, green pepper, and cucumber topped with smoky strips of barbecued beef or pork. It's served with barbecue sauce or heavy salad dressing, such as French or Thousand Island. Find it at **Roland's Bar-B-Que Company** (200 Higdon Ferry Rd., Hot Springs).

What to buy

Pottery made by the Dryden family for more than half a century is widely coveted. Some pieces produced over the past 55 years have appreciated more than 200 times the original price. The family workshop and showroom in Hot Springs (**Dryden Pottery**, 341 Whittington Ave.), where you can watch a demonstration, provides additional fun. More pottery without a "Made in China" label: the salt-glazed pieces crafted by Jim and Barbara Larkin at **Fox Pass Pottery** (379 Fox Pass, Hot Springs), founded in 1973. He works at the potter's wheel; she hand-builds her pieces.

What to do

Hot Springs Documentary Film Festival, Hot Springs, late October.

For more details about this festival, please see page 186.

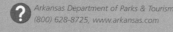

Arkansas Department of Parks & Tourism
(800) 628-8725, www.arkansas.com

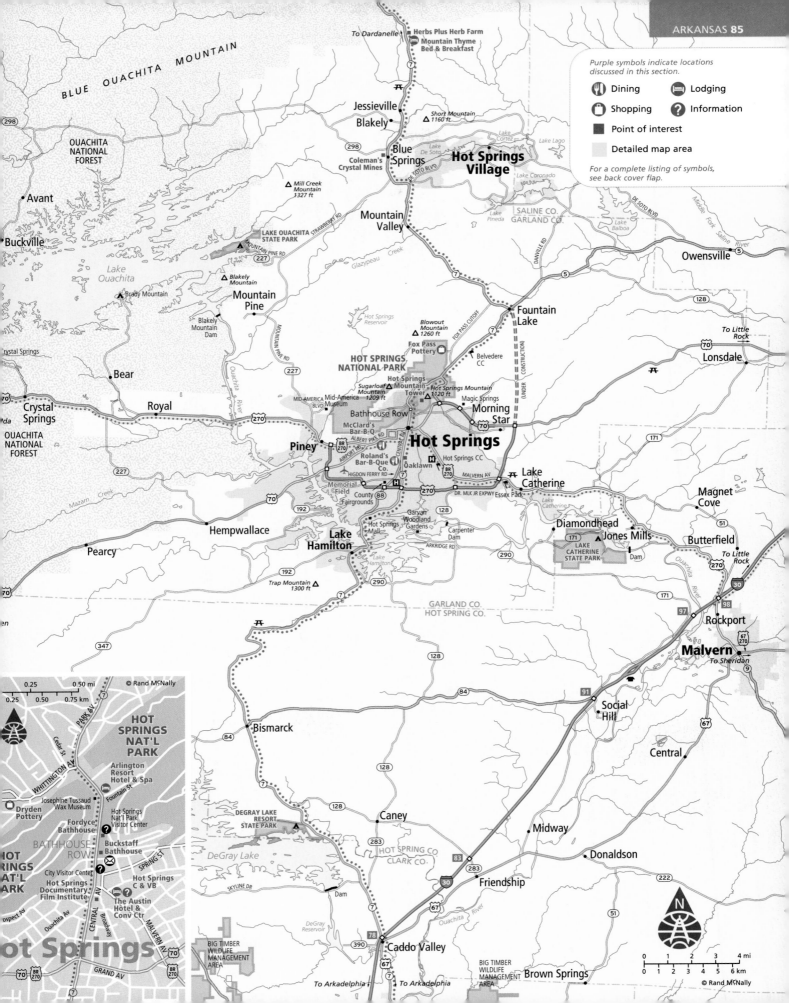

BLUE OUACHITA MOUNTAIN

To Dardanelle

Herbs Plus Herb Farm
Mountain Thyme
Bed & Breakfast

298

OUACHITA
NATIONAL
FOREST

Jessieville

7

Blakely

Short Mountain
1160 ft

Lake
Cortez

Lake Lago

Avant

298

Blue
Springs

Lake
De Soto

Hot Springs
Village

Hot Springs Village

Buckville

Coleman's
Crystal Mines

DE SOTO BLVD

Lake Coronado

Mill Creek
Mountain
1327 ft

Mountain
Valley

Lake
Pineda

SALINE CO.
GARLAND CO.

DE SOTO BLVD

Lake
Balboa

Middle Fork Saline River

LAKE OUACHITA
STATE PARK

STRAWBERRY RD

227

Glazypeau
Creek

7

5

DANVILLE RD

128

Owensville

5

Lake
Ouachita

MOUNTAIN PINE RD

Blakely
Mountain

Brady Mountain

Mountain
Pine

227

Blakely
Mountain Dam

FOX PASS CUTOFF

Fountain
Lake

To Little
Rock

70

Lonsdale

Crystal Springs

MOUNTAIN PINE RD

Bear

Hot Springs
Reservoir

Blowout
Mountain
1260 ft

7

(UNDER CONSTRUCTION)

HOT SPRINGS
NATIONAL PARK

Fox Pass
Pottery

Belvedere
CC

Royal

270

227

Ouachita River

Sugarloaf
Mountain
1209 ft

Hot Springs
Mountain
Tower

Hot Springs Mountain
1120 ft

171

Crystal
Springs

MID-AMERICA
BLVD

Mid-America
Museum

Bathhouse Row

Magic Springs

Morning
Star

OUACHITA
NATIONAL
FOREST

70

McClard's
Bar-B-Q

ALBERT PIKE RD

CENTRAL AV

70

Mazarn Creek

Piney

BR
270

AIRPORT RD

Roland's
Bar-B-Que
Co.

Oaklawn

H

Hot Springs CC

171

Magnet
Cove

BR
270

7

Hot Springs CC

51

HIGDON FERRY RD

270

MALVERN AV

Lake
Catherine

Hempwallace

70

192

88

Memorial
Field

H

DR. MLK JR EXPWY

Essex Park

Lake
Catherine

Diamondhead

Jones Mills

Butterfield

County
Fairgrounds

128

171

LAKE
CATHERINE STATE PARK

Dam

270

To Little
Rock

Pearcy

Lake
Hamilton

Hot Springs
Mall

Garvan
Woodland
Gardens

Carpenter
Dam

290

97

98

30

Rockport

70

192

Trap Mountain
1300 ft

ARKRIDGE RD

Lake
Hamilton

128

171

67
270

9

347

7

290

Ouachita River

Malvern

To Sheridan

GARLAND CO.
HOT SPRING CO.

128

91

Social
Hill

67

Bismarck

84

Central

84

128

7

283

Midway

Caney

HOT SPRING CO.
CLARK CO.

283

83

Donaldson

DEGRAY LAKE
RESORT STATE PARK

128

30

222

DeGray Lake

Dam

67

51

Friendship

SKYLINE DR

7

Dam

N

DeGray
Reservoir

78

390

Caddo Valley

67

BIG TIMBER
WILDLIFE
MANAGEMENT
AREA

To Arkadelphia

7

To Arkadelphia

BIG TIMBER
WILDLIFE
MANAGEMENT
AREA

Brown Springs

0 1 2 3 4 mi
0 1 2 3 4 5 6 km

© Rand McNally

---

0   0.25   0.50 mi

0   0.25   0.50   0.75 km

© Rand McNally

PARK AV

7

HOT SPRINGS NAT'L PARK

Cedar St

Arlington
Resort
Hotel & Spa

WHITTINGTON AV

Fountain St

Josephine Tussaud
Wax Museum

Dryden
Pottery

Hot Springs
Nat'l Park
Visitor Center

?

Fordyce
Bathhouse

Buckstaff
Bathhouse

CENTRAL AV

SPRING ST

BATHHOUSE
ROW

HOT
SPRINGS
NAT'L
PARK

City Visitor Center

?

Hot Springs
Documentary
Film Institute

Hot Springs
C & VB

The Austin
Hotel & Conv Ctr

Broadway

Prospect Av

Ouachita Av

MALVERN AV

ot Springs

70

BR
270

7

GRAND AV

BR
270

**Purple symbols indicate locations
discussed in this section.**

🍴 Dining   🛏 Lodging

🛍 Shopping   ❓ Information

⬛ Point of interest

⬜ Detailed map area

*For a complete listing of symbols,
see back cover flap.*

Mountain Music
Mecca

Mountain View. The name of this tiny community in the heart of the Ozarks says it all. It sits among hills, hollows, and deeply etched valleys, surrounded by misty blue mountains, deep hardwood forests, limestone bluffs, sprawling lakes, and rippling trout streams. Home to dulcimer-makers and banjo pickers, folk art and century-old crafts, and downhome eateries serving barbecue and blackberry cobbler, this is a town that celebrates mountain tradition.

Here you can arrange a float trip and kayaking adventure, splash in a summer swimming hole, or follow a trail through the forest on horseback or mountain bike. Canoeists head for the country's first designated National River, the beautiful, bluff-lined **Buffalo National River**. Visitors also find caves to explore, houseboats to rent, cagey trout to fight, and foot-tapping, soul-stirring music wherever folks gather to relax and enjoy each other.

On warm summer evenings, people gather in Mountain View's historic Courtsquare as mountain music sings out and banjo pickers and fiddlers play the tunes of century-old folk songs. Many listeners bring lawn chairs; some bring their own instruments. Others choose from a variety of indoor music shows and pickin' barns (where fingers pluck strings on instruments such as dobros and banjos).

Just north of Mountain View lies Ozark Folk Center State Park (on AR 382). This living museum preserves Southern mountain folkways and music of a bygone era. Visitors are greeted by master craftspeople quietly explaining their art, and with the sprightly sounds of banjos and fiddles and the alluring aroma of hot pies. The Crafts Village's two dozen buildings and outdoor areas feature craft demonstrations and daytime music programs recalling the period 1820-1920. Master craftspeople demonstrate a wide range of pioneer skills, including furniture making, basketry, blacksmithing, broom making, pottery, printing, and needlecrafts.

Canoeing on the Buffalo National River

Blanchard Springs Caverns

Down through the years, music has made hard times a little better, and mountain music continues to inspire musicians and listeners. During regular performances, all music predates World War II and the cultural changes it brought. The focal point of the sprawling hilltop park: the huge theater where evening music programs feature traditional instruments of the Ozarks—acoustic guitar, five-string banjo, fiddle, mandolin, autoharp, mountain dulcimer, picking bow, and spoons. You'll see jig dancing, square dancing, and clogging and hear instrumentals, ballads, and gospel songs, some dating to Elizabethan times, learned in the homes of friends and family through the strong Ozark oral tradition. Pioneer craft workshops offer a chance to try the dulcimer, autoharp, or fiddle. You can learn hand quilting and how to grow a backyard herb garden. The park cultivates one of the nation's most diverse organic herb gardens, with varieties for home remedies, dye production, and use as scent and in cooking.

Mountain Home is a vacation town tucked between two large recreational lakes, **Bull Shoals** and **Norfork**, with combined shorelines of 1,120 miles. The town offers a clutch of craft and antique shops as well as interesting bed-and-breakfasts and eateries, including Bobbie Sue's (2199 W. US 62 E), which serves stellar barbecue. Just south of town, Stone Creek Ranch (626 Circle B Ln.) offers trail rides on cutting horses and accommodations in attractively furnished cabins with central heat and air, light oak paneling, tin roofs, and fully equipped kitchens.

A dam placed across the White River in 1951 formed 45,440-acre Bull Shoals Lake. With about 1,000 miles of rugged shoreline, it is nationally known for trophy-size bass, crappy, and bream. Besides being an angler's Avalon, this area is stunningly scenic, with roads twisting through rugged mountains where wild rushing streams and rivers, gushing springs, and scenic trails criss-cross the landscape. Many travel this region in spring, when dogwoods bloom, and in fall, when leaves turn burnt orange. At the southern edge of the lake, just below the dam, 732-acre Bull Shoals-White River State Park (129 Bull Shoals Park, Lakeview) is a prime fishing spot. Interpretive programs include guided trail walks and trout-fishing workshops. Norfork Lake is another massive impoundment with excellent fishing (even spear fishing). Take a free tour of Norfork National Fish Hatchery (1414 AR 177 S, Mountain Home), one of the nation's largest federal trout hatcheries.

Cave-fanciers won't want to miss a tour of Blanchard Springs Caverns (15 miles northwest of Mountain View off AR 14, in Ozark National Forest) operated by the U.S. Forest Service. An underground river flows endlessly in this "living" cave. Two guided tours are offered in the warm-weather season (one more strenuous and by reservation only), one tour only in winter.

Ozark Folk Center

Lodging Tips

This region features a wide range of accommodations, including bed-and-breakfasts inns, cabins, cottages, motels, resorts, guesthouses, and lodges. The latter includes the 60-room **Dry Creek Lodge** at Ozark Folk Center State Park, with a swimming pool and rooms blending homespun décor and modern amenities, and glass doors that open onto the Ozark forest. For details: Mountain View Chamber of Commerce, (888) 679-2859, www.ozarkgetaways.com.

Dulcimer musician at the Ozark Folk Center

What to eat

Staples of mountain cooking include ham hocks and beans, turnip greens, corn bread, peach butter, and blackberry cobbler. Sample these and other home-style southern recipes at **The Skillet** restaurant at Ozark Folk Center State Park near Mountain View. From its hilltop perch, it overlooks a butterfly garden and wildlife feeding stations.

What to buy

How about a mountain dulcimer to take home for someone musically inclined—or to learn to play yourself? Shop at **McSpadden's Dulcimers** (1104 Sylamore Ave.), on AR 59 and 14N at the Folk Center turn-off. Prices start at around $290.

What to do

Annual Arkansas Folk Festival, Mountain View, third full weekend in April.
Off the Beaten Path Studio Tour, Mountain View, third weekend in September.
For more details about these festivals, please see page 186.

Arkansas Department of Parks & Tourism
(800) 628-8725, www.arkansas.com

Bull Shoals Lake

Bull Shoals
Bull Shoals Dam
Rivercliff
Lakeview
BULL SHOALS-WHITE RIVER STATE PARK
Fairview
178

Midway

To West Plains, MO
101

NORFOLK LAKE WILDLIFE MANAGEMENT AREA

Lakeside Terrace

Henderson

NORFOLK LAKE WILDLIFE MANAGEMENT AREA

To Salem

Gepp
62 412

Norfolk Lake

Elizabeth
87

NORFOLK LAKE WILDLIFE MANAGEMENT AREA

Brushy

5

201

BR 62
BR 412

Mountain Home

178
126
Whiteville

Bobbie Sue's
Twin Lakes

62 412

Flippin
'02

62 412

62 412
Cotter
345
Gassville
White River

101

Rea Valley

126
CR 57
201
CARTNEY RD
Buford
CIRCLE B LN
Stone Creek Ranch

Big Creek

342

Briarcliff
5

Norfork National Fish Hatchery
Salesville
Norfork Dam
177

Norfork

BAXTER CO.
IZARD CO.

177
223

Pineville
56

126

Buffalo City

Warrior Creek Mountain 1220 ft

Rush Historic District
Rush Landing

BUFFALO NATIONAL RIVER

Buffalo River

White River

5

Calico Rock

341

OZARK NATIONAL FOREST

Sugarloaf Mountain 1150 ft
5

NF 102

14
268
Buffalo Point

LOAFER'S GLORY WILDLIFE MANAGEMENT AREA

Cozahome
CR 61

MARION CO.
SEARCY CO.

MARION CO.
BAXTER CO.

BAXTER CO.
STONE CO.

SYLAMORE SCENIC BYWAY

BUFFALO NATIONAL RIVER

Buffalo

Evening Star

Barkshead

Mount Olive

LOAFER'S GLORY WILDLIFE MANAGEMENT AREA

Big Flat

TIE RIDGE RD

Gunner Pool

9

341

N Sylamore Creek

Harriet

orning Star

27
Blackjack Knob 1240 ft

14

Lone Pine

74

Round Mountain 1411 ft

263

Landis

14

Blanchard Springs
Blanchard Springs Caverns

Fifty-Six

Sylamore
Allison

White River

9

Onia

SEARCY CO.
STONE CO.

Barr Mountain 1779 ft

Alco

Panther Mountain 1472 ft

Newnata

66

66

OZARK FOLK CENTER STATE PARK

87

The Skillet
Dry Creek Lodge
382

McSpadden's Dulcimers

Marshall

Timbo

Strand Knob 1840 ft

263

Courtsquare

Mountain View
Mountain View Chamber of Commerce

5
14
14

65
Ozark Heritage Arts Center & Museum

Oxley
66

Collins Hill 1340 ft
9

Dodd Mountain 1410 ft

Leslie
To Clinton

N

---

0 1 2 3 4 mi
0 2 4 6 km

© Rand McNally

Orlando

Beyond
the Theme Parks

Mickey Mouse and Shamu may define Central Florida to millions of travelers, but there's a whole world beyond the theme parks. Thirty miles northeast of the big attractions lies the little town of **Winter Park**, developed in the late 1800s to lure visitors from the cold North to Florida's first planned city.

A relaxing way to get acquainted with the area: the Scenic Boat Tour (312 E. Morse Blvd.), an old-fashioned pontoon boat that cruises the breezy Winter Park chain of lakes and canals where loggers once hauled trees to a nearby sawmill. Most riders gawk at the mansions built for well-to-do Northerners at the turn of the 20th century, but you also might spot an eagle or an alligator as your boat captain spins tales on the hour-long tour. On the tour, you'll see the eponymous Albin Polasek Museum and Sculpture Gardens (633 Osceola Ave.), former home of the Czech-American sculptor, sitting on three lush lakefront acres. Though Polasek wasn't well known (he died in 1965 at the age of 86), his *Man Carving His Own Destiny* sculpture is probably most recognizable, and it appears along with dozens more of his creations, inside and on the lakefront lawn.

Just blocks from the boat launch, chic Park Avenue boasts sidewalk cafés, doggie bowls with fresh water for four-footed friends, and shops with everything from haute couture to jewelry and antiques. National retailers have moved in, including Nicole Miller, Williams-Sonoma, Restoration Hardware, and Pottery Barn, but locally owned shops like Tuni's boutique and Timothy's Gallery bring a European flair to 10 blocks of shopping with more than 100 stores.

Sower, Albin Polasek Museum and Sculpture Gardens

At the north end of Park Avenue, the world's largest collection of the works of Louis Comfort Tiffany awaits at the Charles Hosmer Morse Museum of American Art (445 Park Ave. N.), including the beautifully restored chapel created by Louis Comfort Tiffany for exhibition at the 1893 World's Columbian Exposition in Chicago. Tiffany's famous stained glass gets the most oohs and ahs, but the collection also includes classic American art pottery and late 19th- and early 20th-century American paintings and decorative arts. This jewel box of a museum shows only a small part of the collection at a time, so return visitors always get a chance to see more.

Orlando's Loch Haven Park houses the Orlando Museum of Art (OMA) (2416 N. Mills Ave.) and the Mennello Museum of American Folk Art (900 E. Princeton St.). OMA, one of Florida's cultural gems, focuses its collection on American art from the 19th century to the present, African art, and art of the ancient Americas. The whimsical folk art museum collects and preserves American folk art, such as a large collection of paintings by Earl Cunningham and work by other important 20th-century self-taught artists.

In **Little Vietnam**, a bustling neighborhood along Colonial Drive, leave the U.S. without a passport. Browse the fascinating Asian supermarkets, or stop for a steaming bowl of noodle soup (called "pho") at Pho 88 (730 N. Mills Ave.) or summer rolls at Little Saigon (1106 E. Colonial Dr.).

Trendy **Thornton Park** bustles with boutiques and restaurants just a block from the heart of downtown Orlando. An outdoor table at Hue (629 E. Central Blvd.) places lunch or dinner guests at the epicenter of the action. Beautiful **Lake Eola Park** with its distinctive fountain and monuments tells the story of the "City Beautiful."

A shopaholic's first stop: Mall at Millenia (4200 Conroy Rd.), anchored by Bloomingdale's, Neiman Marcus, and Macy's and offering 150 other specialty stores, including Gucci, Chanel, Cartier, and Louis Vuitton. For bargains, hit north International Drive's concentration of hundreds of off-price stores. For more manageable shopping, head straight for Orlando Premium Outlets (8200 Vineland Ave.), which gathers retailers such as Brooks Brothers and Banana Republic in one center.

For R&R, guests can indulge in the signature Canyon Stone Massage at Canyon Ranch Spa Club at the Gaylord Palms Resort (6000 W Osceola Pkwy., Kissimmee) or try a citrus-infused treatment at the Ritz-Carlton Spa at the hotelier's Grande Lakes Resort (4012 Central Florida Pkwy., Orlando). To end any day in high style, book a table with one of Orlando's "celebrity chefs" at Emeril Lagasse's Emeril's Orlando (6000 Universal Blvd., Orlando) or Norman Van Aken's Norman's (in the Ritz-Carlton, Grande Lakes). You may be in the shadow of the theme parks, but miles away in spirit.

Pagoda at Lake Eola Park

Seasons 52

© Rand McNally

🍴 What to eat

Restaurant Row on Sand Lake Road offers everything from American to Thai, Latin, French and Middle Eastern. A favorite: **Seasons 52** (7700 Sand Lake Rd., Orlando), where no entrée on the menu is more than 500 calories.

🛍 What to buy

For products indigenous to Central Florida, visit the **Winter Park Farmers' Market** (200 W. New England Ave.) from 9 a.m. to 1 p.m. every Saturday, or the downtown **Orlando Sunday Eola Market** (south shore of Lake Eola) from 9 a.m. to 3 p.m every Sunday.

Purple symbols indicate locations discussed in this section.

🍴 Restaurant   🍴 Lodging
🛍 Shopping   🏛 Museum
⬛ Point of Interest
⬜ Detailed map area

For a complete listing of symbols, see back cover flap.

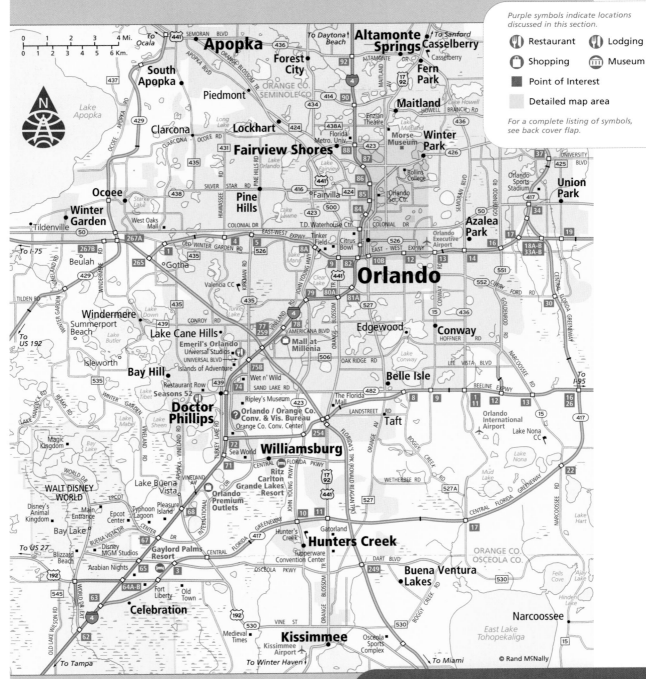

© Rand McNally

❗ What to do

Winter Park Sidewalk Art Festival, third weekend in March.

Florida Film Festival, late March or early April.

For more details about these festivals, please see page 186.

❓ *Visit Florida*
(888) 735-2872, www.visitflorida.com

Lodging Tips

With more than 113,000 rooms, Orlando offers diverse lodging options, from budget and moderately priced hotels to lavish suites. For details: Orlando-Orange County Convention and Visitors Bureau, (407) 363-5872, (800) 972-3304, www.orlandoinfo.com.

Florida's Forgotten Coast

The pace slow downs on this strip of Florida's Gulf coastline, nicknamed the "Forgotten Coast," which lies just minutes from the spring break playground of Panama City Beach. Laid-back **Mexico Beach** marks the western boundary; it stretches east along US 98 to Cape San Blas, **Apalachicola**, St. George Island, **Eastpoint** and **Carabelle**.

No-frills, largely undeveloped **Mexico Beach** presents a mañana sort of personality. Tamed by the St. Joseph Peninsula offshore, gentle waves lap its beaches, with dune walkovers along the town's three-mile length.

For out-of-the way beaches, those in the know head to a peninsula of sand known as Cape San Blas and St. Joseph Peninsula State Park (8899 Cape San Blas Rd.), a 1,650-acre wilderness area at the far end of the cape with camping, beach time, fishing, and wildlife watching. On a map, the skinny peninsula stretches up about 20 miles into St. Joseph Bay. The park lies on the upper half, with nine miles of unspoiled Gulf beach. More than 200 species of birds have been spotted, and monarch butterflies stop here en route to Mexico in the winter. Rent a cabin and leave your cares behind.

Historic **Apalachicola** once served as a bustling seaport for steamboats carrying cotton downriver from Georgia and Alabama to the Gulf of Mexico. Today it's a picturesque fishing town, and succulent oysters are its claim to fame—more than 90 percent of Florida's oysters are harvested here. Downtown's historic buildings, many dating from the 1830s, have been beautifully preserved, with more than 200 antebellum homes and commercial buildings now home to shops, galleries, restaurants, and bed-and-breakfasts. Make a stop at the chamber of commerce (122 Commerce St.) for a self-guided walking tour of the historic district,

St. Joseph Peninsula State Park

which reflects the cultural, social, and economic history of the area. Spend an hour or two strolling past architectural styles that include Colonial Revival, Greek Revival, Queen Anne, and Florida Vernacular. Highlights include the Sponge Exchange and the Cotton Warehouse along the working waterfront, as well as John Gorrie Museum State Park (46 6th St.), which commemorates the 19th-century doctor who invented an ice-making machine to cool patients with yellow fever—the precursor to today's air-conditioning. The original Trinity Episcopal Church (intersection of US 98 and Sixth Street), built in 1836, still holds services today. Seafood fans head to ramshackle Boss Oyster (123 Water St.) with tables overlooking the Apalachicola River. Oyster fans order them freshly shucked by the dozens, but you can order fresh Gulf shrimp, blue crabs, bay scallops, and grouper (or a satisfying cheeseburger).

To get back to the beaches, just across the bay via Gorrie Memorial Bridge sits the town of **Eastpoint**, where seafood docks stretch for miles and you can dine on the bay while watching the shrimp and oyster boats bring in the day's catch. Secluded St. George Island State Park, at the far eastern end of 28-mile-long St. George Island, offers nine miles of pristine white-sand beaches and dunes, along with hiking trails, board-walks, and observation platforms for bird watching. On the beach side, loggerhead and green sea turtles lumber ashore to lay eggs every summer. But don't be fooled by the remote-sounding shores: sunbathers often crowd the beaches on summer days. Late fall through early spring is the best time for bird-watching and peace and quiet. (As of press time, damage from Hurricane Dennis has resulted in limited access to park facilities, but rebuilding is underway. Please call (850) 653-9347, the John Gorrie Museum, for updates.)

Carrabelle's police station

Tiny **Carrabelle's** many docks and marinas offer some of the best charter fishing around. Antique shops and art galleries dot the streetscape, while the smallest police station in the world—the size of a phone booth —is found here. For a break from all the seafood, head to locally owned Hog Wild BBQ (1593 US 98) for hickory-smoked barbecue and the lunch and sup-per buffet.

The Forgotten Coast officially ends at St. Marks National Wildlife Refuge, established in 1931 as a wintering habitat for migratory birds. Take the seven-mile wildlife drive to the lighthouse, one of the oldest in the Southeast. The Visitor Center, three miles south of US 98 on Lighthouse Road, is open daily.

St Marks Lighthouse

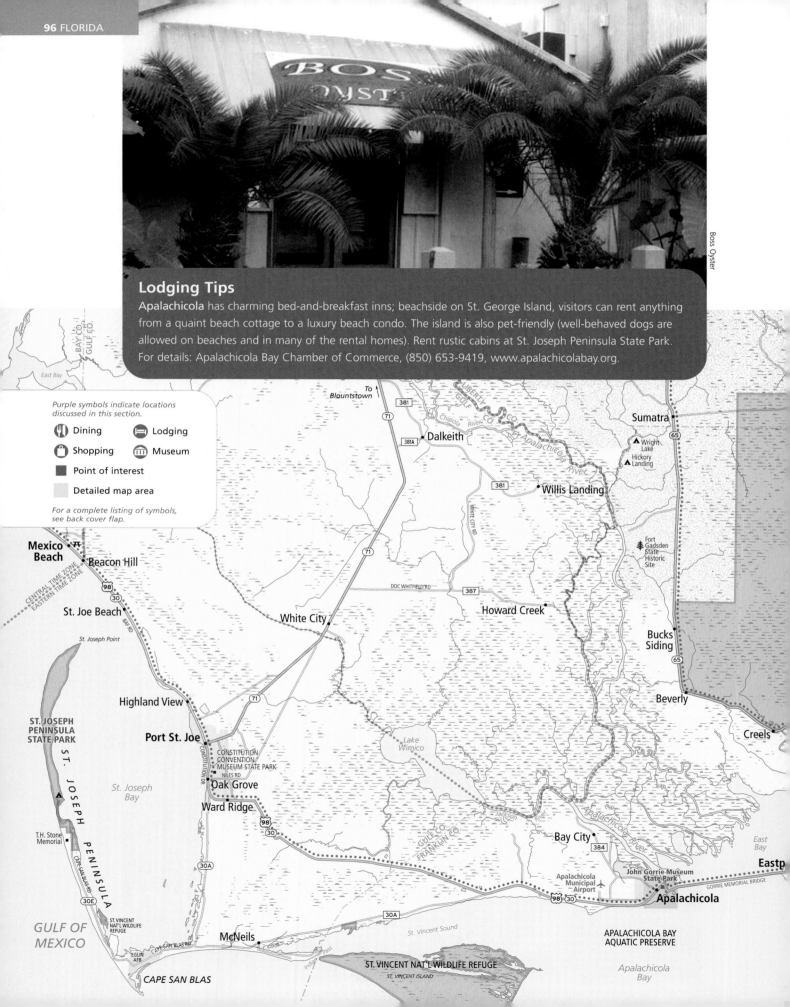

Boss Oyster

Lodging Tips

Apalachicola has charming bed-and-breakfast inns; beachside on St. George Island, visitors can rent anything from a quaint beach cottage to a luxury beach condo. The island is also pet-friendly (well-behaved dogs are allowed on beaches and in many of the rental homes). Rent rustic cabins at St. Joseph Peninsula State Park. For details: Apalachicola Bay Chamber of Commerce, (850) 653-9419, www.apalachicolabay.org.

Purple symbols indicate locations discussed in this section.

- Dining
- Lodging
- Shopping
- Museum
- Point of interest
- Detailed map area

For a complete listing of symbols, see back cover flap.

Map labels

To Blountstown

BAY CO.
GULF CO.

East Bay

LIBERTY CO.
GULF CO.

Chipola River

381

Sumatra

65

381A

Dalkeith

Wright Lake

Hickory Landing

381

Willis Landing

Apalachicola River

WHITE CITY RD

Fort Gadsden State Historic Site

Mexico Beach

Beacon Hill

CENTRAL TIME ZONE
EASTERN TIME ZONE

98

30

71

DOC WHITFIELD RD

387

Howard Creek

Bucks Siding

65

St. Joe Beach

BAY RD

White City

St. Joseph Point

Beverly

Highland View

71

98

Creels

ST. JOSEPH PENINSULA STATE PARK

ST. JOSEPH PENINSULA

Lake Wimico

Port St. Joe

CONSTITUTION DR

CONSTITUTION CONVENTION MUSEUM STATE PARK

NILES RD

Oak Grove

St. Joseph Bay

T.H. Stone Memorial

Ward Ridge

98
30

Jackson River

GULF CO.
FRANKLIN CO.

Bay City

384

East Bay

Eastp

30A

CAPE SAN BLAS RD

Apalachicola River

John Gorrie Museum State Park

GORRIE MEMORIAL BRIDGE

Apalachicola Municipal Airport

98
30

Apalachicola

30E

EGLIN AFB

GULF OF MEXICO

ST. VINCENT NAT'L WILDLIFE REFUGE

CAPE SAN BLAS

30A

McNeils

Indian Pass

St. Vincent Sound

ST. VINCENT NAT'L WILDLIFE REFUGE

ST. VINCENT ISLAND

APALACHICOLA BAY AQUATIC PRESERVE

Apalachicola Bay

What to eat

Oysters, oysters, oysters, and Gulf shrimp, scallops, and the catch of the day—this is the region for seafood fans. Nothing too fancy, but casual restaurants with water views are abundant. **Boss Oyster** (123 Water St., Apalachicola) is the most talked-about seafood restaurant in these parts.

What to buy

Check out Apalachicola's small shopping district with boutiques in historic buildings. Shops on St. George Island carry everything from beach gear, clothing, gifts, and books to gourmet treats, original artwork and jewelry. For antiques, collectibles, and funky vintage finds, head to **Apalachicola Antique Mall**.

What to do

Florida Seafood Festival, Apalachicola, November.

Forgotten Coast Chef Sampler, Apalachicola, February.

For more details about these festivals, please see page 186.

Visit Florida
(888) 735-2872, www.visitflorida.com

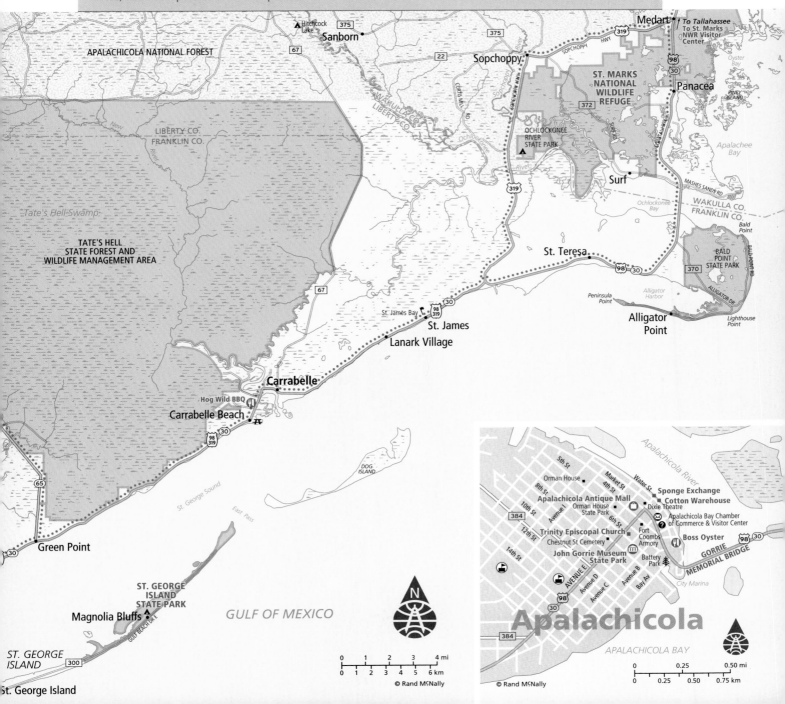

The Lower
Keys

Coral Reefs to
Funky Duval Street

Once you cross the Seven-Mile Bridge just south of **Marathon** in the Middle Keys, you get the feeling that you're actually off the North American continent and out to sea. A narrow ribbon of highway leads to the end of the American road map, Key West.

Entering the Lower Keys, from Bahia Honda Key south, is like taking a step back in time as commercial development drops off and you breeze by thick patches of green. Little green mile markers along the road, starting with MM 113 in Key Largo and ending with MM 1 in **Key West**, note distance.

Bahia Honda State Park (MM 37, 36850 Overseas Hwy.), a favorite of "conchs," or native Key Westers, offers one of the prettiest natural sand beaches in the Keys. Beaches, by the way, are rare in the Keys, so take advantage of this one. You can snorkel, kayak, bicycle, or just stroll, keeping an eye out for an abundance of birds including white or blue herons, gulls, egrets, and pelicans.

Big Pine Key and surrounding islands are home to the elusive Key deer, the small subspecies of the Virginia white-tail deer found nowhere else in the world except the National Key Deer Refuge (MM 30.5, 175 Key Deer Blvd.). The deer are easiest to spot in the early morning and early evening hours.

For snorkeling or diving, many consider Looe Key National Marine Sanctuary the most spectacular reef in the Lower Keys, with 7,000 years' worth of coral growth. About seven miles offshore, you can take an organized trip, like those run by Innerspace Dive Center (MM 30). If you can swim, you can snorkel. No need for scuba tanks—just paddling on top of the water introduces a whole new world. The reef is home to more than 150 species of fish including yellowtail, angelfish, parrotfish, barracuda, sergeant majors, and moray eel. Lucky divers spot sharks and rays.

Duval Street, Key West

For a real Keys' experience, reserve a cottage at Old Wooden Bridge Fishing Camp (1791 Bogie Dr.) on Big Pine Key, then book a kayak tour with Captain Bill Keogh of Big Pine Kayak Adventures. Keogh, an avid photographer and kayaker, takes visitors into both the Great White Heron and Key Deer refuges. He tailors trips for beginners and veterans alike.

Quirky, laid-back Key West, often overrun with tourists, still exudes an irresistible charm. If you don't know your way around, the best way to get your bearings is on the touristy Conch Train, which passes all the important historical sites on a 90-minute tour. Riders learn the lay of the land and gain insights into the rich and famous who loved Key West, among them Ernest Hemingway, John James Audubon, Harry Truman, and Robert Frost. Board the train at Mallory Square (303 Front St.) or Flagler Station (901 Caroline St.).

Get a sense of life in another era with a peek inside the Ernest Hemingway Home and Museum (907 Whitehead St.), or book a room at the Curry Mansion (511 Caroline St.) built by Milton Curry, one of Florida's first millionaires. For an eccentric history lesson, take a tour of the Key West Cemetery. The whitewashed above-ground tombs and statues are fascinating, and a stroll through this historic graveyard can tell as much about Key West's quirky character as any history lesson (with epitaphs like "I told you I was sick").

Sunset Celebration. A circus of vendors works the crowd, with zany performers like the dramatic escape artist who wraps himself Houdini-style in a straight jacket and chains but escapes in minutes to pass the hat.

Street performers at Mallory Square

Eye-popping gold glitters at the Mel Fisher Maritime Museum (200 Greene St.), along with other fabulous treasure from the 17th-century Atocha shipwreck. If you still have energy to burn, climb the 88 steps at the Key West Lighthouse Museum (938 Whitehead St.).

Another of the rare Keys beaches: Clarence S. Higgs Memorial Beach along A1A, which offers picnic tables, shady palms, a café, and a bike path—a great place to people-watch.

Hemingway Days Festival

Compact **Old Town**, a square mile centered around funky **Duval Street**, brims with with boutiques, souvenir shops, restaurants, and galleries. If you've got a sweet tooth, don't miss the decadent frozen key lime pie dipped in dark chocolate sold at the Blonde Giraffe (629 Duval St.). At the end of the street, hundreds throng nightly in Mallory Square for the legendary

For pictures, everyone heads to **Southernmost Point**, an official spot at the corner of South and Whitehead streets. The spot itself isn't much to look at, but a photo seems mandatory to mark the occasion of a visit to the end of the road.

Looe Key Reef

Lodging Tips

The Lower Keys feature plenty of waterfront cottages and cabins. Key West has thousands of rooms, from cottages and condos to more than a dozen charming bed-and-breakfasts in old homes (a number are exclusively gay and lesbian). National hoteliers include the Marriott and Sheraton. For details: Monroe County Tourist Development Council, www.fla-keys.com.

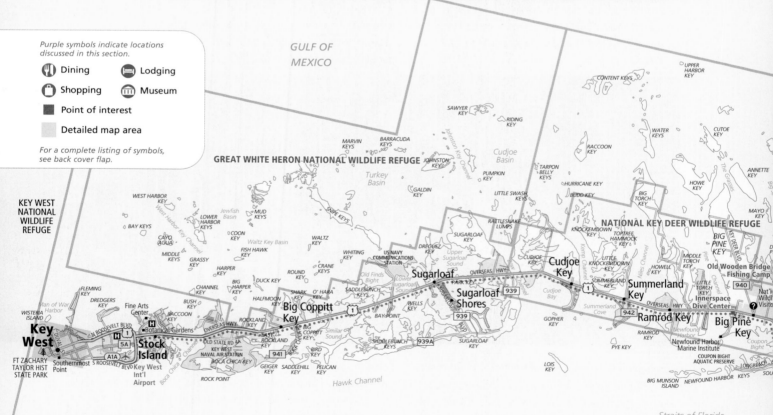

Purple symbols indicate locations discussed in this section.

🍴 Dining   🛏 Lodging

👜 Shopping   🏛 Museum

■ Point of interest

   Detailed map area

For a complete listing of symbols, see back cover flap.

GULF OF MEXICO

KEY WEST NATIONAL WILDLIFE REFUGE

GREAT WHITE HERON NATIONAL WILDLIFE REFUGE

NATIONAL KEY DEER WILDLIFE REFUGE

Turkey Basin

Cudjoe Basin

UPPER HARBOR KEY

CONTENT KEYS

SAWYER KEY

RIDING KEY

MARVIN KEYS

BARRACUDA KEYS

JOHNSTON KEY

PUMPKIN KEY

TARPON BELLY KEYS

LITTLE SWASH KEYS

RACCOON KEY

WATER KEYS

CUTOE KEY

ANNETTE KEY

HOWE KEY

BUDD KEY

HURRICANE KEY

BIG TORCH KEY

MAYO KEY

GALDIN KEY

WEST HARBOR KEY

Jewfish Basin

MUD KEYS

SNIPE KEYS

RATTLESNAKE LUMPS

KNOCKEMDOWN KEYS

TOPTREE HAMMOCK KEY

BIG PINE KEY

LOWER HARBOR KEYS

BAY KEYS

CAYO AGUA

COON KEY

Waltz Key Basin

WALTZ KEY

SUGARLOAF KEY

DREGUEZ KEY

Upper Sugarloaf Sound

CUDJOE KEY

LITTLE KNOCKEMDOWN KEY

HOWELL KEY

MIDDLE TORCH KEY

Pine Channel

Old Wooden Bridge Fishing Camp

MIDDLE KEYS

GRASSY KEY

HARPER KEY

FISH HAWK KEY

WHITING KEY

US NAVY COMMUNICATIONS STATION

Cudjoe Key

Niles Channel

LITTLE TORCH KEY

940

Nat'l Wildl Visitor

FLEMING KEY

DREDGERS KEY

Man of War

CHANNEL KEY

BIG HARPER KEY

DUCK KEY

ROUND KEY

CRANE KEYS

Old Finds Bight

Sugarloaf

OVERSEAS HWY

PARK KEY

1

SUMMERLAND KEY

Summerland Key

Innerspace Dive Center

Cudjoe Bay

BUSH KEY

HALFMOON KEY

SHARK KEY

O'HARA KEY

SADDLEBUNCH KEYS

Lower Sugarloaf Sound

Sugarloaf Shores

939

Summerland Cove

942

Ramrod Key

OVERSEAS HWY

Big Pine Key

WISTERIA ISLAND

Fine Arts Center

RACCOON KEY

ROCKLAND KEY

Big Coppitt Key

1

WELLS KEY

BAY POINT

939

GOPHER KEY

Summerland Cove

RAMROD KEY

Newfound Harbor Marine Institute

Coupon Bight

Key West

DUVAL ST

N ROOSEVELT BLVD

Botanical Gardens

OVERSEAS HWY

BIG COPPITT KEY

Similar Sound

SADDLEBUNCH KEYS

SUGARLOAF KEYS

PYE KEY

COUPON BIGHT AQUATIC PRESERVE

Stock Island

H 1

5A

A1A

S ROOSEVELT BLVD

OLD STATE RD 5A

ROCKLAND KEY

941

KEY WEST NAVAL AIR STATION

BOCA CHICA KEY

BIRD KEY

939A

LOIS KEY

LONGBEACH

FT ZACHARY TAYLOR HIST STATE PARK

Southernmost Point

Key West Int'l Airport

ROCK POINT

GEIGER KEY

SADDLEHILL KEY

PELICAN KEY

Hawk Channel

BIG MUNSON ISLAND

NEWFOUND HARBOR KEYS

Boca Chica Channel

ATLANTIC OCEAN

Straits of Florida

Looe Key Nat'l Marine Sanctuary ■

Lower Keys Underwater Music Festival

What to eat

Conch fritters and key lime pie are specialties, along with fresh seafood. Unassuming roadside diners serve some of the best meals. In Key West, head to Duval Street for the biggest concentration of restaurants. Locals recommend **Mangoes** (700 Duval St.) for the conch chowder and local snapper.

What to buy

Prime shopping lies on Duval Street in Key West in the form of housewares, clothing, artwork, and lots of fun, frivolous merchandise. For the best selection, head to **Fast Buck Freddie's** (500 Duval St.).

What to do

Lower Keys Underwater Music Festival, Looe Key Reef, early July.

Hemingway Days, Key West, July.

For more details about these festivals, please see page 186.

Visit Florida
(888) 735-2872, www.visitflorida.com

© Rand McNally

Georgia
Shores

Dressed in some of Mother Nature's finest handiwork, this stretch of Georgia's coastline promises history and romance. Tales of early settlers, the rich who once wintered here, abound. Today's visitors enjoy historic sites, sandy beaches, swampy places, and the chance to connect with the outdoors.

In **Brunswick**, the **Mary Ross Waterfront Park** (Gloucester and Bay streets) holds the Liberty Ship Memorial Plaza, which honors those who built the ships that helped win World War II. (It's also a strategic vantage point for viewing sunsets over the marshes.) Years before the war, romance flourished beneath the sprawling limbs of Lovers' Oak (Albany and Prince streets), where Native American sweethearts are rumored to have rendezvoued. It's said that under Lanier's Oak (US 17, Brunswick) Georgia poet Sidney Lanier, while viewing the landscape, found inspiration for "The Marshes of Glynn." With streets and squares laid out in 1771 by General James Oglethorpe, **Old Town Brunswick** showcases many restored late 19th- and early 20th-century homes. Particularly interesting are the Mahoney McGarvey House (1709 Reynolds St.) and Old City Hall (Newcastle Street, downtown Brunswick).

Cotton and rice once reigned along Georgia's coast, where plantations flourished from 1760 until the onset of the Civil War. The famed "Avenue of Oaks," which once led to one of the most prosperous local plantations, **Retreat Plantation** (St. Simons Island's southern tip), today forms part of the entrance to the Sea Island Golf Club. Visitors can tour the still-working St. Simons Lighthouse (101 12th St., southern tip of island). Adjacent to the 1872 lighthouse, the keeper's cottage houses a museum and gift shop of the Coastal Georgia Historical Society.

Former Glynn County Courthouse (1907), Brunswick

Remnants of a fort and the town of **Frederica** serve as reminders of the once-thriving town that sprang up in 1736. Part of the Fort Frederica National Monument (6515 Frederica Rd.), the site is open daily and includes an orientation film and ranger-led tours. Interpreter-led tours of Hofwyl-Broadfield Plantation (5556 US 17) explain the life and culture of an 1800s rice plantation.

shore birds, and historic structures. Accessible by passenger ferry (8 miles east of Kingsland at I-95's Exit 3), the 36,415-acre island boasts great biking (rentals are available), backpacking, bird watching, boating, camping, fishing, hiking, and kayaking.

Looking for even more Mother Nature? Hit the Colonial Coast Birding Trail, running between **Savannah** and

Jekyll Island Club Hotel

Memories of old money and good times echo in the National Historic Landmark District on Jekyll Island. Here, from 1888 to 1942, wealthy industrialists and financiers (William Rockefeller, Joseph Pulitzer, and J.P. Morgan among them) spent their winters at the Jekyll Island Club.

While history defines the region, visitors savor ways to connect with the land. Bicycle rentals, golf, miniature golf, horseback riding, nature trails (such as Earth Day Nature Trail, off US 17 at Sidney Lanier Bridge), and ghost walks (St. Simons Island) keep vacationers active. Other options include fishing and party-boat charters, casino cruises, boat and personal watercraft rentals, kayak tours, canoe rentals, sailing charters, and water nature tours.

Okefenokee National Wildlife Refuge (west of Kingsland), a vast wetland area, stretches across 400,000 acres of canals and moss-draped cypress trees. Guided boat tours, kayaks, and canoes provide opportunities to encounter hundreds of species of plant and animal life, such as alligators. Fishing, picnicking, and bike rentals also are available. In the midst of Cumberland Island's salt marshes, dune fields, maritime forests, mud flats, and tidal creeks visitors sometimes spy sea turtles, wild turkeys, wild horses, armadillos,

St. Mary's, where some 300 species of birds have been spotted along shorelines, salt marshes, old rice fields, woodlands, tidal rivers, freshwater wetlands, and other habitats. Watchers might see bald eagles, wood storks, sanderlings, or great egrets. No wonder the Creek Indians called the Georgia coast the Enchanted Land. More chances to get close to nature await at Crooked River State Park (6222 Charlie Smith Sr. Hwy., St. Mary's), which has picnic and group shelters, rental cottages, tent/trailer/RV sites, and places to fish, hike, and bike.

Alligator in Okefenokee Swamp

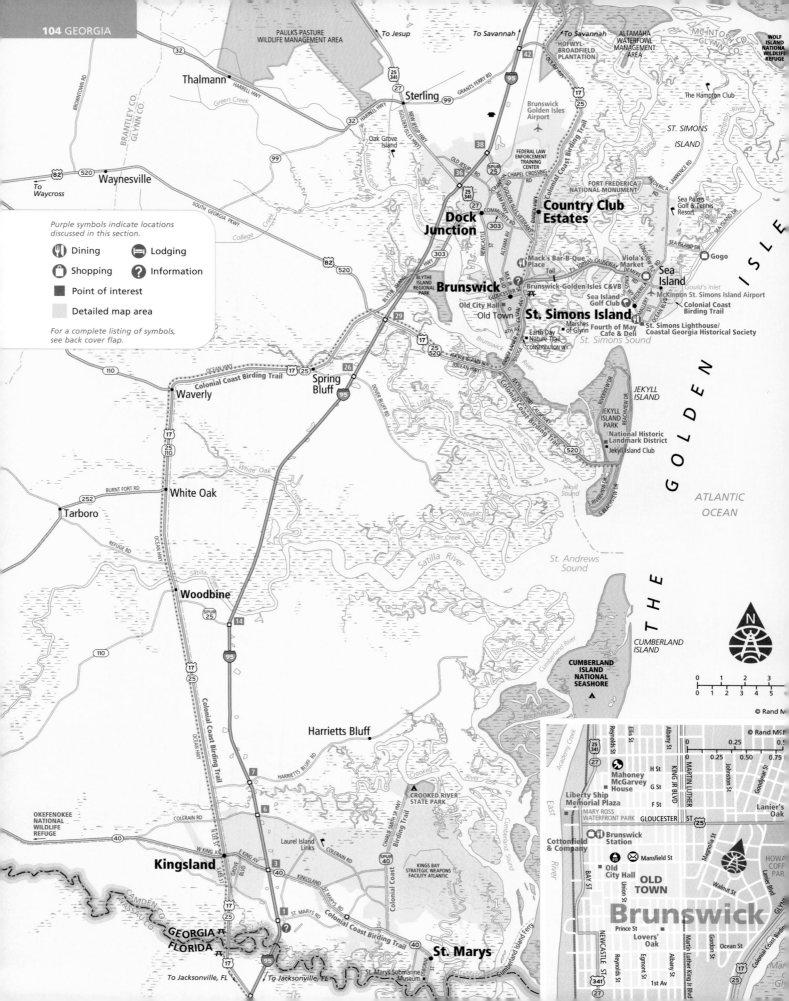

Purple symbols indicate locations discussed in this section.

🍴 Dining 🛏 Lodging
🛍 Shopping ❓ Information
■ Point of interest
▨ Detailed map area

For a complete listing of symbols, see back cover flap.

PAULKS PASTURE WILDLIFE MANAGEMENT AREA

To Jesup   To Savannah   To Savannah

HOFWYL-BROADFIELD PLANTATION

ALTAMAHA WATERFOWL MANAGEMENT AREA

WOLF ISLAND NATIONAL WILDLIFE REFUGE

McINTOSH CO GLYNN CO

The Hampton Club

Thalmann

Sterling

Brunswick Golden Isles Airport

ST. SIMONS ISLAND

FEDERAL LAW ENFORCEMENT TRAINING CENTER

Waynesville

FORT FREDERICA NATIONAL MONUMENT

Sea Palms Golf & Tennis Resort

To Waycross

Dock Junction

Country Club Estates

Mack's Bar-B-Que Place

Viola's Market

Gogo

Sea Island

Brunswick-Golden Isles C&VB

Brunswick

Old City Hall

Old Town

Sea Island Golf Club

McKinnon St. Simons Island Airport

Colonial Coast Birding Trail

St. Simons Island

Marshes of Glynn

Fourth of May Cafe & Deli

St. Simons Lighthouse/Coastal Georgia Historical Society

Earth Day Nature Trail

St. Simons Sound

BLYTHE ISLAND REGIONAL PARK

Spring Bluff

Colonial Coast Birding Trail

Waverly

JEKYLL ISLAND

JEKYLL ISLAND PARK

National Historic Landmark District

Jekyll Island Club

GOLDEN ISLE

White Oak

ATLANTIC OCEAN

Tarboro

OKEFENOKEE NATIONAL WILDLIFE REFUGE

Woodbine

St. Andrews Sound

THE CUMBERLAND ISLAND

Harrietts Bluff

CROOKED RIVER STATE PARK

Laurel Island Links

KINGS BAY STRATEGIC WEAPONS FACILITY ATLANTIC

CUMBERLAND ISLAND NATIONAL SEASHORE

Kingsland

Colonial Coast Birding Trail

GEORGIA
FLORIDA

St. Marys Submarine Museum

St. Marys

To Jacksonville, FL   To Jacksonville, FL

CAMDEN CO
NASSAU CO

Mahoney McGarvey House

Liberty Ship Memorial Plaza

MARY ROSS WATERFRONT PARK

Cottonfield & Company

Brunswick Station

Mansfield St

Old City Hall

OLD TOWN

Lanier's Oak

Brunswick

Lovers' Oak

HOWARD COFFIN PARK

© Rand McNally

Ritz Theatre (1898) in Old Town Brunswick

What to eat

Brunswick, Ga. claims to be the original home of Brunswick Stew, a hearty tomato-based dish that typically includes pork or chicken, beans, potatoes, and more. **Brunswick Station** (1414 Newcastle St., Brunswick) serves a champion stew. Other eateries that offer the dish include **Mack's Bar-B-Que Place** (2809 Glynn Ave., Brunswick) and the **Fourth of May Cafe and Deli** (444 Ocean Blvd., St. Simons Island).

What to buy

Viola's Market (115 Longview Plaza, St. Simons Island) sells local artist Annette Friedrich's mirrors, picture frames, and jewelry boxes, all encrusted in seashells. Illuminated lighthouse sculptures along with artwork by local photographers, artists, and craftspeople are available at **Cottonfield & Company** (1413 Newcastle St., downtown Brunswick). **Gogo** (600 Sea Island Rd., St. Simons Island) sells artist Gogo Ferguson's gold and silver jewelry crafted from shells, bones, and other items found on the beaches of Cumberland Island.

What to do

Blessing of the Fleet, Brunswick, Mother's Day.
Brunswick Stewbilee, Brunswick, second weekend in October.
Catfish Festival, Kingsland, Labor Day weekend.

For more details about these festivals, please see page 186.

Georgia Office of Tourism
(800) 847-4842, www.georgiaonmymind.org

Lodging Tips

Rooms are plentiful, ranging from national chain hotels along I-95 to full-service resorts, chain hotels, and bed-and-breakfast inns. For details: Brunswick-Golden Isles Convention & Visitors Bureau, (800) 933-COAST (2627) or www.bgicvb.com; or Kingsland Convention & Visitors Bureau, (912) 729-5999, (800) 433-0225, www.VisitKingsland.com.

Mining Northern
Georgia

Mountains and sprawling Lake Lanier define a slice of Northern Georgia where gold once was mined and where today's visitors savor relaxing spas and outdoor places to play.

A progressive southern town, **Gainesville** anchors the area with water sports, museums, and southern hospitality. Honoring the inspiration for the town's title as "Poultry Capital of the World," a three-foot statue of a rooster perches atop a 25-foot marble column in Poultry Park (corner of West Academy Street and Jesse Jewell Parkway, Gainesville). With a picturesque streetscape and preserved historic buildings, Gainesville's downtown buzzes with restaurants and retail stores (more than 35 on the downtown square) and hosts special events throughout the year. A walking tour/ scale model of the solar system begins at the square's southeast corner—the sun—and travels northwest to Mercury, Venus, and Earth, eventually ending at Longwood Park's Pluto. Historic Green Street (north of downtown on US 129), laced with many Victorian and neoclassical homes dating from the late-19th and early-20th centuries, captures the town's ambience. The Gainesville-Hall County Convention and Visitors Bureau (117 Jesse Jewell Pkwy.) distributes walking tour brochures. Additional glimpses of the area's past await at the Northeast Georgia History Center (322 Academy St., Gainesville), which remembers 150 years of the region's history and salutes area leaders and sports legends. One highlight, an 18th-century cabin complete with gardens and authentic furnishings, once belonged to Cherokee Indian Chief White Path.

Site of the first American gold rush, **Dahlonega** (north of Gainesville) retains its mountain charm with a historic town square. Visitors learn about the gold rush at Dahlonega Gold Museum (1 Public Square, in the old Lumpkin County Courthouse), which spotlights

The Charters-Smith House on Historic Green Street

the era—20 years before the gold rush in California—when thousands of people flocked here. That blitz resulted in more than $6 million in gold coined in Dahlonega between 1838 and 1861. Visitors walk

erate climate, and picturesque backdrop. The healing powers, almost forgotten after the 1930s, continue today in places such as the Healing Arts Spa on Green Street (635 Green St., Gainesville), which offers

Dahlonega, Georgia

the massive tunnel network and pan for gold at Consolidated Gold Mine (185 Consolidated Gold Mine Rd.) and Crisson Gold Mine (2736 Morrison Moore Pkwy. East), where a 120-year-old stamp mill still crushes quartz rock that contains gold.

massages, body therapies, facials, and acupuncture. Massages and skin-care treatments are available at Mountain Laurel Creek Inn & Spa (202 Talmer Grizzle Rd., Dahlonega).

Before four town leaders in the late 1960s hit on the idea of transforming the old logging town into a Bavarian village with gingerbread-style buildings and cobblestone streets, the hamlet of **Helen** almost disappeared. A visit should begin at the Helen Welcome Center (726 Brucken Strasse), which has brochures, coupons and restaurant and lodging information. Helen has wedding chapels and plenty of places to shop and play outdoors. Nacoochee Village (7025 S. Main St.) is home to restaurants, shops, attractions, and outfitters offering horseback riding and fly fishing. Canoeing and kayaking are nearby. Visitors find antiques, collectibles, candles, and accessories directly from the manufacturer. Also here: the Habersham Winery (with free tastings), one of Georgia's oldest. Birthplace of the original Cabbage Patch Kids, BabyLand General Hospital (73 W. Underwood St., Cleveland) offers self-guided tours that begin (where else?) in the Fathers' Waiting Room. Visitors can see dolls being made and even adopt a soft-sculpture, hand-stitched "baby."

Poultry Park in Gainesville

When not panning, visitors can pamper themselves in the foothills of the Blue Ridge Mountains. As early as the mid-1840s, the area had earned a reputation for the recuperative qualities of its healing waters, mod-

No adoptions are allowed, yet visitors (with reservations) are welcome to make the acquaintance of kangaroos at the Kangaroo Conservation Center (222 Bailey-Waters Rd., Dawsonville), which offers demonstrations, tours, and rides through animal habitats.

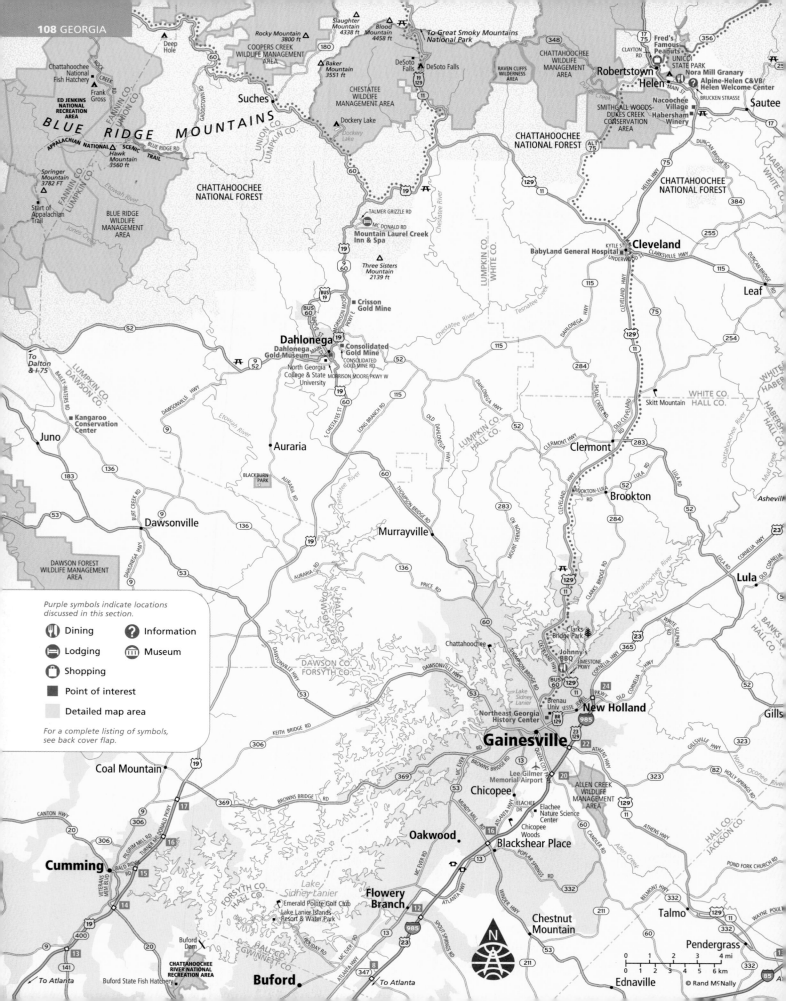

BLUE RIDGE MOUNTAINS

CHATTAHOOCHEE NATIONAL FOREST

CHATTAHOOCHEE NATIONAL FOREST

Deep Hole

Chattahoochee National Fish Hatchery

Frank Gross

ED JENKINS NATIONAL RECREATION AREA

Springer Mountain 3782 ft

APPALACHIAN NATIONAL SCENIC TRAIL

Start of Appalachian Trail

Hawk Mountain 3560 ft

BLUE RIDGE WILDLIFE MANAGEMENT AREA

Rocky Mountain 3800 ft

Slaughter Mountain 4338 ft

Blood Mountain 4458 ft

To Great Smoky Mountains National Park

Baker Mountain 3551 ft

DeSoto Falls

DeSoto Falls

RAVEN CLIFFS WILDERNESS AREA

CHATTAHOOCHEE WILDLIFE MANAGEMENT AREA

Fred's Famous Peanuts

UNICOI STATE PARK

Robertstown

Helen

Nora Mill Granary

Alpine-Helen C&VB/ Helen Welcome Center

Brucken Strasse

Sautee

Nacoochee Village

Habersham Winery

SMITHGALL WOODS-DUKES CREEK CONSERVATION AREA

CHATTAHOOCHEE NATIONAL FOREST

COOPERS CREEK WILDLIFE MANAGEMENT AREA

Suches

CHESTATEE WILDLIFE MANAGEMENT AREA

Dockery Lake

Dockery Lake

CHATTAHOOCHEE NATIONAL FOREST

TALMER GRIZZLE RD

MC DONALD RD

Mountain Laurel Creek Inn & Spa

Three Sisters Mountain 2139 ft

Crisson Gold Mine

Dahlonega

Dahlonega Gold Museum

Consolidated Gold Mine

North Georgia College & State University

BabyLand General Hospital

Cleveland

WHITE CO. HALL CO.

Skitt Mountain

Leaf

Clermont

Brookton

Asheville

Juno

Kangaroo Conservation Center

Auraria

BLACKBURN PARK

Dawsonville

DAWSON FOREST WILDLIFE MANAGEMENT AREA

Murrayville

Lula

Chattahoochee

Clarks Bridge Park

Johnny's BBQ

New Holland

Brenau Univ

Northeast Georgia History Center

Gainesville

Gills

Coal Mountain

Chicopee

Lee Gilmer Memorial Airport

ALLEN CREEK WILDLIFE MANAGEMENT AREA

Oakwood

Blackshear Place

Elachee Nature Science Center

Chicopee Woods

Cumming

Lake Sidney Lanier

Emerald Pointe Golf Club

Lake Lanier Islands Resort & Water Park

Flowery Branch

Chestnut Mountain

Talmo

Buford Dam

CHATTAHOOCHEE RIVER NATIONAL RECREATION AREA

Buford

Buford State Fish Hatchery

To Atlanta

To Atlanta

Ednaville

Pendergrass

Purple symbols indicate locations discussed in this section.

🍴 Dining

❓ Information

🛏 Lodging

🏛 Museum

🛍 Shopping

■ Point of interest

Detailed map area

For a complete listing of symbols, see back cover flap.

N

0   1   2   3   4 mi
0 1 2 3 4 5 6 km

© Rand McNally

What to eat

Pioneer Porridge, made from several grains, simmers in a crock pot at **Nora Mill Granary** (7107 S. Main St., Helen), an operating grist mill on the Chattahoochee River. Taste it here, then buy a packet of porridge mix to take home. Barbecue is tasty at **Johnny's BBQ** (1710 Park Hill Dr., Gainesville), and mouths water for homemade breads at **Two Dog Cafe** (Gainesville's downtown square).

What to buy

Open spring through late fall, **Fred's Famous Peanuts** (17 Clayton Rd., Helen) is the place to find peanut crafts and all sorts of mountain products including jams, jellies, fresh pork rinds, and apple cider. Peanuts—boiled, roasted, or in peanut brittle—are also on offer.

What to do

Polar Bear Swim, Lake Lanier, January.
Magical Nights of Lights, Lake Lanier, late November through early January.
For more details about these festivals, please see page 186.

Georgia Office of Tourism
(800) 847-4842, www.georgiaonmymind.org

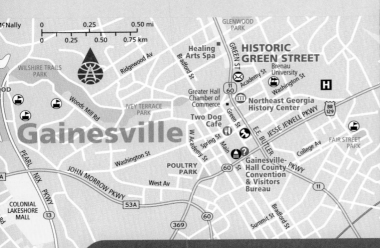

Lodging Tips

Resorts, hotels, cabins, cottages, and bed-and-breakfast inns provide a range of overnight accommodations. For details: Alpine-Helen Convention & Visitors Bureau, (800) 858-8027, www.helenga.org; Gainesville-Hall County Convention and Visitors Bureau, (770) 536-5209, (888) 536-0005, www.gainesvillehallcvb.org; Greater Hall Chamber of Commerce, (770) 532-6206, www.ghcc.com.

Lake Lanier

Mostly
Macon

Established on the banks of the Ocmulgee River, **Macon** has endured and thrived for more than 300 years. The city and surrounding area are peppered with museums, monuments, mounds, and musical moments.

The Deep South pulses in Macon, home to 5,500 individual structures listed on the National Register of Historic Places. Scores of historic houses cluster downtown, including the Hay House (934 Georgia Ave.), known as the "Palace of the South"; the Cannonball House and Museum (856 Mulberry St.), which was struck by a cannonball during the Federal attack on Macon in 1864; and the Sidney Lanier Cottage (935 High St.), birthplace of the eponymous American poet. Lanier's home holds period furnishings, his flute, and writings. Monthly on second Tuesdays, the cottage hosts "Sidney's Salons," featuring poetry readings and music.

It was in Macon that Little Richard, Otis Redding, and James Brown launched their careers in the late '50s and early '60s. Only a decade later, Capricorn Records launched the Allman Brothers Band here. These Georgia music standouts—along with Ray Charles, Alan Jackson, Johnny Mercer, the B-52's, and R.E.M.—are immortalized at the Georgia Music Hall of Fame (200 Martin Luther King Jr. Blvd.), which salutes country legends, big-band sounds, and southern rock in an interactive townscape.

All is not music in Macon. The state's legendary athletic heritage comes to life in the Georgia Sports Hall of Fame (301 Cherry St.), which salutes Olympic champions, professional superstars, and legendary coaches. Hank Aaron, Nancy Lopez, Bill Elliott, and Bobby Jones are among the Georgians remembered.

Woodruff House from Coleman Hill Park

Also downtown: the Tubman African American Museum (340 Walnut St.), where galleries detail the saga of Africans in the United States. Each April, the museum hosts the Pan African Festival with a parade of masquerades, Caribbean steel bands, reggae, African music, dancers, films, children's entertainment, and cultural demonstrations.

Monuments scattered throughout Macon pay tribute to influential Georgians. Side-by-side markers at Rose Hill Cemetery (1091 Riverside Dr.) mark the final resting places of Duane Allman and Berry Oakley of the Allman Brothers. A life-sized bronze statue of Otis Redding overlooks the Ocmulgee River at Gateway Park.

Hay House

The past seems a bit closer at Ocmulgee National Monument & Indian Mounds (1207 Emery Hwy., US 80 off I-16), where visitors can climb ancient mounds, go inside a ceremonial earthlodge, traipse nature trails, and check out hundreds of acres of preserved archaeological remains dating back 12,000 years. Hikers take to Ocmulgee Heritage Trail, where six miles of paths

live animal exhibit, and a 40-million-year-old whale fossil discovered outside of Macon, also intrigues young visitors. The Georgia Music Hall of Fame includes a Music Factory Children's Wing. With three beaches, the Lake Tobesofkee Recreation Area (6600 Mosley Dixon Rd.) invites fishing, swimming, boating, camping, and picnicking. Starcadia Entertainment Park (150

Mural in downtown Macon

trace the Ocmulgee River and connect to the Ocmulgee National Monument. Held annually in September, the Ocmulgee Indian Celebration brings together Native Americans from several nations to fete their heritage with dancing, frontier craftsmen demonstrations, and traditional crafts.

The Macon area offers several attractions of special interest to children. One of them, the five-story Georgia Children's Museum (382 Cherry St.), features an Arts Hall, Young Learner's Exhibition, Black Box Theatre, and Lost Parents Cafe. The Museum of Arts and Sciences (4182 Forsyth Rd.; I-75 to Exit 164), with a planetarium,

Starcadia Circle; I-75 North to Exit 172) packs bumper boats, go-karts, miniature golf, rock climbing, bungee jump, kiddie swings, and picnic areas into a six-acre playground.

One cost-effective way to tour the Macon area: an Around Town tour package—choose an intown or downtown tour or select a combo ticket—that includes trolley transportation and admissions to major attractions with savings of up to 15 percent on additional admissions. The Downtown Welcome Center at Terminal Station sells tickets.

RUM CREEK WILDLIFE MANAGEMENT AREA

PIEDMONT NATIONAL WILDLIFE REFUGE
Jarrell Plantation State Historic Site
OCONEE NATIONAL FOREST
OCONEE NAT'L FOREST
To Athens

Wayside
Bradley
Gray
Clinton

PIEDMONT NATIONAL WILDLIFE REFUGE

Pope's Ferry

To Atlanta

Bolingbroke

Starcadia Entertainment Park
Arkwright

Wesleyan College
Idle Hour CC
Museum of Arts and Sciences
Bellevue
Ingleside
Payne
Cross Keys
Lakeside Hills
Crystal Springs
Bowden
Wheeler Heights

Macon
Mercer Univ
Colonial Mall
OCMULGEE NATIONAL MONUMENT & INDIAN MOUNDS
CENTRAL CITY PARK
(UNDER CONSTRUCTION)
Macon Downtown Airport

Lake Tobesofkee

LAKE TOBESOFKEE RECREATION AREA

Lizella
To Columbus

Macon State College (Macon Campus)
Fincher's Barbecue
ROCKY CREEK RD

Franklinton
To Jeffersonville

JONES CO.
BIBB CO.
Nelsons Lake

BOND SWAMP NATIONAL WILDLIFE REFUGE

BIBB CO.
TWIGGS CO.

Walden

Middle Georgia Regional Airport

Huber
To Savannah

BIBB CO.
HOUSTON CO.

CRAWFORD CO.
PEACH CO.

Byron

Elberta

Bullard
To Cochran

Centerville
Galleria Mall
Homer J Walker Municipal Complex
ROBINS AIR FORCE BASE
Robins AFB

Warner Robins

Museum of Aviation

International City

Bonaire

To Fort Valley

Houston Lake
Kathleen

Perry
To Valdosta
To Hawkinsville

Legend

Purple symbols indicate locations discussed in this section.

- 🍴 Dining
- ❓ Information
- 🛏 Lodging
- 🏛 Museum
- 🛍 Shopping
- 🌳 Park
- ◼ Point of interest
- ▢ Detailed map area

For a complete listing of symbols, see back cover flap.

N

0 1 2 3 4 mi
0 2 4 6 km

© Rand McNally

International Cherry Blossom Festival

🍴 What to eat

Fincher's Barbecue (3947 Houston Ave.) is the only barbecue to have soared into space with NASA. Adding a touch of nostalgia, curb service is available. **Nu-Way Weiners** (430 Cotton Ave.) has served chili dogs since 1916.

🛍 What to buy

Cherry-blossom-related items bloom at the **Cherry Blossom Festival Gift Shop** (577 Mulberry St.), which also sells items "Beyond the Blossoms." The shop is open year-round. At the **Cannonball House & Museum** (856 Mulberry St.), the gift shop offers Southern, Macon, Georgia, and Civil War merchandise.

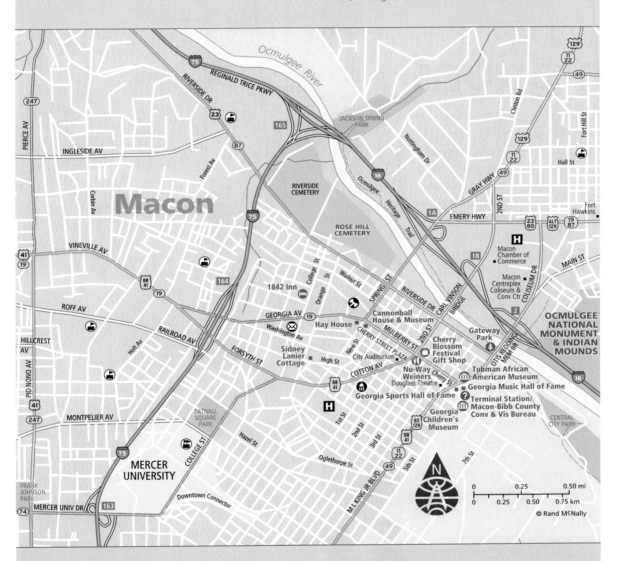

❗ What to do

International Cherry Blossom Festival, March. Bragg Jam Festival, July.

For more details about these festivals, please see page 186.

❓ *Georgia Office of Tourism*
(800) 847-4842, www.georgiaonmymind.org

Lodging tips

Clustered in three distinct areas, accommodations (51 properties with some 4,500 rooms) range from economical and moderately priced hotels and motels to the town's lone bed-and-breakfast, the **1842 Inn** (353 College St.), which Country Inns magazine has named among the nation's top 10 inns. For details (including a Girlfriends' Getaway): Macon-Bibb County Convention and Visitors Bureau, (800) 768-3401, www.maconga.org.

A Pocket of
Plantations

In the heart of Plantation Country, the quaint English village of **St. Francisville** nestles on the bluffs of the Mississippi River, fringed by several plantation homes a few miles from town. On country drives through the gently rolling woodlands, seven resplendent plantations are open for tours; at several, visitors can even spend the night.

Plantations that put out the welcome sign for overnight guests include The Cottage (10528 Cottage Ln., St. Francisville). The home, plus slave quarters, barns, and other original structures, provide an in-depth look at the plantation era. Guests can stay in the main house or in an attached wing. The Butler-Greenwood Plantation (8345 US 61) has remained in the same family since the 1790s. It's filled with priceless antiques, portraits, and family heirlooms and has an exceptional formal Victorian parlor. Enchanting cottages on the oak-lined grounds offer privacy for overnight guests. A visit to Myrtles Plantation (7747 US 61) is not for the faint of heart—it's one of America's most haunted homes. Learn about ghostly encounters on a tour, or spend the night inside the mansion and see for yourself.

Rosedown Plantation State Historic Site

Roadway through West Feliciana Parish, near St. Francisville

Plantations with daily tours include the West Indies-style Oakley Plantation House (11788 LA 965, in the **Audubon State Historic Site**), where John James Audubon painted works for his *Birds of America* series. Rosedown Plantation State Historic Site (12501 LA 10), built by a wealthy cotton planter, features an opulent home and 28 acres of formal gardens. Catalpa Plantation (9508 Old US 61), a late Victorian, overflows with objects collected over the course of a family's five generations. Tours are by appointment only. The Afton Villa Gardens (9247 US 61) feature an impressive lane of live oak trees underplanted in azaleas, elaborate Gothic gates, statuary, terraced lawns, boxwood-bordered parterres, and formal gardens around the ruins of a 1849 Gothic villa. It's open seasonally.

St. Francisville, a picturesque town, holds a historic district of eclectic shops, antiques, homes, and restaurants in restored 19th-century structures. The scenic Tunica Hills around St. Francisville are perfect for outdoor pursuits like biking, hiking, fishing, and birding. Four miles west of the town, discover the beauty of the wetlands by canoe or along hiking trails at Cat Island National Wildlife Refuge, home of the national champion bald cypress tree (the largest tree, of any species, east of the Sierra Nevada). Play golf on the Arnold Palmer championship course at The Bluffs on Thompson Creek.

Across the Mississippi, Pointe Coupee Parish hosts the largest pocket of Creole French architecture in the U.S. today. Most homes are still occupied by families who continue to farm the land of their ancestors. Drive along the scenic False River, an area steeped in the history and traditions of 19th-century Creole Louisiana. Parlange Plantation (8211 False River Rd.), built in 1750, represents a fine example of Creole architecture with magnificent furnishings, paintings, and gardens, and offers tours by appointment only. Mon Reve ("My Dream"—9825 False River Rd.), a lovely French Creole plantation home, is now a bed-and-breakfast with a porch or "gallery" overlooking the False River. Built in 1820, the home comprises cypress, bricks, and bousillage (a mixture of mud, moss, and deer hair). (As of press time, Mon Reve was closed but had plans to reopen.) **New Roads**, a recreational settlement on the False River, features historic Creole homes, churches with Civil War cemeteries, and the Pointe Coupee Parish Museum (8348 False River Rd.).

Afton Villa Gardens

Lodging tips

Staying at a plantation is the ticket here. Some are haunted, others are filled with elegant period furniture and antiques. In some cases, you may stay in caretaker cottages on estate grounds. Small bed-and-breakfast properties, inns, and cottages are found around the St. Francisville historic district and in country settings; all are charming. There's only one motorcoach motel here, along with a lodge with suites at the golf resort. For details: West Feliciana Parish Tourist Commission, (225) 635-4224, (800) 789-422, www.stfrancisville.us.

Purple symbols indicate locations discussed in this section.

🍴 Dining   🛏 Lodging
🛍 Shopping   ⛳ Golfing
⬛ Point of interest
▨ Detailed map area

For a complete listing of symbols, see back cover flap.

© Rand McNally

What to eat

Try Louisiana favorites like a muffaletta, a large round sandwich layered with meats, cheeses, and an olive relish, at **Magnolia Café** (5687 Commerce St., St. Francisville). A po' boy sandwich, best filled with shrimp or crawfish, is popular at **Cypress Grill** (5632 Commerce St.); check out the daily plate special at **Benoit Meats**, too (5712 Commerce St.). Save room for local beers like Dixie Blackened Voodoo or Abita Turbo Dog, served at the **St. Francisville Inn** (5720 Commerce St.).

What to buy

Grandmother's Buttons (9814 Royal St.), housed in a restored 1905 St. Francisville bank building, features a button museum in the old vault. The shop has a vast array of jewelry crafted from 19th-century buttons as well as antiques. Find a selection of local historian and author Anne Butler's published works on Angola prison, children's stories, local history, and personal life stories about growing up on a plantation in the **Butler-Greenwood Plantation's** gift shop (8345 US 1). And as long as you're in Audubon country, stop by **Birdman Coffee & Books** (5689 Commerce St.) to browse the specialty hand-carved birds.

What to do

Audubon Spring Pilgrimage, St. Francisville, third weekend in March.

For more details about this festival, please see page 186.

Louisiana Office of Tourism
(800) 334-8626, (225) 342-8100, www.louisianatravel.com

Statue at Afton Villa Gardens

Kicking It Up in
Cajun
Country

Enjoy a cultural experience like no other in the heart of Cajun country. Cajun heritage and traditions evoke joie de vivre, and one can feel the joy in their music, see it in the tapestry of works by artists and craftspeople, taste it in their distinctive foods, and revel in it during events like Mardi Gras and local festivals.

Feel the pulse of Cajun Country in **Lafayette**, a cultural oasis on the bayou where the old fuses with the new. A good place to begin: the Acadian Cultural Center (501 Fisher Rd.). Watch an outstanding film about the exile of the Acadian people from their native Nova Scotia and how they settled in the bayous and swamps of Louisiana. Lafayette has two unique attractions taking visitors back to the early days of Cajun and Creole life. Vermilionville (300 Fisher Rd.), a living history village, features costumed craftspeople demonstrating cooking, music, and other traditional skills typical of life in Acadia between 1765 and 1890. The Acadian Village (200 Greenleaf Dr.), a folklife museum, contains homes and architectural landmarks of 19th-century Acadia.

Breaux Bridge, the Crawfish Capital of the World, was the first to put crawfish on the menu. Crawfish étouffée was created here. If you're going to try crawfish, this is the place. Many restaurants in town serve it in special ways. Every year the "mud bugs" are honored with their own Breaux Bridge Crawfish Festival (the first full weekend in May) featuring crawfish creations and lots of music.

Cajun and zydeco music reflect the cultures and traditions of the Acadian and Creole people. Cajun music, usually sung in French, tells stories of life on the bayou. Zydeco, a mix of Cajun music and the blues, has roots in the Creoles of African descent. Young and old alike enjoy a fais-do-do, dancing a lively Cajun

Mardi Gras celebration

two-step or swaying to an accordion waltz. Mulate's (325 Mills Ave.) features Cajun food and dancing to live bands. Zydeco breakfasts rock at Café Des Amis (140 East Bridge St.). Head to Angelle's Whiskey River Landing (1365 Henderson Levee Rd., Henderson) any

on Avery Island), home of the famous Tabasco sauce. A fun plant tour explains how peppers are harvested by hand using *le petit baton rouge*, a small red stick, to gauge the perfect color for picking. The gift shop sells everything Tabasco, with lots of free samples.

Mulate's in Breaux Bridge

Sunday just before sunset, when locals gather for a fais-do-do with toe-tapping Cajun tunes. For an encore of history, get a sense of early Louisiana life on a walking tour of the historic houses downtown.

Crawfish cornbread

Breaux Bridge is the gateway to the Atchafalaya Basin, with some of the state's most scenic nature and wildlife habitats. Take a swamp tour by boat to experience the beauty of this mosaic of streams, lakes, bayous, and swamps. Several companies depart from Henderson Levee Road, in **Henderson**.

Iberia Parish is well known for its Cajun and Creole influences in charming towns nestled along the bayou. If you catch a whiff of something peppery in the air, you're close to Avery Island's Jungle Gardens (off LA 329

Avery Island sits on a salt dome surrounded by the pristine beauty of swamps and marshes. Adding to the island's rustic nature, Tabasco creator E.A. McIlhenny planted rare botanical treasures and established a bird sanctuary. In spring, thousands of snowy white egrets and other migratory water birds flock to Bird City, the island's protected rookery.

Take a tranquil escape to Rip Van Winkle Gardens (5505 Rip Van Winkle Rd., Jefferson Island), a 25-acre, semitropical paradise with live oak tree vistas, seasonal explosions of blooms, and drop-dead gorgeous grounds for strolling. Tour the 1870s Southern mansion of Joseph Jefferson, a theater actor best known for his role as Rip Van Winkle. Stay overnight in luxurious Acadian cottages with elegant French furnishings on the estate. Shadows-on-the-Teche, (317 East Main St., New Iberia), one of the most famous antebellum homes in the South, is a stunning 1834 sugar plantation home built by a wealthy planter on the Bayou Teche.

Tour the oldest rice mill in America at Conrad Rice Mill/ Konriko Company Store (307 Ann St., New Iberia). The store offers one-stop-shopping for gourmet rices, sauces, and spices along with Konriko products and locally produced foods. Explore the swamps, bayous, and coves around Iberia Parish with Airboat Tours (Marshfield Landing, Loreauville, March–October). Alligators, ducks, and pelicans make their homes in channels filled with water lilies and grand 200-year-old cypress trees.

🍴 What to eat

A typical Cajun menu includes crawfish, crawfish étouffée, boudin, cracklin's, gumbo, and jambalaya. Check out the menus at **Seafood Connection** (999 Parkview Dr., New Iberia) and **Little River Inn** (833 East Main St., New Iberia).

🛍 What to buy

Red, green, sweet, or spicy—Tabasco products can be purchased at the **Tabasco Country Store** (see main story). For more Cajun spices and sauces, browse the **Konriko Company Store** (see main story). Both stores have music sections, where you can pick up a zydeco or Cajun music CD.

❗ What to do

Breaux Bridge Crawfish Festival, Breaux Bridge, first full weekend in May.

For more details about this festival, please see page 186.

❓ *Louisiana Office of Tourism*
(800) 334-8626, (225) 342-8100, www.louisianatravel.com

Lodging tips:

Hotels, cabins, and bed-and-breakfast inns are available throughout the area. For details: Lafayette Convention and Visitors Commission, (800) 346-1958; Breaux Bridge Visitors Center, (888) 565-5939, www.breauxbridgelive.com/visitor.html; Iberia Parish Convention and Visitors Bureau, (888) 942-3742, www.iberiatravel.com.

Cajun musician

© Rand McNally

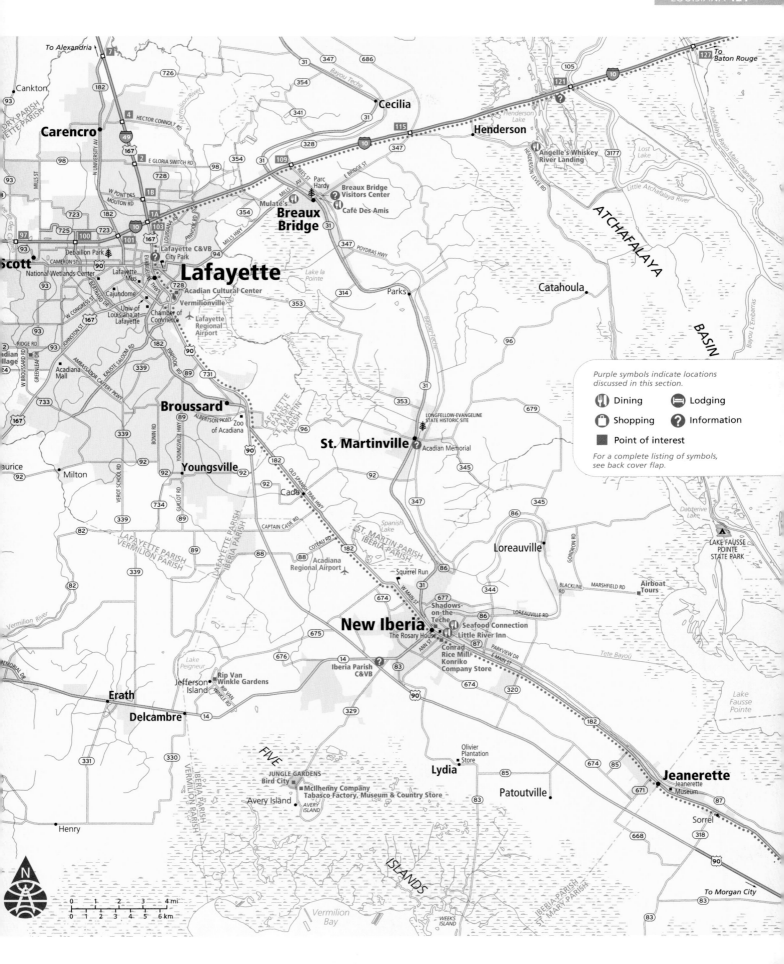

To Alexandria
To Baton Rouge
Cankton
Cecilia
Carencro
Henderson
Scott
Lafayette
Breaux Bridge
Mulate's
Parc Hardy
Breaux Bridge Visitors Center
Café Des-Amis
Angelle's Whiskey River Landing
ATCHAFALAYA
Deballion Park
National Wetlands Center
Lafayette C&VB City Park
Lafayette Mus
Acadian Cultural Center
Vermilionville
Univ of Louisiana at Lafayette
Chamber of Commerce
Lafayette Regional Airport
Lake la Pointe
Parks
Catahoula
BASIN
Broussard
Zoo of Acadiana
LAFAYETTE PARISH
ST. MARTIN PARISH
LONGFELLOW-EVANGELINE STATE HISTORIC SITE
Maurice
Milton
Youngsville
Cade
St. Martinville
Acadian Memorial
Loreauville
Lake Dauterive

Purple symbols indicate locations discussed in this section.

🍴 Dining   🛏 Lodging
🛍 Shopping   ❓ Information
◼ Point of interest

For a complete listing of symbols, see back cover flap.

Acadiana Regional Airport
Squirrel Run
LAFAYETTE PARISH VERMILION PARISH
Airboat Tours
LAKE FAUSSE POINTE STATE PARK
New Iberia
Shadows-on-the-Teche
Seafood Connection
Little River Inn
The Rosary House
Conrad Rice Mill/ Konriko Company Store
Tete Bayou
Erath
Lake Peigneur
Jefferson Island
Rip Van Winkle Gardens
Iberia Parish C&VB
Delcambre
Olivier Plantation Store
Lake Fausse Pointe
FIVE
Lydia
Jeanerette
Jeanerette Museum
JUNGLE GARDENS Bird City
McIlhenny Company Tabasco Factory, Museum & Country Store
Avery Island
Patoutville
Henry
Sorrel
IBERIA PARISH ST. MARTIN PARISH
ISLANDS
Vermilion Bay
WEEKS ISLAND
To Morgan City

N

0   1   2   3   4 mi
0 1 2 3 4 5 6 km

Rolling on the
Red River

Two of the best-kept secrets in northern Louisiana are the vibrant towns of **Shreveport** and **Bossier City**, nestled on opposite banks of the mighty Red River. Riverboat casinos, shopping, museums, art galleries, and gardens beckon visitors.

Five riverboat casinos with Vegas-style gaming moor along the riverbank. From tropical island settings to a 19th-century paddle wheeler and its wild west theme, the casinos offer a variety of dining venues, spa facilities, and entertainment. For gambling landlubbers, Harrah's Louisiana Downs (8000 East Texas St., Bossier City) features casino games along with live Thoroughbred racing at its racetrack.

Let the good times roll at the Red River District, Shreveport's downtown entertainment quarter for live music, shopping, dancing, and dining. Under the Texas Street Bridge (officially, the Long-Allen Bridge), the "Walk of Stars" honors northwest Louisiana celebrities such as Elvis Presley, Hank Williams, blues musician Huddie "Leadbelly" Ledbetter, and PGA golfer Hal Sutton. Murals, mosaics, and embedded implements cover the columns, which pay tribute to the five contributing cultures of Louisiana: African-American, Indian, French, Spanish, and Cajun.

Elvis Presley fans will want to stop by the Municipal Memorial Auditorium (705 Elvis Presley Ave., Shreveport), the site of the Louisiana Hayride, the popular radio show that launched Elvis's career. Inside, the Stage of Stars Museum features a room full of Elvis memorabilia, including many photographs, along with collections from other stars who graced the stage. The stage itself is still there and available for photo ops.

A medley of museums showcases the history and culture of the two cities. The Ark-La-Tex Museum (2021 East Texas St., Bossier City) collects and displays all things Mardi Gras, including floats, costumes, and other accoutrements of the event. At the Louisiana State Oil & Gas Museum (200 South Land Ave., Oil City), tours of historic buildings and exhibits portray the history of Caddo Parish and its foremost industry, oil. Visitors at the Pioneer Heritage Center (1 University Pl., on the campus of LSU-Shreveport) tour Caspiana

Mardi Gras float at Ark-La-Tex Museum

Paddle wheeler casino riverboat in Shreveport

House (the big main home from the former Caspiana plantation) and the Thrasher House, a log "dogtrot," or enclosed passage between a house's two sections. The two houses, both listed on the National Register of Historic Places, join several other buildings and exhibits to form a "history laboratory" depicting life between 1830 and 1900. (Note: the Pioneer Heritage Center is open Sunday during school semesters, and during the week by appointment.)

For those with a botanical bent, this area offers acres of lush gardens. Some notable places: At the Gardens of the American Rose Center (8877 Jefferson Paige Rd., Shreveport), more than 20,000 roses are planted in 60 tranquil gardens. In spring, the azalea gardens on the grounds of R.W. Norton Art Gallery (4747 Creswell Ave., Shreveport) burst into bloom. The gallery itself features American and European paintings. At the Olde Covered Bridge Garden (6905 Greenwood Rd., Shreveport), explore a display garden with flowering plants, a duck pond, and a historic covered bridge. Highlights of the Barnwell Garden & Art Center (601 Clyde Fant Pkwy., Shreveport) include the domed botanical garden conservatory and a fragrance garden.

An after-dark visit to Riverfront Park (601 Clyde Fant Pkwy., Shreveport) reveals the changing colors of the giant steel roses. Daytime visitors enjoy a waterfall as well as the lights and music of the water fountain. For a historical boat tour of the Red River and the wildlife habitats of Cross Bayou, make time for a cruise on Spirit of the Red River (dock is at 821 Clyde Fant Pkwy.) The Sci-Port Discovery Center (820 Clyde Fant Pkwy.) features more than 200 hands-on science exhibits, an IMAX theater, and a new interactive laser planetarium.

Trendy shoppers will enjoy the ambience of the new lifestyle center, the Louisiana Boardwalk (100 Bass Pro Dr., Bossier City). The scenic riverfront invites a stroll, which could also extend to the dozens of outlet shops and restaurants on the music-filled streets. Enjoy a spin on the carousel, ride the trolley, or watch the dancing fountain. The Boardwalk also offers a child's play area, a bowling alley, and a movie theater.

Louisiana's Scenic Byway, LA 2, leaves the twinkling lights behind for a drive through the tranquil countryside. Rolling hills, picturesque farms, and fields of cotton and sunflowers take one back to a bygone era. Detours through rural communities and friendly towns offer snapshots of another way of life. **Vivian** boasts the historic Vivian Depot Museum.

Steel roses in Riverfront Park

Shongaloo's pride is the Log Cabin Museum and the Old Salem Church and Cemetery, built by slaves in 1863. Venture off the byway to sites in **Webster Parish** including the Germantown Colony & Museum (off LA 534, Germantown Road) and Calloway Corners Bed & Breakfast (10782 US 371, Calloway Corners), a home with lovely gardens, cultivated day lilies, magnolias, pecans, and oaks. Once a vacant house, the site inspired a series of romance novels (the Calloway Corners series), which in turn motivated the establishment of the bed-and-breakfast.

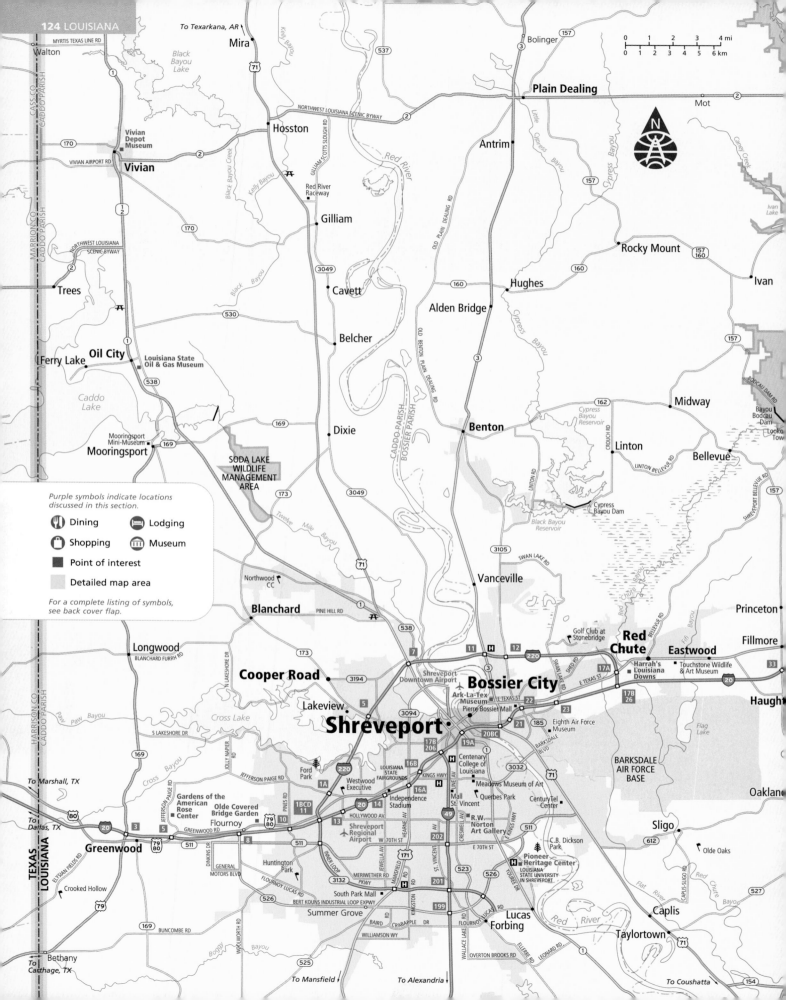

To Texarkana, AR

Walton
MYRTIS TEXAS LINE RD

CASS CO.
CADDO PARISH

Black
Bayou
Lake

Mira

Mot

Bolinger

Plain Dealing

NORTHWEST LOUISIANA SCENIC BYWAY

Hosston

Antrim

Vivian
Depot
Museum

Vivian

VIVIAN AIRPORT RD

NORTHWEST LOUISIANA
SCENIC BYWAY

Red River
Raceway

Gilliam

GILLIAM SCOTTS SLOUGH RD

Rocky Mount

Ivan

Trees

MARION CO.
CADDO PARISH

Cavett

Alden Bridge

Hughes

Ivan
Lake

Belcher

OLD PLAIN DEALING RD

Ferry Lake

Oil City

Louisiana State
Oil & Gas Museum

Caddo
Lake

Midway

Bayou
Bodcau
Dam

Mooringsport
Mini-Museum

Mooringsport

Dixie

OLD BENTON PLAIN DEALING RD

Benton

Cypress
Bayou
Reservoir

Linton

CROUCH RD

Bellevue

Looko
Tow

SODA LAKE
WILDLIFE
MANAGEMENT
AREA

Cypress
Bayou Dam

Black Bayou
Reservoir

HARRISON CO.
CADDO PARISH

Northwood
CC

Blanchard

PINE HILL RD

Vanceville

Princeton

Fillmore

Longwood
BLANCHARD FURRH RD

Cooper Road

Golf Club at
Stonebridge

**Red
Chute**

Eastwood

Haught

Lakeview

Shreveport

Bossier City

Harrah's
Louisiana
Downs

Touchstone Wildlife
& Art Museum

Shreveport
Downtown Airport

Ark-La-Tex
Museum

Pierre Bossier Mall

Eighth Air Force
Museum

Flag
Lake

To Marshall, TX

Ford
Park

Centenary
College of
Louisiana

Meadows Museum of Art

Querbes Park

CenturyTel
Center

BARKSDALE
AIR FORCE
BASE

Oaklan

To
Dallas, TX

**TEXAS
LOUISIANA**

Greenwood

Gardens of the
American
Rose
Center

Olde Covered
Bridge Garden

Flournoy

Westwood
Executive

Louisiana
State
Fairgrounds

Independence
Stadium

Mall
St. Vincent

R.W.
Norton
Art Gallery

Sligo

Olde Oaks

Crooked Hollow

GENERAL
MOTORS BLVD

Huntington
Park

Shreveport
Regional Airport

C.B. Dickson
Park

Pioneer
Heritage Center

Caplis

South Park Mall

BERT KOUNS INDUSTRIAL LOOP EXPWY

LOUISIANA
STATE UNIVERSITY
IN SHREVEPORT

Summer Grove

Lucas
Forbing

Bethany

To
Carthage, TX

To Mansfield

To Alexandria

Taylortown

To Coushatta

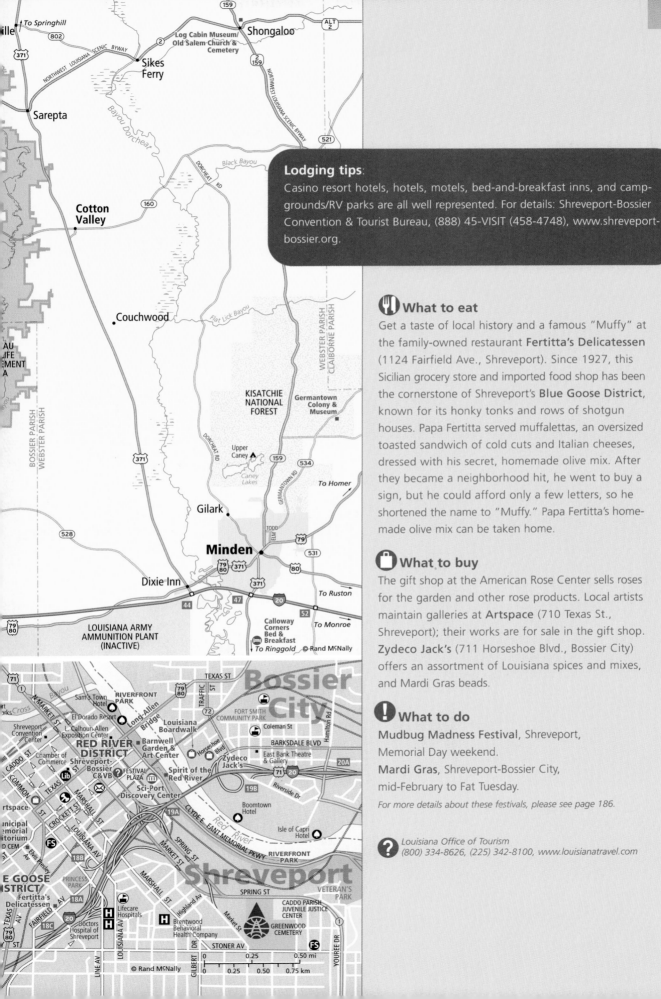

Lodging tips:
Casino resort hotels, hotels, motels, bed-and-breakfast inns, and camp-grounds/RV parks are all well represented. For details: Shreveport-Bossier Convention & Tourist Bureau, (888) 45-VISIT (458-4748), www.shreveport-bossier.org.

What to eat

Get a taste of local history and a famous "Muffy" at the family-owned restaurant **Fertitta's Delicatessen** (1124 Fairfield Ave., Shreveport). Since 1927, this Sicilian grocery store and imported food shop has been the cornerstone of Shreveport's **Blue Goose District**, known for its honky tonks and rows of shotgun houses. Papa Fertitta served muffalettas, an oversized toasted sandwich of cold cuts and Italian cheeses, dressed with his secret, homemade olive mix. After they became a neighborhood hit, he went to buy a sign, but he could afford only a few letters, so he shortened the name to "Muffy." Papa Fertitta's home-made olive mix can be taken home.

What to buy

The gift shop at the American Rose Center sells roses for the garden and other rose products. Local artists maintain galleries at **Artspace** (710 Texas St., Shreveport); their works are for sale in the gift shop. **Zydeco Jack's** (711 Horseshoe Blvd., Bossier City) offers an assortment of Louisiana spices and mixes, and Mardi Gras beads.

What to do

Mudbug Madness Festival, Shreveport, Memorial Day weekend.
Mardi Gras, Shreveport-Bossier City, mid-February to Fat Tuesday.
For more details about these festivals, please see page 186.

Louisiana Office of Tourism
(800) 334-8626, (225) 342-8100, www.louisianatravel.com

Delta Gaming and
the Blues

Explore the Mississippi Delta, from back-street juke joints churning out Delta blues to the excitement of high-stakes gaming at **Tunica's** casinos. Surrounded by catfish ponds and cotton and soy fields, Tunica lies in the heart of this rich and fertile area. Here in the "Casino Capital of the South," a neon wonderland of nine themed casinos showcases blues performers and headline entertainment, restaurants, and gaming in an atmosphere of gracious Southern hospitality.

Bluesville/Blues & Legends Hall of Fame (Horseshoe Casino, 1021 Casino Center Dr., Robinsonville) is a museum and nightclub with collections of blues memorabilia and videos of the Delta's famous blues musicians. By night, the club-style showroom comes alive with a star lineup of performers and groups. The Tunica Museum (One Museum Blvd.) presents the history of the blues along with exhibits on the Civil War, Spanish explorers, and Native Americans.

But Tunica has greens as well as blues. The city's three championship courses include Tunica National Golf & Tennis (1 Champions Lane) with a 360-degree driving range and four innovative Har-Tru clay tennis courts, Cottonwoods (Grand Casino Resort, 13615 Old US 61 North, Robinsonville) with gently rolling fairways and lakes, and the challenging Scottish-style course at River Bend Links (1205 Nine Lake Dr.) featuring sand and grass bunkers, strategically placed mounds, and lakes. For a change of pace, try "golf with a shotgun"— shooting sporting clays from the sky at Willows Trap, Skeet & Sporting Clays (Grand Casino Resort).

At Tunica RiverPark (One RiverPark Dr.), a waterfront museum focuses on the animal life supported by and the ecological impact of the levee system upon the Mississippi River. Here visitors explore aquariums filled with river critters, walk the wetlands on boardwalk trails, cruise the river on board the 120-foot paddle wheeler *Tunica Queen*, or just sit a spell in rocking chairs on the veranda, watching the mighty Mississippi roll by.

Blue Front Cafe

Tunica's RiverPark Museum

US 61, "America's Blues Highway," runs through **Clarksdale**, the cradle of the blues. At the time of the Great Migration, Clarksdale was the first town to welcome Delta farmhands and musicians escaping oppressive sharecropping practices on rural plantations and farms. Hometown legacies like Muddy Waters, W.C. Handy, and Robert Johnson sprang out of this rich blues heritage.

In Clarksdale's historic Blues Alley, the Delta Blues Museum (1 Blues Alley) features the history of musicians who brought blues to the world. Notable exhibits include Muddy Waters's cabin from Stovall Plantation, B.B. King's guitar, and Sonny Boy Williams II's harmonicas. For those in search of a true Delta blues experience, beside the museum is a rockin' blues joint called Ground Zero Blues Club (0 Blues Alley), co-owned by actor Morgan Freeman. Juke joint fare is served for lunch and dinner, with blues bands jamming on the stage several nights a week. For a unique fine dining experience, Morgan also co-owns Madidi (164 Delta Ave.) featuring fresh and innovative French cuisine. Don't miss the legendary crossroads at the intersection of two great blues highways, US highways 61 and 49. Marked by three blue crossed guitars, it's said to be the place where Robert Johnson sold his soul to the devil for the ability to play music like no other.

A few miles from the crossroads lies Hopson Plantation & Commissary, once one of the largest cotton farms in the South. Unchanged from its days as a working plantation, Hopson takes visitors back in time with a walk around the sharecropper shacks, seed houses, and the original cotton gin. Hopson was the first to produce a cotton crop, from planting to baling, entirely by machine. The Commissary (open by appointment) now houses some farming memorabilia. For an overnight cultural experience, stay at the Shack Up Inn/ Cotton Gin Inn (001 Commissary Circle) on the Commissary grounds. The Shack Up Inn rents out a row of authentic, nostalgically furnished shotgun shacks, updated with indoor plumbing, air-conditioning, and other comforts. You can all but see musicians sipping a cold one on the rickety porch and belting out some impromptu blues.

The site of the WROX Museum (257 Delta Ave.) once housed this down-home blues radio station in the 1950s. Many popular bluesmen such as Ike Turner, Sam Cook, and even Elvis broadcasted live from the studio.

Grand Casino Tunica

What to eat

Just south of Tunica sits a bastion of down-home Southern cooking: the **Blue & White Restaurant** (1355 US 61, Tunica). All the Southern favorites are there—greens, grits, chicken and dumplings—as well as a local specialty, fried dill pickles. It's open for breakfast and lunch.

What to buy

Stop by **Cat Head Delta Blues and Folk Art** (252 Delta Ave., Clarksdale) to get some blues CDs for the road. This eclectic shop has works by local folk artists, occasional live music, and book signings. It's a good place to find out what's happening music-wise around town.

What to do

Sunflower River Blues & Gospel Festival, Clarksdale, August.
Tunica Air Races and Air Show, Tunica, first week in June.

For more details about these festivals, please see page 186.

Mississippi Division of Tourism
(800) 927-6378, (601) 359-3297, www.visitmississippi.org

Lodging tips:
Choices run the gamut from casino suites and rooms, hotels, and motels, to bed-and-breakfast inns. For details: Tunica Convention & Visitors Bureau, (888) 4TUNICA (488-6422), www.tunicamiss.org; Clarksdale Convention & Visitors Bureau, (800) 626-3764, www.clarksdaletourism.com.

Natchez's
Antebellum
Elegance

Resting on a bluff overlooking the Mississippi River, **Natchez** showcases graceful antebellum homes and late-19th-century buildings, with antique stores, specialty shops, hotels, and restaurants inside their historic walls. Once the epicenter of cotton production, the region and its rich soil allowed planters to amass great fortunes, which they used to build the area's luxurious mansions and villas.

A relaxed introduction to Natchez's ambience includes taking a horse-drawn carriage through the quaint streets (Southern Carriage Tours start at the **Canal Street Depot**). The ride passes the city's central landmark, St. Mary's Basilica (107 South Union St.), a Gothic Revival-style cathedral with an ornate interior and beautiful stained glass windows, as well as Trinity Episcopal Church (305 South Commerce St.) with its Tiffany-designed windows. Longwood (140 Lower Woodville Rd.) encapsulates tumultuous history in its octagonal walls—it's finished on the exterior but unfinished inside because laborers left at the outbreak of the Civil War. Longwood offers tours, as do Dunleith (84 Homochitto St.), a majestic Greek Revival mansion flanked with 26 Tuscan columns, and Stanton Hall (401 High St.), a magnificent and palatial residence.

More private homes and gardens open for tours during the Spring and Fall Pilgrimages, when homeowners in period costume talk about the history of their homes. A highlight of the Spring event: the Historic Natchez Pageant, a lavish production of scenes from the Old South.

Stanton Hall

Natchez is a gumbo of many cultures. Native Americans were the first to inhabit the region, and the Natchez tribe gave the city its name. The Grand Village of the Natchez Indians (400 Jefferson Davis Blvd.) features a museum, a reconstructed Indian home, and three ceremonial mounds. The Natchez Museum of African American History and Culture (301 Main Pl.) chronicles

dinner parties at this antebellum mansion, guests gather in the antique-furnished study for drinks and hors d'oeuvres, then partake in an elegant five-course meal. Old riverboat days live on at the Cock of the Walk (200 North Broadway St.), where the waitstaff serves cornbread flipped from a sizzling skillet at the table. The signature dish? Secret-recipe fried catfish.

Gardens of Monmouth Plantation

the story of African American life in Natchez from enslavement through the second World War, highlighting both accomplishments and struggles through period art, photographs, and artifacts.

Another side of Natchez appears along the waterfront, where, in the golden age of the South, droves of steamships docked to pick up bales of cotton and offload human cargo—laborers and slaves. **Natchez-Under-The-Hill**, in the shadows of the prosperous Natchez high on the bluff, had a notorious reputation for drinking, gambling, and murder. Riverboat gamblers, thieves, and ladies of the night frequented the saloons and unsavory establishments in this seedy port district.

Today, Natchez-Under-the-Hill has undergone a modern renaissance with restaurants, specialty shops, and gambling at the Isle of Capri Casino (70 Silver St.). Paddle wheeler cruise ships dock at this wonderful place to watch the sun set over the river. Relive the colorful era of the past at a friendly watering hole, Under-the-Hill Saloon (25 Silver St.). Eclectic memorabilia of life in the 1700s line the walls of this 200-year-old building.

A unique Southern dining experience can be had at Monmouth Plantation (36 Melrose Ave.). At nightly

Natchez's hot and humid climate favors the growth of muscadine grapes, a varietal used to make bottles ranging from sweet whites to dry reds. Inspired by his grandmother's winemaking, a local veterinarian founded the Old South Winery (65 South Concord Ave.). The winery offers tours, tastings, and a gift shop.

Frogmore Cotton Plantation & Gins (11054 US 84, Frogmore) lets visitors pick cotton from the fields (except during May and June) against a backdrop of slave cabins and restored buildings. Tours of this 1,800-acre working cotton plantation are also available. **Woodville** was incorporated in the early 1800s; its historic district radiates from the Courthouse Square

Sunset in Natchez

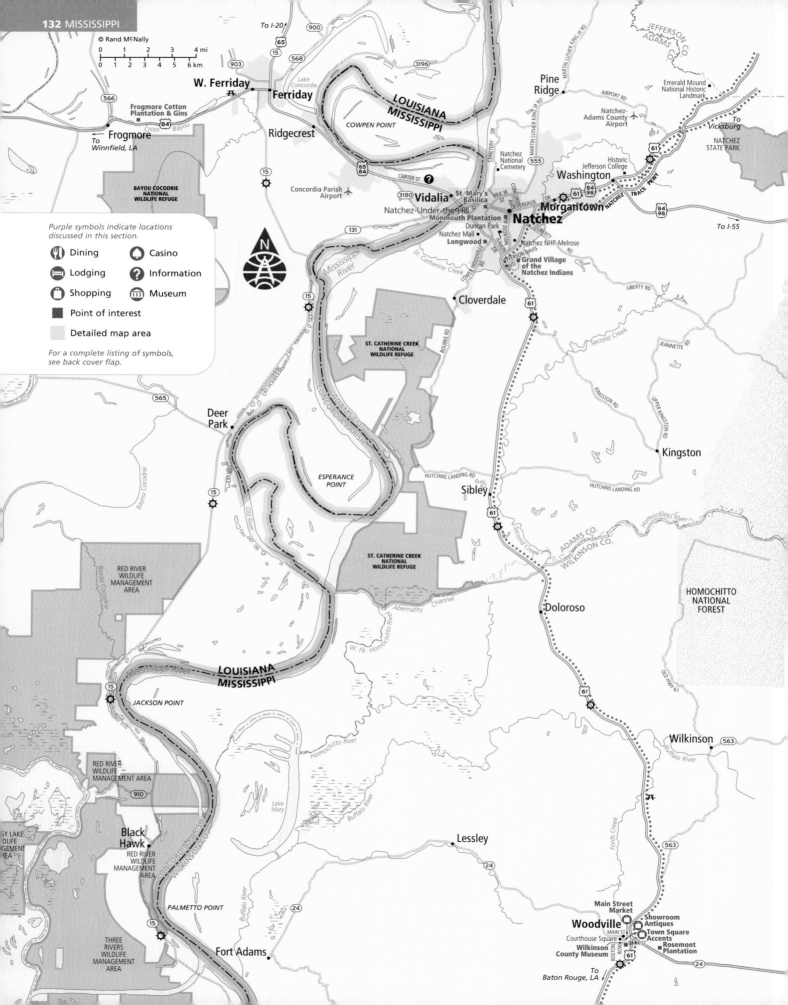

covered in live oak trees. One large oak bears the name of Jefferson Davis, president of the Confederacy, whose boyhood home was at Rosemont Plantation. Open for tours March 1 to December 15, Rosemont (MS 24, Woodville) features many of the Davis family's original furnishings and portraits. Woodville's historic district features 140 19th-century buildings, from Federal style to post-World War II, including more than a dozen historic homes and three of the oldest churches in the state. The Wilkinson County Museum (on Courthouse Square) sits in the former headquarters—built in 1842 —of the West Feliciana Railroad. Antiques, collectibles, and handmade items can be found at Town Square Accents (155 Boston Row), the Main Street Market (613 Main St.), and 21 vendors with booths at Showroom Antiques (368 US 61 North).

What to eat

Try the "Knock You Naked" margarita, gringo pie, and homemade tamales at **Fat Mama's Tamales** (500 S. Canal St.). At **Darby's Famous Fudge** (410 Main St.), chocolate praline proves a perennial favorite. Pick up native muscadine products and wines from **Old South Winery** (65 Concord Ave.).

What to buy

The Historic Natchez Collection represents reproductions, adaptations, and new interpretations of decorative arts and home furnishings typical of the Natchez area. Most pieces hark back to antebellum years. The Historic Natchez Foundation licenses manufacturers to create these pieces, which range from drapery hardware to toleware (enameled or lacquered metalware) to wicker furniture. A list of manufacturers can be found at this site: www.natchez.org/collection.htm.

What to do

Great Mississippi River Balloon Race, Natchez, third weekend in October.

For more details about this festival, please see page 186.

Mississippi Division of Tourism
(800) 927-6378, (601) 359-3297, www.visitmississippi.org

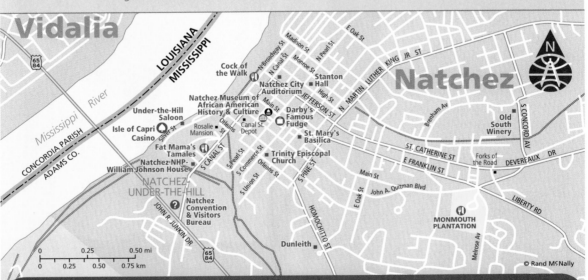

Lodging tips:
40 historic homes feature accommodations in antebellum mansions, Victorian houses, cozy cottages, or rustic cabins. Many include a full authentic Southern breakfast. There is also a full range of hotels, motels, and inns. For details: Natchez Visitors Center, (800) 647-672, www.visitnatchez.com.

Tupelo Country

Although Elvis Presley, the king of rock and roll, was born in **Tupelo**, it's the small-town friendliness and a grab bag of unique attractions that make this "all-American city" a fun place to explore.

Elvis was born in a small shotgun house; today it anchors the 15-acre Elvis Presley Center (306 Elvis Presley Dr.). The museum features a private collection of Elvis memorabilia. The Walk of Life surrounds the house with markers depicting the years of Elvis's life, while the Fountain of Life, a stunning water feature, represents Elvis's life in Tupelo. The story wall recounts tales from boyhood friends. Visitors can relax and reflect in the park or meditate in the chapel, built with donations from fans. The Early Years Driving Tour, a self-guided trip down memory lane, take visitors to places of significance in Elvis's life. Highlights include the Tupelo Hardware Store, where Elvis's mother bought him his first guitar as a Christmas present, and Johnnie's Drive-In, where he spent time with friends and enjoyed cheeseburgers and RC Cola.

Classic and antique car lovers will enjoy the Tupelo Automobile Museum (1 Otis Blvd.), featuring more than 100 exotic automobiles and charting the course of automotive design from the late 1800s on. Classics include Packards, Cadillacs, Duesenbergs, a Tucker, and a host of other foreign and American makes and models. One-of-a-kind vehicles and celebrity cars, like Elvis's Lincoln, are showroom favorites.

Families might want to check out the hungry critters at Tupelo Buffalo Park and Zoo (2272 N. Coley Rd.). On board the Monster Bison Bus, a reconverted school bus with mammoth tires, passengers can see the largest herd of buffalo east of the Mississippi River. Guests can hand-feed the one-ton creatures; sometimes a camel or an elusive pair of zebras show up for a handout, too. The zoo's exotic creatures

Stained glass at the Elvis Presley Memorial Chapel, located at the Elvis Presley Birthplace Park

include a Bengal tiger, monkeys, a reticulated giraffe, a black bear, and reptiles. Pygmy goats, miniature horses, and other friendly animals hang out at the petting zoo.

The Natchez Trace Parkway wends its way through Mississippi and Tennessee and these states' rich past. Presentations at the Visitor Center (2680 Natchez

From its early days as a cotton port, **Aberdeen** has always been a city of riches. This town teems with antebellum architecture, showcasing more than 50 opulent historic homes: Victorians with towers and turrets, turn-of-the-century Queen Annes sporting ornate gingerbread trim, and Greek Revival mansions. Some homes, furnished in original and period antiques, are open to the public.

Longhorn cattle and the Bison Bus at Tupelo Buffalo Park and Zoo

Trace Pkwy., Tupelo) depict the Trace's history. The 444 miles between Natchez and Nashville first served as a wild animal path, then as a Native American trail later used by Spanish explorers, British troops, and southern frontier settlers. Today motorists, cyclists, and hikers favor this scenic byway. Four miles south of the Visitors Center lies the Chickasaw Village, an 18th-century Chickasaw site with exhibits describing their life and history. A nature trail features plants used by the Indians.

The area's history also includes wartime conflict. At Brices Cross Roads National Battlefield (MS 370 and US 45, Baldwyn), Confederate troops under General Nathan Bedford Forrest defeated Union forces attempting to secure General William T. Sherman's supply lines. Adjacent to the battlefield, 95 Confederate soldiers lie buried in Bethany Cemetery. At the Visitor and Interpretive Center, browse through displays of artifacts and view a battlefield diorama. Tupelo National Battlefield (MS 6) commemorates Mississippi's last major battle in the Civil War. On a more modern note, the Tupelo War Museum (in the Mall at Barnes Crossing, 1001 Barnes Crossing Rd.) features extensive collections of World War II artifacts, from German weapons to parts from a Japanese kamikaze plane.

Oxford, a university town rich in culture, sits an hour's drive west on MS 6. The picturesque courtyard square could be lifted straight off the pages of a William Faulkner novel. Ancient oak-lined streets wind to Faulkner's home, Rowan Oak (off of Old Taylor Rd.), where the author penned his famous novels. The University of Mississippi campus boasts museums of Greek and Roman antiquities, southern folk art, and the Blues Archive, with an extensive collection of sultry music. The campus treasure, inside Ventress Hall: a stained glass window depicting the University Greys going to battle in the Civil War.

Tupelo National Battlefield

What to eat

Mallard and Thatch (202 W. Main St.), an Irish pub, serves an eclectic menu of local and Irish fare. Waitresses clad in kilts and black combat boots are known to dance a jig on the bar. Locals get their cat-fish and hush puppies fix at **Este's Catfish and Steakhouse** (2450 State Park Rd.).

What to buy

Come rain or shine, the second weekend of each month (except the furniture market months of February and August) the Tupelo Gigantic Flea Market & Craft Show attracts more than 30,000 shoppers and vendors from a dozen-plus states. The three-day event is held in the climate-controlled buildings at the **Tupelo Furniture Market**, where shoppers can browse in more than 800 vendor booths offering everything from knicknacks to oriental rugs.

What to do

Elvis Presley Festival, Tupelo, first weekend in June.
Blue Suede Cruise, Tupelo, first weekend in May.

For more details about these festivals, please see page 186.

Mississippi Division of Tourism
(800) 927-6378, (601) 359-3297, www.visitmississippi.org

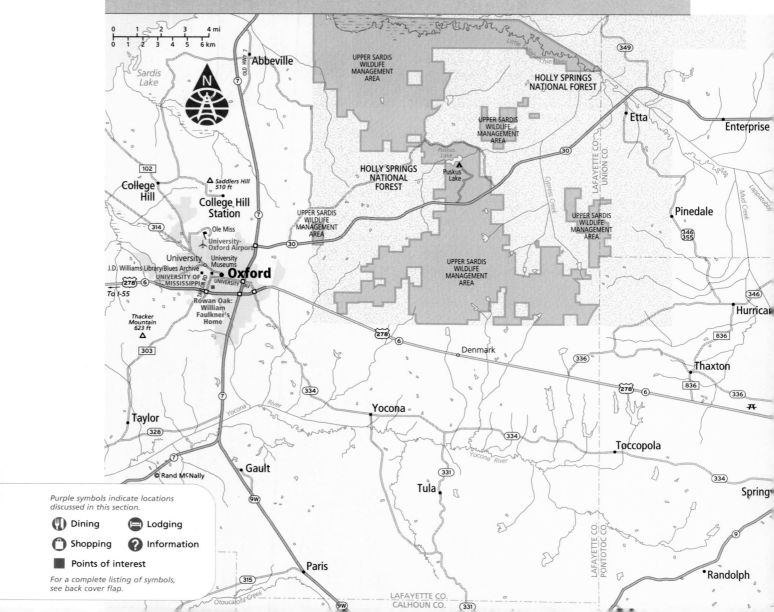

Purple symbols indicate locations discussed in this section.

- 🍴 Dining
- 🛏 Lodging
- 🛍 Shopping
- ❓ Information
- ■ Points of interest

For a complete listing of symbols, see back cover flap.

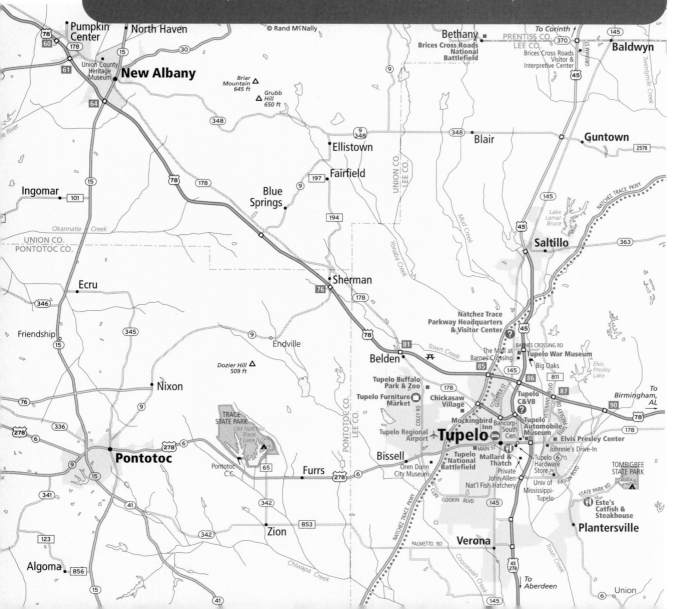

The annual Elvis Presley Festival

Lodging tips:

Accommodations include more than two dozen chain motels, hotels and inns, conveniently located in all parts of the city. **The Mockingbird Inn** (305 North Gloster St.), Tupelo's award-winning bed and breakfast, features eight guest rooms reflecting world themes such as Paris, Africa, and Athens, and complimentary beverages and turn-down treats. For details: Tupelo Convention & Visitors Bureau, (800) 533-061, www.tupelo.net.

© Rand McNally

Asheville: Mountain Hip

Many visitors to **Asheville** come away convinced that not only is it a nice place to visit, but they would also like to live there. They enjoy its art deco skyline, the eclectic shops on Wall Street in its stylish renaissance downtown, and the emphasis on regional arts and crafts. They appreciate its cosmopolitan ambience as they hit the high spots with historic trolley tours and walking tours that focus on art, history, and, popularly, ghosts.

Downtown Asheville boasts more art deco architecture from the late 1920s and early 1930s than any southeastern city other than Miami. Its hip, vaguely Jazz Age-appeal is reflected in its many clubs, coffee bars, sidewalk cafés, trendy restaurants, and galleries galore. Asheville is home to the Southern Highland Craft Guild, the oldest of its kind in the nation, with more than 900 artisan members. Find it at the Folk Art Center that clings to the ridges just east of town, close to scenic Blue Ridge Parkway (382 Blue Ridge Parkway, milepost 382). Shop for traditional and contemporary crafts of the Southern Appalachian region, including wood carvings, pottery, furniture, woven garments, ironwork, jewelry, baskets, and ceramic tiles. Craft demonstrations are given daily March through December.

Discover the world's largest collection of furniture and lighting fixtures from the Arts & Crafts era at the Grove Park Inn Resort & Spa (290 Macon Ave., Asheville). Most of the original 700 custom-made pieces of furniture and 600 hand-hammered copper light fixtures remain. E.W. Grove, who made his fortune in patent medicines, opened the 510-room Grove Park Inn (now listed on the National Register of Historic Places) in 1913. The luxury spa consistently receives high ratings. You can request the room where F. Scott Fitzgerald stayed and wrote (suite 441).

Another of America's literary giants, Thomas Wolfe, was born and raised in Asheville. He spent his boyhood years at his mother's boarding house, Old Kentucky Home, which he immortalized in his autobiographical novel, *Look Homeward, Angel*. A visitor center displays

Flat Iron Building on Wall Street

personal effects from the Wolfe family home and the writer's New York City apartment. An audio-visual program on Wolfe's life and writing is shown hourly, and guided tours of the boarding house are offered (Thomas Wolfe Memorial State Historic Site, 52 N. Market St.). In nearby Pack Square, a statue of an angel is positioned just as Wolfe described in his novel.

Glamorous Biltmore Estate (1 Approach Rd.), the largest private residence in North America, boasts 250 rooms. Built by George W. Vanderbilt and completed

US 64/74A) offers hiking, picnicking, and wonderful long-distance views of up to 75 miles. Head for Little Switzerland, where Mount Mitchell State Park (NC 128) offers views from the highest point east of the Mississippi.

Black Mountain is Asheville in miniature, with art and craft studios, eateries, close to 50 antique stores, and century-old music halls where you can hear blue-grass, jazz, acoustic folk, and classical music—all in a town just 10 blocks long. Golfers intimidated by

Biltmore Estate

in 1895, it's modeled on a 16th-century chateau in France's Loire Valley. Architect Richard Morris Hunt designed the house, and Frederick Law Olmsted, designer of New York's Central Park, landscaped the grounds.

Away from town, visitors enjoy waterfalls that cascade down mountainsides, and photographers rise early to capture the layered peaks of the mountains shimmering in the morning's transparent light. Motorists favor Asheville as a connection point with the famed Blue Ridge Parkway, the scenic highway that crests the southern Appalachian Mountains. Spring brings showy displays of blooming rhododendron. Summer visitors enjoy natural swimming holes and trips via kayak, canoe, and pontoon boat. With autumn come splendid colors that stretch through a six-week season, peaking at progressively lower elevations. Winter gives skiers the best of both worlds, with mountains blanketed in snow and little or no snow in town.

Exhilarating outdoor adventures abound in this region. White-water rafting trips on numerous rivers are organized by Nantahala Outdoor Center (13077 NC 19 W, Bryson City). Chimney Rock Park (25 miles SE on

long par-five holes should beware the par-six at Black Mountain Golf Club (18 Ross Dr.), where one of the world's longest fairways stretches 747 yards.

If any of this photogenic region looks familiar, you should know that filmmakers have been turning their cameras on Asheville and environs since the 1920s. Scenes from *Dirty Dancing* and *Forrest Gump* were filmed here. More recently, Blue Ridge Mountain scenery provided locations for *The Clearing*, the psychological thriller starring Robert Redford. *Last of the Mohicans*, starring Daniel Day Lewis, included scenes shot around Chimney Rock.

Downtown Asheville

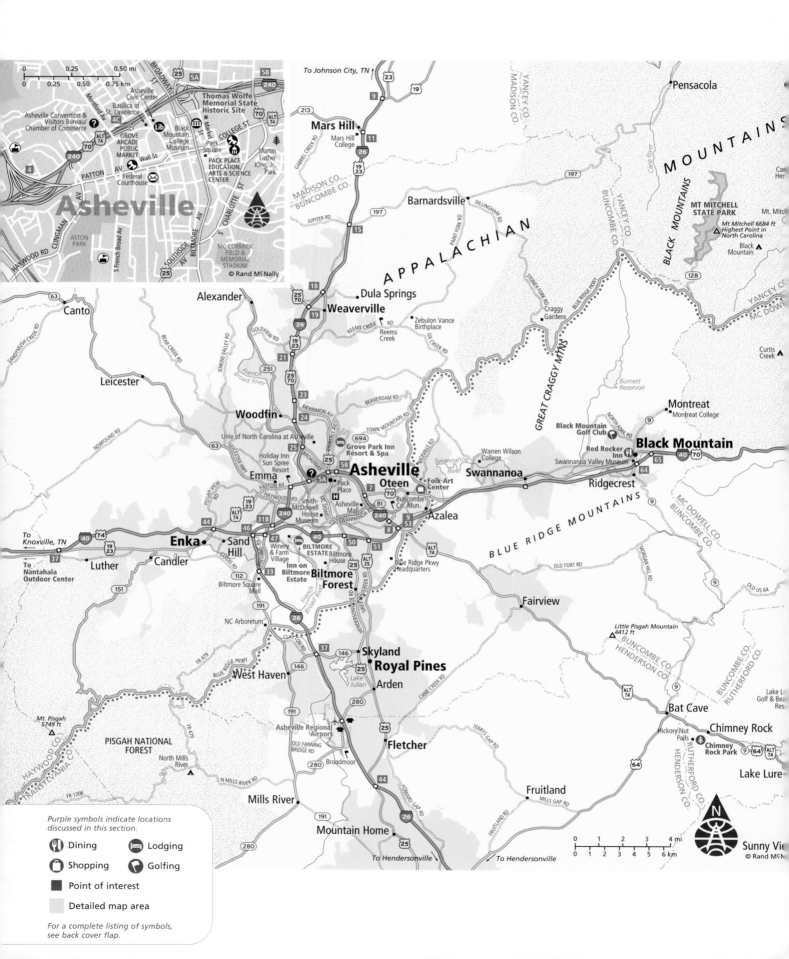

Asheville

To Johnson City, TN

Pensacola

MT MITCHELL STATE PARK
Mt Mitchell 6684 ft
Highest Point in North Carolina

Mars Hill
Mars Hill College

Barnardsville

APPALACHIAN

MOUNTAINS

BLACK MOUNTAINS

Black Mountain

Canto

Alexander

Dula Springs

Weaverville
Zebulon Vance Birthplace
Craggy Gardens

Montreat
Montreat College

Leicester

Woodfin
Univ of North Carolina at Asheville
Holiday Inn Sun Spree Resort

Grove Park Inn Resort & Spa

Warren Wilson College

Black Mountain Golf Club

Red Rocker Inn
Swannanoa Valley Museum

Black Mountain

Emma
Asheville
Pack Place
Oteen
Folk Art Center
Swannanoa
Ridgecrest

Smith-McDowell House Museum
Asheville Mall
Buncombe Co. Mun.
Azalea

BLUE RIDGE MOUNTAINS

To Knoxville, TN
To Nantahala Outdoor Center

Enka
Sand Hill
Winery & Farm Village
BILTMORE ESTATE
Biltmore House
Blue Ridge Pkwy Headquarters

Luther
Candler
Inn on Biltmore Estate
Biltmore Forest
Biltmore Square Mall

NC Arboretum

Fairview

Little Pisgah Mountain 4412 ft

Skyland
Royal Pines
Arden

West Haven

Bat Cave

Chimney Rock

Mt. Pisgah 5749 ft

PISGAH NATIONAL FOREST

North Mills River

Asheville Regional Airport

Fletcher

Hickory Nut Falls
Chimney Rock Park

Lake Lure

Broadmoor

Fruitland

Mills River

Mountain Home

Sunny Vie

To Hendersonville   To Hendersonville

Purple symbols indicate locations discussed in this section.

🍴 Dining   🛏 Lodging

🛍 Shopping   ⛳ Golfing

■ Point of interest

▨ Detailed map area

For a complete listing of symbols, see back cover flap.

© Rand McNally

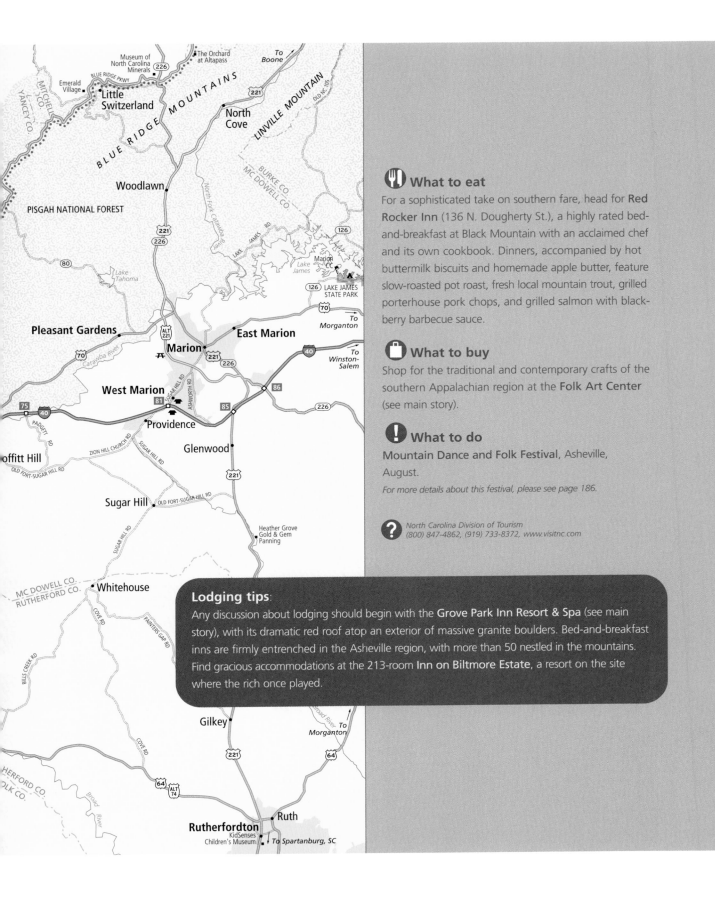

What to eat

For a sophisticated take on southern fare, head for **Red Rocker Inn** (136 N. Dougherty St.), a highly rated bed-and-breakfast at Black Mountain with an acclaimed chef and its own cookbook. Dinners, accompanied by hot buttermilk biscuits and homemade apple butter, feature slow-roasted pot roast, fresh local mountain trout, grilled porterhouse pork chops, and grilled salmon with blackberry barbecue sauce.

What to buy

Shop for the traditional and contemporary crafts of the southern Appalachian region at the **Folk Art Center** (see main story).

What to do

Mountain Dance and Folk Festival, Asheville, August.

For more details about this festival, please see page 186.

North Carolina Division of Tourism
(800) 847-4862, (919) 733-8372, www.visitnc.com

Lodging tips:

Any discussion about lodging should begin with the **Grove Park Inn Resort & Spa** (see main story), with its dramatic red roof atop an exterior of massive granite boulders. Bed-and-breakfast inns are firmly entrenched in the Asheville region, with more than 50 nestled in the mountains. Find gracious accommodations at the 213-room **Inn on Biltmore Estate**, a resort on the site where the rich once played.

Wilmington: Hollywood East

Cape Fear got its forbidding moniker from early sailors wary of its shipwrecking shoals, and the two horror movies that bear its name have only reinforced its spooky reputation. But fear not: This coast welcomes visitors with superb beaches and ocean sports that include sea kayaking, surfing, and surfcasting, and with its fascinating military history.

In the **Kure Beach** area, you'll find colorful shrimp shacks and stylish cafés, as well as Fort Fisher State Historic Site (US 421 S. at Kure Beach). Bristling with cannons and fiber-optic lighting effects, it chronicles the Civil War's fiercest land and sea battles. The state-of-the-art North Carolina Aquarium at Fort Fisher (900 Loggerhead Rd., Kure Beach) showcases the "Cape Fear Shoals" exhibit. This 235,000-gallon tank houses 50 different species, including sharks, lobsters, moray eels, sea turtles, and colorful reef and ocean fishes. At Carolina Beach State Park (1010 State Park Rd., Carolina Beach), the Venus Flytrap Trail preserves six kinds of insect-eating plants.

Wilmington, a major port along this stretch of Atlantic coast, figured prominently in the Revolutionary and Civil wars. Vital to the Confederate cause as the only southern port able to defy the Union blockade and continue exporting income-earning cotton, it also played an important role before and during the Revolution—first as a center of colonial resistance and later as headquarters for British troops. It was from Wilmington in 1781 that British General Cornwallis left for his appointment with destiny in Yorktown. Today, Wilmington earns kudos for its stately old homes and gardens and renovated historic district and waterfront. The USS *North Carolina*, a 35,000-ton superannuated World War II battleship, is a popular attraction. Visitors swivel its gun turrets and study the alligators that swim lazily alongside.

In Wilmington, cobblestone streets and brick warehouses line the Cape Fear River. A National Register Historic District (more than 230 blocks) includes a cluster of bed-and-breakfast inns. Warehouses have been converted to retail space—notably the Cotton Exchange (321 N. Front St.), a 19th-century cotton warehouse with more than 30 shops and restau-

Wilmington riverfront

rants. Charming Front St., the lively heart of town, displays a franchise-free stretch of bookstores, music shops, and other businesses; it often stars in movies as an idyllic Main Street, USA.

Filming *Dawson's Creek* at North Carolina Aquarium at Fort Fisher

Hollywood came calling in 1983 (Dino DeLaurentiis filmed *Firestarter* at the historic 1725 Orton Plantation), and since then Wilmington and the Cape Fear coast have amassed more than 400 credits. The mild climate, island beaches, varied landscapes, and historic communities draw filmmakers. Television credits include *One Tree Hill* and *Dawson's Creek*. Feature films include *Divine Secrets of the Ya-Ya Sisterhood*, *Black Knight*, and *Blue Velvet*. Studio tours and self-guided tours to movie locations are popular diversions.

Wrightsville Beach, with its distinctive stilt houses, lies only 12 miles east of Wilmington. Founded in 1899 and once accessible only by water, it offers an inviting five-mile stretch of white sand.

can be as uncomplicated as renting a bicycle and exploring quiet byways or scudding a sailboat across the ocean. Anglers can cast off a pier or into the surf, or arrange a deep-sea excursion. Net blue crabs from a wharf, buy fresh shrimp right off a commercial fishing boat, or simply stroll one of the long, white beaches, searching for shells and watching darting sandpipers nimbly outpace the incoming tide. Many fine golf courses dot Brunswick County. Players may find themselves sharing the landscape with foxes, deer, herons, egrets, and ospreys.

Just north of the South Carolina line, the tiny fishing village of **Calabash** boasts two major claims to fame. Its restaurants draw visitors with fresh, locally caught seafood. Throughout the Carolinas, the term "Calabash-style" seafood is used generically for lightly battered, deep-fried fish fillets (typically, flounder), oysters, clams, scallops, and tiny, succulent shrimp (also great

Azalea belles at the North Carolina Azalea Festival

By a quirk of geography, some 50 miles of Atlantic shore fronting Brunswick County stretch east-to-west, rather than north-to-south. Protecting this coast is a strand of quiet barrier islands. These include Ocean Isle, with seven miles of Atlantic beach. The casual ambience of an area only an hour's drive north of the bustle of Myrtle Beach charms vacationers. Pleasures

boiled). Calabash sometimes is remembered because of comedian Jimmy Durante's famous show closer: "Goodnight, Mrs. Calabash, wherever you are!" (It originated from an unidentified Calabash woman the entertainer once met.)

To Clinton

Council

BLADEN CO.
COLUMBUS CO.

BLADEN CO.
PENDER CO.

ELWELL FERRY RD

EAST ARCADIA RD

Cape Fear River

PENDER CO.
BRUNSWICK CO.

To Whiteville

Hallsboro

Lake Waccamaw

Depot Museum

LAKE SHORE DR

BELLA COOLA RD

Lake Waccamaw

LAKE WACCAMAW STATE PARK

Bolton

Freeman

Delco

Riegelwood

Northwest

MT. MISERY RD

Maco

Phoenix

Sandy Creek

Malmo

Le

Purple symbols indicate locations discussed in this section.

🍴 Dining   🛏 Lodging

🛍 Shopping   ❓ Information

⬛ Point of interest

Detailed map area

For a complete listing of symbols, see back cover flap.

COLUMBUS CO.
BRUNSWICK CO.

Lanvale

CAMP BRANCH RD NW

Green Swamp

Town Creek

FUNSTON RD

Winnabow

Wilmington Railroad Museum

Cotton Exchange

USS North Carolina Battleship Memorial

The Golden Gallery

Grace St

Thalian Hall Center for the Performing Arts

Chestnut St

Cape Fear Coast Convention & Visitors Bureau

MARKET ST

HISTORIC DISTRICT

Burgwin-Wright House & Gardens

Bellamy Mansion Museum

Dock St

Cape Fear Museum of History & Science

Wilmington Trolley Company

Latimer House Museum

Orange St

Cape Fear Serpentarium

Children's Museum of Wilmington

Ann St

Wilmington

Bolivia

MACHOLA RD NW

Prospect

Little Macedonia

LITTLE MACEDONIA RD NW

Boiling Spring Lakes

© Rand McNally

WOOSTER ST

DAWSON ST

Supply

STONE CHIMNEY RD SW

Carolina National

SUNSET HARBOR RD SE

Shallotte

Varnum

STANBURY RD SW

Oak Island

Grissettown

Thomasboro

Sandpiper Bay

Varnamtown

Sunset Harbor

OAK ISLAND

Yaupon Beach

Crow Creek

Meadowlands

Big Nell's Pit Stop

Gause Landing

Holden Beach

Lockwoods Folly Inlet

Caswell Beach

Carolina Shores Golf & CC

Thistle

Ingram Planetarium

Shallotte Inlet

Calabash

The Pearl

Seaside

Ocean Isle Beach

Museum of Coastal Carolina

Long Bay

Oyster Bay

NORTH CAROLINA
SOUTH CAROLINA

To Myrtle Beach, SC

Sunset Beach

ATLANTIC OCEAN

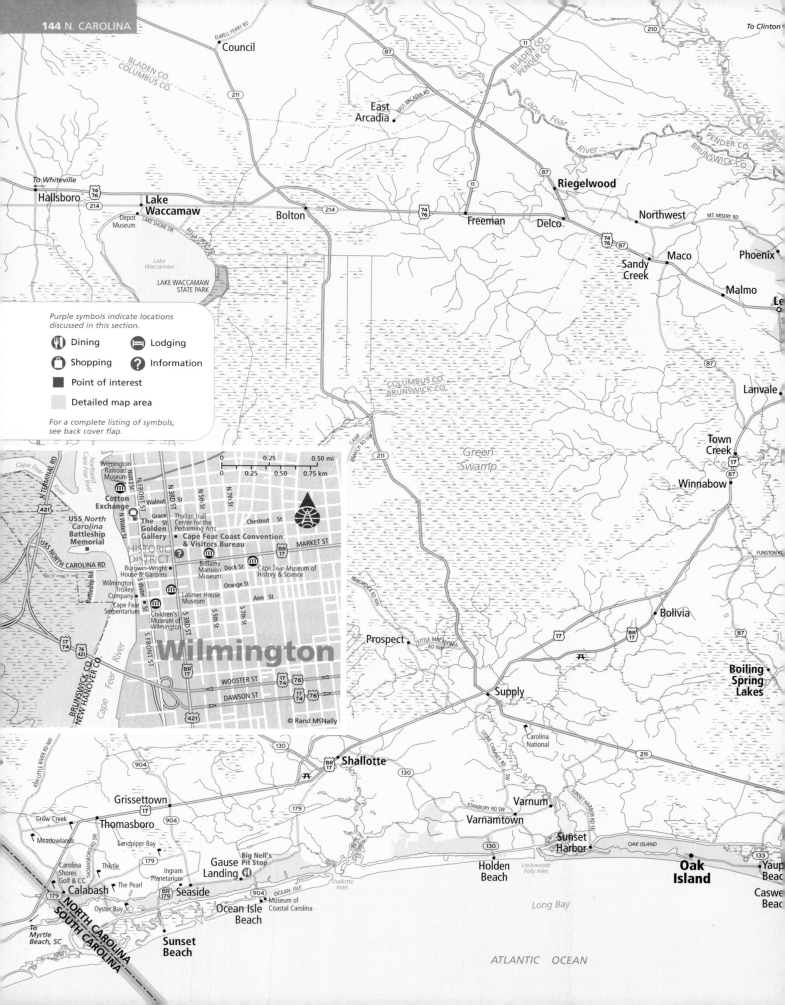

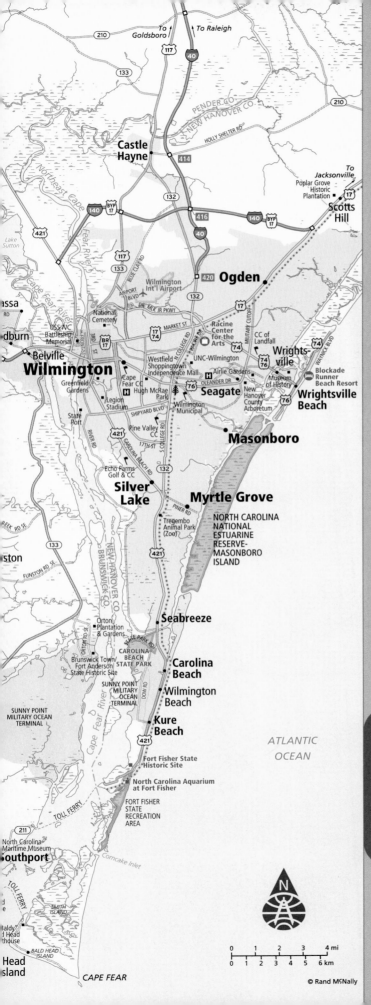

What to eat

Fresh fish and shellfish in its many preparations abound, but the area is known for Calabash-style seafood (see main story). Cathead biscuits drenched with sawmill gravy are served alongside Brunswick stew at **Big Nell's Pit Stop** (179 Seaside) in Brunswick County, which also serves "a bowl of sunshine"(a.k.a. grits).

What to buy

More than 35 art galleries in Wilmington and Cape Fear beaches offer works by local and regional artists. The **Golden Gallery** (307 N. Front St.) in the **Cotton Exchange** sells Mary Ellen Golden's watercolors depicting Cape Fear coastal landscapes. The gallery also displays husband John Golden's regional illustrations and photography. Wilmington's **Racine Center for the Arts** (203 Racine Dr.) houses the Gallery at Racine, featuring renowned Wilmington artists such as George Pocheptsov and Shaw Lakey. Adjacent sit Firebird Pottery Studio and Blue Moon Showcase, with booths featuring the work of approximately 100 artisans representing a variety of media.

What to do

North Carolina Azalea Festival,
first weekend in April.
Riverfest,
first weekend in October.

For more details about these festivals, please see page 186.

North Carolina Division of Tourism
(800) 847-4862, (919) 733-8372, www.visitnc.com

Lodging tips:

Accommodations range from efficiency units to oceanfront villas and luxurious spas. Beach house rentals are a popular alternative to hotels and motels (although major chains are well represented). Choices along the beach include the **Blockade Runner Beach Resort** (275 Waynick Blvd., Wrightsville Beach), which also offers bicycle rentals. Nearly two dozen bed-and-breakfast inns populate the area. For details: Cape Fear Coast Convention & Visitors Bureau, (877) 406-2356, www.cape-fear.nc.us.

Adventures in Piedmont

What do Mayberry and merlot have in common? Both lie within an hour's drive of **Winston-Salem**, and each is a tourist magnet. Sheriff Andy Taylor, Deputy Barney Fife, and gang hang out in **Mount Airy**, the town that served as the prototype for the fictional town of Mayberry on *The Andy Griffith Show*. It's the real-life birthplace of lead actor Andy Griffith.

Mount Airy attracts droves of Mayberry cultists who get their hair trimmed at Floyd's City Barber Shop (129 N. Main St.), where the sign boasts "2 chairs—no waiting," and order pork chop sandwiches at Snappy Lunch (125 N. Main St.), which Andy mentioned on one episode. Or they can ride in a replica of the 1962 squad car that was Barney's pride and joy. The new Andy Griffith Museum (currently under construction, with a projected opening date of late 2006 or early 2007) will hold a huge collection of memorabilia; the annual "Mayberry Days" (last weekend in September) draw huge crowds.

As for merlot, find it in Yadkin Valley Wine Country, home to 19 wineries, where a favorable combination of soil and sunshine produces high-quality grapes and award-winning wines. Visit this region by following the "Wine Trail" along peaceful, winding country roads, either by car or as part as an organized bicycle tour. The 1.4-million-acre valley was approved in 2002 as North Carolina's first American Viticultural Area, enabling wineries to put this designation on labels (provided 85 percent of the grapes are grown in the region). Wineries offer tours and tastings and, in wine country tradition, the valley is sprinkled with fine restaurants, charming bed-and-breakfasts, antique stores, and art galleries. A busy calendar features events combining music, art, and wine.

The real contrast between oenophiles (who may fashionably shun merlot) and the folk of Mayberry (Mount Airy residents play the part to the hilt, favoring porch rocking chairs) is perhaps the difference between the way urban Piedmont is perceived and the way it

Memorabilia at Floyd's City Barber Shop

Interior of Reynolda House

really is. The three cities of the so-called "Triad"— Winston-Salem, **High Point**, and **Greensboro**—are most unlike television's Mayberry. Within them, culture flourishes, business grows (especially in white-collar industries), and higher learning thrives.

Winston-Salem, nestled in the foothills of the Blue Ridge Mountains, often surprises with its zesty, eclectic art scene, epitomized by the downtown Arts District centered on Sixth and Trade streets. It hosts "Gallery Hop" on the first Friday evening of every month, and, seasonally, "Fourth Street Jazz & Blues" on Friday nights and "Summer on Trade" every Saturday night.

Exploring Winston-Salem, you'll find plenty of history relating to the Moravians who traveled south on the Great Wagon Road. In 1753, this group of German-speaking Protestants established a small village and farming center in the North Carolina piedmont. Today this settlement, known as Historic Bethabara Park, is a National Historic Landmark. In 1766, the Moravians established Salem, a congregational town and trading center founded to house professional craftsmen. The Moravians' vision in creating a self-sufficient community made Salem a haven for entrepreneurs. Within a few years the town included a tannery, pottery, brickyard, flour mill, bakery, slaughterhouse, brewery, ironworks, and cloth and furniture makers.

Visitors can see much of this industry in action at Old Salem (900 Old Salem Rd.), an authentic restoration and living history museum with cobblestone streets and white picket fences. Costumed interpreters provide tours and demonstrate early crafts. However, Old Salem is a real community, with homes privately owned and occupied. Don't miss Reynolda House, Museum of American Art and Reynolda Gardens (2250 Reynolda

Rd.). Once the "cottage" of tobacco baron R.J. Reynolds and his wife, Katharine, this 40,000-square-foot house exhibits a fine collection of American art. Pieces date from 1755 to the present and include works by Georgia O'Keeffe, Grant Wood, Jasper Johns, Frederick Church, Jacob Lawrence, and Thomas Eakins. The attic offers a glimpse of bygone fashions with a display of Katharine Reynolds' hats, shoes, and dresses. Visit nearby Reynolda Gardens and Reynolda Village, a collection of elegant shops, boutiques, and restaurants in the former outbuildings and workshops of the Reynolds estate.

Explore the Piedmont plateau at Hanging Rock State Park near Danbury (NC 2015). Among sheer cliffs and peaks of bare rock, quiet forests, and cascading waterfalls, you can rent a vacation cabin and fall asleep to the chorus of frogs. A cool mountain lake nestled in the hills beckons swimmers and anglers. Park amenities include boat rentals and an observation tower.

T. Bagge: Merchant in Old Salem

What to eat

Lexington, just south of Winston-Salem, is ground zero for North Carolina-style barbecue, where the sauce is vinegar-based rather than tomato-based. A pulled pork sandwich is packed with shredded barbecued shoulder pork. Find it at **Lexington Barbecue #1** (10 US 29-70S); in Winston-Salem, and at **Little Richard's Bar-B-Que** (several locations). On a visit to Old Salem, stop at the **Winkler Bakery** (529 Main St.), established in 1800, where they still bake their famous coffeecake and serve it hot from the wood-fired oven.

What to buy

T. Bagge: Merchant in Old Salem offers pewter Christmas tree ornaments and wafer-thin Moravian cookies, remembrances of the Moravian culture that thrives in Winston-Salem. "Texas Pete" sauces, chilies, jams, jellies, marmalades, and salsas are made in Winston-Salem and available at the **T.W. Garner General Store** (4045 Indiana Ave., Winston-Salem).

What to do

Tanglewood Festival of Lights, Winston-Salem, early November to January 1.

For more details about this festival, please see page 186.

North Carolina Division of Tourism
(800) 847-4862, (919) 733-8372, www.visitnc.com

Lodging tips:

Winston-Salem offers a variety of hotels, motels, and bed-and-breakfast inns, from four-star to four rooms. In Old Salem, the atmospheric **Brookstown Inn** (200 Brookstown Ave.), created from an 1837 textile mill, features hand-made bricks and exposed beams. For details: Winston-Salem Convention & Visitors Bureau, (866) 728-4200, www.visitwinston-salem.com.

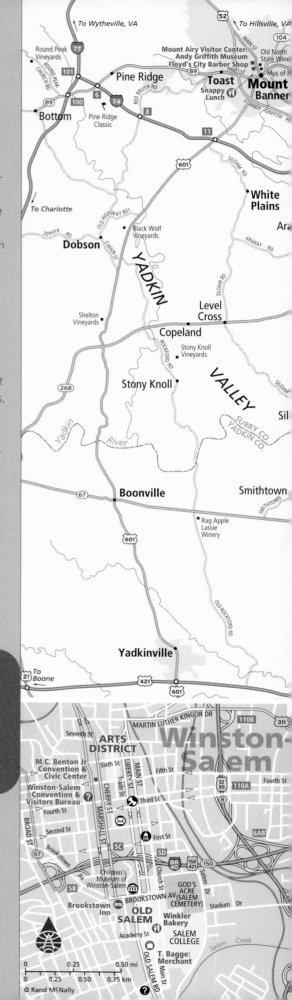

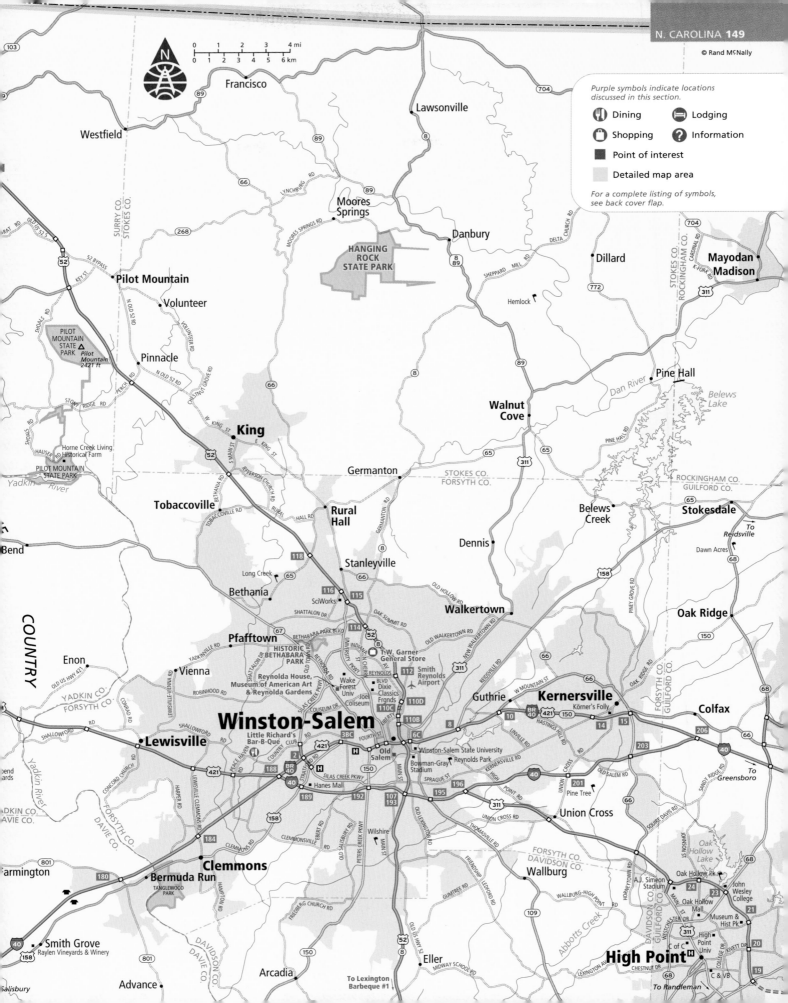

© Rand McNally

103

89

Francisco

Westfield

Lawsonville

704

8

SURRY CO.
STOKES CO.

52 BYPASS
52

89

268

89

Moores
Springs

Danbury

Dillard

DELTA CHURCH RD

STOKES CO.
ROCKINGHAM CO.

704

Mayodan
Madison

311

Pilot Mountain

Volunteer

KEY ST
52

HANGING
ROCK
STATE PARK

8
89

SHEPPARD MILL RD

772

311

CARDINAL RD

K-FOR-E RD

PILOT
MOUNTAIN STATE
PARK

Pilot
Mountain
2421 ft

Pinnacle

66

Hemlock

89

N OLD 52 RD

CHESTNUT GROVE RD

PERCH RD

Dan River

Pine Hall

Belews
Lake

SHOALS RD

STONY RIDGE RD

HAUSER RD

Horne Creek Living
Historical Farm

PILOT MOUNTAIN
STATE PARK

Yadkin River

W KING ST

King

S MAIN ST

E KING ST

Walnut
Cove

65

311

PINE HALL RD

Bend

BETHANIA RD

JEFFERSON CHURCH RD

RURAL HALL RD

Germanton

GERMANTON RD

STOKES CO.
FORSYTH CO.

Belews
Creek

ROCKINGHAM CO.
GUILFORD CO.

65

Stokesdale

To
Reidsville

68

Tobaccoville

TOBACCOVILLE RD

Rural
Hall

8

Dennis

Dawn Acres

COUNTRY

118

Long Creek

65

Stanleyville

66

OLD HOLLOW RD

158

PINEY GROVE RD

Oak Ridge

150

Bethania

116

SciWorks

115

SHATTALON DR

OAK SUMMIT RD

Walkertown

311

NEW WALKERTOWN RD

OLD WALKERTOWN RD

66

OAK RIDGE RD

Enon

67

114

Pfafftown

HISTORIC
BETHABARA
PARK

BETHABARA PARK BLVD

SHATTALON DR

UNIVERSITY PKWY

REYNOLDS RD

INDIANA AVE

52
8

T.W. Garner
General Store

W MOUNTAIN ST

Guthrie

BR
40
421

Körner's Folly

Kernersville

FORSYTH CO.
GUILFORD CO.

Colfax

68

YADKIN CO.
FORSYTH CO.

Vienna

YADKINVILLE RD

ROBINHOOD RD

Reynolda House,
Museum of American Art
& Reynolda Gardens

112

Smith
Reynolds
Airport

LEWISVILLE-VIENNA RD

Wake
Forest
Univ

BLVD
Dixie
Classics
Frgnds

110D

10

HASTINGS HILL RD

150

14

15

203

206

40

66

40
To
Greensboro

YADKIN CO.
DAVIE CO.

CONRAD RD

SHALLOWFORD RD

Lewisville

SHALLOWFORD RD

PEACE HAVEN RD

COUNTRY CLUB RD

Joel
Coliseum

COLISEUM DR

SILAS CREEK PKWY

Little Richard's
Bar-B-Que

110C

110B

BBC

FOURTH ST

Winston-Salem

421

2

LIBERTY ST

6C

Old Salem

Winston-Salem State University

Reynolds Park

KERNERSVILLE RD

REIDSVILLE RD

311

UNIVILLE RD

Pine Tree

201

OLD SALEM RD

SQUIRE DAVIS RD

SANDY RIDGE RD

188

BR
40

STRATFORD RD

40
189

H

H

150

Hanes Mall

SILAS CREEK PKWY

192

107
193

195

Bowman-Gray
Stadium

SPRAGUE ST

196

UNION CROSS RD

Union
Cross

8

311

POINT RD

THOMASVILLE RD

FORSYTH CO.
DAVIDSON CO.

Yadkin River

DAVIE CO.

FORSYTH CO.

HARPER RD

LEWISVILLE CLEMMONS RD

158

Clemmons

184

CLEMMONS RD

CLEMMONSVILLE RD

EBERT RD

OLD SALISBURY RD

PETERS CREEK PKWY

Wilshire

MAIN ST

OLD LEXINGTON RD

Wallburg

FRIENDSHIP LEDFORD RD

WALLBURG-HIGH POINT RD

HORNETOWN RD

Oak
Hollow
Lake

68

Oak Hollow Pk.

A.J. Simeon
Stadium

John
Wesley
College

801

180

Bermuda Run

TANGLEWOOD PARK

HARPER RD

FREEDBERG CHURCH RD

GUMTREE RD

109

Abbotts Creek

DAVIDSON CO.
GUILFORD CO.

MAIN ST

WESTCHESTER DR

24

23

Oak Hollow
Mall

21

Museum &
Hist Pk

Farmington

40

158

Smith Grove
Raylen Vineyards & Winery

801

Advance

Arcadia

Eller

52

8

MIDWAY SCHOOL RD

To Lexington
Barbeque #1

Salisbury

603

Randleman

311

A.J. Simeon
Stadium

High
Point
Univ

C of C

C & VB

LEXINGTON AVE

CHESTNUT DR

COLLEGE DR

KIVETT DR

68

High Point

H

19

20

21

Garden City
of the South

Virtually surrounded by rivers and tidal creeks, with windswept barrier isles nearby, **Charleston** provides an idyllic setting for getaways long or short. The evidence: colorful cobblestone lanes, busy wharves, docks lined with seafood restaurants, an abundance of elegant hostelries, and enough one-of-a-kind shops to imperil the loosest budgets.

Charleston possesses an incomparable grace and beauty that help make it one of the southeast's most captivating travel destinations. Fanciful hand-forged wrought-iron gates lead to gardens where azaleas and magnolia bloom and gnarled live oaks drip with Spanish moss. Grand antebellum homes present an architectural textbook of styles from Colonial and Georgian to Federal and Greek Revival.

To Charleston's charm and beauty, add serious brushes with America's history. It is the oldest city between Virginia and Florida, founded in 1670 by English settlers and named "Charles Towne" for British monarch Charles II. Charleston even had its own nobility during its formative years; major landowners were titled barons, dukes, and earls. The firing on Fort Sumter by Confederate soldiers set off the Civil War, a conflict that saw the world's first successful submarine attack when the Confederate submarine *H.L. Hunley* sank the Union warship *Housatonic* in Charleston Harbor.

Although Charleston itself overflows with diversions, the surrounding countryside and coastline also beckon with attractions such as **Summerville**, a picturesque town built by wealthy planters. 20 miles northwest of Charleston, Summerville's front porches, pine trees, and azalea blooms interweave with a variety of eateries and shops (including many antique emporia) and more than 700 buildings on the National Register of Historic Places.

Charleston Harbor

To the northeast, the quaint, photogenic fishing village of **McClellanville** lures moviemakers, such as cast and crew of the 1991 film *Paradise*. Nearby is Hampton Plantation State Historic Site (1950 Rutledge Rd.), once a sprawling rice plantation. Its restored 18th-century mansion was the ancestral home of South Carolina poet laureate Archibald Rutledge.

Folly Beach Pier

Golfers and tennis players travel to the well-appointed resorts of Kiawah Island. These include the Sanctuary at Kiawah Island Golf Resort, a 255-room luxury resort with ocean-view balconies. Beachwalker Park provides a beautiful stretch of public-access beach. Surfers head

Conservation Corps in the 1930s, Edisto Beach State Park contains a fine shelling beach and is popular with surf and marsh anglers. Edisto Island Museum (8123 Chisolm Plantation Rd.) features displays on sea island plantation life, the Civil War, and Native American history.

In and around Charleston, popular attractions include harbor boat tours, especially those that stop at Fort Sumter National Monument (1214 Middle St., Sullivan's Island). One contemporary military attraction: Patriots Point Naval & Maritime Museum (40 Patriots Point Rd.), where you can visit the Congressional Medal of Honor Museum and board the flight deck of World War II aircraft carrier USS *Yorktown*. Take a horse-drawn carriage ride through Old Charleston or choose from many well-choreographed guided walking tours. They specialize in such topics as the Civil and Revolutionary wars, black history, architecture, and gardens. En route, you'll discover that George Washington did indeed sleep here, in 1791 when he stayed in the Heyward Washington House (97 Church St.). This handsome brick building, dating from 1772, offers tours. East of the Cooper River lies Sullivan's Island, site of a Revolutionary-era fort. Just north is **Isle of Palms**, with palm-lined boulevards, a marina, golf courses, restaurants, and shops along miles of beaches.

Long Bridge at Magnolia Plantation

for Folly Beach, Charleston's nearest beach and the site of many surfing contests. In the 1930s, this beach community was home to big bands such as Tommy Dorsey and Artie Shaw, which played along the boardwalk. Today it offers vibrant nightlife, a clutch of seafood restaurants, tall sand dunes, and choice beach house rentals.

Anglers and beachcombers prize the quiet, natural beauty of Edisto Island. Developed by the Civilian

Drayton Hall (3380 Ashley River Rd.), completed in 1742, is one of the only plantation houses to survive the Revolutionary and Civil wars. Standing on a 125-acre site, it is a masterpiece of Georgian-Palladian architecture now filled with original 18th-century craftsmanship. Special daily tours focus on African American life. Nearby Magnolia Plantation (3550 Ashley River Rd.) displays one of the country's largest collections of azaleas and camellias.

What to eat

Low Country cooking features she-crab soup (crab eggs add a distinctive flavor to this gender-specific soup). The cuisine also includes rice, grits, green tomatoes, and other local produce. Featured dishes include oyster roasts and gumbo-like "Frogmore Stew," a seasoned seafood boil with shrimp and smoked sausage. Try this stew at the upscale **Charleston Grill** (in the Charleston Place Hotel, 205 Meeting St.), where it incorporates fresh shrimp, homemade andouille sausage, crab meat, and corn simmered in a shellfish broth. Many communities host annual oyster roasts, the largest held at **Boone Hall Plantation** (1235 Long Point Rd., Mount Pleasant) every January.

What to buy

Models and movie stars—and plenty of wannabes— buy the chic bags from **Moo Roo Handbags** (316 King St.). Bags are hand-crafted with exotic feathers, skins, and semi-precious stones. The Charleston-based designer personally signs and dates each bag. Yes, that strikingly beautiful blonde may indeed be customer Sharon Stone. *Sex in the City* cast members are also among celebrity clientele. Sweetgrass baskets, made with sewing techniques brought by enslaved blacks from West Africa, are found throughout the Charleston area, including City Market, local gift shops, and at roadside stands along US 17 North.

What to do

Spoleto Festival USA,
late May and early June.
Festival of Houses and Gardens,
mid-March to mid-April.
For more details about these festivals, please see page 186.

South Carolina Department of Parks, Recreation & Tourism
(888) 727-6453, (803) 734-1700,
www.discoversouthcarolina.com

Lodging tips:

Charleston's lodging options range from budget to full-service luxury, with locations at beaches and in the heart of town. City fathers like to boast that guests have included military and government leaders, movie and music stars, and celebrities from George Washington and Prince Charles to Oprah Winfrey. Choices include numerous luxury inns and a wide range of bed-and-breakfasts. Tony **Charleston Place Hotel** (205 Meeting St.) is a top spot in town, with Gucci and Godiva shops, a sweeping staircase straight out of *Gone With the Wind*, and elegant dining and live jazz at the Charleston Grill. For details: Charleston Area Convention & Visitors Bureau, (843) 853-8000, www.charlestoncvb.com.

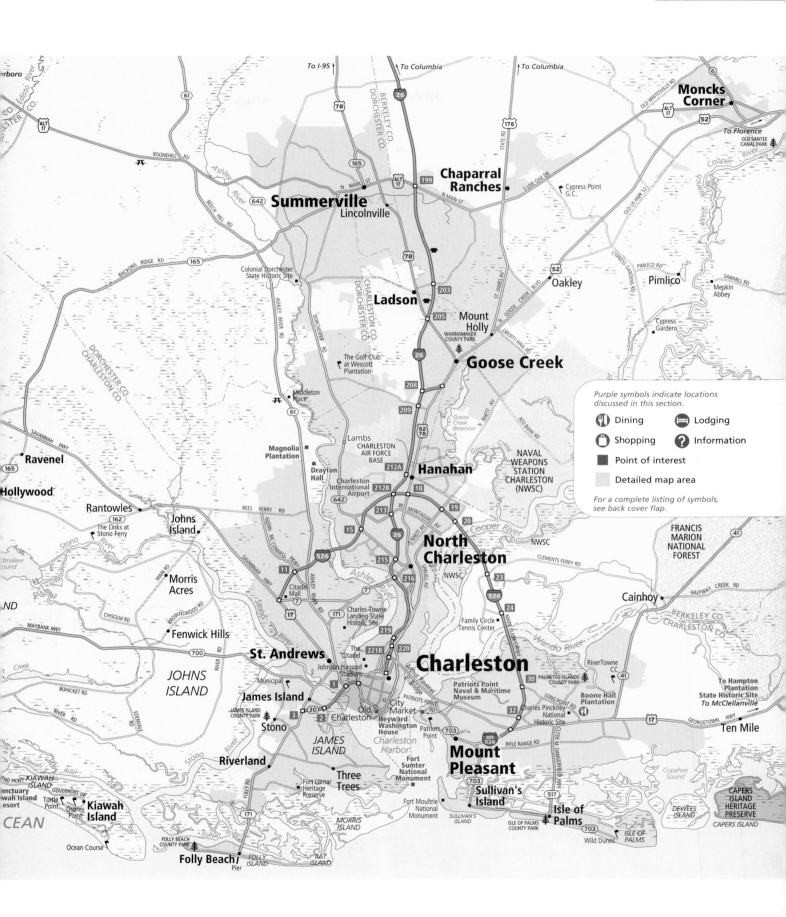

To I-95   To Columbia   To Columbia

Moncks Corner

To Florence

Old Santee Canal Park

Edisto River

61

78

26

ALT 17

642

Summerville

Lincolnville

165

ALT 17

199

N MAIN ST

Chaparral Ranches

S LIVE OAK DR

Cypress Point G.C.

176

STATE RD

Cypress Gardens Rd

Pimlico Rd

Sawmill Rd

Pimlico

Mepkin Abbey

Cooper River

West Branch Cooper River

BOONEHILL RD

Ashley River

BEECH HILL RD

BACKONS RIDGE RD

165

642

N MAIN ST

78

Colonial Dorchester State Historic Site

Ladson

203

205

Mount Holly

WANNAMAKER COUNTY PARK

26

52

Oakley

OLD US HWY 52

N GOOSE CREEK BLVD

ST JAMES AV

LIBERTY HALL RD

Cypress Gardens

The Golf Club at Wescott Plantation

Goose Creek

208

209

Goose Creek Reservoir

RED BANK RD

N RHETT AV

Middleton Place

61

Lambs

52 78

NAVAL WEAPONS STATION CHARLESTON (NWSC)

Magnolia Plantation

CHARLESTON AIR FORCE BASE

212A

Hanahan

18

Drayton Hall

Charleston International Airport

642

212B

213

15

W MONTAGUE AV

19

20

Goose Creek

Ravenel

165

Hollywood

SAVANNAH HWY

Rantowles

162

The Links at Stono Ferry

BEES FERRY RD

Johns Island

GLENN MCCONNELL PKWY

26

NWSC

Cooper River

CLEMENTS FERRY RD

NWSC

FRANCIS MARION NATIONAL FOREST

41

Stono River

Imalaw Island Sound

Morris Acres

MAIN RD

CHISOLM RD

BROWNSWOOD RD

SAVANNAH HWY

526

11

Ashley River

215

North Charleston

216

SPRUILL AV

23

526

24

Cainhoy

HALFWAY CREEK RD

BERKELEY CO CHARLESTON CO

Citadel Mall

7

Charles Towne Landing State Historic Site

Family Circle Tennis Center

MARK CLARK EXPY

Fenwick Hills

700

RIVER RD

St. Andrews

171

219

221B

220

The Citadel

Johnson Hagood Stadium

RiverTowne CC

41

Wando River

JOHNS ISLAND

MAYBANK HWY

BOHICKET RD

EDENVALE RD

Municipal

1

James Island

JAMES ISLAND COUNTY PARK

30

3

Stono

Charleston

Arthur Ravenel Jr. Bridge

Patriots Point

PATRIOTS POINT RD

Patriots Point Naval & Maritime Museum

Palmetto Islands County Park

LONG POINT RD

Boone Hall Plantation

30

To Hampton Plantation State Historic Site
To McClellanville

17

Ten Mile

GEORGETOWN RD

CLYDE M. DANGERFIELD HWY

Creek

MORRIS ISLAND

KIAWAH ISLAND

Sanctuary uah Island sort

GOVERNORS DR

Turtle Point

Osprey Point

Kiawah Island

Ocean Course

CEAN

2

Old Charleston

Riverland

FOLLY RD

James Island

2

JAMES ISLAND

City Market

Heyward Washington House

Charleston Harbor

Three Trees

Fort Lamar Heritage Preserve

Fort Sumter National Monument

Fort Moultrie National Monument

Mount Pleasant

703

Sullivan's Island

517

Charles Pinckney National Historic Site

32

RIFLE RANGE RD

Isle of Palms

703

Wild Dunes

ISLE OF PALMS

Copahee Sound

DEWEES ISLAND

CAPERS ISLAND HERITAGE PRESERVE

CAPERS ISLAND

171

FOLLY BEACH COUNTY PARK

Folly Beach
Pier

FOLLY ISLAND

RAT ISLAND

Ocean Course

Purple symbols indicate locations discussed in this section.

🍴 Dining   🛏 Lodging

🛍 Shopping   ❓ Information

⬛ Point of interest

Detailed map area

For a complete listing of symbols, see back cover flap.

The British
Were Here

Without Paul Revere's dramatic warnings of imminent British arrival, the redcoats came and occupied central South Carolina. **Camden** became headquarters in the south for Lord Charles Cornwallis and the British Army during the Revolutionary War. As the oldest existing inland town in the state, it is part of a township plan ordered by King George II in 1730. British influences abound, especially in the seven-county tourism region tagged "Olde English District." Its inherent "Englishness" shows in a love of horses and a full calendar of equestrian events that include polo matches, hunt meets, and (shades of *National Velvet*) steeplechase racing.

Camden welcomes spring with the Carolina Cup, a premier steeplechase event at which extravagant tailgating parties bring out the best crystal and women arrive in bright sundresses and straw hats. A second major steeplechase event—the Colonial Cup in November, held at the Springdale Race Course (200 Knights Hill Rd.)—climaxes a weeklong festival. History buffs head for Historic Camden Revolutionary War Site (222 S. Broad St.), where Lord Cornwallis and 2,500 British soldiers spent a rough year following the siege of Charleston. The 107-acre outdoor museum complex includes the town site of 18th-century Camden, the restored and furnished 1789 Craven House, and the Kershaw-Cornwallis House, built in 1777 and reconstructed in 1977. There is a smithy and two early 19th-century log cabins. Old Camden Trace offers a three-mile walk through Historic Camden, which includes the 1758 Quaker Cemetery.

Columbia, the South Carolina capital created in 1786 to succeed Charleston as seat of government, is a city of wide boulevards and redbrick buildings. It sits along the banks of the Congaree River, virtually at the geographical center of the state. Yes, George Washington did sleep here (in 1791) and, yes, Sherman's troops set fire to the city during the Civil War (in 1865).

Kershaw-Cornwallis House at Historic Camden Revolutionary War Site

Finlay Park Fountain and the Columbia skyline

The Columbia Museum of Art (1515 Main St.), a downtown department store transformed in 1998 into a sleek, airy, light-filled space, features 25 galleries. Highlights include Claude Monet's impressionistic view of Giverny and an American collection that includes work by Remington, Sully, and Stuart, as well as the glass art of Louis Comfort Tiffany. Notable collections of European and American fine and decorative art include Italian Renaissance and Baroque masterpieces from the Samuel H. Kress Collection. One of the museum's jewels is a large and rare Nativity fresco by preeminent Florentine Renaissance artist Sandro Botticelli.

Although inevitably referred to by locals as "swamp," Congaree National Park (100 National Park Rd.) is a magnificent preserve with huge, ancient trees and creeks for canoeing and kayaking. Activities include hiking, primitive camping, birdwatching, kayaking, and ranger-guided interpretive walks and canoe tours. The park preserves primeval forest that contains America's largest contiguous tract of old-growth bottomland hardwood forest. Known for giant hardwoods and towering pines, the park's floodplain forest includes one of the highest canopies in the world and some of the tallest trees in the eastern United States. **Sumter**, a city of about 40,000 with a collection of pretty antebellum mansions, takes its name from Revolutionary War hero General Thomas Sumter, a.k.a. the "Fighting Gamecock." A major downtown landmark: historic Sumter Opera House (21 N. Main St.) with its landmark clock tower. Its performance schedule features a lively mix of film, dance, theater, and concerts. Sumter is best known for Swan Lake Iris Gardens (822 W. Liberty St.), showcasing 150 acres of Japanese iris, magnolias, azaleas, and a variety of seasonal flowers. Gorgeous, scented blooms surround Swan Lake, home to all eight species of the world's swans—including black Australian varieties. The garden hosts Sumter Iris Festival each Memorial Day weekend. Also popular is "Fantasy of Lights" (late November), with more than 100 lighted figures and more than one million lights illuminating the lake.

More holiday flavor awaits at Poinsett State Park (6660 Poinsett Park Rd.), at least in name. Joel R. Poinsett is credited with introducing the poinsettia from Mexico to the United States. The park's diverse terrain ranges from swamp and sand hills to mountain bluffs and hardwood forests. Cabins, shelters, and other historic structures provide excellent examples of the craftsmanship of the Civilian Conservation Corps, which built them as part of Depression-era work programs. Rental fishing boats provide access to bass, bream, and catfish in a 10-acre lake. The Palmetto Trail for hiking and mountain biking winds through the park, where curious travelers may find unmarked Revolutionary War sites and the remains of gristmills.

Cypress trees in Congaree National Park

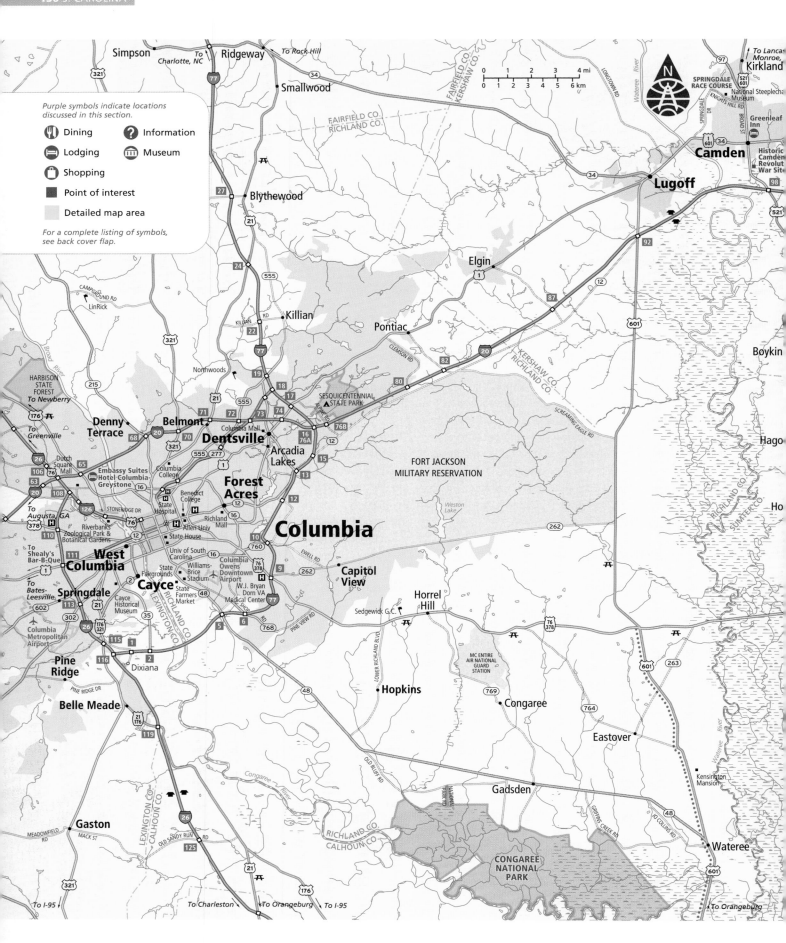

Purple symbols indicate locations discussed in this section.

🍴 Dining   ❓ Information
🛏 Lodging   🏛 Museum
🛍 Shopping
■ Point of interest
▨ Detailed map area

For a complete listing of symbols, see back cover flap.

0   1   2   3   4 mi
0   1   2   3   4   5   6 km

N

Simpson
Ridgeway
To Rock Hill
To Charlotte, NC
Smallwood
SPRINGDALE RACE COURSE
National Steeplechase Museum
Greenleaf Inn
Kirkland
To Lancaster, Monroe
Camden
Historic Camden Revolut. War Site
Lugoff
Elgin
Blythewood
Killian
Pontiac
Boykin
Northwoods
SESQUICENTENNIAL STATE PARK
Hago
HARBISON STATE FOREST
To Newberry
Denny Terrace
Belmont
Dentsville
Arcadia Lakes
FORT JACKSON MILITARY RESERVATION
Weston Lake
Ho
To Greenville
Dutch Square Mall
Embassy Suites Hotel Columbia-Greystone
Columbia College
Forest Acres
Columbia
To Augusta, GA
Benedict College
State Hospital
Allen Univ
Richland Mall
Riverbanks Zoological Park & Botanical Gardens
State House
To Shealy's Bar-B-Que
West Columbia
Univ of South Carolina
Columbia Owens Downtown Airport
Capitol View
To Bates-Leesville
Cayce
Springdale
State Fairgrounds
Williams-Brice Stadium
State Farmers Market
W.J. Bryan Dorn VA Medical Center
Sedgewick G.C.
Horrel Hill
Cayce Historical Museum
Columbia Metropolitan Airport
MC ENTIRE AIR NATIONAL GUARD STATION
Pine Ridge
Dixiana
Hopkins
Congaree
Belle Meade
Eastover
Kensington Mansion
Gaston
Gadsden
CONGAREE NATIONAL PARK
Wateree
To I-95
To Charleston
To Orangeburg
To I-95
To Orangeburg

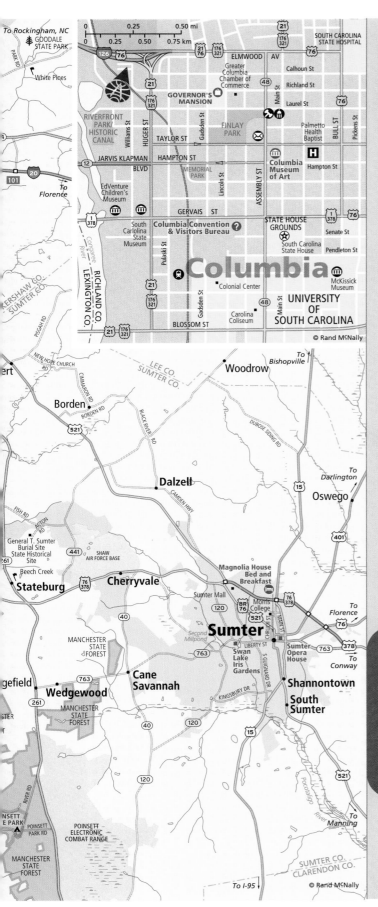

What to eat

Mustard-based barbecue sauce is the style in this area. One of its most popular purveyors is **Shealy's Bar-B-Que** (340 East Columbia Ave., Batesburg-Leesville). It's about 40 miles southwest of the statehouse, but many government workers find it well worth the trip for barbecued pork, beef, chicken, and ribs. Founded in 1969, Shealy's is well regarded statewide—and beyond. It bottles its own sauces, including the original mustard-based variety and a vinegar-and-pepper sauce.

What to buy

Stop by the **Governor's Mansion** (800 Richland St., Columbia), not only to see the building, but also to do a bit of shopping. A gift shop brims with products and crafts made in South Carolina. Included are hand-woven sweetgrass baskets, jewelry incorporating the state's signature palmetto tree design, beautifully sculpted pottery, and framed or unframed prints by local artists plus note cards and an array of jams and relishes.

What to do

Revolutionary War Field Days, Camden, first full weekend in November.
Iris Festival, Sumter, late May.
For more details about these festivals, please see page 186.

South Carolina Department of Parks, Recreation & Tourism
(888) 727-6453, (803) 734-1700
www.discoversouthcarolina.com

Lodging tips:

In Columbia, as in other state capitals, hoteliers cater to legislators and lobbyists with relatively upscale properties such as the **Embassy Suites Hotel Columbia-Greystone** (200 Stoneridge Dr.). In Camden, try the 10-room **Greenleaf Inn** (1308 Broad St.); in Sumter, **Magnolia House Bed and Breakfast** (230 Church St.). For details: Columbia Convention & Visitors Bureau, (803) 545-000, (800) 264-4484, www.columbiacvb.com.

Grand
Along the Strand

It's called the Grand Strand, the 60-mile stretch of ocean shore running from historic **Georgetown**, laid out by English colonists in 1730, to the North Carolina border. And grand it is. With wide, sandy Atlantic beaches and water warmed by the Gulf Stream, it appeals to golfers and birders, seafood lovers and nature lovers, anglers and shell collectors.

Georgetown, the state's third oldest city, lures history buffs. Surrounded by rivers and marshlands, it became the center of America's rice industry. Indigo, cotton, and lumber contributed to the city's wealth and spawned a rich plantation culture. Take a plantation boat tour with Cap'n Rod's Lowcountry Plantation Tours (711 Front St., Georgetown) or Captain Sandy's Plantation Tours (Front Street Harbor Walk, Georgetown). Also available from Georgetown: shell-collecting boat trips.

History lurks even in the region's fascination with the ancient game of golf. In 1927, the Ocean Forest Country Club (now Pine Lakes International Country Club) opened an 18-hole course. Today, more than 100 golf courses make the Grand Strand popular for golfing getaways, earning it the sobriquet "Seaside Golf Capital of the World" (although St. Andrews undoubtedly doesn't feel threatened). The Grand Strand attracts such notable course designers as Robert Trent Jones, Jack Nicklaus, and Pete Dye. Their signature courses, carved out of the Carolina Low Country, offer beauty as well as challenge, with magnificent live oaks, loblolly pines, and fluttering palmettos. Swept by ocean breezes, many of these elite, well-manicured courses border meandering waterways and wetlands teeming with wildlife.

The Grand Strand

Mural in Georgetown

One of the best-preserved beaches on the Grand Strand is protected by sand dunes and flanked by sea oats and loblolly pines in Huntington Beach State Park (16148 Ocean Hwy., Murrells Inlet). Diverse habitats range from fresh water lagoon to salt marsh, attracting marsh hens, snowy egrets, and great blue herons. More than 300 other bird species recorded in the park make it a premier birding site. Find exceptional wildlife viewing along hiking and interpretive trails and board-walks. The park incorporates historic Atalaya Castle, former winter home and studio of prominent sculptress Anna Hyatt Huntington and philanthropist husband Archer Milton Huntington.

Myrtle Beach State Park (4401 S. Kings Hwy.) draws visitors to its mile-long strand of sandy beach, fishing pier, and Coastal Appreciation Programs offering a chance to learn about whales, sharks, and sea turtles, and catch a crab and search for shells. This 312-acre oceanfront preserve is South Carolina's oldest state park, built by the Civilian Conservation Corps in the 1930s. Its Sculptured Oak Nature Trail provides a rare opportunity to see one of the last stands of maritime forest on the northern coast of South Carolina.

Arts lovers head for Brookgreen Gardens (1931 Brookgreen Dr., Murrells Inlet), containing the Huntington Sculpture Garden, which showcases more than 550 works of American sculpture. Brookgreen occupies the site of four former rice plantations purchased by the Huntingtons, converted into gardens, and opened to the public in 1932. Daily programs include garden strolls and a sculpture tour. Brookgreen's Low Country History and Wildlife Preserve contains several thousand acres of native plants and animals. Creek excursions and "Trekker" rides take visitors through three ecosystems and to various historic sites including a rice mill and remains of a Civil War fort.

Alligator Adventure (US 17 South, adjacent to Barefoot Landing in North Myrtle Beach), an expansive reptile park, displays hundreds of American alligators, giant Galapagos tortoises, West African dwarf croco-diles, mambas, pythons, boas, anacondas, and king cobras. Ripley's Aquarium (1110 Celebrity Circle, Myrtle Beach) is home to more than 6,000 fish.

Anglers will find eight fishing piers, surf-casting hot spots, and productive fishing in backwater creeks between Georgetown and Little River (where crabbing is great, too). Offshore, bottom-fishing excursions on head boats and deep-sea sport fishing in the Gulf Stream await.

Richard McDermott Miller's *Saint James Triad* at Brookgreen Gardens

Perhaps nothing better symbolizes the relaxed way of life of the coastal Low Country than Original Pawleys Rope Hammocks (10880 Ocean Hwy., Pawleys Island). Soft cotton-rope hammocks are made by hand, as they have been since 1889, when a local riverboat pilot designed the prototype. Visit the factory to watch workers (often, multigenerational families) weave more than a quarter-mile of white cotton rope into the sturdy and artistic pattern that makes the body of each hammock. This weave is then attached to a bentwood frame cut from seasoned Carolina red oak (the warp of which gives the hammock its comfortable sway) with traditional self-tightening nautical knots. As craftspersons weave, you may hear the lyrical Gullah dialect of the southern Low Country, which has its roots in West African languages and Elizabethan English.

Lodging tips:

With 72,400 accommodation units, the Myrtle Beach area offers a wide range of choices, from luxurious beach houses and roomy condos to quaint mom-and-pop motels. Included are a total of about 47,000 hotel and motel rooms. For details: Myrtle Beach Area Convention & Visitors Bureau, (843) 626-7444, (800) 356-3106, www.myrtlebeachinfo.com.

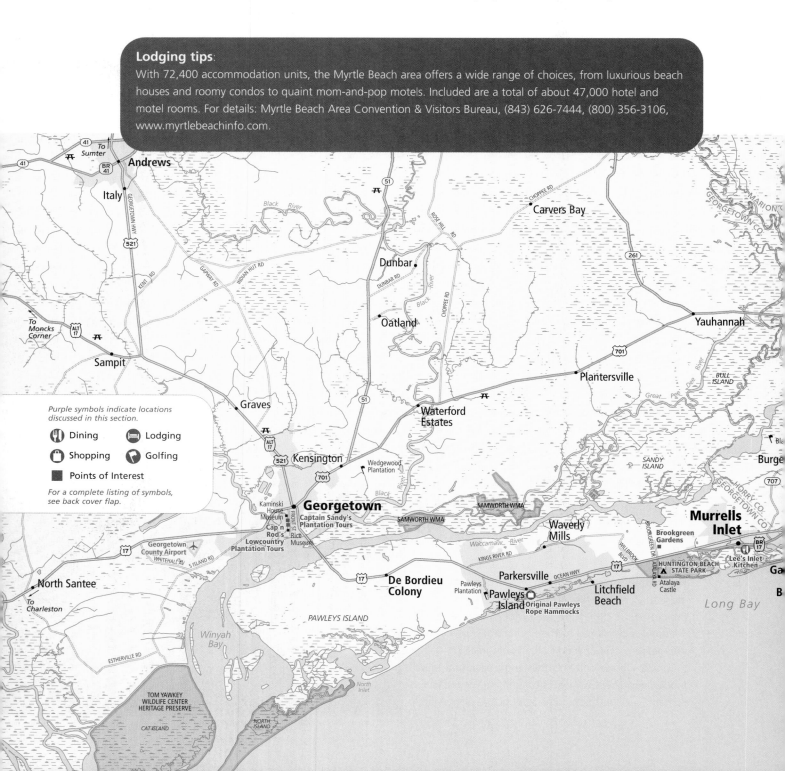

What to eat

Blending African, French, Spanish, and Caribbean culinary traditions, Low Country cuisine features such perennially popular dishes as shrimp Creole, oyster pie, baked fish, and barbecued ribs and chicken. So-called Calabash-style seafood refers to the lightly battered, deep-fried fish and shellfish found along the coastal Carolinas. Sample these at **Lee's Inlet Kitchen** at Murrells Inlet (4460 US Bus. 17), established in 1948, and at the **Sea Captain's House** on the oceanfront in Myrtle Beach.

What to buy

Find handcrafted hammocks at the factory retail outlet of **Original Pawleys Rope Hammocks** (see main story).

What to do

Myrtle Beach Sun Fun Festival, early June.

Atalaya Arts and Crafts Festival, Huntington Beach State Park, fourth weekend in September.

For more details about these festivals, please see page 186.

South Carolina Department of Parks, Recreation & Tourism (888) 727-6453, (803) 734-1700, www.discoversouthcarolina.com

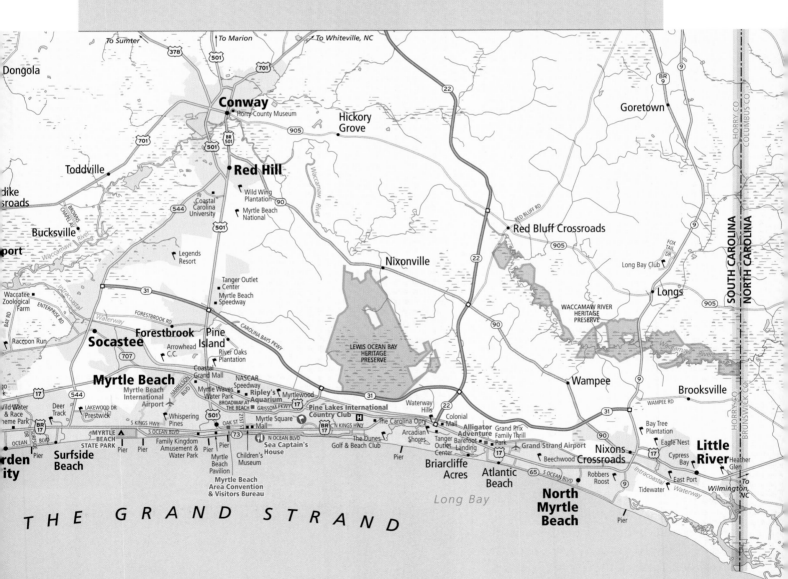

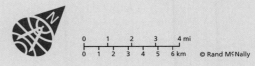

Sweet
Mountain Music

Mountain culture Smokies-style nowadays means more than banjos and down-in-the-holler lore. Visitors to this area can expect expertly interpreted outdoor rambles, urban nightlife, and artisanal shopping throughout the winding, wispy hills.

Blackberry Farm seems an unlikely find in rural East Tennessee. Nestled in a cove at **Walland**, just south of Knoxville on the border of Great Smoky Mountains National Park, this resort offers total elegance and incomparable comfort. It perennially appears on respected "best" lists and bears the whimsical sobriquet "Ritz in the Woods." Three and a half miles of paved trails wind through Blackberry Farm's 4,200 acres, as well as hundreds of miles of hiking paths. On nature walks, guides identify trees and plants and discuss their use as food, medicine, and dyes. Close to an overgrown trail leading up the mountain, you may find the prints of black bear, about 1,700 of which live in Great Smoky Mountains National Park.

For a customized interpretive hike or ramble, contact Just Get Outdoors (3340 E. Wearwood Dr., Sevierville), originated and operated by Liz Domingue, a trained naturalist and wildlife biologist. Whether you're interested in birds, wildflowers, trees, or simply enjoying mountain scenery and cultural history, you'll discover the remarkable diversity of plants and animals inhabiting the Smokies, just as renowned botanist and naturalist William Bartram did when visiting in 1775.

Also appealing—especially to photographers—is Great Smoky Mountains National Park's Cades Cove, where waterfalls, trout streams, abundant wildlife, and stunning mountain views offer a sample of the Smokies' offerings. More than a dozen hiking and horseback trails originate at Cades Cove. Access it via an 11-mile driving loop and discover historic pioneer farms and churches, a gristmill, barns, and log cabins. (On Wednesdays and Saturdays during peak season, the loop is restricted to bicyclists and hikers until 10 a.m.)

Clogging at the Tennessee Fall Homecoming

Patrick Sullivan's Steakhouse and Saloon in Knoxville's Historic Old City

Knoxville is a vibrant university town with dogwood-lined residential streets. In Historic Old City, a revitalized warehouse section, restored buildings more than a century old house cafés and coffee houses, antique shops and fashion boutiques, nightclubs and restaurants. Another historic downtown area with an eclectic mix of galleries, shops, and restaurants: Market Square. It is the hub of many special events, including "First Friday" (of every month), which features openings, shows, and exhibitions, plus food and drink. Every Saturday morning May-November the square hosts a farmers' market plying fresh organic and regional produce, flowers, herbs, and baked goods. Take a stroll through 200 years of Knoxville history alongside the Tennessee River. Volunteer Landing Park offers a one-mile paved walkway, with audio, text, and photographs chronicling early life in the river town.

The well-regarded Knoxville Zoo (3500 Knoxville Zoo Dr.) houses collections of big cats and gorillas, along with the elephants, giraffes, zebras, and elands that occupy the "Grasslands Africa!" exhibit. The zoo's preservation and breeding programs are internationally renowned. The Women's Basketball Hall of Fame (700 Hall of Fame Dr.) takes visitors on a journey from the ladylike game of the 1890s to the intensity of the modern locker room, where you can listen in on half-time talks with some of the country's top coaches. Interactive displays test your skills on the courts as you shoot hoops, race around the dribbling course, learn shooting skills, and measure your vertical leap. "The Huddle," another interactive display, puts you on the court during an actual NCAA game to hear what coaches say during time outs.

The Smokies are liberally sprinkled with artisan studios and galleries that play peek-a-boo with motorists winding around country backroads. But for sheer numbers, the **Pigeon Forge** area won't be outdone, with shopping at six outlet malls. Pigeon Forge is the home of Dollywood (1020 Dollywood Ln.), Dolly Parton's flamboyant theme park that stages country music on multiple stages (and features occasional appearances by Dolly herself). The park has plenty of rides, wet and dry, but its focus on local mountain culture and areas where you can watch mountain artisans at work appeals to adults, too.

For more mountain culture, travel to **Norris** to visit the Museum of Appalachia, tucked among picturesque peaks and quaint hollows. Its collection of more than 35 authentic log cabins and buildings includes the Tennessee home of Samuel Clemens's (Mark Twain) family. Corn, squash, beans, and tomatoes sprout in gardens enclosed by split-rail fences. Cattle, mules, sheep, and goats graze in pastures near a huge cantilever barn. Special events bring together country musicians to pick tunes on a porch, while quilters, potters, and broommakers work at their crafts and visitors sample fried apple pie and sassafras tea.

Clemens family home at the Museum of Appalachia

What to eat

Sample country cooking at Pigeon Forge's **Old Mill Restaurant** (3344 Butler St.) and **Pottery House Restaurant** (3341 Old Mill St.). Both are known for baked goods made from flour and cornmeal ground at the 1830 Old Mill. Diners at the Old Mill Restaurant favor biscuits, cornbread, and pastries along with chicken and dumplings, fried catfish, and pot roast with gravy. Specialties at Pottery House Restaurant include homemade soups, sandwiches made with a variety of fresh-baked breads, and made-from-scratch pastries.

What to buy

With close to 300 factory outlet stores, the Pigeon Forge region draws shopaholics. For original arts and crafts, visit **Old Mill Square**. Stop at a **Jim Gray Gallery** in Pigeon Forge or Gatlinburg to purchase a painting or print of a serene Smokies' landscape (perhaps of Cades Cove) as a lasting memory of your visit.

What to do

Dogwood Arts Festival, Knoxville, mid- to late April.

Tennessee Fall Homecoming, Museum of Appalachia, second full weekend in October.

For more details about these festivals, please see page 186.

Tennessee Department of Tourist Development
(800) 462-8366, (615) 741-2159, www.tnvacation.com

Lodging tips:

At the top of the luxury scale, you won't do better than at **Blackberry Farm**, dubbed the "Ritz in the Woods" (see main story). Another option is to rent a mountain "cabin"—a bit of a misnomer for lodgings that feature fireplaces, hot tubs, and fully equipped kitchens. In Pigeon Forge, **Hilton's Bluff** (2654 Valley Heights Dr.) is a 10-room bed-and-breakfast with scenic mountain views and rocking chairs from which to enjoy them. Knoxville has a wide selection of lodgings, including representatives of major budget and luxury chains. For details: Knoxville Tourism & Sports Corporation, (800) 727-8045, www.knoxville.org; Pigeon Forge Department of Tourism, (800) 251-9100, www.mypigeonforge.com.

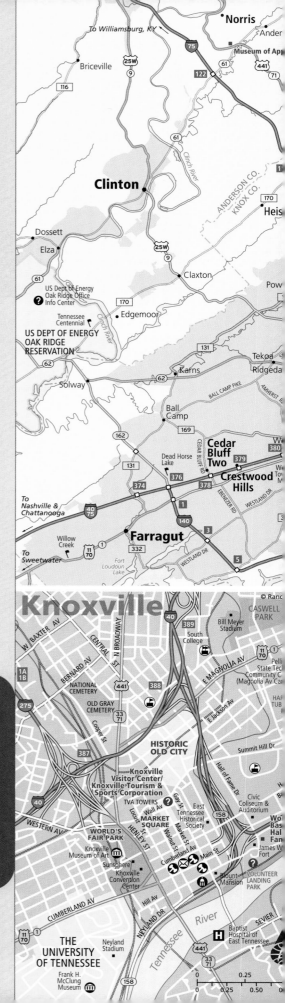

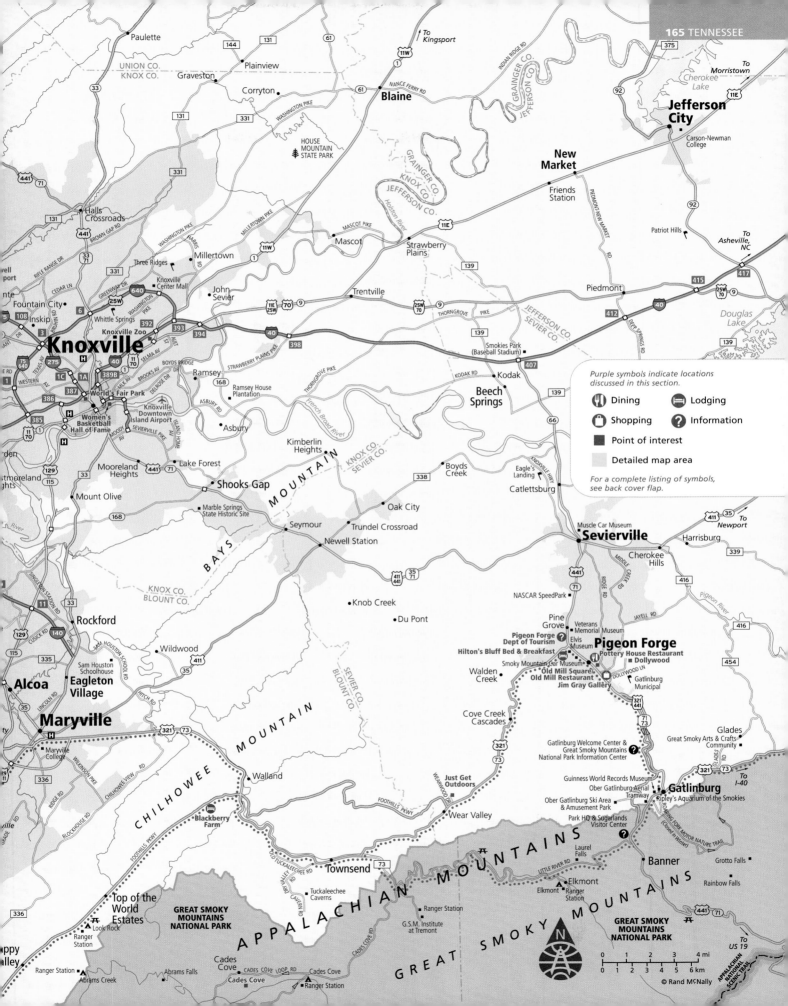

Paulette

Plainview

Graveston

144   131

131

61

To Kingsport

11W
1

Morristown   To
Cherokee
Lake

375

UNION CO.
KNOX CO.

33

Corryton

61

NANCE FERRY RD

WASHINGTON PIKE

Blaine

92   11E

**Jefferson
City**

Carson-Newman
College

441   71

131

331

331

Halls
Crossroads

BROWN GAP RD

441

131

WASHINGTON PIKE

Three Ridges

Millertown

MASCOT PIKE

Mascot

Strawberry
Plains

11E

139

**New
Market**

Friends
Station

PIEDMONT-NEW MARKET RD

92

Patriot Hills

To
Asheville,
NC

RIFLE RANGE DR
CEDAR LN

Knoxville
Center Mall

640

25W

MILLERTOWN PIKE

Holston River

Piedmont

415   417

33
71

108   6

Whittle Springs

392   393

John
Sever

1

11W

Trentville

11E/70
9

GRAINGER CO.
KNOX CO.

JEFFERSON CO.

11E

25W
70

9

THORNGROVE PIKE

139

JEFFERSON CO.
SEVIER CO.

412   40

25W
70   9

Douglas
Lake

Fountain City
Inskip

3

Knoxville

Knoxville Zoo

394

40

398

40

Smokies Park
(Baseball Stadium)

407

139

75
640   275

11
70

40

11
70

389B

World's Fair Park

Ramsey

168

STRAWBERRY PLAINS PIKE

Ramsey House
Plantation

THORNGROVE PIKE

KODAK RD

Kodak

66

139

WESTERN AV

386   387

Knoxville
Downtown
Island Airport

Asbury

French Broad River

**Beech
Springs**

11
70   1

Women's
Basketball
Hall of Fame

385

SEVIERVILLE PIKE

MOODY AV

Kimberlin
Heights

KNOX CO.
SEVIER CO.

Boyds
Creek

Eagle's
Landing

KNOXVILLE HWY

Catlettsburg

411   35
To
Newport

Mooreland
Heights

441   71

Lake Forest

Shooks Gap

BAYS   MOUNTAIN

338

Muscle Car Museum

Sevierville

Harrisburg

129
115

33

Mount Olive

Marble Springs
State Historic Site

168

Oak City

Cherokee
Hills

RIDGE RD

416

339

Seymour

Trundel Crossroad

Newell Station

NASCAR SpeedPark

MIDDLE CREEK RD

JAYELL RD

416

KNOX CO.
BLOUNT CO.

411
441

35
71

Pine
Grove

Veterans
Memorial Museum

Pigeon Forge
Dept of Tourism

Elvis
Museum

Pigeon River

11

SINGLETON STATION RD

33

Rockford

Knob Creek

Du Pont

Hilton's Bluff Bed & Breakfast

Smoky Mountain Car Museum

Pigeon Forge

Pottery House Restaurant
Dollywood

454

129

140

Wildwood

411

Walden
Creek

Old Mill Square
Old Mill Restaurant
Jim Gray Gallery

DOLLYWOOD LN

Gatlinburg
Municipal

115   335

35

SEVIER CO.
BLOUNT CO.

321
441

Alcoa

Sam Houston
Schoolhouse

**Eagleton
Village**

HITCH RD

Cove Creek
Cascades

71
73

Glades

Great Smoky Arts & Crafts
Community

Maryville

Maryville
College

321   73

Gatlinburg Welcome Center &
Great Smoky Mountains
National Park Information Center

321   73

WILKINSON PIKE

336

RIDGE RD

CHILHOWEE VIEW RD

Walland

Just Get
Outdoors

WEARWOOD DR

321
73

Guinness World Records Museum

Ober Gatlinburg Aerial
Tramway

Gatlinburg

To
I-40

Ober Gatlinburg Ski Area
& Amusement Park

Ripley's Aquarium of the Smokies

ROARING FORK MOTOR NATURE TRAIL
(Closed in Winter)

BLOCKHOUSE RD

CHILHOWEE   MOUNTAIN

FOOTHILLS PKWY

Wear Valley

Park HQ & Sugarlands
Visitor Center

APPALACHIAN   MOUNTAINS

Blackberry
Farm

OLD TUCKALEECHEE RD

Townsend   73

LITTLE RIVER RD

Laurel
Falls

Banner

Grotto Falls

Rainbow Falls

Top of the
World
Estates

Look Rock

Ranger
Station

DRY VALLEY RD

Tuckaleechee
Caverns

CADES COVE RD

Ranger Station

G.S.M. Institute
at Tremont

**GREAT SMOKY
MOUNTAINS
NATIONAL PARK**

Elkmont
Elkmont
Ranger
Station

**GREAT SMOKY
MOUNTAINS
NATIONAL PARK**

441   71

N

To
US 19

Ranger Station

Abrams Creek

Cades
Cove

CADES COVE LOOP RD   Cades Cove

Cades Cove

Ranger
Station

Abrams Falls

GREAT   SMOKY   MOUNTAINS

0   1   2   3   4 mi
0 1 2 3 4 5 6 km

© Rand McNally

APPALACHIAN SCENIC TRAIL

Memphis
Mud and Music

Named for its Egyptian sister city on the Nile, **Memphis** not only leads nationally in high-tech start-ups, but also houses some quirky venues. There's a hotel with marching ducks, the world's third-largest pyramid, and the A. Schwab Dry Goods Store (163 Beale St.), founded in 1876, with an inventory ranging from baseball caps, overalls, and American flags to incense and voodoo supplies.

An important Mississippi River port, Memphis is accessed by the scenic Great River Road that traces "Old Muddy" for much of its length. For incomparable views of the river, head for 1,642-acre Fort Pillow State Park (3122 Park Rd., Henning) on the Chickasaw Bluffs, site of a Civil War battle and a strategic fort mostly controlled by Union forces. A museum displays military artifacts and screens a video of the 1864 battle re-enactment. A designated wildlife observation area, the park is popular with bird watchers and marked with interpretive signs identifying species and habitat. Another popular preserve is Meeman-Shelby Forest State Park, a 13,467-acre park bordering the Mississippi River at Millington (910 Riddick Rd.). It largely comprises hardwood forests of large oak, cypress, and tupelo. The park contains two lakes, hiking trails, and a nature center offering canoe trips and pontoon boat rides.

Memphis supports an important music industry, styling itself both "Birthplace of Rock and Roll" and "Home of the Blues." Graceland, Elvis Presley's lavish estate (3734 Elvis Presley Blvd.), is among the five most visited homes in America. Visitors can tour the mansion, car museum (containing the singer's famed Cadillacs), and the "Lisa Marie," Elvis's custom jet (complete with gold bathroom fixtures). Another major draw: Sun Studio (706 Union Ave.), where on July 5, 1954, 19-year-old Elvis recorded "That's All Right," his first hit. Memphis remains an active recording center with more than two dozen studios and independent labels.

Beale Street storefront

Sun Studio

Explore colorful Beale Street, with its clutch of bars and clubs, theaters and eateries. In its heyday, Beale Street was choked with saloons, pawnshops, dance halls, and gambling dens. Now called the "Birthplace of the Blues," it's a major tourist draw, although many locals prefer a stretch of Madison in Midtown as an eating-and-drinking neighborhood.

Visitors who arrive in Memphis in the morning can make a breakfast stop at Arcade Restaurant (540 S. Main St.). It was Elvis's favorite diner, and hard-core fans can duplicate his favorite sandwich—peanut butter and banana on white bread. With Presley impersonators so thick on the ground in Memphis, you may also wonder if Elvis has left the building.

Another celebrity eatery, the Rendezvous (52 S. Second St.)—"the 'Vous" in local parlance—opened in 1948 in an alley across from the Peabody. Order a hefty slab of loin back ribs with mustard-based slaw and beans or perhaps pork shoulder sandwich. This bustling eatery was the setting for a scene in John Grisham's *The Firm*. The movie version of this legal thriller featured an exhilarating chase sequence with bad guys pursuing Tom Cruise on the monorail connecting downtown with Mud Island. Ride this tram to Mud Island River Park with its scale model of the lower Mississippi River and its tributaries. Five blocks long, it faithfully reproduces the lower river's every twist and turn. The Mississippi River Museum features 18 galleries of exhibits, including a section that traces the music about the river.

Mississippi River model at Mud Island River Park

A must stop, even if you don't stay there, is The Peabody Memphis (149 Union Ave.). The Peabody is the South's grand hotel, where William Faulkner and Charles Lindbergh were frequent visitors. Ducks occupy penthouse quarters and travel by elevator each morning to spend the day in the lobby fountain. A red carpet is rolled out, Sousa marches are piped in, and the ducks waddle between elevator and fountain to the vast amusement of the assembled crowd. The ceremony is reversed each evening.

Newer Memphis attractions include a $10 million expansion of the National Civil Rights Museum (450 Mulberry St.), site of Dr. Martin Luther King Jr.'s assassination. A China exhibit at the Memphis Zoo (2000 Prentiss Pl.) introduces a pair of giant pandas. The National Ornamental Metal Museum (374 Metal Museum Dr.), the nation's only museum devoted to the conservation and advancement of fine metalwork, also stages blues concerts on the bluffs.

Lodging Tips

Memphis offers the wide range of accommodations you'd expect in the state's largest city (18th largest in the nation). **The Peabody Memphis**, with its elegant lobby and famous ducks, is a fun and comfortable place to stay. Across from Graceland, Elvis Presley's **Heartbreak Hotel** (3677 Elvis Presley Blvd.) features suitably kitschy décor. For details: Memphis Convention & Visitors Bureau, (901) 543-5350, www.memphistravel.com.

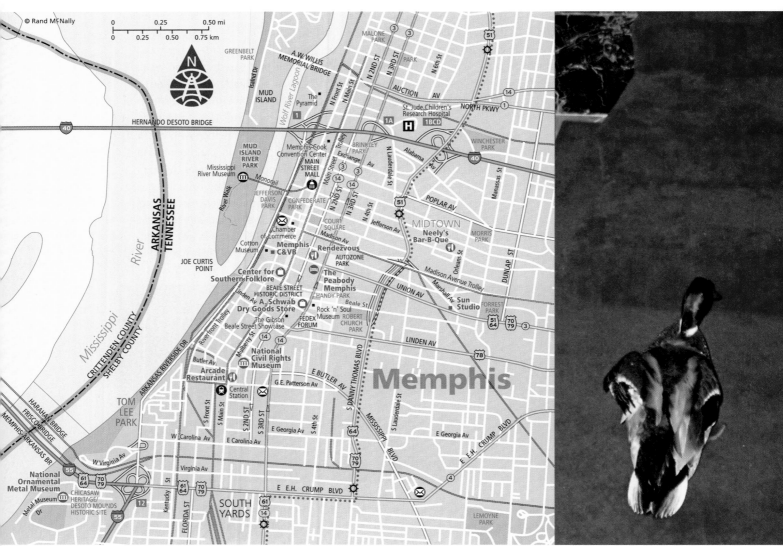

Duck on the red carpet of The Peabody Memphis hotel

What to eat

Many rib fanciers regard Memphis as the epicenter of barbecue (Kansas City notwithstanding). Here, barbecue essentially means pork ribs and shoulder and dry-rub preparation. The river town has about 100 bar-becue restaurants, including the famed **Rendezvous** (see main story). Other well-regarded barbeque eateries are **Neely's Bar-B-Que** (5700 Mount Moriah Rd.) and **Corky's Ribs & BBQ** (5259 Poplar Ave.). Sweet potato pancakes and smoky country ham are favorites at the **Arcade** restaurant (see main story).

What to buy

Visit the **Center for Southern Folklore** (119 S. Main in Pembroke Sq.) for a variety of regional folk art (including wearable art) and handicrafts, plus music videos. Look for funky suspenders at **A. Schwab** (163 Beale St.), along with baseball cards for that favorite nephew.

Purple symbols indicate locations discussed in this section.

- Dining
- Lodging
- Shopping
- Information
- Museum
- Point of interest
- Detailed map area

For a complete listing of symbols, see back cover flap.

© Rand McNally

What to do

Memphis in May,
May.

Beale Street Music Festival,
May.

For more details about these festivals, please see page 186.

Tennessee Department of Tourist Development
(800) 462-8366, (615) 741-2159, www.tnvacation.com

More Than
a Little Bit Country

First-time visitors to **Nashville** receive a sophisticated surprise. This city of half a million people boasts a score of sushi bars, a liberal sprinkling of art galleries and museums, and a modern skyline spiked with glass-and-steel high-rises.

Yet Nashville remains more than just a little bit country. Cowboy hats and hand-tooled boots are still de rigueur, and legions of recording companies, music publishers, and agents crowd famed "Music Row." Music—a $2 billion annual business in middle Tennessee—still attracts itinerant wannabes toting battered guitar cases and scribbled lyrics. On Music Row, tour historic RCA Studio B (316 Broadway), a cradle of the "Nashville Sound," where Hank Snow, Eddy Arnold, Willie Nelson, and Dolly Parton cut hit records. Elvis Presley recorded more than 200 songs at this, the city's oldest surviving recording studio. Gritty honky-tonks along Broadway such as Tootsie's Orchid Lounge (422 Broadway), where Patsy Cline once performed, and Robert's Western World (416 Broadway), which doubles as a bar and shoe store, draw tourists. Alongside sits Hatch Show Print Gallery (316 Broadway), one of America's oldest working letterpress print shops, producing distinctive theatrical handbills.

Ryman Auditorium (116 Fifth Ave. North) is the "Mother Church of Country Music." Every Saturday for 31 years, from 1943 to 1974, the music of the Grand Ole Opry rang out across America from its stage. Its acoustics are said to be second only to those of the Mormon Tabernacle, surpassing even Carnegie Hall. After lying dormant for about 20 years, this old brick tabernacle was restored in 1994 at a cost of $8.5 million. It contains the original rows of oak pews; restorers were instructed to remove chewing gum, but leave the nicks and scars. Although the Grand Ole Opry now makes its permanent home in a larger, modern facility northeast of town, it returns to limited engagements at Ryman. Tour this National Historic Landmark building and you can almost hear echoes of great country performers of the past. Showcases packed with memorabilia, framed photographs of huge crowds

The Stage honky-tonk on Broadway

standing in line for Opry tickets, and the old ticket booth, now a recording studio where you can cut your own CD, are among the attractions. A backstage tour takes visitors into performers' dressing rooms, including those of Minnie Pearl, Johnny Cash, and June Carter Cash. Guests can pose center stage with a prop guitar for a souvenir picture.

Johnny Cash exhibit at the Country Music Hall of Fame and Museum

In 2001, the Country Music Hall of Fame and Museum (222 Fifth Ave. South) acquired a colossal, $37-million new home. This storehouse of historic instruments and flamboyant costumes chronicles the history of the genre through archival film clips and sound bites and interactive displays. An incredible storehouse of memorabilia includes Patsy Cline's cowgirl outfit and Elvis Presley's 1960 "Solid Gold" Cadillac limousine.

Many regional attractions lie well beyond Nashville's downtown core. Pretty Williamson County, immediately south of Nashville, brims with historic places, notably **Franklin**, site of an important Civil War battle and of Carnton Plantation (1345 Carnton Ln., Franklin), a restored antebellum house and garden. It provides a setting for *The Widow of the South*, which made the 2005 *New York Times* bestseller list.

In the countryside west of Nashville sits the community of **Leiper's Fork**, where Puckett's Grocery and Restaurant (4142 Old Hillsboro Rd.) provides home-cooked meals and occasional casual country music performances. The surrounding area of horse farms and large estates evokes the horse country around Lexington, Kentucky. Here you'll find the pastoral Harpeth River, snaking and doubling back on itself. It's popular for float trips, with one of the best and easiest around the Narrows of Harpeth. A trip of 11 miles or so takes about three hours (with outfitting by a canoe livery aptly named Tip-A-Canoe).

A trio of outlying attractions reflects the wealth and gracious lifestyles of the Old South. Cheekwood Botanical Garden & Museum of Art (1200 Forrest Park Dr.) features artwork in the original 1932 Georgian mansion. The surrounding 55 acres include an interactive learning center, 10 botanical gardens, and the Woodland Scupture Trail. At The Hermitage, the elaborate mansion home of President Andrew Jackson (4580 Rachel's Ln., Hermitage), costumed interpreters detail how Jackson and his beloved wife Rachel raised their family and prospered in a two-story farmhouse.

The Hermitage, home of President Andrew Jackson

Dubbed "Queen of the Tennessee Plantations," Belle Meade Plantation (5025 Harding Rd.) is an 1853 Greek Revival mansion that was once internationally known as a Thoroughbred stud farm (the racehourse Seabiscuit traces its lineage to Belle Meade). Costumed guides conduct tours of the mansion, grounds, and colossal carriage house.

What to eat

"Meat and threes" is local argot for an entrée and three side dishes, usually served cafeteria-style. Entrées might include meatloaf, country-fried steak, fried or rotisserie chicken, pork chop, beef tips, and turkey and dressing. Vegetable sides run the gamut from turnip greens, creamed corn, mashed potatoes, and squash to green beans, macaroni and cheese, candied yams, and okra. **Swett's** (2725 Clifton Ave.) rules the genre, but other good spots include **Arnold's Country Kitchen** (605 8th Ave. South).

What to buy

Rhinestone-studded jeans and hand-tooled leather boots (with a side of music) at **Robert's Western World** (see main story). In West Nashville, **Crystal's for Fine Gifts** (4550 Harding Rd.), owned by country-western superstar Crystal Gayle, offers Waterford and Lalique crystal as well as porcelain by Lladró and Herend. The **Country Hall of Fame and Museum Store** carries more than 10,000 books, CDs, and tapes by country music artists.

What to do

CMA Music Festival,
June.

Dancing in the District,
weekly June–September.

For more details about these festivals, please see page 186.

Tennessee Department of Tourist Development
(800) 462-8366, (615) 741-2159, www.tnvacation.com

Lodging tips:

Within a short walk of major downtown attractions, including the **Country Music Hall of Fame**, **Ryman Auditorium**, and the Broadway honky-tonks, is the all-suite **Nashville Hilton Downtown**. For a splurge, the elegant downtown **Hermitage Hotel**, opened in 1910, is the state's only five-diamond property. For leaner budgets, the economy chains are well represented throughout the metropolitan area. For details: Nashville Convention & Visitors Bureau, (800) 657-6910, www.visitmusiccity.com.

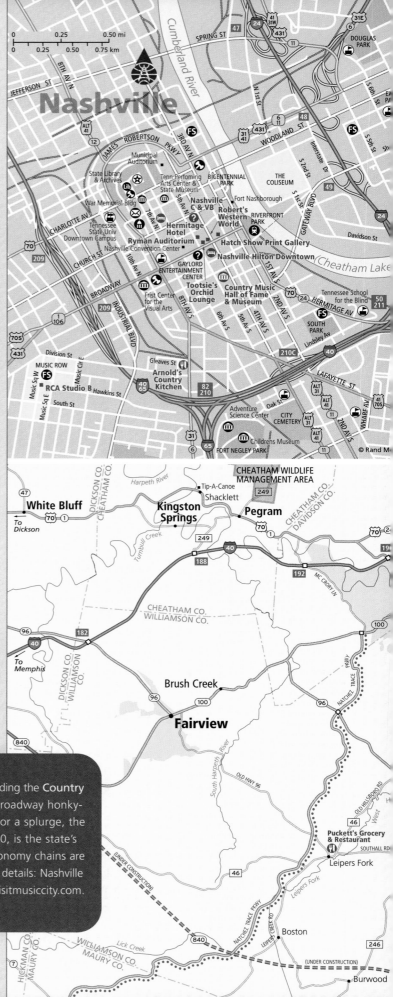

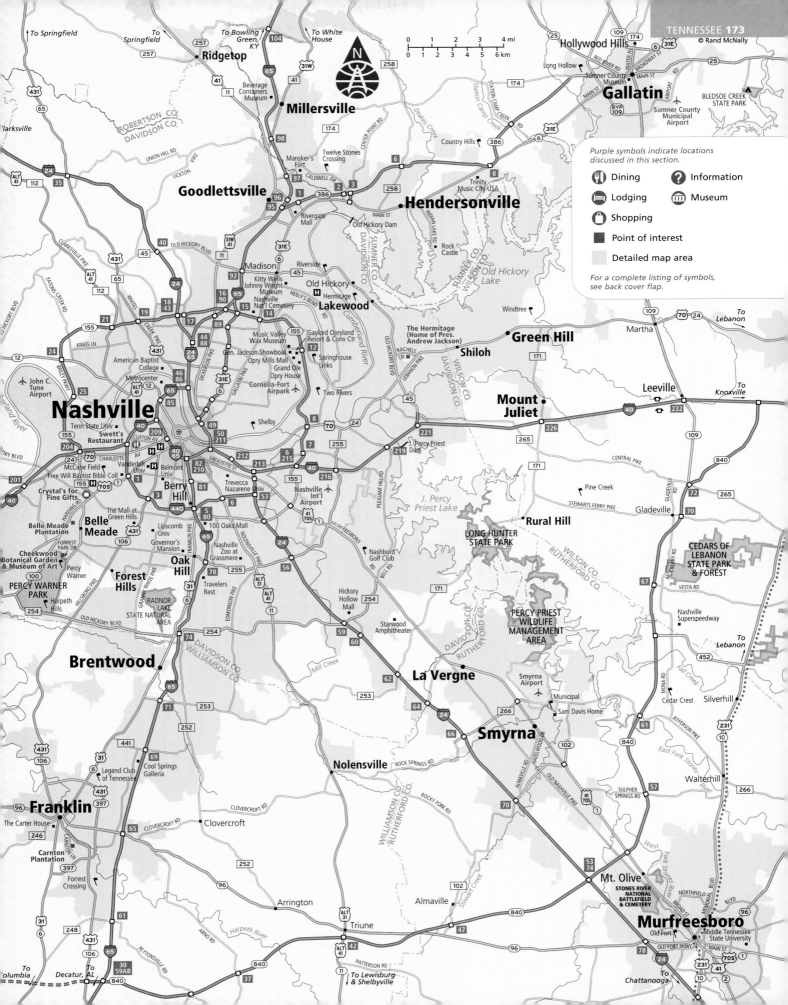

To Springfield
To Springfield
To Bowling Green, KY
To White House
Ridgetop
257
257
104
258
31W
65
41
Hollywood Hills
109
174
25
31E
174
Red River Rd
Broadway Ave
Main St
7
25
Springfield Pike
31E
Gallatin
Long Hollow
Sumner County Museum
Main St
BYP
109
Sumner County Municipal Airport
BLEDSOE CREEK STATE PARK
ROBERTSON CO.
DAVIDSON CO.
Beverage Containers Museum
11
41
Millersville
174
258
Station Camp Creek
31E
Clarksville
431
ALT
41
112
24
35
98
174
31E
Country Hills
386
8
Union Hill Rd
LICKTON
Mansker's Fort
Twelve Stones Crossing
6
Trinity Music City USA
Indian Lake Rd
WILSON CO.
SUMNER CO.
431
Goodlettsville
96
97
CALDWELL DR
3
258
Rock Castle
65
95
1
386
2
Rivergate Mall
MAIN ST
Hendersonville
Old Hickory Dam
40
31W
41
OLD HICKORY BLVD
11
31E
DAVIDSON CO.
SUMNER CO.
Old Hickory Lake

Purple symbols indicate locations
discussed in this section.

🍴 Dining   ❓ Information

🛏 Lodging   🏛 Museum

🛍 Shopping

⬛ Point of interest

▨ Detailed map area

For a complete listing of symbols,
see back cover flap.

Clarksville Pike
Eatons Creek Rd
431
45
112
65
Whites Creek Pike
92
Madison
6
Riverside
45
Kitty Wells Johnny Wright Museum
Old Hickory
H
Hermitage
Lakewood
Windtree
109
70
24
To Lebanon
Martha
21
16
90
15
14
Music Valley Wax Museum
155
Gaylord Opryland Resort & Conv Ctr
The Hermitage (Home of Pres. Andrew Jackson)
Green Hill
171
Kings Ln
18
43
17
44
88
89
Gen. Jackson Showboat
Opry Mills Mall
Grand Ole Opry House
Springhouse Links
RACHELS LN
Shiloh
24
65
American Baptist College
Metrocenter
46
86
DICKERSON PIKE
GALLATIN PIKE
Cornelia-Fort Airpark
Two Rivers
LEBANON PIKE
WILSON CO.
DAVIDSON CO.
Leeville
To Knoxville
John C. Tune Airport
25
ALT
12
65
85
31E
6
8
70
24
45
Mount Juliet
40
232
orland River
155
Nashville
209
Tenn State Univ
Swett's Restaurant
H
H
Shelby
221
226
265
109
CENTRAL PIKE
204
24
70
McCabe Field
Free Will Baptist Bible Coll
1
Vanderbilt Univ
82
210
212
213
49
50
211
7
255
6
215
219
J. Percy Priest Dam
171
Pine Creek
STEWARTS FERRY PIKE
Gladeville
72
265
201
155
H
70S
Crystal's for Fine Gifts
3
Belmont Univ
Berry Hill
81
Trevecca Nazarene Univ
53
Nashville Int'l Airport
40
216
J. Percy Priest Lake
70
40
Belle Meade Plantation
Belle Meade
431
106
Lipscomb Univ
Governor's Mansion
65
5
80
100 Oaks Mall
155
41
70S
1
MURFREESBORO PIKE
Nashboro Golf Club
BELL RD
LONG HUNTER STATE PARK
Rural Hill
CEDARS OF LEBANON STATE PARK & FOREST
Cheekwood Botanical Garden & Museum of Art
Percy Warner
Oak Hill
FRANKLIN PIKE
Nashville Zoo at Grassmere
56
Nashville Superspeedway
67
VESTA RD
100
Forest Hills
78
NOLENSVILLE PIKE
EDMONSON PIKE
24
WILSON CO.
RUTHERFORD CO.
PERCY WARNER PARK
Harpeth Hills
GRANNY WHITE PIKE
31
255
Travelers Rest
ALT
41
31
171
Hickory Hollow Mall
254
PERCY PRIEST WILDLIFE MANAGEMENT AREA
Nashville
254
RADNOR LAKE STATE NATURAL AREA
6
OLD HICKORY BLVD
11
Starwood Amphitheater
Silverhill
Cedar Crest
74
DAVIDSON CO.
WILLIAMSON CO.
59
60
La Vergne
Smyrna Airport
MONA RD
452
To Lebanon
Brentwood
65
62
Municipal
Sam Davis Home
ALMAVILLE RD
HAZELWOOD DR
OLD NASHVILLE PIKE
266
To Lebanon
71
253
64
24
102
840
East Fork Stones River
61
JEFFERSON PIKE
10
231
252
441
66
Smyrna
69
Cool Springs Galleria
SULPHER SPRINGS RD
57
Walterhill
31
6
Legend Club of Tennessee
252
Nolensville
ROCK SPRINGS RD
41
70S
1
266
Franklin
96
431
397
65
CLOVERCROFT RD
Clovercroft
ROCKY FORK RD
WILLIAMSON CO.
RUTHERFORD CO.
70
Stewart Creek
The Carter House
246
Carnton Plantation
397
Forrest Crossing
ARNO RD
96
252
102
Almaville
840
53
74
Mt. Olive
STONES RIVER NATIONAL BATTLEFIELD & CEMETERY
NORTHFIELD BLVD
MEMORIAL BLVD
31
61
248
Arrington
ALT
31
Triune
96
Old Fort
OLD FORT PKWY
Murfreesboro
BROAD ST
MAIN ST
70S
431
106
Harpeth River
ALT
31
42
PATTERSON RD
To Lewisburg & Shelbyville
47
Middle Tennessee State University
78
24
231
41
1
6
30
59AB
840
37
11
To Chattanooga
10
To Decatur, AL
To Columbia

0 1 2 3 4 mi
0 1 2 3 4 5 6 km

Hunt Country

Horse farms and undulating terrain are common throughout northern and central Virginia, but nowhere is equine culture more visible than among the hills of Loudoun and Fauquier counties between Washington Dulles International Airport and the Blue Ridge Mountains. Fox hunting in the colonial tradition, fortunes, and fine Thoroughbreds began to reign there in the early 20th century, and the traditions continue today. A cruise along the back roads and Virginia scenic byways in any season pampers the eye, as horse farms, stone fences, elegant manses, picturesque villages, and country inns come into view. Sampling the horsemania is easy; there's a year-round roster of equine events, such as steeplechase racing, dressage, and jumping.

Middleburg, generally considered the heart of Hunt Country, is where Jacqueline Kennedy Onassis used to indulge her love of riding. These days, it's celebrities like Robert Duvall or Willard Scott who might turn up in the Middleburg Safeway or at table in the Coach Stop restaurant (9 East Washington St.). It's easy to find all manner of essential Hunt Country tack, décor, and attire in shops like English Country Classics, Hunt Country Yarns, Thrill of the Hunt Antiques, The Tack Box, Cuppa Giddy Up (all on Washington and Federal streets). In the center of town, the historic Red Fox Inn (2 East Washington St.) retains its original 1728 stone structure, and its low-beamed ceilings, pewter dishes, and equestrian prints set the mood for light lunch dining on crab cakes, sandwiches, or grilled fish. Three rooms and suites on the inn's second floor have wide-plank floors, 18th-century furnishings, and fireplaces.

Deep inside Hunt Country, some of the region's wealthiest residents live and farm in tiny Upperville and its pastoral surroundings. Visitors who pause for sleep or repast at either Hunter's Head Tavern (9040 John Mosby Hwy., a.k.a. US 50) or 1763 Inn (10087 John Mosby Hwy./US 50) will sample the Old World ambience and possibly encounter some of the local denizens.

Steeplechase event at Glenwood Park, Middleburg

Red Fox Inn

Leesburg boasts more than 200 years of history as well, and its charming historic district streets are laden with boutiques, antique shops, and galleries housed in 18th- and 19th-century buildings. The city's edges are now fully entrenched suburbia; visitors can browse at Leesburg Corner Premium Outlets (241 Fort Evans Rd. NE), where more than 110 designer and national brand outlets offer savings. Just five miles west of Leesburg (via VA highways 7 and 9) lies enchanting Waterford Village, a National Historic Landmark, which was established by Pennsylvania Quakers in the 18th century. Many of the 90 or so 18th- and 19th-century village buildings remain, and farmland and pasture vistas add to the ambience. Pick up a self-guided walking tour map in the Waterford Foundation office at the corner of Main and Second streets.

Oatlands Plantation's 300 acres (20850 Oatlands Plantation Ln.) hold several points of interest, including a Federal-style-cum-Greek-Revival manse that dates to 1810. Its greenhouse is one of the oldest in America, and the gardens are worth a stroll. Now operated by the National Trust for Historic Preservation, Oatlands hosts many annual events, such as a garden fair in May and a Christmas tour in December.

Civil War sites compose part of the Hunt Country landscape. At nearby Manassas National Battlefield Park (Exit 47B off I-66; visitors center at 6511 Sudley Rd.), North and South fought two major battles at Bull Run in 1861 and 1862, including the war's first great conflict. A visitor's center presents historical background, and acres of rolling hills throughout the park invite hiking and walking. The region's most illustrious and notorious resident of the era: John Singleton Mosby, the famous Confederate raider known as the "gray ghost" who made life miserable for the Yankees. His legacy turns up often in the region, including the cemetery in Warrenton where he rests and such sites

as The Gray Ghost Vineyards & Winery (14706 Lee Hwy., Amissville). Mosby's namesake is just one of the wineries that pop up with regularity along byways and back roads of Hunt Country. The area is one of Virginia's top grape-growing regions. Soil conditions, temperate climate, and skilled winemakers all con-

Oatlands Plantation

tribute to the output. Tarara Winery (13648 Tarara Ln., Leesburg) devotes 50 of its 475 acres to grape products. Its 6,000-square-foot cave, tasting room, and miles of hiking trails invite picnicking and pursuit of tranquility. For those who wish to imbibe in the winery tasting rooms without reserve and ride the scenic byways in style, there's Reston Limousine Wine Tours. Riders can choose winery tour transport from among the company's buses, minibuses, and stretch limos.

Manassas offers more than Civil War history. Old Town Manassas (VA 28, downtown Manassas) is a great district to browse the galleries, shops, and museums, then have lunch. This was a vital railroad junction during the Civil War, and the railroad still passes through this part of the city.

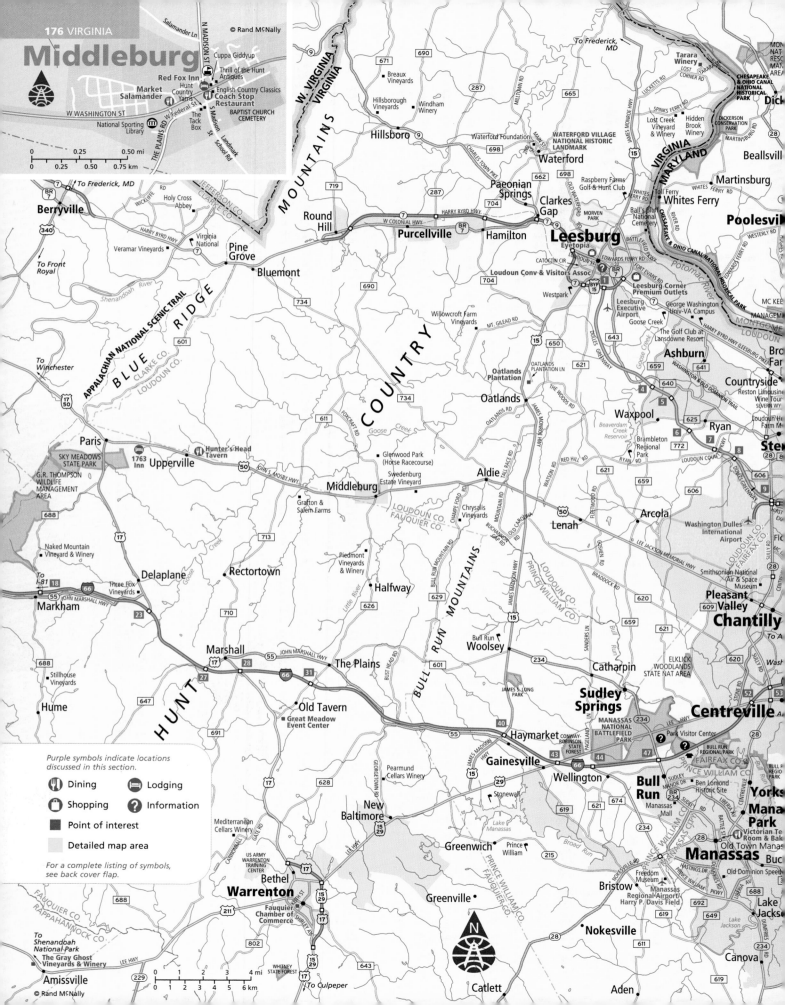

Middleburg

© Rand McNally

Salamander Ln
N Madison St

Cuppa Giddyup
Thrill of the Hunt Antiques
Red Fox Inn
Market Salamander
Hunt Country Yarns
English Country Classics
Coach Stop Restaurant
Baptist Church Cemetery
The Plains Rd
W Federal St
The Tack Box
S Madison St
Landmark School Rd
National Sporting Library
W Washington St

0   0.25   0.50 mi
0   0.25   0.50   0.75 km

Legend

Purple symbols indicate locations discussed in this section.

🍴 Dining   🛏 Lodging

🛍 Shopping   ❓ Information

■ Point of interest

Detailed map area

For a complete listing of symbols, see back cover flap.

What to eat

Traditional Virginia fare includes crab cakes and peanut soup. **Market Salamander** (200 W. Washington St., Middleburg) offers gourmet on the go, while the **Victorian Tea Room and Bakery** (9413 Battle St., Manassas) provides small treats and lunch for ladies in the midst of Old Town.

What to buy

Eyetopia in Leesburg (102 Loudon St. SW) has been called "Girl Heaven" for all ages, with premier accessories like funky handbags and handcrafted jewelry.

What to do

Virginia Gold Cup, Great Meadow Event Center, first Saturday in May.
Upperville Colt & Horse Show, Upperville, early June.
Waterford Homes Tour & Crafts Exhibit, Waterford, first weekend in October.

For more details about these festivals, please see page 186.

Virginia Tourism Corporation
(800) 321-3244, (800) 847-4882, www.virginia.org

Lodging tips:
National chain hotels, inns, and bed-and-breakfasts are plentiful throughout the region. For details: Loudoun Convention & Visitors Association, (800) 752-6118, www.visitloudoun.org; Fauquier Chamber of Commerce, www.fauquierchamber.org/visitors_guide/index.

Market Salamander cooking class

Valley
<u>Meandering</u>

The bucolic, historic Shenandoah Valley is not only one of Virginia's best destination gems, it's one of the most scenic regions in the eastern United States. Small towns and farms—some dating to the early 1700s—dot the landscape amid the Blue Ridge, Shenandoah, and Allegheny mountain ranges. Scotch-Irish and German immigrants built their farmhouses of stone there, and so some parts of the valley look like Pennsylvania. During the Civil War, the Shenandoah's rich farmland served Robert E. Lee's Army of Northern Virginia and saw several tragic wartime clashes. The 1965 film *Shenandoah*, starring Jimmy Stewart, immortalized the region in a story about a peace-loving family surrounded by conflicting forces.

Most visitors explore at least a portion of Shenandoah National Park atop the Blue Ridge Mountains. It offers riveting landscapes, hiking, train rides, and a section of the Maine-to-Georgia Appalachian Trail. Skyline Drive, one of America's most scenic routes, runs the full length of the park and connects with the Blue Ridge Parkway, which continues into North Carolina.

One of the best sections to explore in the valley, which extends 150 miles north-south from Winchester to the Natural Bridge, lies near the intersection of interstates 81 and 64. Settled well before the American Revolution, **Staunton** (pronounced Stan-ton) was a major junction for pioneers heading west. Valley pioneer history comes alive in the Frontier Culture Museum (1290 Richmond Rd.) just outside town, where several 17th-, 18th-, and 19th-century farms brought from Europe depict life in pre-Civil War Shenandoah. In the early 1800s, Staunton served as the eastern terminus of the Staunton-Parkersburg Turnpike (now US 250), a link between the valley and the Ohio River. The Central Virginia Railroad arrived in 1854, making the town even more of a regional center.

Step into Staunton's charming and compact historic downtown for arts encounters, a visual feast of

Sunrise at Shenandoah National Park

Charlottesville's historic Downtown Mall

restored architecture, and some shopping along Beverley Street and the Wharf District. Boutiques, galleries, and premier art emporia, such as the Frame Gallery (21 Market St.) and Sunspots Studios (202 W. Lewis St.), are often housed in restored warehouses and fine homes. Restaurants occupy some of the antique edifices, too. The Pullman Restaurant (36 Middlebrook Ave.) in the restored train station makes a great lunch or cocktail stop, while the Mill Street Grill (One Mill St.), inside a former flour mill building, serves up great ribs, steaks, and seafood. Some call the Dining Room (29 N. Augusta St.) the valley's best choice for fine dining.

Staunton's most famous home is the mid-19th-century Presbyterian Manse where the 28th U.S. president, Woodrow Wilson, was born in 1856. The Woodrow Wilson Presidential Library (18-24 N. Coalter St.) encompasses the home, boxwood gardens, research library, and gift shop, all of which characterize the president's connections to education, public service, and world peace.

The Blackfriars Playhouse (10 S. Market St.) constitutes reason enough for a Staunton stop. It's the world's only authentic re-creation of Shakespeare's original indoor theater, and has a year-round playbill of the Bard's creations done in the Elizabethan manner, as well as musical productions and other plays. If there isn't time to catch a performance, a guided tour of the theater enlightens visitors about theater in Shakespeare's day.

In **Harrisonburg**, a college town with deep roots in the agrarian valley, it's easy to find old-fashioned markets like Dayton Farmers Market (3105 John Wayland Hwy., a.k.a. VA 42) and Shenandoah Heritage Farmers Market on US 11. More country pleasures lie in Tutwiler's Virginia Country Store (124 S. Main St.), with all manner of Virginia-made items such as peanuts, wines, spices, spreads, pretzels, and the famous Route

11 Potato Chips. The Virginia Quilt Museum (301 S. Main St.) displays contemporary and antique pieces in a historic house.

It's not really a valley town, but because it's only 30 minutes east of Staunton, **Charlottesville** is worth a detour. This sophisticated small city was once hometown of presidents Thomas Jefferson and James Monroe. The legacies of both men, especially Jefferson, continues today on the University of Virginia campus, the university Jefferson founded. A visit to Jefferson's grand domed home, Monticello (VA 53, a.k.a. Thomas Jefferson Pkwy.), and its gardens deserves at least half

Monticello, home of Thomas Jefferson

a day. Monroe's much smaller home, Ash Lawn-Highland (1000 James Monroe Pkwy.), has a dramatic hilltop location for vantage on the rolling terrain both men knew and loved. Don't miss Charlottesville Historic Downtown Mall, the city's pedestrian mall chocked with 120 shops and 30 restaurants. One unique eatery popular with both town and gown people: the Hardware Store (316 E. Main St.). It offers light fare and a fully stocked bar amid old rolling ladders and stacks of oak drawers that once held all the hardware basics.

What to eat

Enjoy Route 11 Potato Chips in not just barbecue and dill pickle flavors, but also Mama Zuma's Green Chile Enchilada. Local stores such as **Tutwiler's Virginia Country Store** (see main story) carry the chips.

What to buy

Antique stops abound, along with farm markets, art galleries, and outlets for Virginia products such as wine, peanuts, and crafts. The **Dayton Farmer's Market** (see main story) draws enthusiastic crowds to more than 20 shops offering furniture, meats, locally created art, quilts, and specialty foods among its impressive array of goods.

What to do

Virginia Hot Glass Festival, Staunton, last Saturday and Sunday in April.

Virginia Festival of the Book, Charlottesville, third week in March.

For more details about these festivals, please see page 186.

Virginia Tourism Corporation
(800) 321-3244, (800) 847-4882, www.virginia.org

Lodging tips:

Headliners are Staunton's newly restored **Stonewall Jackson Hotel & Conference Center** (don't miss the working 1920s Wurlitzer in the lobby) at 24 S. Market St., and **Keswick Hall** near Charlottesville, a grand Italianate country estate (701 Club Dr., Keswick). National chains are plentiful in the region; so are inns and bed-and-breakfasts. **Belle Grae Inn** in Staunton (515 W. Frederick St.) is a wonderful Victorian base for local exploration. For details: Harrisonburg-Rockingham Chamber of Commerce, (540) 434-3862, www.hrchamber.org; Charlottesville-Albemarle County CVB, (434) 977-1783, www.charlottesville.org; Staunton-Augusta Visitor Center, (540) 332-3972, www.ci.staunton.va.us.

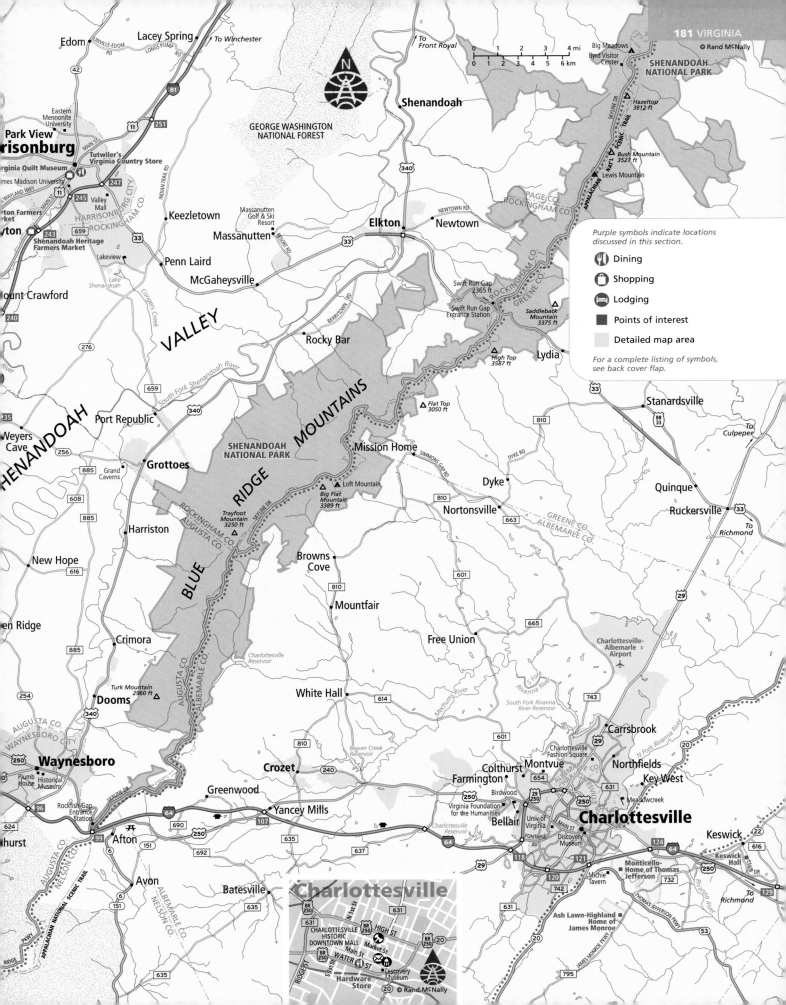

Edom
Lacey Spring
To Winchester
To Front Royal

Park View
rrisonburg
Eastern Mennonite University
Tutwiler's Virginia Country Store
Virginia Quilt Museum
James Madison University
Valley Mall
Shenandoah Heritage Farmers Market
rton Farmers Market
on
Mount Crawford

GEORGE WASHINGTON NATIONAL FOREST

Shenandoah

Big Meadows
Byrd Visitor Center

SHENANDOAH NATIONAL PARK

Hazeltop 3812 ft

Bush Mountain 3527 ft
Lewis Mountain

Keezletown
Massanutten Golf & Ski Resort
Massanutten
Penn Laird
McGaheysville

Elkton
Newtown

VALLEY

Rocky Bar

Swift Run Gap 2365 ft
Swift Run Gap Entrance Station

Saddleback Mountain 3375 ft

Lydia

High Top 3587 ft

Legend

Purple symbols indicate locations discussed in this section.

🍴 Dining
🛍 Shopping
🛏 Lodging
■ Points of interest
▨ Detailed map area

For a complete listing of symbols, see back cover flap.

Stanardsville
To Culpeper

Weyers Cave
HENANDOAH

Port Republic
South Fork Shenandoah River

SHENANDOAH NATIONAL PARK

Mission Home

Flat Top 3050 ft

Dyke

Quinque

Ruckersville
To Richmond

Grottoes
Grand Caverns

BLUE RIDGE MOUNTAINS

Loft Mountain

Nortonsville

GREENE CO. ALBEMARLE CO.

Harriston
Trayfoot Mountain 3250 ft
Big Flat Mountain 3389 ft

New Hope

Browns Cove

en Ridge

Mountfair

Free Union

Charlottesville-Albemarle Airport

Crimora

Charlottesville Reservoir

Turk Mountain 2960 ft
Dooms

White Hall

S Fork Rivanna River

South Fork Rivanna River Reservoir

Carrsbrook

Northfields

AUGUSTA CO. WAYNESBORO CITY

Beaver Creek Reservoir

Crozet

Colthurst
Montvue
Key West
Meadowcreek

Waynesboro
Plumb House
Historical Museum

Greenwood

Yancey Mills

Charlottesville Fashion Square

Farmington
Birdwood
Virginia Foundation for the Humanities
Bellair
Univ of Virginia

Charlottesville

Keswick

Rockfish Gap Entrance Station

Afton

Avon

Batesville

Discovery Museum

Monticello-Home of Thomas Jefferson
Michie Tavern

Keswick Hall
To Richmond

Ash Lawn-Highland Home of James Monroe

Charlottesville (inset map)

CHARLOTTESVILLE HISTORIC DOWNTOWN MALL
Market St
HIGH ST
Main St
WATER ST
Discovery Museum
Hardware Store
© Rand McNally

Northern
Neck

It lies near the nation's capital region, but Virginia's pristine Northern Neck region presents a tranquil contrast to urban centers. Laden with picturesque farming and fishing communities, waterfront homes, and historic sites, the peninsula between the Potomac and Rappahannock rivers stretches about 90 miles from **Fredericksburg** to the Chesapeake Bay. This, Virginia's oldest region, echoes the Commonwealth's earliest beginnings. Favorite sons George Washington and Robert E. Lee were born there, and visits to their home sites are among the area's draws. A good day trip onto the upper portions of the Neck begins at Fredericksburg and continues along VA 3 about 40 miles.

Founded in 1728, Fredericksburg brims with history, especially that of the Civil War era. The town lies equidistant (50 miles from each) between Washington, D.C. and Richmond, capital of the Confederacy, so it was the platform for several major battles. A must-see: Kenmore Plantation and Gardens (1201 Washington Ave.), one of Virginia's finest 18th-century houses and the home of Betty Fielding Lewis, sister of George Washington. Extensive plasterwork from the colonial era distinguishes the site. Though there's other history to explore, including battlefields and homes in which Washington, Jefferson, and other colonists domiciled, the city today has plenty more to explore. It's a good sleep-and-eat base for touring the Neck as well as the local historic district, which has an array of shops, restaurants, and attractions. Caroline Street, the center of the 40-block area of town that's preserved on the National Register Historic District, is a trove of shops for antiques and collectibles shoppers.

LibertyTown Arts Workshop (916 Liberty St.), a new enclave of 20 studios, 40 artists, a gallery, pottery school, and art classes venue, gives new creative vitality to a former plumbing supply building. First Friday events feature exhibit openings in downtown galleries from 6 to 9:30 p.m. and include refreshments and live music in some venues. Fredericksburg's most famous

Statue of Hugh Mercer, Fredericksburg

artist—past or present—is Gari Melchers. Belmont (224 Washington St.), the 27-acre hillside estate where he and his wife Corinne resided from 1916 until his death in 1932, overlooks the Rappahannock River. It contains not only his work, but others by Brueghel, Morisot, and Rodin. The estate and gardens contain a

Stratford Hall

formidable array of art treasures in the manor house and Melchers' studio, spectacular European antiques, and family heirlooms.

East from Fredericksburg on VA 3 is the way to the 550-acre George Washington Birthplace National Monument (1732 Popes Creek Rd., Colonial Bead), where the first president was born in 1732 on Pope's Creek Plantation. Young George spent the first three years of his life and some of his teen years on his father's farm. Though the original house was destroyed by fire, park rangers present a glimpse of 18th-century farm life. The peaceful riverside site includes the brick foundation of the original house and the Washington family cemetery where George's father, grandfather, and great-grandfather rest. A visitor's center introduces the site with a film and exhibits.

Commemorative marker at the Washington Family Burial Ground, George Washington Birthplace

About six miles along VA 3 lies the turn for Stratford Hall Plantation (485 Great House Rd., Stratford), the stunning Lee family plantation and mansion. This 1,600-acre operating farm contains what could be anointed the grandest historic house in the Commonwealth of Virginia. Situated high on bluffs overlooking the Potomac River, the 1720 Georgian mansion has an elegant interior, furnishings, and walls which seem to carry the voices of the great men who were born there and assumed vital roles in shaping a young America. Thomas Lee built the house, and he and wife Hannah reared two daughters and six sons there, including two signers of the Declaration of Independence (Richard Henry and Francis Lightfoot). Robert E. Lee was born and lived at Stratford until age four.

Along the way to both birthplace sites, Ingleside Plantation Vineyards & Winery (5872 Leedstown Rd., Oak Grove) offers tours, tastings, and good gift shop picking. There's scenic beauty, hiking, camping, cabins, fishing, boating, and swimming in Westmoreland State Park (1650 State Park Rd., Montross). Also in the vicinity: Westmoreland Berry Farm (1235 Berry Farm Ln., Oak Grove), where visitors can pick their own blueberries, raspberries, strawberries, blackberries, and apples or buy jams, jellies, and ice cream made with the farm's fruit. Soaring eagles, miles of woodland trails, and observation points abound in adjacent Voorhees Nature Preserve (next to Westmoreland Berry Farm) on the Rappahannock River. Oak Crest Vineyard & Winery (8215 Oak Crest Dr.) in King George has not only vino to taste and buy, but also a formidable gift shop laden with stained glass artifacts, pottery, gardens —and a woodland deck for picnicking.

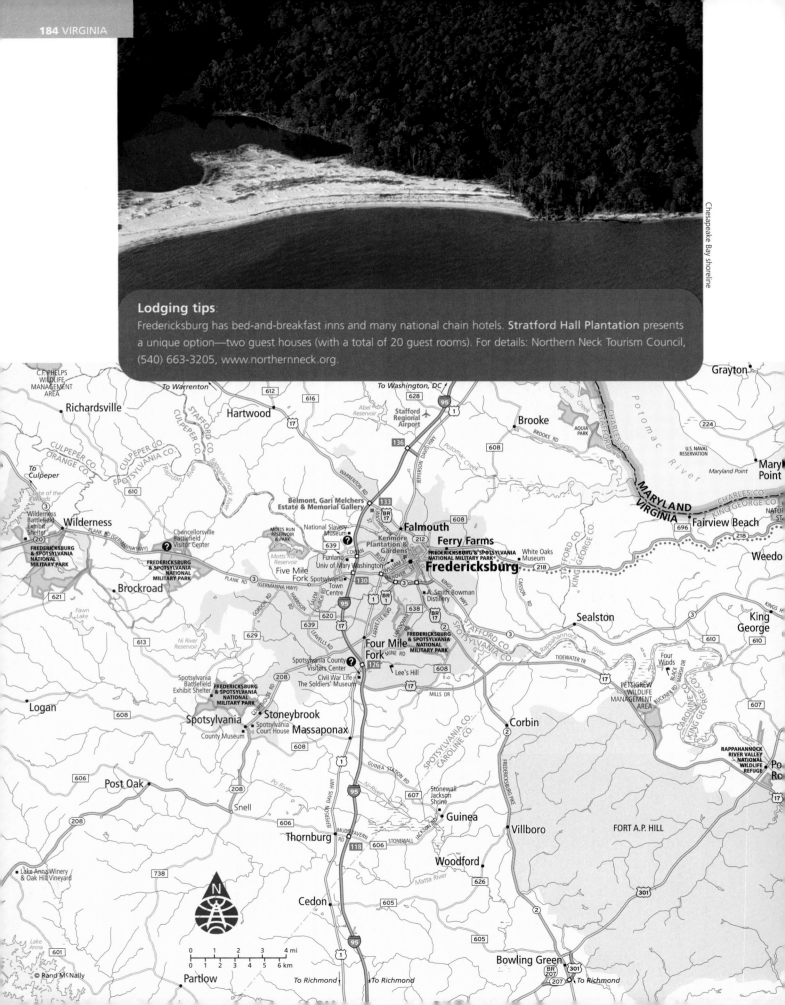

Chesapeake Bay shoreline

Lodging tips:

Fredericksburg has bed-and-breakfast inns and many national chain hotels. **Stratford Hall Plantation** presents a unique option—two guest houses (with a total of 20 guest rooms). For details: Northern Neck Tourism Council, (540) 663-3205, www.northernneck.org.

🍴 What to eat

The Stratford Hall Plantation's **Log Cabin Dining Room** is great for Virginia fare like ham and biscuits, crab soup, and crab cakes. The **Westmoreland Berry Farm** offers ice cream made from the farm's fruit.

🛍 What to buy

Pick up Virgina wine at Ingleside and Oak Crest vineyards along VA 3. Gift shops at Washington's birthplace, Stratford, Westmoreland Berry Farm, and wineries offer Virginia-made products, art, and crafts. Antiques, collectibles, and an array of original art including Civil War prints and paintings are plentiful in Fredericksburg galleries and shops.

❗ What to do

Rappahannock River Waterfowl Show, White Stone, third weekend in March.
For more details about this festival, please see page 186.

❓ *Virginia Tourism Corporation*
(800) 321-3244, (800) 847-4882, www.virginia.org

FESTIVAL INFORMATION

More details about all the festivals listed earlier in the book can be found on these pages. The festivals are grouped by state, then arranged alphabetically by title. Even more details about the festivals can be found by contacting state or local tourism boards.

ALABAMA

Annual National Shrimp Festival
(see page 66 for destination details)
On the public beach at the intersection of highways 59 and 182 in Gulf Shores, the Annual National Shrimp Festival serves up shrimp (fried, grilled, broiled, and steamed), along with other seafood and non-seafood dishes. Also on offer: arts, crafts, an international marketplace, a sand castle-building contest, live music, children's games, and activities. **Second full weekend in October**

Helen Keller Festival
(see page 74 for destination details)
In honor of America's "First Lady of Courage," the week-long Helen Keller Festival in Tuscumbia includes arts, crafts, entertainment, concerts, demonstrations, exhibits, tours of historic sites, puppet shows, and sports tournaments. Staged at Keller's birthplace, Ivy Green, the outdoor drama "The Miracle Worker" is held on weekends from early June through mid-July. **Third weekend in June**

Mullet Toss
(see page 66 for destination details)
The Flora-Bama Lounge (17401 Perdido Key Dr., Pensacola, Fla.) serves as the annual harbinger of spring with a Mullet Toss. Throwing a mullet across the state line from Alabama to Florida traditionally brings folks out to welcome spring and enjoy a great beach party with beer and live music. **Last full weekend in April**

Sidewalk Moving Picture Festival
(see page 70 for destination details)
In downtown Birmingham, the Sidewalk Moving Picture Festival draws filmmakers from across the country and around the world to screen their work. Food and live music are available. **September**

Vines & Waldrep City Stages
(see page 70 for destination details)
The three-day City Stages festival, held in downtown Birmingham, showcases musical talent, both local and national. Food and beverages are plentiful. **Father's Day weekend, June**

W.C. Handy Music Festival
(see page 74 for destination details)
Florence's W.C. Handy Music Festival—with athletic events, educational programs and exhibits, theater, riverside jazz, children's events, a parade, jam sessions, and a gala concert—salutes the musical heritage of the Florence native known as the "Father of the Blues." **Early August**

ARKANSAS

Annual Arkansas Folk Festival
(see page 86 for destination details)
The Annual Arkansas Folk Festival in Mountain View coincides with the blooming of dogwood trees. Musicians and music lovers flock to town, where festivities include a parade, an arts and crafts fair, and plenty of downhome food. **Third full weekend in April**

Hope Watermelon Festival
(see page 82 for destination details)
The Hope Watermelon Festival was one of Bill Clinton's favorite festivals when he was Arkansas's governor. View melons weighing 150-200 pounds; enjoy ice-cold slices of sweet, juicy melons; and look for tennis tournaments, tug-of-war competitions, clogging demonstrations, a dog show, and arts and crafts. **Second weekend in August**

Hot Springs Documentary Film Festival
(see page 82 for destination details)
The Hot Springs Documentary Film Festival draws special guest scholars, filmmakers, and celebrities who participate in forums and lectures. More than 90 films are screened, including the current year's Academy Award nominees in nonfiction categories. **Late October**

Jonquil Festival
(see page 78 for destination details)
The Jonquil Festival heralds the coming of spring with thousands of blooms to welcome craftspeople, entertainers, and visitors to Old Washington Historic State Park near Hope. Look for unique crafts and plenty of downhome cooking. **Mid-March**

Off the Beaten Path Studio Tour
(see page 86 for destination details)
For something a little different, join the fifth annual Off the Beaten Path Studio Tour, a free self-guided driving tour to the private studios of artists in and around Mountain View. **Third weekend in September**

FLORIDA

Florida Film Festival
(see page 90 for destination details)
The Florida Film Festival features top American independent and foreign films. It's held at the Enzian Theater in Maitland, central Florida's only full-time, not-for-profit alternative theater. **Late March or early April**

Florida Seafood Festival
(see page 94 for destination details)
The Florida Seafood Festival, a three-day event in Apalachicola's Battery Park, is the area's biggest. The festival features seafood, arts and crafts exhibits, and seafood-related events and displays. Events include oyster eating, oyster shucking, a parade, a 5K run, and the Blessing of the Fleet. **November**

FESTIVAL INFORMATION

FLORIDA *(continued)*

Forgotten Coast Chef Sampler
(see page 94 for destination details)

The Forgotten Coast Chef Sampler showcases chefs from the region sharing their most creative dishes at the historic Fort Coombs Armory in Apalachicola. **February**

Hemingway Days
(see page 98 for destination details)

For nearly a week, Key West residents and visitors from around the world celebrate the legacy of Ernest Hemingway, who called Key West home for almost 10 years. Short, stocky, bearded contestants vie for top billing at the look-alike competition. Lorian Hemingway, the writer's granddaughter, announces the winners of the eponymous short story contest. Other activities include a family boat-building workshop, a sailing regatta, a Caribbean street fair, and a fishing competition. **Third week in July**

Lower Keys Underwater Music Festival
(see page 98 for destination details)

Each July, the Lower Keys Underwater Music Festival highlights the bountiful biodiversity of the coral barrier reef here. As many as 600 divers and snorkelers typically gather each year for underwater musical highjinks at Looe Key Reef, part of North America's only living coral reef. **Early July**

Winter Park Sidewalk Art Festival
(see page 90 for destination details)

During the Winter Park Sidewalk Art Festival, about 300 artists show their work in Central Park. More than 350,000 visitors attend the three-day event; Friday afternoon or Sunday morning are best for art viewing. **Third weekend in March**

GEORGIA

Blessing of the Fleet
(see page 102 for destination details)

The Blessing of the Fleet takes place annually on Mother's Day at Brunswick's Mary Ross Park. **Mother's Day**

Bragg Jam Festival
(see page 110 for destination details)

Macon's Bragg Jam Festival salutes Macon brothers Braxx and Tate Bragg. Festival activities abound: arts, children's activities, live music, the River Bank Bash, and the Ocmulgee Adventure Race, a six- to 10-hour race with canoeing, trekking, cycling, and orienteering. **July**

Brunswick Stewbilee
(see page 102 for destination details)

Held in Brunswick's Mary Park, the Stewbilee showcases local culinary teams competing for honors. First-rate Brunswick stew, of course, is the highlight. **Second weekend in October**

Catfish Festival
(see page 102 for destination details)

Crispy southern-fried catfish and country music abound during the annual Catfish Festival, held in historic downtown Kingsland on Labor Day Weekend. The festival includes a parade, arts, crafts, food booths, antiques and collectibles, children's activities, a 5K run, and a bicycle ride. **Labor Day weekend**

International Cherry Blossom Festival
(see page 110 for destination details)

With more than 275,000 yoshino cherry trees blooming each March, Macon hosts the 10-day International Cherry Blossom Festival. The festival includes more than 500 events such as home tours, parades, concerts, fireworks, amusement rides, an air show, and a balloon fest. The festival's fine art program includes a fine art print, a porcelain series, and a festival pin. **March**

Polar Bear Swim
(see page 106 for destination details)

Chili and portable hot tubs comfort those who dip into Lake Lanier's frigid waters during early January's Polar Bear Swim. The lake also hosts Magical Nights of Lights (late November through early January) with Santa, amusement rides, and food. **Early January**

LOUISIANA

Audubon Spring Pilgrimage
(see page 114 for destination details)

Every March, the Audubon Spring Pilgrimage pays tribute to painter John James Audubon with tours of private homes, gardens, and churches with hosts dressed in period costumes of the 1820s. Candlelight tours of the historic district, graveyard tales, food, and festivities are offered throughout St. Francisville. **Third weekend in March**

Breaux Bridge Crawfish Festival
(see page 118 for destination details)

Held in Breaux Bridge's Parc Hardy, the Crawfish Festival celebrates the area's best-known crustacean with live music, cooking competitions, crawfish-eating contests, dancing lessons, and sometimes even crawfish races.
First full weekend in May

Mardi Gras
(see page 122 for destination details)

Mardi Gras is just as big in Shreveport-Bossier City as anywhere else in Louisiana. Local festivities include events and parades—even a pet parade. Mardi Gras dates depend on Easter; the celebration begins in mid-February and continues to Fat Tuesday, the day before Ash Wednesday and the beginning of Lent. **Mid-February**

FESTIVAL INFORMATION

MISSISSIPPI

Blue Suede Cruise
(see page 134 for destination details)

Classic cars and music from the '50s and '60s highlight Tupelo's Blue Suede Cruise, which features a parade of classic and antique cars, swap meet, and cruising tour of area attractions. **First weekend in May**

Elvis Presley Festival
(see page 134 for destination details)

The annual Elvis Presley Festival celebrates the legacy of Elvis, Tupelo's most famous native son, with live music, including gospel, blues, country, and rock 'n roll, a pet parade, and a weekend of fun, Elvis-inspired events.
First weekend in June

Great Mississippi River Balloon Race
(see page 130 for destination details)

The Great Mississippi River Balloon Race, a three-day event in Natchez, offers a balloon glow, early morning flights and barge drop, fireworks, and a sky filled with balloons. At the balloon glow, balloons inflate at dusk and, while tethered, light their burners in sync with others to create a glowing light show. **Third weekend in October**

Sunflower River Blues & Gospel Festival
(see page 126 for destination details)

The Sunflower River Blues & Gospel Festival is a three-day event jam-packed with live blues and gospel performances. Local musicians, the festival's focus, take the stage in venues around Clarksdale. **August**

Tunica Air Races and Air Show
(see page 126 for destination details)

The Tunica Air Races and Air Show features an entire week of activities such as aviation exhibits, qualifying air runs, and an incredible acrobatic air show. **First week in June**

NORTH CAROLINA

Mountain Dance and Folk Festival
(see page 138 for destination details)

The Mountain Dance and Folk Festival in downtown Asheville, the oldest of its kind in the nation, celebrates music indigenous to the Blue Ridge and Great Smoky mountains. The mountain music and clog dancing performed at the festival have evolved over 200 years, with roots in the Welsh, Irish, Scottish, and English cultures of the pioneers who settled there. **August**

North Carolina Azalea Festival
(see page 142 for destination details)

Wilmington's North Carolina Azalea Festival celebrates millions of pink, red, and white azaleas that bloom each spring along the Cape Fear coast. Festivities include a street fair, parade (with Southern belles), live entertainment, home and garden tours, a juried art show, a tent circus, a coin show, and a horse show. **First weekend in April**

Riverfest
(see page 142 for destination details)

A 28-year tradition, Wilmington's Riverfest celebrates life and culture on the Cape Fear River. A downtown street fair winds along the river with continuous live entertainment, a KidZone, arts and craft vendors, food, garden tours, a classic car show, and skateboard and wakeboard competitions.
First weekend in October

Tanglewood Festival of Lights
(see page 146 for destination details)

From storybook scenes to holiday themes, more than 100 displays with almost a million lights fill Winston-Salem's Tanglewood Park during the Tanglewood Festival of Lights, one of the largest and most spectacular light shows in the southeast. **Early November-January 1**

SOUTH CAROLINA

Atalaya Arts & Crafts Festival
(see page 158 for destination details)

Atalaya Castle, a National Historic Landmark in Huntington Beach State Park, hosts a prestigious annual juried arts and crafts festival every fall that attracts thousands of visitors.
Fourth weekend in September

Festival of Houses and Gardens
(see page 154 for destination details)

The Festival of Houses and Gardens features interior tours of 150 privately owned homes and gardens in 11 historic Charleston neighborhoods, plus oyster roasts at Drayton Hall Plantation. **Mid-March to mid-April**

Iris Festival
(see page 150 for destination details)

The Iris Festival in Sumter showcases thousands of irises in full bloom at Swan Lake Iris Gardens. Festival events include a food fair, flower shows, music, and a beauty pageant.
Late May

Myrtle Beach Sun Fun Festival
(see page 158 for destination details)

The Myrtle Beach Sun Fun Festival has been celebrated annually for more than 50 years. It features an air show, concerts, and other entertainment, plus parades and events such as sand sculpting, beach tennis, volleyball, and a 5K run and 5K walk. **Early June**

Revolutionary War Field Days
(see page 150 for destination details)

At the Revolutionary War Field Days, Revolutionary reenactors and living history interpreters pitch camp in Camden on grounds occupied by the British in 1780. Highlights include a daily skirmish, a court martial, a period fashion show, 18th-century tradesmen, and crafters selling period merchandise.
First full weekend in November

FESTIVAL INFORMATION

SOUTH CAROLINA *(continued)*

Spoleto Festival USA
(see page 154 for destination details)

The Spoleto Festival USA began in Charleston in 1977. Named after a similar event in Spoleto, Italy, this major citywide celebration includes dance; opera; theater; jazz; orchestral, chamber, and contemporary music; and literary and visual arts. **Late May and early June**

TENNESSEE

CMA Music Festival
(see page 170 for destination details)

The CMA Music Festival is a four-day musical event in downtown Nashville. Each year, 30,000 fans converge on "Music City" to hear approximately 200 artists perform more than 40 hours of live music. Daytime events include autograph signings, fishing and archery tournaments, and artists' Q&A sessions. **June**

Dancing in the District
(see page 170 for destination details)

At Dancing in the District, a weekly summer concert series held every Thursday night June–September, local, regional, and national bands perform on Nashville's downtown Riverfront Park stage. **June-September**

Dogwood Arts Festival
(see page 162 for destination details)

The Dogwood Arts Festival in Knoxville features visual arts, crafts, performing arts, photography, music, cook-offs, children's activities, public and private gardens on display, and tours of dogwood trails. The event kicks off with the Festival on Market Square, with various arts and crafts shows, nature tours, musical events, and a parade through downtown Knoxville. **Mid- to late April**

Memphis in May
(see page 166 for destination details)

The month-long Memphis in May celebration salutes a different country each year with cultural presentations, sporting events, and concerts. It includes an annual international barbecue cook-off and the Beale Street Music Festival. **May**

Beale Street Music Festival
(see page 166 for destination details)

Held in tandem with the Memphis in May celebration, the Beale Street Music Festival draws dozens of performers and acts to several stages in Tom Lee Park. **Early May**

Tennessee Fall Homecoming
(see page 162 for destination details)

During the four-day Tennessee Fall Homecoming, held at the Museum of Appalachia near Norris, more than 400 old-time musicians, singers, craftspeople, and artisans celebrate Appalachian culture and heritage. Musicians occupy four stages continuously while demonstrators work on mountain activities such as boiling molasses and sawmilling. **Second weekend in October**

VIRGINIA

Rappahannock River Waterfowl Show
(see page 178 for destination details)

Artists, carvers, decoy makers, sculptors, and jewelry makers from as far away as Vermont and Florida converge upon White Stone to display their creations, all of which feature local waterfowl. Many items are for purchase; all are for browsing enjoyment. **Third weekend in March**

Upperville Colt & Horse Show
(see page 174 for destination details)

The Upperville Colt & Horse Show, first held in 1853, ranks as the nation's oldest horse show. For seven days kids, internationally famous riders, and everyone else strut their stuff on ponies and champions. **Early June**

Virginia Festival of the Book
(see page 182 for destination details)

Nationally known authors such as Alexander McCall Smith participate in Charlottesville's Virginia Festival of the Book. Along with readings, programs have included bookbinding workshops, children's storytelling, and panels about running your own book clubs. **Third week in March**

Virginia Gold Cup
(see page 174 for destination details)

Watching the upper-crust attendees at the Virginia Gold Cup is as much fun as watching the horses. This premier steeplechase event is held at the Great Meadow Event Center (Fauquier County). **First Saturday in May**

Virginia Hot Glass Festival
(see page 182 for destination details)

Held during Staunton's Victorian Festival, the Virginia Hot Glass Festival at Sunspot Studios features glassblowing demonstrations by local artists in addition to bead making and sand casting. Visitors may purchase pieces. **Last Saturday and Sunday in April**

Waterford Homes Tour & Crafts Exhibit
(see page 174 for destination details)

Every October Waterford closes its streets to cars for the Waterford Homes Tour & Crafts Exhibit. This event draws thousands of visitors for old-fashioned family fun, musical entertainment, Civil War reenactments, regional food, and crafts. **First weekend in October**

A Drive through the Deep South

The rolling landscape of the Cumberland Plateau and the long ridges and valleys of the southernmost Appalachians provide the setting for this Best of the Road™ trip. The route stretches from Birmingham to Huntsville to Chattanooga. Along the way travelers find Civil War battlefields to visit, caves to explore, and great spots for boating, bird-watching, hiking, and mountain biking. Topping it all off: the down-to-earth friendliness of the people who call this area home.

Among the dominant features of Birmingham's skyline as seen from Vulcan Park are the massive silo-shaped blast furnaces and tall smokestacks of Sloss Furnaces. The furnaces closed in 1971, but the site has been preserved as Sloss Furnaces National Historic Landmark. Guides explain the workings of the blast furnaces and point out highlights such as an underground railroad line and a vintage steam shovel. The grounds also include some of the original "shotgun shacks" built to house workers and their families.

A short distance from downtown lies the leafy Forest Park neighborhood, home to a funky gallery called Naked Art. "Naked" in the name refers to a lack of pretense. Owner Veronique Vanblaere, a native of Belgium, believes that art should be fun, functional, and affordable. Her offerings include lamps made from recycled materials, colorful handbags made entirely of duct tape, and terra-cotta planters with inlaid mosaics. Most of the pieces come from local artists.

Leaving Birmingham, the route heads due north to Cullman, home to one of the best-known dining spots in Alabama. The All Steak Restaurant, a fixture since 1938, serves a variety of mouth-watering steaks. You don't have to be a steak-lover to enjoy a meal at the All Steak: the menu also includes excellent seafood dishes such as blackened snapper fillet and coconut fried shrimp as well as chicken and pasta. But what keeps customers coming back are the famous orange rolls. These delicious pastries—sort of like orange-flavored cinnamon rolls—arrive warm with every meal.

Hurricane Creek Park/William "Buddy" Rodgers Natural Area, about eight miles north of Cullman, is a 67-acre natural area highlighted by a 500-foot-deep gorge, waterfalls, steep cliffs, and dramatic rock formations. Several miles of hiking trails wind up, down, and around the gorge, crossing and re-crossing the Hurricane Creek via stepping stones and a swinging bridge. For mountain bikers, the park offers easy-to-moderate wide-track trails and technical single-track trails. Birders might spot wild turkeys, little blue herons, turkey vultures, and any of 50 other species.

Cumberland Plateau, Tennessee

Burritt on the Mountain

About 10 miles beyond the park sits the town of Hartselle. The downtown area, with its well-preserved brick buildings, brick sidewalks, and old-fashioned awnings, looks much as it did in 1926. Today, most visitors come looking for antiques. More than 30 antiques and specialty shops, with names like The Dowry Chest and Spinning Wheel Antiques, line Main and Railroad Streets.

A few miles east of Decatur lies Mooresville, Alabama's oldest incorporated town. It retains the look and feel of a 19th-century town, with tall cedars and magnolias shading streets lined with white picket fences and handsome Federal-style homes. The best way to see the town is to pick up a guidebook at the tiny 1840 post office and stroll around on foot. (The homes are private residences and not open to the public.)

The route continues eastward to Huntsville, a prosperous city filled with great things to see and do—most notably, the U.S. Space and Rocket Center, which exhibits an Apollo capsule and a full-size model of a space shuttle. Visitors to Huntsville will also find an excellent children's museum, an expansive and kid-friendly botanic garden, many antebellum homes, and a historic district called Alabama Constitution Village. Somewhat less well-known: Burritt on the Mountain, a park that overlooks the city from the domed summit of Roundtop Mountain. The park's centerpiece is the X-shaped mansion of physician and inventor Dr. William Burritt, which features period furnishings and historical exhibits. Adjacent to the mansion is the Historic Park, a collection of 19th-century Alabama farmsteads. Barnyard animals roam the grounds, heirloom crops grow in small plots, and costumed interpreters demonstrate period farming techniques and crafts.

One of the most interesting places to shop in the Huntsville area is located near Brownsboro on the east side of Monte Sano. Interior Marketplace contains some 35 shops, boutiques, and galleries operated by independent artisans and merchants. Shoppers can browse for everything from furniture, rugs, and lighting to clothing, candles, and gifts. At Cyn Shea's Garden Café, specialties include a Vermont maple salad, a Cajun grilled chicken salad sandwich, and fresh tomato and caper Chilean sea bass.

Huntsville Museum of Art

The limestone that underlies much of northern Alabama is a Swiss cheese of caves, underground river channels, and sinkholes. One of the most impressive caves lies below Gunter's Mountain between Huntsville and Scottsboro. Cathedral Caverns takes its name from a cluster of stalagmites that an early visitor described as a great cathedral. Walking tours take visitors three-quarters of a mile into the cave as guides point out highlights such as a massive stalagmite and a stalactite formation resembling a frozen waterfall. The cave's entrance gapes 126 feet wide and 25 feet high beneath a thin ledge of rock. *(continued)*

When airline passengers lose or fail to claim their baggage, it often ends up in the Unclaimed Baggage Center in Scottsboro. This unique outlet buys some 500,000 pieces of lost and unclaimed baggage each year, then sifts out the good stuff and resells it, often at bargain prices. The Unclaimed Baggage Center ranks as one of Alabama's most popular attractions, drawing roughly one million visitors each year.

Crossing into Tennessee, the route heads east to Chattanooga. Located along a bend in the Tennessee River, the city boasts a newly revitalized riverfront. Highlights of the downtown area include the Creative Discovery Museum for children, the historic Chattanooga Choo-Choo train station, an IMAX theater, and the Tennessee Aquarium, one of the largest freshwater aquariums in the world.

Another great area to explore is the Bluff View Art District. This charming neighborhood of museums, galleries, studios, bed-and-breakfasts, and cafés sits atop a limestone bluff along the Tennessee River just a short walk from downtown Chattanooga. Its best-known attraction is the Hunter Museum of American Art, which houses a large and highly regarded collection of paintings, sculpture, furniture, and glass. Across the street, the humbler Houston Museum of Decorative Art displays antique glass, china, and furniture from the 18th and 19th centuries. After rambling around the district, many visitors head to Rembrandt's Coffee House, a European-style café offering fresh pastries, homemade chocolates, and a spacious garden patio.

Lookout Mountain, Chattanooga's most famous natural landmark, looms over the southern edge of the city. At its base sits the St. Elmo National Historic District, which encompasses more than 600 properties listed on the National Historic Register. After exploring the district, visitors can grab a bite to eat at Mojo Burrito. This popular little restaurant allows diners to build their own burritos, choosing from a list of 15 or so fillings.

Lookout Mountain Incline Railway provides the most thrilling way to reach the top of the mountain. Built in 1895, the railway has the distinction of being the steepest passenger incline railway in the world: Near the top, the grade becomes almost vertical. Glass-roofed cars allow maximum enjoyment of the panorama that unfolds during the 2,000-foot climb, which takes about eight minutes.

Point Park, a few blocks' walk from the incline's mountaintop station and part of Chickamauga and Chattanooga National Military Park, preserves the site of a famous Civil War encounter known as the "Battle above the Clouds." Plaques, monuments, and a small museum tell the story of the battle and the events leading up to it.

This tranquil park marks the endpoint of Lookout Mountain and a long line of ridges that stretches all the way back to Red Mountain and Birmingham, where this trip began. ●

Point Park

Unexpected
Arkansas

This trip starts in northwestern Arkansas in Eureka Springs, a laid-back hamlet wedged between limestone formations in the Ozarks. It's famous for its historic district of original Victorian buildings and its penchant for music—this town hosts a bluegrass festival and Opera in the Ozarks. The easiest way to see the sights is to hop on and off the Eureka Springs Trolley. The Red Route takes visitors by landmarks like the historic Crescent Hotel & Spa, many of the new spas, neighborhood boutiques such as Frog Fantasies, and most of the town's bed-and-breakfasts.

The sign on the door of Frog Fantasies says it all: A frogs-only gift shop. Frog Fantasies is also part museum. The museum area exhibits a private collection of frog figures in excess of 8,000 pieces. The shop sells frog-themed merchandise from salt shakers to jewelry boxes and earrings to put inside.

Up the hill is the Mount Victoria B&B, owned by an antique dealer who operates a shop on the first floor. Though the furnishings are antique, the décor is not over-the-top frou-frou. Guests can help themselves to breakfast buffets on the landings, dine in their rooms, or take a plate to the veranda and watch the world wake up. The kitchen specialty: blueberry muffin crowns made from berries hand-picked at nearby Drake's Farm. "Are you left- or right-handed?" usually isn't asked at a u-pick farm, but it is at Drake's. Raspberry pickers are issued a glove for the "hold-back" hand, the one that holds back the prickly branches while the other hand picks the berries.

(continued)

Historic downtown Eureka Springs

The drive to Bentonville is full of switchbacks so tight that the locals say you can see your tail lights as you make a turn. When the road does stretch out, the intermittent vistas of the valley provide spectacular photo opportunities. Bentonville has a town square that looks as if it's straight out of New England. US 71 toward Fort Smith has been designated a scenic drive by a number of organizations. It isn't often that a major highway is considered scenic, but looking out at the Ozark National Forest that shoulders the big sky along this route, it's easy to understand why this one has been so honored.

First stop in Fort Smith: the Fort Smith Convention and Visitors Center, which is located in the old Riverfront Hotel that doubled as a bordello until 1904. Locals always called the hotel "Miss Laura's," and the name has stuck. Restored in 1973, the two-story clapboard building with mansard roof represents the only bordello on the National Registry of Historic Places. It also hosts Miss Laura's Players, a theatrical group that presents a musical production about the story of Miss Laura, Fort Smith, and its role on the American frontier.

Perhaps one of Fort Smith's most famous residents was Judge Isaac C. Parker, the "Hanging Judge." During his 21 years on the bench, he sentenced 160 men to hang. The Fort Smith National Historic site includes his courthouse. On tours, visitors can walk inside the early basement jail once considered so horrid it was called "Hell on the Border," referring to its location at the last stop before Indian Territory. Just outside the court-house stands a reconstruction of the gallows.

Fort Smith National Historic Site

On the way back toward US 71, a drive through the Belle Grove Historic District with its unique residences gives a peek at 130 years of varying architectural home styles. The district was named to the National Register of Historic Places in the early 1970s.

At the junction of US 270, roadside stands selling souvenir t-shirts, flags, and concrete statuary greet you as you turn toward the Ouachita Mountains.

The Ouachita is the only mountain range in the United States that runs east to west. The forest that engulfs it encompasses abundant animal and plant life. With creeks, rivers, and Lake Ouachita, outdoor activities abound. The drive through the forest is pep-pered with small populated areas anchored by camp-ing and canoe outfitters, and RV parks. In this area of Arkansas, fishing for stripers is rivaled only by digging for quartz or crystal. If digging doesn't appeal, try one of the many rock shops that appear all the way through the forest and in downtown Hot Springs.

Hot Springs owes its 47 mineral springs to the moun-tains, especially Hot Springs Mountain, from beneath which bubble up nearly a million gallons of water each day. Its temperature? 143° F. For decades the warmth of the water and its reputed cures brought people to

Lake Hamilton near Hot Springs

Arkansas from all over the world. It still does. The water also brings people to the downtown area with milk jugs and other containers to fetch mineral-rich drinking water from free public fountains. "Taking the waters" is still the most popular thing to do in town. Today most of the spas are associated with hotels, like the legendary Arlington Resort Hotel, circa 1875, and its sister hotel, the Majestic, both in the downtown area.

A short drive out of town leads to Lake Hamilton, a hot spot for jet and water skiing, swimming, and houseboating. Garvan Woodland Gardens, one of the few woodland gardens in the country, lies on a 210-acre peninsula in Lake Hamilton. Garvan is considered Arkansas' botanical garden. Visitors can ride a golf cart or stretch their legs along the many walkways. The plantings provide spectacular color within the woodland setting replete with streams, waterfalls, and all those wonderful trees.

Like most of the highways in Arkansas, US 70 and 67 have their share of hardwoods; this time the route they border leads to the state capital, Little Rock.

Little Rock has a five-star museum dedicated to a native son, five-star General Douglas MacArthur, and the newest presidential library in the country, the William J. Clinton Presidential Center.

Located on 30 acres along the south bank of the Arkansas River, the Center houses the largest archival collection in American presidential history. It is part of a campus that includes a pavilion, an amphitheater, a playground, and walking and biking trails, plus the University of Arkansas Clinton School of Public Service.

Little Rock's River Market sits on the "city side" of the river in the River Market District, which anchors the downtown entertainment area. By day the market offers fresh produce and flowers, teas and gourmet coffee, meats, sushi, and even gift stalls. A monthly cooking class is a favorite with residents and visitors. The cost? $10. At night, the Riverfront area jumps with nightspots like the Flying Saucer for flights of beer and fish dishes, and Sticky Fingerz Rock 'n' Roll Chicken Shack for finger food and live music.

River Market, Little Rock

Most attractions in Little Rock are free—the Old State House Museum, the State Capitol, Central High School National Historic Site, and the Cox Creative Center, to name a few. Even Little Rock's welcome center is a draw. Located in the restored Walters-Curran-Bell home now called Curran Hall, the garden and home reflect the antebellum period of the 1840s.

At trip's end, unexpected Arkansas becomes a travel journal of delightful experiences that simply can't be found anywhere else. ●

Historic Waterfront
Georgia and Florida

Live oaks thrive in the Low Country, which stretches flat and finger-like along the south-eastern seaboard. Laden with moss, the massive trees at once evoke a sense of the past and of history in the making. Travelers experience both, especially when visiting Savannah, Ga., and stops along US 17 on the way to Florida.

Founded in 1733, Savannah was designed with six public squares where the townspeople could meet while drawing water from public wells. Today, there are 21 squares in Savannah. Though elaborate fountains have replaced the wells, people still gather in the park-like settings now surrounded by landmarks.

Some of the landmark buildings require a ticket for admission, like the birthplace of Girl Scouts of the U.S.A. founder, Juliette Gordon Low. At the Gordon house, visitors learn about Mrs. Low (or "Daisy," as her family called her) and see examples of her art and sculpture. Built in 1831 for Savannah's mayor, the English Regency house was home to four generations of Gordons before the property was sold to the Girl Scouts organization.

City Hall and the Savannah River, Savannah

Telfair Academy of Arts & Sciences, Savannah

Guests at the award-winning Gastonian B&B step back into an elegant era when they enter this Regency Italianate house, c.1868. Nonetheless, they receive all the pampering of the present—a choice of breakfast menu and serving time, evening cordials by candlelight, and exclusive views of one of only 17 side gardens in the city.

Near the other end of the historic district, Factor's Walk joins River Street or Riverfront Plaza. This area follows the curve of the harbor and brims with galleries, restaurants, and shops.

Savannah is also home to the South's oldest art museum, the Telfair Museum of Art, and to art colonies like City Market with rows of working studios.

Tybee Island, between the Intracoastal and the Atlantic, makes a terrific day trip from Savannah. On the way, a stop at Fort Pulaski provides lessons in fort design, weaponry, and the reason that Americans celebrate Casimir Pulaski Day. It's also the site of early baseball games, as photos in the welcome center attest. One Tybee art stop is the Gallery by the Sea, located next to the Tybee Visitor Center and managed by members of the Tybee Arts Association. It's on the island's main drag, US 80.

Further south on US 17 sit Brunswick and Georgia's Golden Isles. Brunswick's entire downtown is on the National Registry of Historic Places. Buildings from the turn of two centuries ago have been transformed into professional offices, shops, and restaurants. One local favorite: Hungry Hannah's Café. Named for the daughter of a previous owner, the menu offers a signature burger accented with a secret blend of herbs, not spices.

Over the causeway on St. Simons Island, the Village Inn and Pub is a bed-and-breakfast built around a 1930s beach cottage. Its innkeeper provides guests with the name of a staff member on call to assist them throughout their stay. It's a few blocks from St. Simons Lighthouse, up the street from Barbara Jean's Restaurant (where award-winning crab cakes are served) and across the street from a "tree spirit."

Tree spirits are sculptures carved on live oak trees. Created by local artists, the carvings were created as tributes to sailors lost at sea and in homage to the shipbuilding industry that St. Simons served for so many years. Oak from St. Simons was used to build the USS *Constitution*. Its strength, it's said, is one reason the ship bears the nickname "Old Ironsides."

Jekyll Island hosts the Tidelands Nature Center, where visitors can sign up for kayaking and other water activities. Inside the center, exhibits of local marine life are built lower to the floor, to better accommodate young visitors.

(continued)

Back on the mainland, US 17 meanders across the state line and eventually into Jacksonville, Fla., where it joins FL 211 at Riverside Avenue, at the edge of the Riverside Historic District. Riverside has one of the most diverse collections of historical residential architecture in Florida. This area hosts the prestigious Cummer Museum of Art and Gardens. At the Cummer, visitors can view Thomas Moran's *Ponce de Leon in Florida* and one of the foremost collections of Meissen porcelain in the world. Outside, statuary, arbors, and fountains can be found under the bending branches of the Cummer oak, estimated to be nearly 300 years old. The tree boasts a limb span of more than 175 feet and is nearly 75 feet high.

Cummer Museum of Art and Gardens

Riverside Avenue leads to the downtown area and Jacksonville Landing, a shopping, dining, and entertainment center on the north shore of the St. Johns River. It's easy to spend a half a day at the Landing. For the other half? Hop a water taxi to the south side for an afternoon along Museum Circle where Friendship Fountain, the Museum of Science and History, and the Jacksonville Maritime Museum can be found.

St. Augustine isn't far from Jacksonville. There's so much to see in St. Augustine that visitors are encouraged to take a trolley tour. They can hop off for a closer look at the Lightner Museum, the St. Augustine Alligator Farm Zoological Park, Ripley's Believe It or Not! Museum, or Flagler College. Visitors may also tour landmarks on a sightseeing cruise. St. Augustine Lighthouse, Castillo de San Marcos, the site of Admiral Pedro Menendez de Aviles Landing in 1565, the Bridge of Lions, and other sites hug the water's edge.

While St. George Street anchors the downtown shopping area, antique lovers haunt the Uptown District where the number of shops, rare book stores, and restaurants is growing. Reenactments in St. Augustine are particularly popular, so it's common to see residents of the nation's oldest city dressed in a style of a bygone era. Specialty shops and restaurants dot a five-block, pedestrian-only section of the historic district. The district lies alongside St. Augustine's town square where, like other stops along the Intracoastal Waterway, great limbs of centuries-old, live oak trees provide a shady respite for residents and tourists alike. ●

Old Spanish Village, St. Augustine

North Carolina's Outer Banks
and Southern Shores

Mystery envelops so much of North Carolina's coastal history that it's hard to tell where fact ends and legend begins. But that's exactly what makes this trip magical. Who can resist the intrigue of pirates, a vanished colony, back-alley ghosts, and fly-gobbling plants? (And you thought this trip would be nothing but a good book and the almighty beach. Think again.)

What follows: unforgettable experiences on the Outer Banks and Southern Shores, beginning around Kitty Hawk and continuing south to the Cape Fear Coast around Wilmington. Some are new twists on old favorites, and some are memorable moments waiting to be had in nearly undiscovered places.

On Roanoke Island, the best way to escape summer crowds and still learn about the Lost Colony (Roanoke Island's most fascinating story) is by hiring a guide to lead a kayak eco-tour under the bow of the re-created 16th-century *Elizabeth II*. Locals have their own take on the popular story of the early explorers who mysteriously disappeared here in Roanoke Sound. Along the way, great blue heron, nesting egrets, or backyard crabbing pots frequently come into view. Non-seafarers learn about the Lost Colony on board the (tethered) *Elizabeth II* or at the Lost Colony Outdoor Drama in Waterside Theater.

(continued)

North Carolina beach

Across Roanoke Sound lies a thin strip of land (and sand) reachable via US 64. Perched on a Kill Devil Hills hilltop, the Wright Brothers National Memorial, honoring Orville and Wilbur, marks the site of the world's first powered airplane flight in 1903. The visitor center here includes a replica of the original "Wright Flyer."

Orville and Wilbur Wright telegraphed word of their first flight from a telegraph in Kitty Hawk. Once a life-saving station (with the town's only telegraph), the building now houses the Black Pelican Oceanfront Café. For travelers not into museums, this is the perfect stop. A copy of the telegraph and a few flight photos look down from the walls while visitors munch wood-fired gourmet pizza. The white seafood pizza, with shrimp, scallops, and a white sauce, is one of the most popular.

A couple miles south, hang gliders swoop from the mountainous dunes of Jockey's Ridge State Park. Year-round gusty winds make this Nags Head park an ideal spot for kite-flying, too. Spectacular sunsets are visible from the Atlantic Coast's tallest sand dune.

Sam & Omie's, also in Nags Head, serves a 7 a.m. breakfast favored by local fishermen and on offer to visitors, too. Locals say this quaint diner (a 70-year-old icon) serves up the best breakfast in the Outer Banks. Don't leave without trying the crabmeat Benedict weekend special.

Wright Brothers National Memorial

A drive down NC 12 and through the Pea Island National Wildlife Refuge brings the Chicamacomico Life-Saving Station in Rodanthe. Before the U.S. Coast Guard existed, life-saving station volunteers rescued crew members from sinking ships just off shore. Self-guided tours of the station, one of the Outer Banks originals, and its various buildings are offered April through November. June through September, visitors enjoy weekly programs such as rescue stories told during evening beach bonfires.

More tourists flock to the 208-foot Cape Hatteras Lighthouse than to any other natural or historic attraction on the Cape Hatteras National Seashore, the country's first. In a monumental engineering effort, the lighthouse was moved 1,600 feet inland in retreat from the encroaching sea. Visitors can climb the black-and-white, spiral-striped lighthouse April through October.

Cape Hatteras Lighthouse

State Route 12 continues south via ferry from Pea Island to Ocracoke Island. According to locals, a government ordinance ensures that Howard Street, the island's oldest street and a modest dirt road, will never be paved. The best time for checking out the historic houses, old family cemeteries, moss-covered fences, and Village Craftsmen store: just after a rain, when the tree-canopied street drips a fresh, woodsy scent. Teach's Hole, Blackbeard's retail lair for kids, is packed with eye patches, pirate flags, and treasure chest booty of all kinds. Young mates actually enjoy learning history at the store's fun Edward Teach (a.k.a. Blackbeard) exhibit.

Back on the mainland and down US 70, Beaufort is home to the Maritime Museum. Cannon balls and platters from Blackbeard's ship, *Queen Anne's Revenge*, are on display, along with other artifacts from the 18th-century vessel, discovered off the coast here in 1996. From atop this museum visitors view the fishing village's historic homes with their rooftop widow's walks, balconies where the wives of sailors and fishermen would wait and watch for their husbands to return (or not) from sea.

The Beaufort Grocery Company decorates its walls with unusual art: whimsical fish and lobsters made from retired surfboards. By day this bistro in Beaufort's historic district serves homemade deli sandwiches. At night the restaurant turns slighty upscale with excellent seafood burritos, crab cakes, and an extensive wine list.

Springers Point, Ocracoke

Wild horses run free on Shackleford Banks, across the water from Beaufort. Ancestors of these Spanish horses survived 16th-century shipwrecks by swimming to shore here. No fences separate you from the island's animals, whose coats shine red in the late afternoon light. (But remember, these are wild animals, not petting-zoo ponies.) Boats and private ferries run to Shackleford Banks from Harkers Island, Beaufort, or Morehead City. The horses can also be seen from Beaufort's waterfront.

A meander down the coast—you'll drive NC 24, NC 172, then US 17—brings Wilmington, famous for Hollywood studios and the Cotton Exchange. Perhaps less well-known is the Ghost Walk tour of Old Wilmington. Guides recount shivering tales of murder and betrayal on this 1.5-hour tour of haunted back alleys, cemeteries, and historic landmarks. These same guides say people experience ghosts about 35 times each year on the walks.

South of Wilmington, Carolina Beach State Park hosts fly-munching plants on the Venus Flytrap Trail. If you're lucky, you'll hit lunchtime in the mostly-pine forest and see a fly gobbled by one of these carnivores, which are native within only a 75-mile radius of Wilmington.

At the tip of the Fort Fisher peninsula, the Cape Fear River's fresh water mixes with the salty ocean. Some say the wind whips 10 miles per hour faster here than at Wrightsville Beach (up near Wilmington), making it easier for kitesurfers to jump as high as 30 feet. Local sports outfitters help novices end their Outer Banks drive on an adventurous note. ●

CITIES AND TOWNS

Alabama - Arkansas

Arkansas

Arkansas - Florida

District of Columbia

Florida

Florida

Florida - Georgia

Georgia - Kentucky

ningtown, 75 44 H3
or, 400 43 I12
sfield, 392 31 H9
etta, 58,748 31 G6
ow, 350 44 D5
shallville, 1,335 43 D8
tinez, 27,749 32 H2
t, 90 31 E7
thews, 150 44 A2
k, 60 43 D6
eys, 210 31 G10
day 54 A2
field, 150 31 I12
sville, 1,247 31 E9
aysville, 1,071 31 C6
onough, 8,493 31 I7
ntyre, 718 43 B10
innon, 75 44 H3
ae, 2,682 43 E11
gs, 1,090 43 I7
drim, 450 44 E5
ades, 130 44 E3
lo, 485 30 E3
rillville, 120 53 A10
shon, 200 44 H2
ena, 250 31 H12
asville, 80 31 G12
calf, 130 53 B10
ter, 3,879 44 D3
ville, 457 44 B2
way, 1,100 44 F5
way 44 E3
n, 1,012 43 E11
ord, 60 43 H6
edgeville, 18,757 43 A10
en, 3,492 44 B3
wood, 180 43 H12
ler, 522 43 A7
tead, 1,500 31 H8
chell, 173 43 A12
doc, 40 44 C2
ena, 475 43 B6
ncrief 53 B9
niac 54 C4
nroe, 11,407 31 G9
ntezuma, 3,999 43 D7
ntgomery, 4,134 45 F6
nticello, 2,428 31 I9
ntrose, 154 43 C10
ra, 75 43 H11
rgan, 1,464 43 G6
rganton, 299 31 C7
rris, 75 42 F4
rven, 634 53 A11
ultrie, 14,387 43 I8
untain City, 829 31 C10
untain Park, 11,753 31 G7
unt Pleasant, 60 44 H4
unt Vernon, 1,949 43 E12
untville, 200 42 B5
unt Zion, 1,275 30 H4
xley, 100 44 B1
lberry Grove, 100 42 C4
nnerlyn, 50 44 B3
rphy, 100 43 I8
rrays Crossroads 43 D7
rrayville, 800 31 E8
stic, 300 43 G10
unta, 930 44 I3
hville, 4,697 43 I10
ylor 54 A2
edmore 54 B3
ese, 130 31 F10
vils, 185 44 E4
wborn, 520 31 H9
w Branch, 60 44 E2
w Elm 43 H8
w England, 175 30 C3
w Era 43 E7
w Georgia 30 G5
w Holland, 1,200 31 E8
w Hope 32 G1
w Hope, 150 30 G5
wington, 322 44 C4
wnan, 16,242 30 I5
wton, 851 43 H6
holls, 2,024 43 G12
holson, 1,247 31 F9
cklesville 43 C10
ole, 150 30 C4
rcross, 8,410 31 G7
rman Park, 849 43 H9
ristown, 150 44 D1
rth Canton, 900 31 F6
rth High Shoals, 439 31 G9
rwood, 299 31 H12
berg, 130 31 E11
nez, 131 44 D2
kfield, 200 43 F8
kman, 150 30 D5
k Park, 366 44 D2
kwood, 2,689 31 F8
nlocknee, 605 53 A10
lla, 3,270 43 G10
onee, 280 43 B11
essadale, 150 42 B5
um, 414 44 G3
ferman, 403 44 H2
lethorpe, 1,200 43 D7
oopee, 70 44 E2
efenokee 44 I2
d Damascus 42 H5
ver, 253 44 D4
naha, 115 42 E4
nega, 1,340 43 H9
chard Hill, 230 43 A7
ierfield, 100 43 G10
ford, 1,892 31 H8
metto, 3,400 31 H6
Panola, 200 31 H7
Panthersville, 11,791 31 H7
Parkerville 43 H8
Parrott, 156 43 F6
Patterson, 627 44 H2
Pavo, 711 53 A11
Payne, 178 43 B8
Peachtree City, 31,580 31 I6
Pearson, 1,805 43 H11
Pelham, 4,126 43 I7
Pembroke, 2,379 44 E4
Penfield, 150 31 H10
Perkins, 200 44 B3
Perry, 9,602 43 D8
Phillipsburg, 887 43 H9
Philomath, 150 31 G11
Phinizy, 50 32 H2
Pine Grove, 50 44 F1
Pine Harbor, 125 44 G5
Pinehurst, 307 43 E8
Pine Log, 150 30 E5
Pine Mountain, 1,141 42 B5
Pine Mountain Valley, 950 42 C5
Pine Park, 200 53 A9
Pineview, 532 43 E9
Pitts, 308 43 F9
Plainfield, 140 43 D10
Plains, 637 43 E6
Plainville, 257 30 E4
Pleasant Hill, 50 43 B6
Point Peter, 50 31 F11
Pooler, 6,239 44 E5
Popes Ferry, 30 43 B8
Portal, 597 44 C3
Porterdale, 1,281 31 H8
Potterville, 170 43 D7
Poulan, 946 43 G8
Powder Springs, 12,481 30 G5
Powelton, 40 31 I11
Preston, 453 43 E6
Pretoria 43 G7
Pridgen, 50 43 G11
Primrose, 100 42 A5
Pulaski, 261 44 D3
Putney, 2,998 43 H7
Queensland, 140 43 F10
Quitman, 4,638 53 B11
Racepond, 130 44 I2
Radium Springs, 1,400 43 G7
Raoul, 1,816 31 E9
Raybon, 200 44 H3
Ray City, 746 43 I10
Rayle, 139 31 G11
Rebecca, 246 43 F9
Recovery, 30 53 B7
Redan, 33,841 31 G7
Redbud, 100 30 D5
Red Rock, 85 43 G8
Reed Creek, 2,148 31 E11
Register, 164 44 D3
Reidsville, 2,235 44 E2
Remerton, 847 53 A12
Renfroe 42 E5
Reno, 100 53 B9
Rentz, 304 43 D11
Reo 30 D4
Resaca, 815 30 D5
Rex, 950 31 H7
Reynolds, 1,036 43 C7
Reynoldsville, 50 53 A7
Rhine, 422 43 F10
Riceboro, 736 44 G5
Richland, 1,794 42 E5
Richmond Hill, 6,959 44 F5
Rico, 70 30 H5
Riddleville, 124 43 B12
Ridgeville, 300 44 H5
Rincon, 4,376 44 D5
Ringgold, 2,422 30 C4
Rising Fawn, 110 30 D3
Riverdale, 12,478 31 H6
Rivertown, 150 30 H5
Roberta, 808 43 C7
Rochelle, 1,415 43 F9
Rockingham, 30 44 G1
Rockledge, 250 43 D12
Rockmart, 3,870 30 F4
Rock Spring, 300 30 C4
Rockville, 60 31 I10
Rocky Face, 1,000 30 C4
Rocky Ford, 186 44 C3
Rome, 34,980 30 E4
Roopville, 177 30 I4
Roscoe, 200 30 H5
Rosier 44 B2
Roswell, 79,309 31 F7
Round Oak, 200 43 A9
Royston, 2,493 31 E10
Rupert, 100 43 D7
Russell, 850 31 G9
Rutledge, 707 31 H9
Rydal, 200 30 E5
Saint Clair, 150 44 A2
Saint George, 350 54 C5
Saint Marks, 45 42 A5
St. Marys, 13,761 55 B7
Saint Simons Island, 13,381 44 I5
Sale City, 319 43 H7
Salem, 339 43 A7
Sandersville, 6,144 43 B11
Sand Hill, 200 30 H5
Sandy Cross, 260 31 E10
Sandy Springs, 85,781 31 G6
Sapelo Island, 150 44 H5
Sardis, 1,171 44 B4
Sargent, 900 30 I5
Sasser, 393 43 G6
Sautee, 500 31 D9
Savannah, 132,985 45 E6
Scarboro, 40 44 C3
Scotland, 300 43 E11
Scott, 140 43 C12
Screven, 702 44 G3
Sea Island, 700 44 I5
Senoia, 1,738 31 I6
Seville, 200 43 F9
Shady Dale, 242 31 I9
Shannon, 1,682 30 E4
Sharon, 105 31 H12
Sharpsburg, 316 31 I6
Shawnee, 70 44 D5
Shell Bluff 44 A3
Shellman, 1,166 42 G5
Shellman Bluff, 450 44 G5
Shenandoah, 45 30 I5
Silk Mills, 200 31 F11
Siloam, 331 31 H11
Skidaway Island, 6,914 45 F6
Smarr, 350 43 B8
Smithville, 774 43 F7
Smyrna, 40,999 31 G6
Snellville, 15,351 31 G8
Snipesville, 50 43 F12
Social Circle, 3,379 31 H9
Sonoraville 30 E5
Soperton, 2,824 43 D12
South Cobb, 4,400 31 G6
Spalding, 60 43 D7
Sparks, 1,755 43 I9
Sparta, 1,522 31 I11
Spring Bluff 44 I4
Springfield, 1,821 44 D5
Spring Place, 270 30 D5
Springvale, 60 42 F5
Stapleton, 318 43 A12
Statenville, 650 54 B2
Statesboro, 22,698 44 D3
Statham, 2,040 31 G9
Stephens, 110 31 G10
Stewart 31 I8
Stilesboro, 150 30 F5
Stillmore, 730 44 D2
Stillwell, 30 44 D5
Stilson, 150 44 D4
Stockbridge, 9,853 31 H7
Stockton, 200 54 A2
Stone Mountain, 7,145 31 G7
Strouds, 45 43 B7
Subligna, 60 30 D4
Suches, 160 31 D8
Sugar Hill, 11,399 31 F8
Summertown, 140 44 C2
Summerville, 4,556 30 E3
Sumner, 309 43 G8
Sumter, 35 43 F7
Sunbury, 150 44 F5
Sunnyside, 1,385 44 H2
Surrency, 237 44 G2
Suttons Corner 42 G5
Suwanee, 8,725 31 F7
Swainsboro, 6,943 44 C2
Swords, 90 31 H10
Sycamore, 496 43 G9
Sylvania, 2,675 44 C4
Sylvester, 5,990 43 G8
Talbotton, 1,019 43 C6
Tallapoosa, 2,789 30 G4
Tallulah Lodge, 130 31 D10
Talmo 43 H12
Tarrytown, 100 43 D12
Tate, 1,000 31 E6
Tazewell, 130 43 D6
Temple, 2,383 30 G4
Tennga, 400 30 C5
Tennille, 1,505 43 B11
Texas 42 A4
Thalmann, 50 44 H4
The Rock 43 B7
Thomaston, 9,411 43 B6
Thomasville, 18,162 53 A10
Thomson, 6,828 32 H1
Tifton, 15,060 43 H9
Tignall, 653 31 G12
Tilton 30 D5
Toccoa, 9,323 31 D10
Toccoa Falls, 900 31 D10
Toomsboro, 622 43 B10
Towns, 90 43 E12
Townsend, 200 44 G4
Traders Hill, 150 54 B5
Travisville, 100 43 I12
Trenton, 1,942 30 C3
Trion, 1,993 30 D4
Troutman, 50 42 F5
Tucker, 26,532 31 G7
Tunnel Hill, 1,209 30 C4
Turnerville, 300 31 D9
Twin City, 1,752 44 C2
Twin Lakes, 950 54 B1
Tybee Island, 3,392 45 E6
Tyrone, 3,916 31 H6
Tyrone 31 H11
Ty Ty, 716 43 H9
Unadilla, 2,772 43 E8
Union 30 G5
Union City, 11,621 31 H6
Union Point, 1,669 31 H11
Unionville, 2,074 43 H9
Upton 43 G11
Uvalda, 530 43 E12
Vada, 80 43 I6
Valdosta, 44,268 53 A12
Van Wert, 275 30 G4
Varnell, 1,531 30 C5
Veal, 90 30 I4
Veazey, 50 31 H10
Vesta, 60 31 G11
Vidalia, 10,491 44 E1
Vidette, 112 44 B2
Vienna, 2,973 43 E8
Villanow 30 D4
Villa Rica, 4,134 30 G5
Vinings, 9,677 31 G6
Wadley, 2,085 44 B1
Waleska, 616 31 E6
Walnut Grove, 1,241 31 G8
Walthourville, 4,030 44 F4
Waresboro, 400 44 H1
Wares Crossroads, 50 42 A4
Warm Springs, 485 42 B5
Warner Robins, 48,804 43 C9
Warrenton, 2,118 31 I12
Warthen, 250 43 A11
Warwick, 430 43 F8
Washington, 4,295 31 G12
Watkinsville, 2,097 31 G10
Waverly, 400 44 I4
Waverly Hall, 709 42 C5
Wax, 100 30 F4
Waycross, 15,333 44 H1
Waynesboro, 5,813 44 A3
Waynesville, 450 44 H3
Wayside, 130 43 A9
Weber 43 H10
Wenona, 200 43 F8
West Green, 300 43 G12
Weston, 75 42 F5
West Point, 3,382 42 B4
Whigham, 631 53 A9
White, 693 30 E5
Whitemarsh Island, 5,824 45 E6
White Oak, 250 44 I4
White Plains, 283 31 H11
Whitesburg, 596 30 H5
Whitestone, 150 31 D6
Whitesville, 100 42 B4
Wildwood, 200 30 C3
Willacoochee, 1,434 43 H11
Willard 31 I9
Williamson, 297 43 A6
Wilmington Island, 14,213 45 E6
Winder, 10,201 31 F9
Winokur, 100 44 I3
Winston, 350 30 H5
Winterville, 1,068 31 G10
Woodbine, 1,218 55 A6
Woodbury, 1,184 43 B6
Woodcliff, 100 44 C4
Woodland, 432 43 C6
Woodstock, 10,050 31 F6
Woodville, 400 31 H11
Woolsey, 175 31 I6
Worthville, 100 31 I8
Wray, 100 43 G11
Wrens, 2,314 44 A1
Wrightsville, 2,223 43 C12
Yatesville, 408 43 B7
Young Harris, 604 31 C8
Zebulon, 1,181 43 A6

Illinois

CITY, Population Page Grid
Anna, 5,136 16 B3
Boles, 90 16 B4
Boskydell, 30 16 A3
Brownfield, 75 16 B5
Cairo, 3,632 16 D3
Carbondale, 25,597 16 A3
Carrier Mills, 1,886 16 A5
Carterville, 4,616 16 A3
Cave-In-Rock, 346 17 B6
Cobden, 1,116 16 B3
Crab Orchard, 450 16 A4
Creal Springs, 702 16 A4
Cypress, 271 16 B3
Dongola, 806 16 B3
Eagle Point Bay, 350 16 A4
East Cape Girardeau, 437 16 B2
Eddyville, 153 16 B5
Elizabethtown, 348 17 B6
Equality, 721 16 A5
Golconda, 726 16 B5
Goreville, 938 16 B4
Gorham, 256 16 A2
Grand Tower, 624 16 A2
Grantsburg, 150 16 B4
Harrisburg, 9,860 16 A5
Herod, 70 16 A5
Hillerman, 35 16 C4
Jacob, 50 16 A2
Jonesboro, 1,853 16 B3
Joppa, 409 16 C4
Junction, 139 17 A6
Karbers Ridge, 45 17 A6
Karnak, 619 16 C4
Lick Creek, 60 16 B3
Makanda, 419 16 A3
Marion, 16,035 16 A4
McClure, 600 16 B2
Metropolis, 6,482 16 C4
Midway, 25 16 C5
Mill Creek, 76 16 B3
Miller City, 70 16 C2
Mound City, 692 16 C3
Mounds, 1,117 16 C3
Mount Pleasant, 50 16 B3
Murphysboro, 8,694 16 A2
New Burnside, 242 16 A4
New Columbia, 150 16 C4
New Grand Chain, 233 16 C3
New Liberty, 70 16 C5
Old Shawneetown, 278 17 A6
Olive Branch, 600 16 C2
Olmsted, 299 16 C3
Ozark, 110 16 B4
Pankeyville, 200 16 A5
Paulton, 150 16 A4
Pomona, 80 16 A2
Reevesville, 160 16 B4
Rosiclare, 1,213 16 B5
Saline Mines, 25 17 A6
Shawneetown, 1,410 17 A6
Simpson, 54 16 B4
Stonefort, 292 16 A4
Tamms, 1,192 16 C3
Ullin, 779 16 C3
Vienna, 1,234 16 B4
Ware, 260 16 B2
Wolf Lake, 300 16 B2

Kansas

CITY, Population Page Grid
Altamont, 1,092 13 C7
Altoona, 485 13 A6
Angola, 50 13 C6
Arkansas City, 11,963 12 C2
Arma, 1,529 13 A9
Ashton, 25 12 C1
Atlanta, 255 12 B2
Augusta, 8,423 12 A2
Bartlett, 124 13 C7
Baxter Springs, 4,602 13 C9
Beaumont, 200 12 A3
Belle Plaine, 1,708 12 B1
Benedict, 103 13 A6
Brazilton, 80 13 A8
Buffalo, 284 13 A6
Burden, 564 12 B2
Cambridge, 103 12 B3
Caney, 2,092 12 C5
Cedar Vale, 723 12 C3
Chanute, 9,411 13 A6
Chautauqua, 113 12 C4
Cherokee, 722 13 B8
Cherryvale, 2,386 13 B6
Chetopa, 1,281 13 C7
Climax, 64 12 A4
Coffeyville, 11,060 13 C6
Columbus, 3,396 13 C8
Coyville, 71 12 A5
Crestline, 110 13 C9
Dearing, 409 13 C6
Dennis, 150 13 B7
Derby, 17,807 12 A1
Dexter, 364 12 C3
Douglass, 1,813 12 A2
Earlton, 80 13 A6
Edna, 423 13 C7
Elgin, 82 12 C4
Elk City, 305 12 B5
Elk Falls, 112 12 B4
Erie, 1,211 13 A7
Fall River, 156 12 A5
Farlington, 75 13 A8
Faulkner, 30 13 B8
Floral, 40 12 B2
Fredonia, 2,600 12 A5
Frontenac, 2,996 13 B9
Galena, 3,287 13 C9
Galesburg, 150 13 B7
Garland, 100 13 A9
Geuda Springs, 212 12 C1
Girard, 2,773 13 B8
Greenwich Heights, 960 12 A1
Grenola, 231 12 B3
Hackney, 25 12 C2
Hallowell, 200 13 C8
Havana, 86 12 C5
Haverhill, 50 12 A2
Hepler, 154 13 A8
Hewins, 40 12 C4
Hiattville, 60 13 A8
Howard, 808 12 B4
Independence, 9,846 13 C6
Jefferson, 50 12 C5
Labette, 68 13 C7
Lafontaine, 100 12 B5
Lakeland Estates, 300 12 A5
Latham, 164 12 A3
Leon, 647 12 A2
Liberty, 95 13 C6
Longton, 394 12 B5
Maple City, 20 12 C2
McCune, 426 13 B8
Mecca Acres, 285 12 A1
Melrose, 50 13 C8
Moline, 457 12 B4
Montana, 55 13 B7
Morehead, 50 13 B6
Mound Valley, 418 13 C7
Mulberry, 577 13 A9
Mulvane, 5,155 12 B1
Neodesha, 2,848 13 B6
New Salem, 80 12 B2
Niotaze, 122 12 C5
Oaklawn, 3,000 12 A1
Oak Valley, 25 12 B5
Opolis, 130 13 B9
Oswego, 2,046 13 C7
Oxford, 1,173 12 B1
Parkerfield, 300 12 C2
Parsons, 11,514 13 B7
Peru, 183 12 C4
Piedmont, 250 12 A4
Pittsburg, 19,243 13 B9
Riverton, 600 13 C9
Rock, 80 12 B2
Rose Hill, 3,432 12 A1
St. Paul, 646 13 B7
Scammon, 496 13 B8
Sedan, 1,342 12 C4
Severy, 359 12 A4
Sherman, 50 13 C8
Sherwin, 40 13 C8
Silverdale, 50 12 C2
Stark, 106 13 A7
Sycamore, 200 13 B6
Thayer, 500 13 B6
Tyro, 226 12 C5
Udall, 794 12 B1
Urbana, 30 13 A7
Valeda, 70 13 C6
Walnut, 221 13 A8
Weir, 780 13 B8
Wichita, 346,753 12 A1
Wilmot, 30 12 B2
Winfield, 12,206 12 C2

Kentucky

CITY, Population Page Grid
Aaron, 70 18 D4
Aberdeen, 200 17 C11
Adairville, 920 17 E10
Adolphus, 150 17 E12
Albany, 2,220 18 E4
Allegre, 100 17 D9
Allensville, 189 17 E9
Amandaville 18 D3
Amos, 50 18 E1
Anco, 360 19 C10
Anna 17 C11
Annville, 589 19 B7
Anton, 200 17 B8
Apex 17 C9
Argyle 18 C5
Arjay, 600 19 D8
Arlington, 395 16 D3
Artemus, 800 19 D8
Ashland, 21,981 8 F1
Athol, 75 19 A9
Auburn, 1,444 17 D10
Aurora, 200 17 E6
Austin, 150 18 D1
Auxier, 900 19 A11
Bandana, 300 16 C4
Barbourville, 3,589 19 D8
Bardwell, 799 16 D3
Barlow, 715 16 C3
Baxter, 800 19 D9
Bayou 16 C5
Bays, 25 19 A10
Beattyville, 1,193 19 A8
Beaumont, 100 18 D2
Beauty, 600 8 I1
Beaver Dam, 3,033 17 B10
Beech Grove, 250 17 A8
Beechmont, 600 17 C9
Bee Spring, 150 17 C12
Bell City 16 E5
Bells Run 17 A10
Benham, 599 19 D11
Bennettstown, 35 17 E8
Benton, 4,197 16 D5
Berea, 9,851 19 A6
Bernstadt 19 C7
Bethany, 65 19 A9
Bethelridge, 30 18 C5
Betsy Layne, 450 19 A11
Beulah Heights, 50 19 D6
Big Clifty, 300 17 B12
Big Creek, 300 19 C9
Bighill, 200 19 A7
Big Laurel, 120 19 D10
Blackey, 153 19 C10
Blackmont, 300 19 D9
Black Snake, 200 19 D9
Blandville, 99 16 D4
Boaz, 20 16 D5
Bobs Fork, 175 19 C9
Bon Ayr, 60 18 D1
Bonnieville, 354 18 B2
Boone Heights, 800 19 D8
Booneville, 111 19 B8
Botto, 150 19 C8
Bowling Green, 49,278 17 D11
Bradfordsville, 304 18 B4
Breeding, 60 18 D3
Bremen, 365 17 B9
Brewers, 125 16 E5
Briensburg, 250 17 D6
Brodhead, 1,193 19 B6
Brooklyn, 40 17 C11
Broughtentown, 50 19 B6
Browder, 300 17 C9
Browns Crossroads, 80 18 E4
Brownsville, 921 17 C12
Bryantsville, 130 18 A5
Buckhorn, 144 19 B9
Buffalo, 400 18 B2
Buford, 75 17 A10
Burgin, 874 18 A5
Burkesville, 1,756 18 D3
Burna, 300 16 C5
Burnaugh, 175 8 G1
Burning Springs, 100 19 C8
Buttonsberry, 90 17 B9
Cabell, 50 18 D4
Cadiz, 2,373 17 D7
Calhoun, 836 17 B9
Calloway, 100 19 B7
Calvary, 60 18 B4
Calvert City, 2,701 16 D5
Campbellsville, 10,498 18 B3
Campton, 424 19 A9

Kentucky - Louisiana

Louisiana

Louisiana - Maryland

Maryland

CITY, Population	Page	Grid

Maryland - Mississippi

Mississippi - North Carolina

North Carolina

North Carolina - Oklahoma

Oklahoma - South Carolina

Jay, 2,482 13 F8
Jenks, 9,557 12 G5
Jennings, 373 12 G4
Johnson, 223 24 A1
Jumbo 24 E5
Justice, 1,311 13 F6
Kansas, 685 13 G8
Kaw City, 372 12 D2
Keefton, 100 13 I7
Kellyville, 50 13 D9
Kellyville, 906 12 H4
Kemp, 144 24 G3
Kendrick, 138 12 H2
Kenefic, 192 24 F3
Kent 24 F5
Kenwood, 120 13 F8
Keota, 517 25 B7
Kiefer, 1,026 12 G4
Kildare, 92 12 D1
Kingston, 1,390 24 F2
Kinta, 243 25 B6
Kiowa, 693 24 D4
Konawa, 1,479 24 C1
Krebs, 2,051 24 C5
Lafayette, 40 25 B7
Lamar, 172 24 B3
Lane, 300 24 E4
Langley, 669 13 F8
Langston, 1,670 12 G1
Lawrence Creek, 119 12 G3
Leach, 220 13 G8
Lebanon, 400 24 F2
Le Flore, 168 25 C7
Lehigh, 315 24 E3
Lenapah, 298 13 D6
Lenna, 40 24 A5
Leonard, 550 12 H5
Lequire, 250 25 B7
Lewisville 25 B6
Liberty, 184 12 H5
Limestone, 745 12 F5
Little, 100 24 A2
Little Chief, 30 12 E3
Little City, 150 24 F2
Locust Grove, 1,412 13 G7
Longtown, 2,397 24 B5
Lost City, 809 13 G7
Lotsee, 11 12 G4
Lula, 30 24 D2
Luther, 612 12 H1
Lynn Addition, 350 12 E4
Madill, 3,410 24 F1
Mannford, 2,095 12 G4
Mannsville, 587 24 F1
Maramec, 104 12 F3
Marble City, 242 13 I8
Marland, 280 12 E1
Martin 13 I7
Mason, 100 12 I4
Matoy 24 F4
Maud, 1,136 24 B1
Mazie, 88 13 G7
McAlester, 17,783 24 C5
McBride, 80 24 G2
McCord, 1,711 12 E2
McCurtain, 466 25 B7
McKey, 135 13 I8
McMillan, 25 24 F1
Mead, 123 24 F2
Meeker, 978 12 I2
Mehan, 45 12 G2
Meridian, 54 12 H1
Miami, 13,704 13 D8
Midlothian, 25 12 I2
Milburn, 312 24 E2
Milfay, 170 12 H3
Mill Creek, 340 24 E1
Miller 24 E5
Millerton, 359 25 F7
Monroe, 200 25 C9
Moodys, 170 13 G8
Moon, 100 25 G8
Morris, 1,294 12 I5
Morrison, 636 12 F2
Mounds, 1,153 12 H4
Mount Herman, 150 25 E8
Moyers, 100 24 E5
Muldrow, 3,104 25 A8
Muse, 200 25 D8
Muskogee, 38,310 13 H7
Nashoba, 150 25 E6
New Alluwe, 95 13 E6
Newkirk, 2,243 12 D1
New Lima, 130 24 B2
Non, 40 24 C3
Notchietown, 430 13 I7
Nowata, 3,971 13 E6
Nuyaka, 150 12 I4
Oak Grove, 200 12 G3
Oak Grove 24 D1
Oakhurst, 2,731 12 G5
Oakland, 674 24 F1
Oaks, 412 13 G8
Oberlin 24 G4
Ochelata, 494 12 E5
Oglesby, 100 12 E5
Oilton, 1,099 12 G3
Okay, 597 13 H7
Okemah, 3,038 24 A3
Okesa, 120 12 E4
Okfuskee 12 I4
Okmulgee, 13,022 12 I5
Oktaha, 327 13 I6
Oleta, 50 25 F6
Olive, 200 12 G3
Olney, 130 24 E3
Onapa 24 A5
Oneta, 800 13 G6
Oologah, 883 13 F6
Osage, 188 12 F3
Owasso, 18,502 12 F5
Paden, 446 12 I3
Page, 25 25 D8
Panama, 1,362 25 B8
Panola, 300 25 C6
Park Hill, 3,936 13 H8
Parkland, 50 12 H2
Patton, 100 13 F7
Pawhuska, 3,629 12 E4
Pawnee, 2,230 12 F2
Payson, 30 12 I2
Pearsonia 12 D3
Peckham, 75 12 D1
Peggs, 180 13 G7
Peoria, 141 13 D9
Perkins, 2,272 12 G1
Pershing, 50 12 E4
Pettit, 771 13 H8
Pharoah, 100 24 A3
Picher, 1,640 13 D8
Pickens, 170 25 E7
Pickett, 400 24 C1
Pittsburg, 280 24 D4
Pleasant Hill, 50 25 G8
Plunkettville, 80 25 E9
Pocola, 3,994 25 B9
Ponca City, 25,919 12 E1
Pontotoc, 200 24 D2
Porter, 574 13 H6
Porum, 725 25 A6
Poteau, 7,939 25 B8
Prague, 2,138 12 I2
Preston, 500 12 H5
Proctor, 130 13 G8
Prue, 433 12 F4
Pryor Creek, 8,659 13 F7
Pyramid Corners, 45 13 D7
Quapaw, 984 13 D8
Quay, 47 12 G2
Quinton, 1,071 25 B6
Ralston, 355 12 E2
Ramona, 564 12 E5
Rattan, 241 25 F6
Ravia, 459 24 E1
Reagan, 50 24 E2
Redbird, 153 13 H6
Red Oak, 581 25 C7
Red Rock, 293 12 E1
Remus, 150 24 B1
Remy, 411 25 A8
Rentiesville, 102 13 I6
Ripley, 444 12 G2
Rock Island, 709 25 B9
Roff, 734 24 D1
Roland, 2,842 25 A9
Rose, 100 13 F8
Rufe, 200 25 F7
St. Louis, 206 24 B1
Salina, 1,422 13 F7
Sallisaw, 7,989 25 A8
Sand Bluff 24 F5
Sand Point, 200 24 F2
Sand Springs, 17,451 12 G4
Sapulpa, 19,166 12 G4
Sasakwa, 150 24 C2
Savanna, 730 24 C4
Sawyer, 274 25 F6
Schulter, 600 12 I5
Scipio, 50 24 B4
Scraper, 475 13 G8
Scullin 24 D1
Seminole, 6,899 24 B2
Sequoyah, 671 13 F6
Shady Grove, 185 25 A6
Shady Point, 848 25 B8
Shawnee, 28,692 24 A1
Shidler, 520 12 D3
Short, 328 13 I9
Silo, 282 24 F2
Skedee, 102 12 F3
Skiatook, 5,396 12 F5
Slick, 148 12 H4
Smithville, 123 25 E8
Snow, 130 25 E6
Soper, 300 25 F5
South Coffeyville, 790 13 D6
Sparks, 137 12 I2
Spaulding, 62 24 B2
Spavinaw, 563 13 F8
Spencerville, 200 25 F6
Sperry, 981 12 F5
Spiro, 2,227 25 B8
Steel Junction, 40 25 F8
Stidham, 23 24 A5
Stigler, 2,731 25 B7
Stillwater, 39,065 12 G1
Stilwell, 3,276 13 H9
Stonebluff, 300 12 H5
Stonewall, 465 24 D2
Stratford, 1,474 24 C1
Stringtown, 396 24 E4
Stroud, 2,758 12 H3
Stuart, 220 24 C4
Sulphur, 4,794 24 D1
Summerfield, 150 25 C7
Summit, 226 13 H6
Sumner, 230 12 F1
Swink, 83 25 F6
Sycamore, 183 13 F9
Taft, 349 13 H6
Tahlequah, 14,458 13 H8
Talala, 270 13 E6
Talihina, 1,211 25 D7
Tamaha, 198 25 A7
Tecumseh, 6,098 24 B1
Tenkiller, 549 13 H8
Teresita 13 G8
Texanna, 2,083 25 A6
Ti 24 D5
Timber Brook, 1,000 13 G6
Tishomingo, 3,162 24 E2
Tom, 150 25 G8
Troy, 40 24 E1
Tryon, 448 12 H2
Tulsa, 393,049 12 G5
Tupelo, 377 24 D2
Turley, 3,231 12 F5
Tushka, 345 24 E3
Tuskahoma, 100 25 D6
Unger 24 F4
Union Valley, 110 24 D2
Valliant, 771 25 F7
Vamoosa, 80 24 C2
Vera, 188 12 F5
Verdigris, 223 13 F6
Vernon, 60 24 B4
Vian, 1,362 13 I8
Vinco, 70 12 G1
Vinita, 6,062 13 E7
Wade, 70 24 G4
Wagoner, 7,669 13 G7
Wainwright, 197 13 I6
Wann, 132 12 D5
Wapanucka, 445 24 E2
Wardville 24 D4
Warner, 1,430 13 I7
Warwick, 235 12 H2
Watova, 150 13 E6
Watson, 300 25 E8
Watts, 316 13 G9
Webb City, 95 12 D2
Webbers Falls, 726 13 I7
Welch, 597 13 D7
Weleetka, 1,014 24 A3
Welling, 669 13 H8
Wellston, 825 12 H1
Welty, 120 12 I3
Westport, 264 12 F3
West Siloam Springs, 877 13 G9
Westville, 1,596 13 G9
Wetumka, 1,451 24 B3
Wewoka, 3,562 24 B2
Whippoorwill, 100 12 D4
Whitefield, 231 25 B6
White Oak, 100 13 E7
Whitesboro, 220 25 D7
Wilburton, 2,972 25 C6
Wister, 1,002 25 C8
Wolco, 30 12 E4
Woodall, 741 13 H8
Wright City, 848 25 F7
Wyandotte, 363 13 D9
Wynona, 531 12 E4
Yale, 1,342 12 G2
Yanush, 60 25 D6
Yeager, 67 24 B3
Yost Lake, 10 12 F2
Yuba, 60 24 G3
Zoe 25 C8

Pennsylvania

CITY, Population Page Grid
Addison, 214 9 B11
Amaranth 10 A3
Arendtsville, 848 11 A6
Atglen, 1,217 11 A9
Bard, 50 10 A2
Bendersville, 576 11 A6
Berlin, 2,192 9 A12
Big Cove Tannery, 200 10 A3
Biglerville, 1,101 11 A6
Bobtown, 1,100 9 B9
Brave, 200 9 B8
Breezewood, 300 10 A3
Brogue, 200 11 A8
Carroll Valley, 3,291 10 B5
Casselman, 99 9 A11
Centerville, 125 10 A2
Chadds Ford, 1,200 11 A11
Chalkhill, 400 9 A10
Chambersburg, 17,862 10 A4
Chaneysville, 80 10 A2
Chatham, 300 11 A10
Chester, 36,854 11 A11
Cito, 20 10 A3
Clearville, 200 10 A2
Coatesville, 10,838 11 A10
Collinsville, 150 11 A8
Confluence, 834 9 A11
Crystal Spring, 100 10 A3
Delroy, 200 11 A8
Delta, 741 11 B8
Dott, 40 10 A3
Dover, 1,815 11 A7
Downingtown, 7,589 11 A10
Earlston, 250 10 A2
East Berlin, 1,365 11 A6
East York, 8,782 11 A7
Edenville, 150 10 A4
Fairdale, 1,955 9 A9
Fairhope, 50 9 A12
Farmington, 250 9 A10
Fayetteville, 2,774 10 A5
Fort Loudon, 1,200 10 A4
Gap, 1,611 11 A9
Garrett, 449 9 A11
Gettysburg, 7,490 11 A6
Glen Rock, 1,809 11 B7
Glen Savage, 15 9 A12
Graysville, 160 9 A8
Greencastle, 3,722 10 B4
Guilford, 1,835 10 A5
Hampton, 633 11 A6
Hanover, 14,535 11 A6
Haydentown, 120 9 A9
Holbrook, 40 9 A8
Hyndman, 1,005 10 A1
Jefferson, 631 11 A7
Kennett Square, 5,273 11 A10
Kingwood, 120 9 A11
Lake Meade, 1,832 11 A6
Lewisville, 225 11 B10
Littlestown, 3,947 11 B6
London Grove, 250 11 A10
Mainsville, 300 10 A5
Markleysburg, 282 9 B10
Masontown, 3,611 9 A9
Mather, 1,000 9 A8
McConnellsburg, 1,073 10 A3
McCracken, 60 9 A7
McSherrystown, 2,691 11 A6
Media, 5,533 11 A11
Mercersburg, 1,540 10 A4
Metzler, 135 9 A11
Meyersdale, 2,473 9 A12
Millersville, 7,774 11 A8
Mill Run, 400 9 A10
Mont Alto, 1,357 10 A5
Morrisville, 1,443 9 A8
Mount Morris, 1,300 9 B8
Needmore, 300 10 A3
Nemacolin, 1,034 9 A9
New Bridgeville, 320 11 A8
New Freedom, 3,512 11 B7
New Freeport, 100 9 B7
New Park, 300 11 B8
New Texas, 100 11 B9
Newtown Square, 11,300 11 A11
Nineveh, 125 9 A8
Ohiopyle, 77 9 A10
Oliver, 2,925 9 A10
Oxford, 4,315 11 B9
Paradise, 1,028 11 A9
Parkesburg, 3,373 11 A10
Parkville, 6,593 11 B7
Pequea, 300 11 A8
Philadelphia, 1,517,550 11 A12
Point Marion, 1,333 9 B9
Purcell, 25 10 A2
Quarryville, 1,994 11 A9
Rainsburg, 146 10 A2
Red Lion, 6,149 11 A8
Republic, 1,396 9 A9
Rockwood, 954 9 A11
Saint Thomas, 900 10 A4
Salisbury, 878 9 B11
Seven Valleys, 492 11 A7
Shiloh, 10,192 11 A7
Shimpstown, 80 10 A4
Shrewsbury, 3,378 11 B7
Smithfield, 854 9 A9
Smock, 600 9 A9
South Connellsville, 2,281 9 A10
South Uniontown, 3,500 9 A9
Spraggs, 30 9 B8
Spring Grove, 2,050 11 A7
State Line, 1,100 10 B4
Stewartstown, 1,752 11 B8
Strasburg, 2,800 11 A9
Susquehanna Trails, 2,134 11 B8
Uniontown, 12,422 9 A10
Ursina, 254 9 A11
Wayne Heights, 1,805 10 B5
Waynesboro, 9,614 10 B5
Waynesburg, 4,184 9 A8
West Chester, 17,861 11 A10
West Grove, 2,652 11 A10
White House, 80 9 B9
Williamson, 200 10 A4
Willow Street, 7,258 11 A9
Wind Ridge, 200 9 A7
Windsor, 1,331 11 A7
Wittenberg, 15 9 A12
York, 40,862 11 A7

South Carolina

CITY, Population Page Grid
Abbeville, 5,840 32 F1
Adamsburg, 80 32 C4
Adams Run, 600 45 C8
Aiken, 25,337 32 H3
Aiken West, 3,000 32 H3
Alcolu, 600 33 G8
Allendale, 4,052 44 B5
Alvin, 100 33 I10
Anderson, 25,514 31 D12
Andrews, 3,068 33 H10
Angelus, 35 33 D8
Arial, 2,607 31 C12
Ashland 33 E8
Ashton, 80 45 B6
Ashwood 33 F8
Awendaw, 1,195 45 B10
Aynor, 587 33 F11
Baileys Landing, 40 45 D6
Ballentine, 730 32 F5
Bamberg, 3,733 33 I6
Barnwell, 5,035 32 I5
Batesburg-Leesville, 5,517 32 G4
Baton Rouge 32 D5
Bayboro, 40 33 F12
Beaufort, 12,950 45 D7
Beckhamville, 360 33 D6
Belle Meade, 400 33 G6
Belton, 4,461 32 D1
Belvedere, 5,631 32 H3
Bennettsville, 9,425 33 D10
Bethera, 100 45 A10
Bethune, 352 33 E8
Beufordtown, 50 33 I10
Bingham, 90 33 E10
Bishopville, 3,670 33 F8
Blacksburg, 1,880 32 B4
Blackstock, 200 32 D5
Blackville, 2,973 32 I5
Blair, 60 32 E5
Blenheim, 137 33 D10
Bluffton, 1,275 45 E6
Blythewood, 170 33 F6
Boiling Springs 44 A5
Bolentown, 60 33 H6
Bonneau, 354 33 I9
Bonneau Beach, 200 33 I9
Bordeaux 32 G1
Borden, 80 33 F7
Bounty Land, 250 31 D11
Bowling Green, 500 32 B5
Bowman, 1,198 33 I7
Bradley, 171 32 F2
Branchville, 1,083 33 I6
Briarcliffe Acres, 470 34 G2
Bristow, 25 33 E10
Brittons Neck, 600 33 G11
Brookdale, 4,724 33 H6
Brunson, 589 44 B5
Buck Hall, 80 45 A11
Buckingham Landing, 100 45 E7
Bucksport, 1,117 33 H12
Buffalo, 1,426 32 D4
Bullock Creek 32 C4
Burton, 7,180 45 D7
Cades, 300 33 G10
Cainhoy, 200 45 B10
Calhoun Falls, 2,303 31 F12
Callison, 50 32 F2
Camden, 6,682 33 E7
Cameron, 449 33 H7
Canadys, 200 45 A7
Capitol View, 4,000 33 G6
Carlisle, 496 32 D4
Cartersville, 110 33 F9
Carvers Bay, 30 33 H11
Cashville 32 C2
Cassatt, 70 33 E8
Catarrah, 30 33 D8
Catawba, 400 33 C6
Centenary, 500 33 F11
Centerville, 5,181 31 D12
Central, 3,522 31 D11
Chaparral Ranches, 5,000 45 A9
Chapin, 628 32 F5
Chappells, 100 32 F3
Charleston, 96,650 45 B9
Cheraw, 5,524 33 D9
Cherryvale, 2,461 33 G8
Chester, 6,476 32 D5
Chesterfield, 1,374 33 D9
Clarks Hill, 376 32 H2
Clearwater, 4,199 32 H3
Clemson, 11,939 31 D11
Clinton, 8,545 32 E3
Clio, 774 33 D10
Clover, 4,014 32 B5
Club House Crossroads, 50 32 G5
Clyde 33 E8
Cokesbury, 279 32 E2
Colliers 32 G2
Columbia, 115,877 33 F6
Congaree 33 G6
Converse, 1,200 32 C3
Conway, 11,788 33 G12
Cool Spring, 100 33 G12
Coosawhatchie, 300 45 C6
Cope, 107 33 I6
Cordesville, 90 45 A10
Cornwell, 50 32 D5
Cottageville, 707 45 B8
Coward, 650 33 F10
Cowpens, 2,279 32 C3
Crestview, 1,700 33 E10
Cross, 300 33 I8
Cross Anchor, 350 32 D3
Cross Hill, 601 32 E3
Cross Keys, 100 32 D3
Cummings, 100 45 C6
Dacusville 32 C1
Dale, 150 45 C7
Dalzell, 2,260 33 F8
Darlington, 6,720 33 E9
Davis Station, 150 33 H8
De Bordieu Colony, 3,000 33 I12
Dekalb 33 E7
Delta 32 D4
Denmark, 3,328 32 I5
Dentsville, 13,049 33 F6
Dillon, 6,316 33 E11
Donalds, 354 32 E2
Dorchester, 450 45 A8
Dovesville, 200 33 E9
Du Bose Park, 200 33 E7
Due West, 1,209 32 E1
Duford, 70 33 F12
Dunbar, 450 33 H11
Duncan, 2,861 32 C2
Eadytown, 50 33 I9
Earlwood Park, 35 33 E9
Early Branch, 150 45 C6
Easley, 17,754 31 C12
East Gaffney, 3,349 32 B4
Eastover, 830 33 G7
Edgefield, 4,449 32 G3
Edgemoor, 350 33 C6
Edisto Beach, 641 45 D8
Edisto Island, 100 45
Edmund, 50 32
Effingham, 230 33
Ehrhardt, 614 45
Elgin, 2,426 33
Elgin, 806 33
Elko, 212 32
Elliott, 650 33
Elloree, 742 33
Enoree, 1,100 32
Estill, 2,425 44
Eureka Mill, 1,737 32
Eutawville, 344 33
Evergreen, 120 33
Fairfax, 3,206 44
Fair Play, 400 31
Fairview, 1,200 32
Fairview Crossroads, 60 32
Fenwick Hills, 300 45
Filbert, 300 32
Fingerville, 380 32
Five Forks, 8,064 32
Florence, 30,248 33
Folly Beach, 2,116 45
Foreston, 100 33
Fork, 280 33
Fork Shoals, 180 32
Fort Lawn, 864 33
Fort Mill, 7,587 33
Fort Motte, 150 33
Fountain Inn, 6,017 32
Frogmore, 300 45
Furman, 286 44
Gable, 200 33
Gadsden, 300 33
Gaffney, 12,968 32
Galivants Ferry, 180 33
Gantt, 13,962 32
Garden City, 9,357 33
Gaston, 1,304 32
Georgetown, 8,979 33
Gilbert, 500 32
Gillisonville, 200 45
Givhans, 200 45
Glenn Springs, 110 32
Glymphville 32
Good Hope 32
Goose Creek, 29,208 45
Goretown, 110 34
Gourdin 33
Govan, 67 44
Grahamville, 250 45
Gramling, 350 32
Gray Court, 1,021 32
Grays 45
Great Falls, 2,194 33
Greeleyville, 452 33
Green Pond, 200 45
Green Sea, 200 33
Greenville, 55,988 32
Greenwood, 22,228 32
Greer, 16,843 32
Gresham, 200 33
Grover, 180 45
Gurley, 100 33
Guthries, 50 32
Hampton, 2,837 45
Hanahan, 12,937 45
Hannah, 50 33
Hardeeville, 1,793 45
Harleyville, 685 45
Hartsville, 7,556 33
Hebron, 90 33
Helena, 300 32
Hemingway, 573 33
Hendersonville, 240 45
Hickory Grove, 337 32
Hickory Tavern, 300 32
Hilda, 436 32
Hilton Head Island, 33,862 45
Holly Hill, 1,421 33
Holly Springs, 50 31
Hollywood, 3,879 45
Homeland Park, 6,337 31
Honea Path, 3,504 32
Honey Hill, 110 45
Horatio, 300 33
Hyman, 100 33
Irmo, 11,039 32
Irvines Landing, 400 32
Islandton, 100 45
Isle of Palms, 4,583 45
Italy, 80 33
Iva, 1,156 31
Jackson, 1,625 32
Jacksonboro, 500 45
Jamestown, 97 33
Jefferson, 704 33
Jenkinsville, 250 32
Joanna, 1,609 32
Jocassee, 60 31
Johns Island, 500 45
Johnsonville, 1,418 33
Johnston, 2,400 32
Jonesville, 982 32
Jordan, 50 33
Jordanville, 40 33
Kelton, 150 32
Kensington, 600 33
Kershaw, 1,645 33
Ketchuptown, 30 33
Kiawah Island, 1,163 45
Kinards, 250 32
Kings Creek, 200 32
Kingstree, 3,617 33
Kirksey, 60 32
Kitchings Mill 32
Kline, 238 44

South Carolina - Tennessee

Tennessee - Texas

Texas

Texas - Virginia

Virginia

Virginia

Virginia - West Virginia

West Virginia

This map shows both the distance and the approximate driving time between many cities across the Southeast region.

You can get even more mileages and driving times at **randmcnally.com**

MILEAGES

277 Black numerals indicate mileage in statue miles.

DRIVE TIMES

7:55 Blue numbers indicate driving time. Driving time shown is approximate under normal conditions. Consideration has been given to topography, number of towns along the route, congested urban areas, and the speed limit imposed by each state. Allowances should be made for night driving and unusually fast or slow drivers.

POINTS OF INTEREST

❶ Cape Hatteras C-11
❷ Great Smoky Mountains D-8
   National Park
❸ Hilton Head Island E-9
❹ Land Between the Lakes C-6
❺ Mammoth Cave National Park C-7
❻ Monticello B-10
❼ Rehoboth Beach B-11
❽ Shenandoah National Park B-10
❾ Walt Disney World G-9
❿ Williamsburg C-11

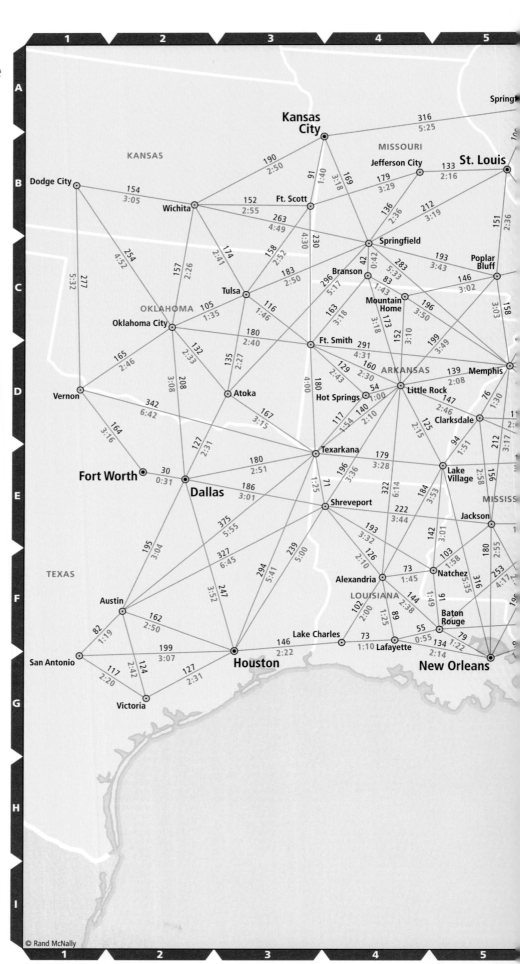

© Rand McNally

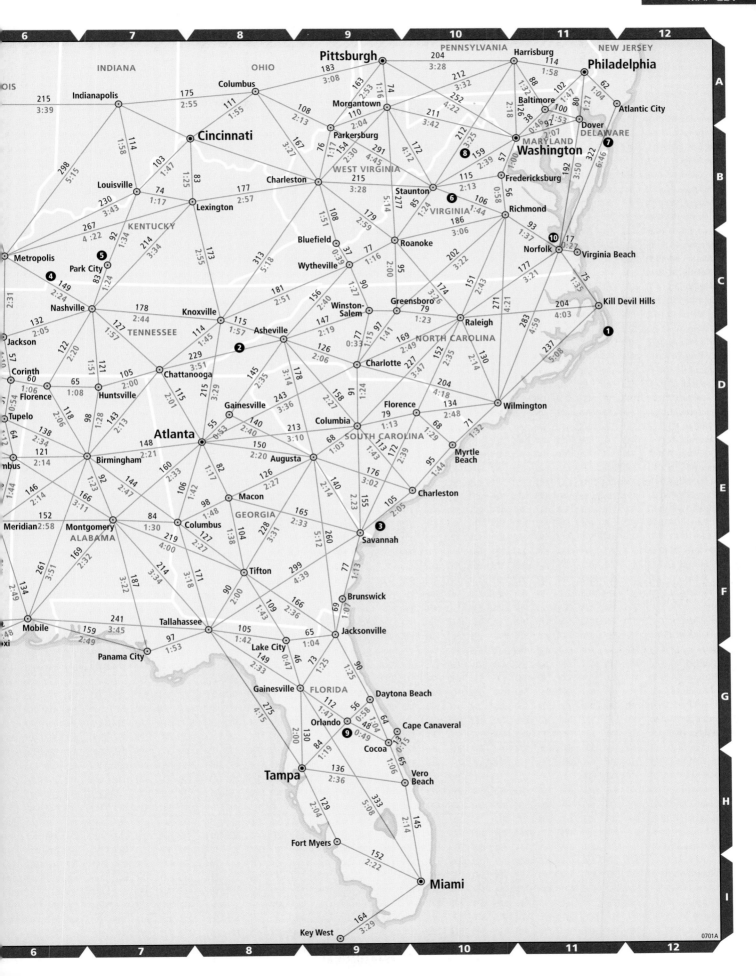

0701A

Grid references following the city names refer to locations on the mileage and driving times map on pages 220-221.

	Asheville, NC (D-8)	Atlanta, GA (D-8)	Baltimore, MD (A-11)	Baton Rouge, LA (F-5)	Biloxi, MS (F-6)	Birmingham, AL (E-7)	Branson, MO (C-4)	Brunswick, GA (F-9)	Cape Canaveral, FL (G-9)	Charleston, SC (E-10)	Charleston, WV (B-9)	Charlotte, NC (D-9)	Clarksdale, MS (D-5)	Columbia, SC (D-9)	Dallas, TX (E-2)	Dover, DE (A-11)	Florence, AL (D-6)	Fredericksburg, VA (B-10)	Gainesville, GA (D-8)	Hot Springs, AR (D-4)	Houston, TX (F-3)	Huntsville, AL (D-7)	Jackson, MS (E-5)	Jacksonville, FL (F-9)	Key West, FL (I-9)	Knoxville, TN (C-8)	Lafayette, LA (F-4)	Lake City, FL (F-8)	Little Rock, AR (D-4)
Asheville, NC (D-8)		195	498	720	584	344	761	383	602	267	285	126	574	158	955	552	401	425	147	692	992	334	581	443	946	115	774	479	640
Atlanta, GA (D-8)	195		674	525	389	149	664	277	490	321	503	244	398	213	794	731	226	585	51	581	797	181	386	346	823	216	579	288	529
Baltimore, MD (A-11)	498	674		1181	1063	783	1091	679	898	563	369	436	985	512	1366	104	812	92	635	1103	1453	745	1023	739	1242	526	1235	799	1051
Baton Rouge, LA (F-5)	720	525	1181		144	399	532	670	747	841	968	769	328	733	447	1235	419	1110	576	438	272	493	170	603	1080	655	54	545	358
Biloxi, MS (F-6)	584	389	1063	144		321	606	534	611	705	886	633	324	597	591	1120	383	974	440	460	416	408	170	467	944	573	198	409	432
Birmingham, AL (E-7)	344	149	783	399	321		516	426	612	470	570	393	250	362	649	837	119	701	200	433	671	98	241	468	945	257	453	410	381
Branson, MO (C-4)	761	664	1091	532	606	516		941	1126	985	762	890	319	877	461	1190	422	1086	729	220	602	489	436	982	1459	646	579	924	174
Brunswick, GA (F-9)	383	277	679	670	534	426	941		230	179	587	324	675	229	986	736	503	590	324	858	942	458	578	71	574	486	724	131	806
Cape Canaveral, FL (G-9)	602	490	898	747	611	612	1126	230		398	806	543	860	448	1145	955	729	809	537	1043	1019	671	737	159	354	705	801	203	991
Charleston, SC (E-10)	267	321	563	841	705	470	985	179	398		471	208	719	113	1115	620	547	474	308	902	1113	502	707	239	742	370	895	299	850
Charleston, WV (B-9)	285	503	369	968	886	570	762	587	806	471		265	670	355	1051	455	536	324	430	788	1170	504	810	647	1150	313	1022	707	736
Charlotte, NC (D-9)	126	244	436	769	633	393	890	324	543	208	265		642	92	1038	493	478	347	205	807	1041	411	630	384	887	230	823	444	755
Clarksdale, MS (D-5)	574	398	985	328	324	250	319	675	860	719	670	642		611	466	1039	191	903	449	203	520	260	158	716	1193	459	382	658	151
Columbia, SC (D-9)	158	213	512	733	597	362	877	229	448	113	355	92	611		1007	569	439	423	199	794	1005	394	599	289	792	261	787	349	742
Dallas, TX (E-2)	955	794	1366	447	591	649	461	986	1145	1115	1051	1038	466	1007		1420	602	1284	845	292	247	669	408	1001	1478	840	397	943	315
Dover, DE (A-11)	552	731	104	1235	1120	837	1190	736	955	620	455	493	1039	569	1420		866	149	692	1157	1507	799	1077	796	1299	580	1289	856	1105
Florence, AL (D-6)	401	226	812	419	383	119	422	503	729	547	536	478	191	439	602	866		730	267	339	691	67	249	585	1062	286	473	527	287
Fredericksburg, VA (B-10)	425	585	92	1110	974	701	1086	590	809	474	324	347	903	423	1284	149	730		546	1021	1382	663	941	650	1153	444	1164	710	969
Gainesville, GA (D-8)	147	51	635	576	440	200	729	324	537	308	430	205	449	199	845	692	267	546		632	848	200	437	393	870	187	630	335	580
Hot Springs, AR (D-4)	692	581	1103	438	460	433	220	858	1043	902	788	807	203	794	292	1157	339	1021	632		411	406	290	899	1376	577	388	841	52
Houston, TX (F-3)	992	797	1453	272	416	671	602	942	1019	1113	1170	1041	520	1005	247	1507	691	1382	848	411		765	442	875	1352	927	222	817	434
Huntsville, AL (D-7)	334	181	745	493	408	98	489	458	671	502	504	411	260	394	669	799	67	663	200	406	765		335	527	1004	219	547	469	354
Jackson, MS (E-5)	581	386	1023	170	170	241	436	578	737	707	810	630	158	599	408	1077	249	941	437	290	442	335		593	1070	497	224	535	262
Jacksonville, FL (F-9)	443	346	739	603	467	468	982	71	159	239	647	384	716	289	1001	796	585	650	393	899	875	527	593		503	546	657	64	847
Key West, FL (I-9)	946	823	1242	1080	944	945	1459	574	354	742	1150	887	1193	792	1478	1299	1062	1153	870	1376	1352	1004	1070	503		1039	1134	536	1324
Knoxville, TN (C-8)	115	216	526	655	573	257	646	486	705	370	313	230	459	261	840	580	286	444	187	577	927	219	497	546	1039		709	504	525
Lafayette, LA (F-4)	774	579	1235	54	198	453	579	724	801	895	1022	823	382	787	397	1289	473	1164	630	388	222	547	224	657	1134	709		599	411
Lake City, FL (F-8)	479	288	799	545	409	410	924	131	203	299	707	444	658	349	943	856	527	710	335	841	817	469	535	64	536	504	599		789
Little Rock, AR (D-4)	640	529	1051	358	432	381	174	806	991	850	736	755	151	742	315	1105	287	969	580	52	434	354	262	847	1324	525	411	789	
Macon, GA (E-8)	272	81	698	549	413	230	745	196	413	270	541	278	479	187	839	755	307	609	128	662	821	262	431	269	746	297	603	211	610
Mammoth Cave NP, KY (C-7)	310	332	676	675	590	280	520	609	822	565	307	425	370	456	751	762	236	631	338	488	870	204	505	678	1155	195	729	620	436
Memphis, TN (D-5)	503	391	914	382	378	243	274	668	853	712	599	618	73	604	454	968	149	832	442	191	573	216	212	709	1186	388	436	651	139
Metropolis, IL (C-6)	442	392	817	559	555	340	329	669	882	697	448	557	254	588	637	907	210	771	398	374	756	264	389	738	1215	327	613	680	322
Miami, FL (I-10)	786	661	1082	918	782	783	1297	414	194	582	990	727	1031	632	1316	1139	900	993	708	1214	1190	842	908	343	164	877	972	374	1162
Mobile, AL (F-6)	524	329	1003	200	64	261	626	470	547	645	826	573	344	537	598	1060	328	914	380	480	472	357	190	403	880	513	254	345	452
Montgomery, AL (E-7)	355	160	834	365	229	92	606	349	520	476	657	404	340	368	655	891	209	745	211	523	637	188	247	376	853	344	419	318	471
Mountain Home, AR (C-4)	670	583	1049	574	570	435	83	860	1045	904	680	785	265	796	465	1135	341	999	634	202	584	408	404	901	1378	555	561	843	156
Myrtle Beach, SC (E-10)	299	357	470	877	741	506	1021	278	497	95	434	171	755	145	1151	527	583	381	340	938	1149	538	743	338	841	402	931	398	886
Nashville, TN (C-7)	293	243	704	584	499	189	470	520	733	548	391	408	282	439	663	758	145	622	249	400	782	113	417	589	1066	178	638	531	348
Natchez, MS (F-5)	695	500	1137	89	223	355	443	712	789	821	900	744	218	713	385	1191	344	1055	551	292	322	449	114	645	1122	611	143	587	269
New Orleans, LA (G-5)	663	468	1124	79	87	342	597	613	690	784	911	712	338	676	526	1178	411	1053	519	451	351	436	180	546	1023	598	133	488	423
Orlando, FL (G-9)	585	440	881	697	561	562	1076	213	59	381	789	526	810	431	1095	938	679	792	487	993	969	621	687	142	391	656	751	153	941
Panama City, FL (F-7)	480	285	959	360	224	280	794	334	411	502	788	529	504	441	758	1016	397	870	336	640	632	376	350	267	744	498	414	209	612
Parkersburg, WV (A-9)	360	578	323	1043	961	645	787	662	881	546	75	340	745	430	1126	409	611	368	505	863	1245	579	885	722	1225	388	1097	782	811
Philadelphia, PA (A-11)	600	772	102	1283	1161	885	1148	777	996	661	476	534	1087	610	1468	86	914	190	733	1205	1555	847	1125	837	1340	628	1337	897	1153
Raleigh, NC (C-10)	247	407	295	932	796	556	1019	396	615	280	325	169	818	229	1199	352	645	206	368	936	1204	578	793	456	959	359	986	516	884
Richmond, VA (B-10)	370	530	144	1055	919	679	1078	535	754	419	316	292	895	368	1276	201	722	55	491	1013	1327	655	916	595	1098	436	1109	655	961
Savannah, GA (E-9)	309	252	605	700	564	401	916	80	299	105	513	250	650	155	990	662	478	516	299	833	972	433	582	140	643	412	754	200	781
Shreveport, LA (E-3)	803	608	1245	265	392	463	364	800	959	929	932	852	281	821	186	1299	483	1163	659	173	239	557	222	815	1292	719	215	757	196
Staunton, VA (B-10)	305	505	195	988	894	590	975	589	808	473	213	267	792	357	1173	249	619	115	466	910	1260	552	830	649	1152	333	1042	709	858
Tallahassee, FL (F-8)	456	265	898	440	304	305	819	230	307	398	729	466	553	375	838	955	422	809	312	736	712	401	430	163	640	481	494	105	684
Tampa, FL (H-8)	641	458	937	715	579	580	1094	269	127	437	845	582	828	487	1113	994	697	848	505	1011	987	639	705	202	404	674	769	171	959
Texarkana, AR (E-3)	780	676	1191	336	460	531	308	868	1027	997	876	895	291	889	180	1245	427	1109	727	117	292	494	290	883	1360	665	286	825	140
Tulsa, OK (C-3)	907	796	1236	613	705	648	223	1073	1258	1117	907	1022	418	1009	262	1372	554	1236	847	244	505	621	535	1114	1591	792	563	1056	273
Tupelo, MS (D-6)	480	285	891	338	309	137	380	562	747	606	605	529	110	498	560	945	82	809	336	297	610	147	168	603	1080	365	392	545	245
Virginia Beach, VA (C-11)	412	572	246	1097	961	721	1184	561	780	445	422	334	983	394	1364	192	810	157	533	1101	1369	743	958	621	1124	524	1151	681	1049
Washington, DC (B-11)	458	636	38	1141	1025	743	1128	641	860	525	366	398	945	474	1326	93	772	54	597	1063	1413	705	983	701	1204	486	1195	761	1011
Wilmington, NC (D-10)	331	421	410	941	805	570	1085	376	595	167	456	207	819	209	1215	467	647	321	404	1002	1213	602	807	436	939	466	995	496	950
Winston-Salem, NC (C-9)	144	321	374	846	710	470	916	405	624	289	218	83	715	173	1096	431	542	285	282	833	1118	475	707	465	968	256	900	525	781
Wytheville, VA (C-9)	153	374	344	836	754	438	827	458	677	342	133	136	640	226	1021	398	467	262	298	758	1108	400	678	518	1021	181	890	578	706

Grid references following the city names refer to locations on the mileage and driving times map on pages 220-221.

Memphis, TN (D-5)	Metropolis, IL (C-6)	Miami, FL (I-10)	Mobile, AL (F-6)	Montgomery, AL (E-7)	Mountain Home, AR (C-4)	Myrtle Beach, SC (E-10)	Nashville, TN (C-7)	Natchez, MS (F-5)	New Orleans, LA (G-5)	Orlando, FL (G-9)	Panama City, FL (F-7)	Parkersburg, WV (A-9)	Philadelphia, PA (A-11)	Raleigh, NC (C-10)	Richmond, VA (B-10)	Savannah, GA (E-9)	Shreveport, LA (E-3)	Staunton, VA (B-10)	Tallahassee, FL (F-8)	Tampa, FL (H-8)	Texarkana, AR (E-3)	Tulsa, OK (C-3)	Tupelo, MS (D-6)	Virginia Beach, VA (C-11)	Washington, DC (B-11)	Wilmington, NC (D-10)	Winston-Salem, NC (C-9)	Wytheville, VA (C-9)	
503	442	786	524	355	670	299	293	695	663	585	480	360	600	247	370	309	803	305	456	641	780	907	480	412	458	331	144	153	**Asheville, NC (D-8)**
391	392	661	329	160	583	357	243	500	468	440	285	578	772	407	530	252	608	505	265	458	676	796	285	572	636	421	321	374	**Atlanta, GA (D-8)**
914	817	1082	1003	834	1049	470	704	1137	1124	881	959	323	102	295	144	605	1245	195	898	937	1191	1236	891	246	38	410	374	344	**Baltimore, MD (A-11)**
382	559	918	200	365	574	877	584	89	79	697	360	1043	1283	932	1055	700	265	988	440	715	336	613	338	1097	1141	941	846	836	**Baton Rouge, LA (F-5)**
378	555	782	64	229	570	741	499	223	87	561	224	961	1161	796	919	564	392	894	304	579	460	705	309	961	1025	805	710	754	**Biloxi, MS (F-6)**
243	340	783	261	92	435	506	189	355	342	562	280	645	885	556	679	401	463	590	305	580	531	648	137	721	743	570	470	438	**Birmingham, AL (E-7)**
274	329	1297	626	606	83	1021	470	443	597	1076	794	787	1148	1019	1078	916	364	975	819	1094	308	223	380	1184	1128	1085	916	827	**Branson, MO (C-4)**
668	669	414	470	349	860	278	520	712	613	213	334	662	777	396	535	80	800	589	230	269	868	1073	562	561	641	376	405	458	**Brunswick, GA (F-9)**
853	882	194	547	520	1045	497	733	789	690	59	411	881	996	615	754	299	959	808	307	127	1027	1258	747	780	860	595	624	677	**Cape Canaveral, FL (G-9)**
712	697	582	645	476	904	95	548	821	784	381	502	546	661	280	419	105	929	473	398	437	997	1117	606	445	525	167	289	342	**Charleston, SC (E-10)**
599	448	990	826	657	680	434	391	900	911	789	788	75	476	325	316	513	932	213	729	845	876	907	605	422	366	456	218	133	**Charleston, WV (B-9)**
618	557	727	573	404	785	171	408	744	712	526	529	340	534	169	292	250	852	267	466	582	895	1022	529	334	398	207	83	136	**Charlotte, NC (D-9)**
73	254	1031	344	340	265	755	282	218	338	810	504	745	1087	818	895	650	281	792	553	828	291	418	110	983	945	819	715	640	**Clarksdale, MS (D-5)**
604	588	632	537	368	796	145	439	713	676	431	441	430	610	229	368	155	821	357	375	487	889	1009	498	394	474	209	173	226	**Columbia, SC (D-9)**
454	637	1316	598	655	465	1151	663	385	526	1095	758	1126	1468	1199	1276	990	186	1173	838	1113	180	262	560	1364	1326	1215	1096	1021	**Dallas, TX (E-2)**
968	907	1139	1060	891	1135	527	758	1191	1178	938	1016	409	86	352	201	662	1299	249	955	994	1245	1372	945	192	93	467	431	398	**Dover, DE (A-11)**
149	210	900	328	209	341	583	145	344	411	679	397	611	914	645	722	478	483	619	422	697	427	554	82	810	772	647	542	467	**Florence, AL (D-6)**
832	771	993	914	745	999	381	622	1055	1053	792	870	368	190	206	55	516	1163	115	809	848	1109	1236	809	157	54	321	285	262	**Fredericksburg, VA (B-10)**
442	398	708	380	211	634	340	249	551	519	487	336	505	733	368	491	299	659	466	312	505	727	847	336	533	597	404	282	298	**Gainesville, GA (D-8)**
191	374	1214	480	523	202	938	400	292	451	993	640	863	1205	936	1013	833	173	910	736	1011	117	244	297	1101	1063	1002	833	758	**Hot Springs, AR (D-4)**
573	756	1190	472	637	584	1149	782	322	351	969	632	1245	1555	1204	1327	972	239	1260	712	987	292	505	610	1369	1413	1213	1118	1108	**Houston, TX (F-3)**
216	264	842	357	188	408	538	113	449	436	621	376	579	847	578	655	433	557	552	401	639	494	621	147	743	705	602	475	400	**Huntsville, AL (D-7)**
212	389	908	190	247	404	743	417	114	180	687	350	885	1125	793	916	582	222	830	430	705	290	535	168	958	983	807	707	678	**Jackson, MS (E-5)**
709	738	343	403	376	901	338	589	645	546	142	267	722	837	456	595	140	815	649	163	202	883	1114	603	621	701	436	465	518	**Jacksonville, FL (F-9)**
186	1215	164	880	853	1378	841	1066	1122	1023	391	744	1225	1340	959	1098	643	1292	1152	640	404	1360	1591	1080	1124	1204	939	968	1021	**Key West, FL (I-9)**
388	327	877	513	344	555	402	178	611	598	656	498	388	628	359	436	412	719	333	481	674	665	792	365	524	486	466	256	181	**Knoxville, TN (C-8)**
436	613	972	254	419	561	931	638	143	133	751	414	1097	1337	986	1109	754	215	1042	494	769	286	563	392	1151	1195	995	900	890	**Lafayette, LA (F-4)**
651	680	374	345	318	843	398	531	587	488	153	209	782	897	516	655	200	757	709	105	171	825	1056	545	681	761	496	525	578	**Lake City, FL (F-8)**
139	322	1162	452	471	156	886	348	269	423	941	612	811	1153	884	961	781	196	858	684	959	140	273	245	1049	1011	950	781	706	**Little Rock, AR (D-4)**
472	473	584	353	184	664	331	324	545	492	363	254	616	796	415	554	171	653	543	188	381	721	877	366	580	660	395	359	412	**Macon, GA (E-8)**
299	201	993	539	370	433	597	91	600	618	772	558	382	783	554	623	584	632	520	583	790	576	703	305	729	673	661	451	376	**Mammoth Cave NP, KY (C-7)**
	180	1024	398	333	193	748	211	307	392	803	521	674	1016	747	824	643	335	721	546	821	279	406	107	912	874	812	644	569	**Memphis, TN (D-5)**
180		1053	599	430	242	729	151	484	569	832	618	523	924	686	763	644	518	660	643	850	462	484	229	851	813	793	583	508	**Metropolis, IL (C-6)**
1024	1053		718	691	1216	681	904	960	861	229	582	1065	1180	799	938	483	1130	992	478	254	1198	1429	918	964	1044	779	808	861	**Miami, FL (I-10)**
398	599	718		169	590	681	448	242	143	497	160	901	1101	736	859	539	412	834	240	515	480	725	277	901	965	745	650	694	**Mobile, AL (F-6)**
333	430	691	169		525	512	279	361	308	470	188	732	932	567	690	335	469	665	213	488	537	738	227	732	796	576	481	525	**Montgomery, AL (E-7)**
193	242	1216	590	525		940	378	425	584	995	713	755	1156	914	991	835	346	888	738	1013	290	235	299	1079	1041	1004	811	736	**Mountain Home, AR (C-4)**
748	729	681	681	512	940		580	857	820	480	601	509	568	187	326	204	965	433	497	536	1033	1153	642	352	432	71	217	305	**Myrtle Beach, SC (E-10)**
211	151	904	448	279	378	580		512	527	683	467	466	806	537	614	495	544	511	492	701	488	615	217	702	664	644	434	359	**Nashville, TN (C-7)**
307	484	960	242	361	425	857	512		175	739	402	975	1239	907	1030	696	199	944	482	757	267	542	263	1072	1097	921	821	792	**Natchez, MS (F-5)**
392	569	861	143	308	584	820	527	175		640	303	986	1226	875	998	643	344	931	383	658	415	692	337	1040	1084	884	789	779	**New Orleans, LA (G-5)**
803	832	229	497	470	995	480	683	739	640		361	864	979	598	737	282	909	791	257	83	977	1208	697	763	843	578	607	660	**Orlando, FL (G-9)**
521	618	582	160	188	713	601	467	402	303	361		863	1057	719	815	403	572	790	98	379	640	926	415	884	921	699	606	659	**Panama City, FL (F-7)**
674	523	1065	901	732	755	509	466	975	986	864	863		430	400	391	588	1007	288	804	920	951	932	680	497	324	531	293	208	**Parkersburg, WV (A-9)**
1016	924	1180	1101	932	1156	568	806	1239	1226	979	1057	430		393	242	703	1347	297	996	1035	1293	1293	993	280	136	508	472	446	**Philadelphia, PA (A-11)**
747	686	799	736	567	914	187	537	907	875	598	719	400	393		151	322	1015	258	615	654	1024	1151	692	191	257	132	107	196	**Raleigh, NC (C-10)**
824	763	938	859	690	991	326	614	1030	998	737	815	391	242	151		461	1138	107	754	793	1101	1228	801	105	106	266	230	254	**Richmond, VA (B-10)**
643	644	483	539	335	835	204	495	696	643	282	403	588	703	322	461		804	515	299	338	872	1048	537	487	567	302	331	384	**Savannah, GA (E-9)**
335	518	1130	412	469	346	965	544	199	344	909	572	1007	1347	1015	1138	804		1052	652	927	71	352	387	1180	1205	1029	929	900	**Shreveport, LA (E-3)**
721	660	992	834	665	888	433	511	944	931	791	790	288	297	258	107	515	1052		731	847	998	1125	698	213	155	373	184	151	**Staunton, VA (B-10)**
546	643	478	240	213	738	497	492	482	383	257	98	804	996	615	754	299	652	731		275	720	951	440	780	860	595	547	600	**Tallahassee, FL (F-8)**
821	850	254	515	488	1013	536	701	757	658	83	379	920	1035	654	793	338	927	847	275		995	1226	715	819	899	634	663	716	**Tampa, FL (H-8)**
279	462	1198	480	537	290	1033	488	267	415	977	640	951	1293	1024	1101	872	71	998	720	995		279	385	1189	1151	1097	921	846	**Texarkana, AR (E-3)**
406	484	1429	725	738	235	1153	615	542	692	1208	926	932	1293	1151	1228	1048	352	1125	951	1226	279		512	1316	1278	1217	1048	973	**Tulsa, OK (C-3)**
107	229	918	277	227	299	642	217	263	337	697	415	680	993	692	801	537	387	698	440	715	385	512		857	851	706	606	546	**Tupelo, MS (D-6)**
912	851	964	901	732	1079	352	702	1072	1040	763	884	497	280	191	105	487	1180	213	780	819	1189	1316	857		208	292	272	360	**Virginia Beach, VA (C-11)**
874	813	1044	965	796	1041	432	664	1097	1084	843	921	324	136	257	106	567	1205	155	860	899	1151	1278	851	208		372	336	304	**Washington, DC (B-11)**
812	793	779	745	576	1004	71	644	921	884	578	699	531	508	132	266	302	1029	373	595	634	1097	1217	706	292	372		238	327	**Wilmington, NC (D-10)**
644	583	808	650	481	811	217	434	821	789	607	606	293	472	107	230	331	929	184	547	663	921	1048	606	272	336	238		89	**Winston-Salem, NC (C-9)**
569	508	861	694	525	736	305	359	792	779	660	659	208	446	196	254	384	900	151	600	716	846	973	546	360	304	327	89		**Wytheville, VA (C-9)**

Mileages in this chart are based upon the routes usually followed by motorists. Highway systems involved include interstate, U.S., and state highways.

ROAD CONSTRUCTION
AND ROAD CONDITIONS RESOURCES

Most of the hotlines and websites listed here offer information on both road construction and road conditions. For those that provide only one or the other, we've used an orange cone ⚠ to indicate road construction information and a blue snowflake ❄ to indicate road conditions information.

ALABAMA
www.dot.state.al.us

ARKANSAS
(800) 245-1672 ❄
(501) 569-2374 ❄
www.arkansashighways.com

FLORIDA
511
www.511tampabay.com
www.fl511.com

GEORGIA
(404) 635-8000
www.dot.state.ga.us

KENTUCKY
511
(866) 737-3767
www.511.ky.gov

LOUISIANA
www.511la.org

MARYLAND
(800) 327-3125 ❄
(800) 541-9595 ❄
(410) 582-5650
www.chart.state.md.us

MISSISSIPPI
(601) 987-1211 ❄
(601) 359-7301 ⚠
www.mdot.state.ms.us

MISSOURI
(800) 222-6400 (in MO) ❄
www.modot.mo.gov

NORTH CAROLINA
511
(877) 511-4662
www.ncsmartlink.org/aboutITS
/511.html

OKLAHOMA
(405) 425-2385 ❄
(888) 425-2385 ❄

SOUTH CAROLINA
www.dot.state.sc.us

TENNESSEE
(800) 342-3258 ❄
(800) 858-6349 ⚠
www.tdot.state.tn.us/travel.htm

TEXAS
(800) 452-9292
www.dot.state.tx.us

VIRGINIA
511
(800) 367-7623 ❄
(800) 578-4111
www.511virginia.org

WASHINGTON, D.C.
www.ddot.dc.gov ⚠

WEST VIRGINIA
(877) 982-7623 ❄
www.wvdot.com

Get the info from the 511 hotline

The U.S. Federal Highway Administration has begun implementing a national system of highway and road conditions/construction information for travelers. Under the new plan, travelers can **dial 511 and get up-to-date information on roads and highways.** Implementation of 511 is the responsibility of state and local agencies. For more details, visit: www.fhwa.dot.gov/trafficinfo/511.htm

LODGING RESOURCES

AmericInn
(800) 634-3444
www.americinn.com

Baymont Inns & Suites
(800) 301-0200 or
(866) 999-1111
www.baymontinn.com

Best Western
(800) 780-7234
www.bestwestern.com

Budget Host
(800) 283-4678
www.budgethost.com

Clarion Hotels
(877) 424-6423
www.clarioninn.com

Comfort Inns
(877) 424-6423
www.comfortinn.com

Comfort Suites
(877) 424-6423
www.comfortsuites.com

Courtyard by Marriott
(800) 321-2211
www.courtyard.com

Crowne Plaza Hotel & Resorts
(877) 227-6963
www.crowneplaza.com

Days Inn
(800) 329-7466
www.daysinn.com

Doubletree Hotels & Guest Suites
(800) 222-8733
www.doubletree.com

Drury Hotels
(800) 378-7946
www.druryhotels.com

Embassy Suites Hotels
(800) 362-2779
www.embassysuites.com

Fairfield Inn by Marriott
(800) 228-2800
www.fairfieldinn.com

Fairmont Hotels & Resorts
(800) 257-7544
www.fairmont.com

Hampton Inn
(800) 426-7866
www.hamptoninn.com

Hilton Hotels
(800) 445-8667
www.hilton.com

Holiday Inn Hotels & Resorts
(800) 465-4329
www.holiday-inn.com

Homewood Suites
(800) 225-5466
www.homewood-suites.com

Hyatt Hotels & Resorts
(888) 591-1234
www.hyatt.com

InterContinental Hotels & Resorts
(888) 424-6835
www.intercontinental.com

Jameson Inns
(800) 526-3766
www.jamesoninns.com

Knights Inn
(800) 843-5644
www.knightsinn.com

La Quinta Inn & Suites
(866) 725-1661
www.lq.com

Le Meridien Hotels
(800) 543-4300
www.lemeridien.com

Loews Hotels
(800) 235-6397
www.loewshotels.com

MainStay Suites
(877) 424-6423
www.mainstaysuites.com

Marriott International
(888) 236-2427
www.marriott.com

Omni Hotels
(888) 444-6664
www.omnihotels.com

Preferred Hotels & Resorts
(800) 323-7500
www.preferredhotels.com

Quality Inns & Suites
(877) 424-6423
www.qualityinn.com

Radisson Hotels & Resorts
(800) 333-3333
www.radisson.com

Ramada Inn/Ramada Limited/Ramada Plaza Hotels
(800) 272-6232
www.ramada.com

Renaissance Hotels & Resorts
(888) 236-2427
www.renaissancehotels.com

Sheraton Hotels & Resorts
(800) 598-1753
www.sheraton.com

Signature Inns
(800) 822-5252
www.signatureinns.com

Sleep Inn
(877) 424-6423
www.sleepinn.com

Super 8 Motel
(800) 800-8000
www.super8.com

Travelodge Hotels
(800) 578-7878
www.travelodge.com

Westin Hotels & Resorts
(888) 625-5144
www.westin.com

Wyndham Hotels & Resorts
(877) 999-3223
www.wyndham.com